Contributions to the Sociology of Language 3

Edited by

Joshua A. Fishman

Multilingualism in the Soviet Union

Aspects of Language Policy and its Implementation

by

E. GLYN LEWIS

1972 – MOUTON – THE HAGUE • PARIS

LIBRARY OF CONGRESS CATALOG CARD NUMBER 72-88222

Printed in The Netherlands by Mennen Printers, Asten.

Er cof am fy rhieni

Preface

Joshua A. Fishman

There are several reasons why the current volume by Glyn Lewis promises to be of unusual importance to many students of the sociology of language. All of these reasons taken together make this volume a true contribution to the field as a whole as well to this particular series of publications.

To begin with, the fact that it deals with the Soviet Union is in itself a matter of great importance. Except for a very few translations of small segments of the work of one or two Soviet sociolinguists (e.g. Desheriyev 1965, Guxman 1960), hardly any sociolinguistic facts, figures or theoretical integrative attempts are available to the English reader in connection with the work that has been done there during the past two decades. If we but consider that few regions of the world have witnessed as much language planning as has the Soviet Union (See e.g., Lencek 1971), in connection with as large and as diversified a set of speech communities and languages, it immediately becomes clear that any attempt to present (as does Glyn Lewis) the major policies, sociolinguistic practices and consequences that pertain to the Soviet Union, is performing yeoman's service in connection with filling a huge gap in our sociolinguistic map. Indeed, it may very well be that Glyn Lewis' service in this connection will be as great vis-a-vis students, scholars and practitioners of sociology of language *within the Soviet Union per se* as it will be for their counterparts in other corners of the globe.

Above and beyond his splendid contribution to furthering our knowledge concerning the sociolinguistic situation in a huge part of the world about which we have hitherto been woefully ignorant, Glyn Lewis' study must be welcomed as an example of the interdisciplinary and multi-level inquiries that our field so needs. The data he examines and analyzes are linguistic, historical demographic, chronological and educational. The questions that he seeks to answer via these data are both synchronic and diachronic, both theoretical and applied, both descriptive and predictive. As a result, I am convinced that no serious student of bilingual education anywhere in the world, or of language planning anywhere in the world, or of language maintenance and language shift anywhere in the world, will be able to ignore Glyn Lewis' work for a good many years to come. Quite the contrary. I am certain that it will become and remain a fundamental work in all of the sociology of language for a good long time to come.

What particularly excites me about Glyn Lewis' work (coming as it does after years of exhaustive and exhausting contacts with Soviet scholars, schools, and publications) is that it is able both to grapple with the overall trend of developments, as well as to preserve our awareness for the variation (in policies, practices and outcomes) that also obtains. In a world in which no-one can view the Soviet Union dispassionately Glyn Lewis reveals himself to be uncommonly able to avoid both broad condemnation and broad commendation, and, at the same time, not to overlook the forest for the trees, nor the trees for the forest. A byproduct of this, one would hope, would be the more rapid 'opening' of the Soviet Union to sociologists of language more generally, particularly to such that would hope to engage in studies at a more micro-level than that on which Glyn Lewis has here focused his attention.

There is, once again, a flourishing sociology of language (at least numerically so) within the Soviet Union (as demonstrated by the thirty-some papers presented by Soviet academicians at the sessions of the Seventh World Congress of Sociology, Varna, Bulgaria, Sept 14-19, 1970). There are sections on sociolinguistics at the Academies of Sciences of many of the Soviet Republics. Soviet sociologists of language have indicated their interest in establishing closer contacts with colleagues outside the Soviet Union (Kjolseth and Sock 1972) via joint conferences, joint publications, and joint participation in the work of the Research Committee on Sociolinguistics of the International Sociological Association (RCS-ISA) and its *Newsletter*. Thus, Glyn Lewis' admirable work comes at a very favorable juncture. One can only hope that both the non-Soviet and the Soviet reader (and there should be many of both sorts) will be able to utilize his intriguing first steps in order to further and deepen the co-operative contacts already underway as well as in order to advance the sociology of language as a whole. It is a sign of my high regard for this work that I conclude that it is very likely to contribute handsomely in both of these respects.

Jerusalem, 1972.

REFERENCES

Desheriyev, Yu. et al,

1965 "The Development and mutual enrichment of the languages of the USSR",
Kommunist, no. 13, 55-56. English translation in *The Current Digest of the
Soviet Press* 1965, 17, no. 47, 14-19.

Guxman, M. M.,

1960 "Some general regularities in the formation and development of national
languages", in M. M. Guxman (ed.), *Voprosy Formirovanija i Razvitija
Nacional 'nyx Jazykov*, Moscow, 295-307. English translation in J. A. Fishman (ed.), *Readings in the Sociology of Language* (The Hague, Mouton,
1966), 766-779.

Kjolseth, Rolf and Fritz Sock (eds.),

1972 "Toward a Sociology of Language (Selected Contribution from the 7th
World Congress of Sociology in Varne, Bulgaria, September 14-19. 1970)".
Special Anthology Edition (Number 15) of *The Koelner Zeitschrift für Sozio-
logie und Sozialpsychologie*. (Cologne and Opladen, Westdeutsche Verlag).

Lencek, Rado L.

1971 "Problems in Sociolinguistics in The Soviet Union" *(Georgetown University
Monograph Series on Languages and Linguistics*, 1971, 24, 269-301*).*

Acknowledgements

I am greatly indebted to many friends, colleagues and scholars interested in the areas of research represented in the present study. I have tried to acknowledge this wherever possible; but there are some whose interest and assistance it is impossible to refer to adequately in any specific references in the text and the bibliography. Among these are, first, the late Professor G. P. Serdyuchenko from whom I first obtained valuable information, materials and bibliographical references when he attended the International Seminar on Bilingualism at Aberystwyth, which I was privileged to organize and report upon for UNESCO (U.K. Commission). Subsequent meetings in Moscow and at international conferences deepened my regard for him and increased my indebtedness. I am similarly indebted to many teachers of English in the USSR who have visited Wales as guests of the British Council over several years, and who have been helpful in discussing several aspects of the language situation of the Soviet Union. I hope that the intention of this study, if not the outcome, will not be unacceptable to them and will help to repay in part their kindness. This is especially the case with teachers, schools inspectors and administrators whom I have met in Leningrad, Tbilisi and Erevan, as well as Moscow.

To my former colleague and Chief Inspector, Dr. William Thomas I am indebted for placing me in charge of bilingual education in the Ministry of Education and encouraging my initial researches. Professor J. A. Fishman has encouraged this particular study almost from its inception and his patience in fostering its completion has been unfailing.

Much of the research was conducted when I was one of Her Majesty's

Inspectors in the Ministry of Education and later when I was a Director
of the Languages Research Project for the Schools Council at the University College, Swansea. The Ministry of Education (together with the
British Council) invited me to take charge of a small delegation to study
language teaching in the USSR, and the Ministry subsequently made it
possible for me to visit and study similar problems in East and West
Africa, Canada and the United States. Without the assistance and kindness of the staff of the Ministry of Education Library and that of the
Library of the University Colleges of Swansea and Cardiff I could not
have contemplated the wide ranging reading involved in this study. The
views expressed in the book do not reflect the attitude of the Ministry of
Education, however.

Finally, the enormous assistance and encouragement of my wife entitle
her to be regarded in every way as jointly responsible for whatever is of
value in this study.

Contents

Contents   XVII

List of Tables

Distribution
of Soviet Nationalities
and Languages

Chapter 1

INTRODUCTION

A. LEVELS OF INVESTIGATION

The historical universality of language contact and consequent bilingualism, together with the intensification of such contacts in contemporary society, makes it almost unnecessary to justify a study such as this. It is doubtful whether there exists any community or any language which has been isolated from and free of contact with other communities and other languages. In fact there is no reason to doubt that polyglottism is the earliest condition of large numbers of people and the exclusive cultivation of a single language has been a concession to political philosophies of a nationalistic tendency. The exaggerated significance of nationalism in our modern age makes such a study ever more desirable. The apotheosis of linguistic nationalism, especially among small countries, which we have witnessed in recent times, has not been entirely advantageous: language enables people to assert their separateness just as it enables them to communicate and to co-operate. It is as true now as it was for Sapir that "national languages constitute a huge system of vested interests which sullenly resists critical enquiry" (Sapir, 1949, 118). Sapir could hazard the guess that "revivalist movements" and the investment of great emotional capital and intellectual effort in the attempt to save languages from the consequence of contact would "come to be looked upon as little more than eddies in the more powerful stream [...] which set in at the end of the medieval period" (p. 88). However, these eddies are still very strong and the identification of language maintenance with national or group self-interest and separatism, although not new, arising as it does from a conjunction of the forces of Romantic philosophy, anti-quarianism and the democratic need for and insistence on the use of the vernacular in education, is of increasing significance.

Nor does the choice of the Soviet Union as an area in which these forces are studied require any justification, though the form which the study takes does. Like all protagonists to a debate it is desirable that I should declare 'my interest', which is not in the Soviet Union as a special area of study. Nor am I a 'Sovietologist', my main preoccupations having been the place of bilingualism in education and the study of the considerations which affect that problem. It is very largely because the USSR, in my experience, is the one area, apart from the Republic of South Africa, which takes this matter seriously (and organizes its system of education to take bilingualism into account at almost all levels and in respect of nearly all the population), that this study was undertaken. For this reason too the study itself is concerned with general forces and general consequences rather than with a detailed investigation of one community or even one nationality,[1] or with the operation of one set of factors or of one aspect of the linguistic situation of several nationalities. For reasons which are discussed subsequently the USSR as a whole is the area of study and the interaction of several factors within that area determines the structure of the investigation. Consequently although detail is used to illustrate or substantiate the conclusions arrived at, the study is compre-hensive and general rather than meticulous and microscopic. The detail is deployed to illuminate general tendencies and the working of general forces, rather than simply to build up a picture of the Soviet situation, although I hope that such a picture does emerge.

Although not the same degree of attention is devoted to all of them the present study is pursued on four levels. The first concerns the contem-porary situation, and the current operation of the most significant variables – the synchronic-descriptive level. On the second level the study has been concerned with the historical context of language contact. With-out attempting a consistently exhaustive comparative approach occasion has been taken to relate the Soviet experience to that of other colonizing powers such as the Greeks, Romans, French and British who have created similar multilingual situations, or have had to operate within existing ones. A similar historical and comparative approach is possible in respect of the various Soviet countries themselves under different political regimes, such as the Tsars or in the case of the Baltic countries independently, and under German or Swedish influence. This is the comparative-historical level of analysis and it is a vitally necessary one if we are to be able to distinguish what is peculiar to the immediate problem

[1]   For a prototype instance of such a study beautifully planned and implemented see Fishman et al. (1968b).

from what is universal in multilingual complexes. The third level might be best described as the synchronic-comparative level, and is concerned with instituting some comparisons with contemporary complex linguistic situations in other parts of the world, or between different national and language groups within the Soviet Union, especially between groups which belong to different language families and different races. On this level of interest two lines of attack are open – the first attempts to discover the similarities and differences between several political and social systems in the operation of a language policy; and the second looks at the operation of the same or single policy, and ideally the influence of the same or single language, on several other languages and communities. The USSR is an area where both these lines may be pursued. Whatever of value may be gained from the description of the situation of the Soviet Union at the present time it may be that it provides one of the best opportunities for the study of the interaction of some of the most important sociolinguistic variables synchronically and diachronically, and can enable a student of bilingualism, especially of bilingualism in education, to undertake useful comparative descriptions. It is because, in my view, both the historical and the comparative socio-linguistic approach within the area of multilingualism are necessary in order to establish the necessary characteristics of the contemporary situation that these lines have been adumbrated in this study, with the expectation that more comprehensive historical and comparative studies will follow.

There is a fourth level on which the present study has been pursued – the relationship of changes affecting languages (their inherent characteristics, demographic pattern of distribution and role-status, for instance) and changes affecting the social pattern and the culture of the country within which the languages are spoken. It is usually assumed that the interaction of two languages means the interaction of two cultures as well (Fox, 1968, 456) but this is not necessarily the case at present, nor has it been invariably the case in the past. In fact bilingualism has frequently continued for centuries after the ethnic and political assimilation of linguistic communities. This was the case in Southern Italy so far as concerned Greek, Latin, and Messapic. It is true of Wales as well, since the significant cultural differences between the two linguistic groups English and Welsh are minimal, although there is very considerable bilingualism. On this fourth level of interest lies also the consideration of possible differences between social change as it affects groups speaking genetically related languages on the one hand, and on the other genetically unrelated groups of languages involved in the same dynamic social processes. Greenberg has referred to this question and concludes that of the two ways of grouping languages – according to consanguinity or contiguity, it is the relationship between social and cultural change and languages of the same geographical area rather than of the same genetic family which will be most uniform (Greenberg, 1963, 68). The USSR offers a remarkably good opportunity to test this conclusion. We find languages of different families existing within the same geographical and cultural area, and languages of the same family dispersed very widely and embracing several culture areas. The linguistically complex Ferghana valley is an instance of the first, and the diffusion of Slavic languages throughout the Soviet Union is an instance of the second. Generally speaking it will be found that Greenberg's conclusion is confirmed. For instance Turkic and non-Turkic languages in the same geographical area reflect the same social and cultural changes, and in much the same way; while Slavic languages in the West reflect the cultural milieu of that area and the same languages reflect different social and cultural changes in Central Asia. At the same time it is possible in the USSR to substantiate a converse proposition – that a culturally uniform area has a different effect from a culturally heterogenous area on language maintenance, and consequently on the inherent characteristics of a language. Immigrants who remain within the Central Asian cultural complex are more likely to retain their native language even when they move into a different language area than immigrants who move not simply into another language area but out of the Central Asian Republics altogether. It would be interesting to compare this finding to what happens to, say, Italian immigrants who move into other parts of Europe and those who move out of the European context altogether.

Again on this fourth level of interest, it is necessary that some consideration should be given to the whole problem of linguistic and cultural 'merging'. Whatever may be said about the motivation for or the speed with which 'merging' is taking place the consequences of such an occurrence are there for all to see. One of the aspects to be considered is the extent to which this phenomenon is regionalized (that is the creation of blocks of converging languages, as might be the case in Daghestan or the North Caucusus for instance); or is uniform and general throughout the USSR under the dominant influence of one language; or the extent to which the regional and the general processes relate and interact. The question at issue is the extent to which it may be possible to observe in the USSR the development of what others have observed historically in Western Europe, namely the emergence of a 'sprachbund'. It has been claimed that languages used within the same socio-cultural area may be subjected to reciprocal influences at all linguistic levels – phonology, grammar and vocabulary (Sommerfelt, 1962, 139). Latin has exerted such an influence in Europe, and English in large areas of Africa. It may be that Russian will produce the same kinds of consequences in the USSR. At the same time, since the element of 'language planning' and of social engineering, including the promotion of other languages, is an aspect of the Soviet situation which, until the 20th Century, could not have affected the Western European area, it may be that the 'sprachbund' if it is a reality will be a matter not simply of the general influence of Russian but of that together with more limited and more numerous language alliances produced by the convergence of non-Russian languages within the various regions.

In considering the relationship of language to cultural and social change in the USSR, there is a need to pursue the question of the extent to which society itself is exposed to structural strains because of language contacts of a new sort, and particularly because of the penetration of a lingua franca such as Russian. It is possible to mention at least three aspects of society where restructuring may occur because of changes in the relationship between languages. Vocabulary is a major element in the style of life which sets off different status groups; and specialised ways of talking and writing within various strata and spheres of society are important. Status groups tend to close their ranks by means of language differences even when the society is monolingual. The introduction of another language altogether, or the privileged promotion of one already spoken in the area, is calculated to do much more. On the one hand the new language, especially if it is prestigious, cuts across the existing divisions in society; and on the other it is likely to help set up new status groups (Lewis, 1962b).

Related to the existence of status groups, in terms of language differences, is the problem of the relation of language to traditional social classes. Chadwick (1945) refers to bilingualism as a manifestation of the stratification of society in pre-War Poland, where Polish peasants spoke Russian dialects and the upper classes Polish. In Java the nobility speak Noko and the commoners Kromo. This demarcation of classes may be affected by the introduction of an exotic or a prestigious language. On the one hand the prestige language or the 'official language' may be spoken by all classes, or it may be spoken by a particular section of society, or it may be used by a cross section of society which comes to constitute a new class – for instance a class of administrators, as is the case in the USSR. Nor is this all, for an intrusive language may affect relations between the different age groups in the whole of society. These effects may be temporary or transitional but they may have considerable influence on the structure of family life. The young, especially if they are taught the language in school and learn other subjects by means of it, will have a different attitude towards it, to say nothing of greater competence in handling it than their parents. Consequently there may be a lug between the internal relationships of languages within a family and the relationships of the languages within the wider society. This in turn may help promote a cleavage between two types of cultural milieu for the languages, one an intimate and 'group culture' milieu and the other an impersonal, more formal and 'civic' milieu. Furthermore, even within the family, differences may be noted – a child will be willing to speak his native tongue only to the grandparents since the intermediate generation is felt to be committed to the intrusive language. As the child develops a more positive attitude towards this prestigious or intrusive language and uses it increasingly in ever broader domains the reaction against the language of the older groups intensifies and almost automatically this transfers to a reaction against the older groups as persons. This is certainly the case in some bilingual countries, Wales for instance; and there is no reason to doubt that it may characterise the Soviet situation.

The restructuring is not confined to the organization or stratification of society but affects the cultural life of a community. The different languages in any new realignment of their relationships may not simply appropriate to themselves different roles or continue to be used in the traditional roles, but the roles themselves may be so polarised as to suggest the emergence of two distinct types of culture. It is quite commonplace for different languages to be used mainly in private or personal or intimate roles on the one hand, and on the other in transactional and public roles. But so far as the Soviet Union is concerned the premium placed upon political awareness, and the importance attached to a severely political ideology, the emergence of an administrative class or elite operating from a prestigious centre through the medium, in the main, of one prestigious language have tended to bring into being an independent political or "civic culture" which stands outside the traditional pattern of cultures in much the same way as a culture related to a religious organization, church or set of ecclesiastical institutions has tended in the past to separate itself from the secular elements of a culture or to dominate those elements. There is no question but that there is this polarization of a 'civic' and a 'group' culture in the USSR, and that its existence is largely influenced by if not synonymous with the polarization of attitudes to the Russian and the local languages.

B. SELECTION OF VARIABLES FOR STUDY

i. *Limitation of Choice*

The variables which were selected for a study of the Soviet Union are those which a judgment of the operation of bilingualism elsewhere, and especially bilingualism in education appeared to indicate were relevant. In that sense the choice of variables may be somewhat arbitrary. The present study did not begin by distinguishing all the variables which appeared to operate in the Soviet context, nor has it been the aim of the study to examine all the inter-relationships of the variables that actually were selected. Furthermore where a variable has been identified and where it is considered in its relationships with other variables it has not always been the case that it has been given the degree of consideration commensurate with its importance. For instance the importance of religion is recognised in the study, but for various reasons it has not been examined separately in any depth. Then again, within the sphere of economic forces which are taken into account 'job opportunities' for speakers of one rather than another language is an important factor, but it has not been examined in any detail. All this is inevitable, but it is hoped that such special aspects when they are treated in the future will be the better understood for being placed in a wider context.

Then again, it is necessary to distinguish between variables which are the precondition of bilingualism-*primary* variables; and those which determine the nature of the bilingualism which actually emerges – *secondary* variables. Among the primary variables may be identified geographical, historical, demographic and purely linguistic. It would have been exciting to have been able to treat all these, but from my standpoint the ones which offer most opportunities for useful comparison with other bilingual countries are the demographic and historical. Consequently it is to these primary variables that most of the attention of the investigation is devoted. Similarly there are several variables which can be termed secondary or shaping factors – political decision and policy, educational administration and pedagogy, and language planning as envisaged by the strict or pure linguist, are some of these. Here again the choice has been made according to their presumed usefulness for further comparative studies, and, it must be confessed, by my own inclination. It will be observed that, first, education, then political policy, and last language planning strictly interpreted appear in that order of importance.

ii. *Political Variables*

The most generally interesting if not the most important of all the factors, and one which straddles the distinction between primary and secondary variables, is the political. This has called for fairly detailed consideration, partly because it provides one of the most fruitful areas for comparative study and partly because it not only influences but actually controls the operation of other variables. Strange as it may seem the political factor operates retroactively even and influences the operation of history in determining attitudes to languages in the USSR. Soviet historiography has distorted the manner in which history has influenced Soviet international relations, and to that extent the interpretation of history has been used by political agencies to produce one rather than another form of language contact. The case of the Central Asian nationalities and especially the Tadzhiks is much to the point here.

The social and political policy is looked at, I hope, with sympathy, and from a standpoint which, for the purposes of this study, is well within Soviet socialist political theory, rather than from an exclusively critical standpoint and against an external background of a radically different political theory. In other words what I have done, as far as possible, is to accept the Soviet point of view, to examine how it works and the consequences; and only then to make a judgment concerning its consistency or inherent duplicity, as the case may be. I suggest that a lack of objectivity, however excusable, is as much to be deplored in critics of the USSR as it is in the writings which appear from inside the Soviet Union. Both have impeded a true understanding of the situation of the nationalities and their languages. One consequence of the approach which has been adopted is the elaboration of the theory of the 'two paths', an examination of the relationship of that theory to the belief in the possibility of a development which is in truth 'nationalist in form and socialist in content', and finally a judgment of the essential consistency of Soviet policy even if the implementation of that policy is characterised by periodical readjustments. Such an objective, even sympathetic approach, does not preclude the possibility of a critical conclusion to the effect that the Soviet languages policy is consistent possibly because it is mechanical and dogmatic, essentially static and to that extent sterile. It provides no basis for development, and is therefore inconsistent with Marxist-Leninist philosophy.

iii. *Physical Variables*

The physical conditions in which the languages are spoken and have contact with each other are obviously important, and an attempt is made to consider the influence of geographical isolation such as that of the Daghestan languages or the Pamiri dialects, or the isolation experienced by speakers of large numbers of languages in the deserts of Central Asia or the icy desolation of the North, or by speakers of languages isolated by the nature of their occupations, nomads and dwellers of rural areas. Similarly the break down of isolation and the development of urban life, the improvement of communications and transport are taken into account in the analysis of the varying degrees to which languages are maintained in different geographical and social situations. Among the most important of the forces working towards the breakdown of isolation is the movement of populations either from the immediate localities of towns or across vast distances. If we are to understand the nature of that influence some attention has to be given to the operation of sub-factors of migration, namely the stability or otherwise of the immigrant group, its size and diffusion, the extent to which it is reinforced, as well as its linguistic status before arrival, whether for instance it was already bilingual, or what languages it had contact with previously. Similarly the linguistic and cultural distance between the immigrants' native language and that of the locality in which they now live has to be considered. In all these matters the importance of the element of social planning is taken into account, and the extent to which such planning influences the nature of present day language contact, compared with traditional forms.

iv. *Social-cultural Variables*

Social and cultural characteristics constitute another set of variables. The differences between languages have to be examined along a develop-mental co-ordinate – ranging from relatively primitive tribal groups speaking a variety of small dialects, to major nations possessing classical cultures and standardized languages of great stability. The language groups need to be considered also on a horizontal scale – the way in which they differ among themselves according to the variety of uses to which they are put, the nature of the social and cultural milieux they re-flect, as well as the kinds of contact situations in which they may partic-ipate. For this reason a typology of Soviet languages along both dimen-sions is proposed for examination. Similarly the changing structure of the groups speaking the languages is a subject for discussion. Reference has been made to the importance of the age and sex composition of immigrant groups, of the original communities to which they belonged, as well as of the host populations. But these two features of age and sex distribution have a significance beyond the migrant groups. Differences in the fertility of families in different nationalities and between rural and urban popula-tions are important in the context of high levels of natural population growth in some areas and the consequence of this for the maintenance of Russian dominance. High fertility rates may help to maintain local languages even when the language community is losing its relative im-portance demographically within a national territory. Then again, in most developing countries bilingualism is almost always a characteristic of the male population. The women are far more restricted in their social and linguistic contacts and they are, for other reasons also, more conserv-ative linguistically. At the same time and for the same reasons that establish them as conserving factors, women in isolated and rural areas tend not to be active in promoting the use of the languages for other than the most limited and often trivial purposes. The disturbance of the sex balance caused by migration is relevant here. The consequence of intermarriage, both as a feature of urbanization and as an independent variable has also to be examined, and the consequences of intermarriage for language maintenance illustrated.

v. *Religion*

This factor is immensely important in any consideration of bilingualism and lends itself very well as a basis for the comparative study of our subject. It is perhaps the most potent factor in the maintenance of the Welsh language in Wales, and it enters into the consideration of the same phenomenon in Canada, The Republic of South Africa, Belgium and Ireland, to name only a few of the areas where comparison is relevant. Historically, too, the relationship of religion and the maintenance of the vernacular has been extremely close. Religion is one of the bastions of traditionalism and in consequence it exerts a considerable influence on the speed with which peoples pass through the various stages of bilingualism leading to ultimate monolingualism. However, though all these considerations affect the situation of languages in the USSR the exhaustive treatment of religion has not been attempted in this study. This is due in the main to a personal inadequacy, secondly to the fact that the work of Benningsen and Quelquejay makes a further study at the moment somewhat redundant, thirdly any treatment of the religious factor would of necessity have to give considerable attention to the situation of the Jews and they, I am convinced, have to be the subject of a separate study initially since in their case religion and nationality and language are difficult to disentangle. In addition there are features of the present religious situation in the USSR and of the relationship of religion to political ideology which require a preparatory study. For instance though traditional religions exert, over the whole of the Soviet Union a decreasing influence in determining the choice of language, there is no doubt that just as Christianity reached the heart of the Roman Empire through the intermediary of Greek, reaching out from Greek enclaves in Rome, so the homogenous influence of the Communist ideology, as we try to show, is promoted mainly through the influence of Russian, whether directly when it is used in the communication of the fundamental tenets of the dogma, or indirectly when it exerts its influence on the other languages, especially their political and ideological vocabularies.

vi. *Education*

The interaction of the educational with the other social, political, demographic and linguistic factors constitute the central point of interest of the Soviet Union from my point of view, though quite obviously this need not be the case for everybody. Consequently the analysis of how educational administration and pedagogy reflect and reinforce language policy generally, the comparison of Soviet policy and its implementation in education with the approaches adopted in other multilingual communities, and the part played by the linguistic aspects of the school curriculum in promoting the social uniformation of the USSR, as well as the cultural 'rapprochment' of the many language communities – these are the main lines of the treatment of the operation of education factors in the multilingual situation of the Soviet Union. Some consideration is also given to the changes which have occurred in the nature of Soviet bilingualism under the influence of education, from oral to literate, and from fortuitous to planned. At the same time such a study as this cannot avoid considering the fact that education is not exclusively a socializing factor but is directed towards the development of the minds and capacities of individual children without regard for their national or linguistic affiliations. Consequently in a discussion of the pedagogic aspect of education in the USSR the psychological considerations are touched upon. A satisfactory treatment of these individualistic aspects of Soviet bilingualism is important enough to deserve a more extensive and deeper study.

vii. *Language Variables*

Whatever may be said about social and political factors, about the changes in the distribution and the relative sizes of language groups and nationalities, and about the various aspects of education, in the end the focal point of language contact studies must be the fate of the languages themselves, and it is the recognition of this fact which makes Weinreich's classical study seminal. The present study has not attempted to traverse within the USSR the same ground which Weinreich explored on such a broad scale, but it has tried to profit from his work and that of others such as Haugen. The differences between dialect contact and language contact are important in the USSR, and the varying degrees of intelligibility among dialects, the different levels of standardization and the varying traditions of literary cultures enter into the discussion, too. The types of contact have to be analyzed and categorized and these types have to be seen in the context of different types of ethnic communities – national; minority (traditional or immigrant); dispersed, or concentrated in close enclaves etc. In addition there is the functional differentiation between languages in contact – relationships determined by 'division of labour', whereby they may undertake all the social roles indifferently, or maintain a flexible compartmentalization of use, or become rigidly related to some uses and not others, as might be the case with a diglossic situation where one dialect was developed exclusively for a religious function. These all occur within the USSR. Some Soviet languages are in process of standardization, and are made up of several distinct and sometimes extreme dialects; they are spoken by groups for whom the tradition of education and of literacy is relatively short and its incidence shallow, and there are cleavages between urban and rural communities speaking the same language. Such a conjunction of circumstances establishes a diglossic contact situation which though it does not conform strictly with Ferguson's definition is nevertheless an exemplification of one aspect of that concept. The Tadzhik language is a case in point.

But perhaps the most important aspect of the study of the operation of the linguistic variables is the change which has been brought about by the planned intervention under the control of central agencies, resulting in the development of mass or popular bilingualism where previously there existed only a limited bilingualism. Second is the fact that this popular bilingualism is literate where previously it was almost entirely oral, and third, the fact that foreign languages are now no longer the prerogative of a few (constituting an élitist bilingualism), but part of the educational system which reaches all children. It is also a fact that the pressure on the acquisition of a foreign language is such as to ensure that a foreign language enters into a pattern of popular bilingualism almost at the same level as the Russian language does in the Central Asian Republics, for instance.

Finally there are the 'linguistic consequences' for the Soviet languages, arising out of increased and intensified contact, and of the changes in the nature of those contacts. The discussion of these matters embraces several of the non-Russian languages but the main interest lies with the fate of the Russian language. Meillet suggests that the result of bilingualism is the down grading of the native language – "alors l'ancienne langue tend a se dégrader" (Meillet 1952, 77). But from a study of the developments in the USSR this is not the case when there are interventionist and planning policies directed at the native languages. The consequences for these languages are governed by the nature of the social and linguistic engineering policies which are adopted and pursued. In spite of intensified and extended contact there is no denying that sociologically the 'national languages' of the Union Republics have gained considerably over the last fifty years, though in relation to Russian they may still be underprivileged; and it is also the case that many of the languages of much smaller groups than those which speak the recognised 'national languages' are far from having experienced either sociological or linguistic retreat. The position is somewhat anomalous – relative to their past histories the non-Russian languages are in much better shape and have gained in prestige and in viability as media for the purposes of more extensive and more sophisticated communication. On the other hand relative to Russian their situation is if anything less satisfactory, and there are signs of the increasing encroachment of that language in domains of use which were, within their native territories, the prerogative of the 'national languages'; and there is increasing conflict between them. What does emerge however is the fact that the planning policies pursued by governments have a radical effect on the kinds of relationship which, it has been customary to maintain, characterized contact situations.

viii. *Russian*

Whatever the sociological standing of the non-Russian languages may be the influence of Russian upon them is very considerable. The current use of a Cyrillic alphabet influences all languages, but not all languages equally or all languages in like manner. This is what one would expect among these languages: some belong to the same family of languages as Russian, and some of those which do not belong have had very long and very close contact with that language. Others have been isolated from Russian, until comparatively recently, partly because of geographical distance, and partly because of extreme difference in the culture and ways of life which they reflect. Differences emerge in any comparison of the ways in which Slavic, Turkic and some Paleoasiatic languages have reacted to contact with Russian. It is interesting to note that some language groups appear to be conservative in their reactions while others are more receptive, and this is something one would expect from observation of contact elsewhere. For instance, speakers of French in France are more reluctant to introduce English words into their language than speakers of French in Belgium. It is also the case that the speakers of the two languages within Belgium, French and Flemish, are dissimilar in their attitude to the adoption of foreign words and importations. These differences are observable in the Soviet Union too. Speakers of Beludzhi are more conservative in Turkeminstan than the speakers of the same language in Tadzhikstan, thus bearing out the differences observed between French speakers in France and Belgium. It is also the case that vis-a-vis the same language, Russian, there is a tendency for Georgians to be more conservative than Armenians, bearing out the observation of the differences in the attitude of French and Flemish speakers in Belgium.

However the changes which the extension of Russian influence may have brought about on other languages may, in the long run be nothing like as important as the changes which extended influence may induce in the Russian language itself. Maxim Gorky was heard on more than one occasion to inveigh against the possible dialectization of the Russian language. The policies which were pursued in and continued after his time would have given him no reassurance. The history of Greek and

Latin would have been in his mind, perhaps. The great classicist Richard Bentley argued that if he had "to name some of the causes of the changes and mixture of the Greek or indeed of any other tongue, he would have pitched upon empire in the first place. For even common sense will tell one, that if a nation extends its conquests over other countries of a different speech [...] it may extinguish the ancient language of the conquered; but its own must needs have a little mixture and imbibe something from the tongue that it destroys". The tendency for Russian as for any language which serves as a lingua franca is not only to be dialectized, but generally to be simplified, and for what is most characteristic of the Russian language to become less evident. At the same time as this attenuation of Russian is occurring there is a tendency that non-native speakers of Russian, especially on formal occasions, and even more so when it comes to writing, may be over-zealous in their search for correctness. In this too they are no different from non-native speakers of English in Africa or India. These two processes, dialectization and hyper-correctness in the more formal domains of use may lead, in the view of some observers in the USSR, to the emergence, very gradually, of dual norms for Russian among non-native speakers, neither of which conforms very closely to the norms observed by native speakers.

However, what may have happened to other languages which have extended their domain may not be a true guide to the fate of Russian. The centralized control of planning and planned agencies may retard as well as govern the direction of change. Malkiel has spoken of the time scale on which changes occur and refers to a "critical gap, ranging from four to six hundred years according to zone and language". We observe that many centuries of unplanned, fortuitous contact has not, so far as concerns most of the languages of the USSR and especially the major languages, altered either their inherent character or their demographic standing substantially – it is unlikely that it will be very much faster in future. And now that many of the languages are taught in school for the first time and are used as teaching languages with an increasing literary repertoire for teachers and readers to draw on, it may be that the pace of change will become even slower. The history of the Albanian language is significant. It has endured the successive domination of Romans, Slavs and Turks for over two thousand years and it still survives. The main conclusion to be drawn from this study is that in spite of many interventions by central planning agencies, indeed partly because of these interventions, the non-Russian national languages are strong, and these languages, unquestionably, will remain within a very complex pattern of bilingual and multilingual situations. It may be that what the Soviet educationist has to do is not to deny that fact or seek to invalidate it by new measures, but to ensure that educational and broader social policy maximizes the advantages and minimizes the disadvantages which inevitably appear.

Chapter 2

THE BACKGROUND OF LINGUISTIC HETEROGENEITY

A. HISTORICAL SETTING

i. *Developmental Differences*

The linguistic complexity of the Soviet Union is the heritage of a long history as well as the consequence of policies pursued during the last fifty years. The military and expansionist policies of the Tsars not only created the framework within which any subsequent 'nationalities' policy had to operate, but to a large extent, and perhaps inevitably, determined some of the directions which such policies followed. Russian expansion may be said to begin in earnest with Ivan the Terrible. In 1552 he took Kazhan and thus put an end to the subjugation imposed on the Russians by the Tartar Khans, which had confined them geographically and isolated them from other Slavs, like the Ukrainians and Poles. About the middle of the Seventeenth Century the Cossaks and Ukrainians were brought under Russian control, and following this, under Peter the Great and Katherine, the Baltic peoples, parts of Poland and later still, areas of the Caucusus were incorporated. By 1881 the expansion was virtually complete, with the acquisition of Turkestan by Alexander II. As a result the Russian Empire became an immense multilingual state, consisting of about 180 different linguistic groups. Some of these had been brought up in a Western European tradition, as was the case with the Russians and Ukrainians. Others, like the Armenians and Georgians, belonged to different though in many respects equally great traditions. Others again had histories which even more widely separated them from the West, and

from each other. These consisted of the very complex Tatar-Turkic
Muslim groups.

Not only did the Bolsheviks inherit this vast linguistic conglomerate
but in their preparations for the Revolution and later, when in power,
they were committed to rectify much of the harm the previous rulers and
administrators had perpetrated. Having incorporated such diverse national groups the Tsars had pursued a policy of ruthless assimilation; but
more important, from the point of view of subsequent events, they prac-
tised an equally ruthless suppression of national minorities. Their policy
blocked the development of the national languages of even such large
populations as the Belorussians and Ukrainians. Attempts to develop national cultures, to enrich the existing languages and to create alphabets
were frustrated. This, from the despotic Tsarist point of view, perfectly
logical policy was applied rigorously in the schools that existed, so that
non-Russian peoples, with very few and isolated exceptions, were denied
education in their native tongue, even if education was available to them
at all.

When the Revolution had been inaugurated the Bolsheviks had to
tackle the problem of the co-existence of social organizations and communities on several levels of development, spread over vast distances and
inhabiting extremely different kinds of land, or enjoying different types
of climate and consequently, different ways of life. Not only was the
range of heterogeneity very considerable but it was derived from many
diverse sources. There were differences in economic development, especially between European and Asian peoples; differences in social structure between, for instance the advanced nations and the small, almost
tribal communities of the North; differences in education at various levels
from elementary to University, and in the nature of the support for such
provision – secular in the West and mainly religious in Central Asia;
differences in the kind of religious affiliation and its degree, especially
between Christian, Muslim and Jew; differences in degree of participation in social organizations, especially as between urban and rural areas;
differences in political traditions, in values and norms of public and
private behaviour, in patterns of family life and in the basic psychological
traits of the very numerous large and small nationalities.

These societies represented, in fact almost a complete picture of the
mode of development of human communities, according to Soviet
theory. Briefly, this theory postulated the existence, first, of small clans
and tribal (ethnic) groups, *narod* which were associated with a primitive
and communal system. Later with the development of the early class
societies, a new type of community emerged which was no longer based
on blood relationship – namely the *narodnost*, with a degree of linguistic,
cultural and territorial unity as well as economic ties. The *narodnost*

precedes and is very much less stable than the *natsiya* (nation) which is characterized by its relative stability in language, shared and common settlement of a territory, economic life and basic cultural features. It does not follow that there is an immutable law of development from one stage to the next; and it does happen, and in fact in some instances in the Soviet Union no discouragement is offered, when a *narodnost* for various reasons is unable to consolidate as a nation and comes to adopt the fundamental or defining characteristics of a nation with which it has close relations. But if we make reasonable allowances for the inevitable simplification and distortion which any kind of categorization involves it is possible to identify at least four levels of development among Soviet communities and ethnic groups at the beginning of the 20th century.

First, there were the peoples who had attained a high level of industrial development, had created a relatively sophisticated culture and civilization and had become self-conscious national entities. They could be said to have developed, to all intents and purposes, something like the normal concept of the modern national state. These were the republics on the western marches and to the south. In addition to Russia itself, this group included the Ukraine, Belorussia, Georgia, Latvia, Lithuania, Armenia, Estonia and Moldavia. For these any further development was regarded in almost exclusively political terms – the transformation of 'bourgeois' into 'socialist' nations. Second, there were those nationalities which, though less advanced than the first group, had nevertheless embarked on a process of industrialization and national unification and mobilization. Some of them had become *narodnost* in the Middle Ages, but their development had been retarded and they were in many instances no more than a congeries of small, isolated ethnic groups at the third or fourth level of development which we describe below. Their social organization, taken as a whole, retained features of feudalism. This group includes the Uzbeks, Turkmens, Kazakhs and Tatars.

The third group includes Kirgiz, Uygurs, Kara-Kalpaks, Maris, Udmurts, Yakuts and many others. According to Stalin they preserved "the pastoral and tribal forms of life, [...] or they have not yet progressed completely beyond the semifeudal life." In many cases they were splintered communities – separated enclaves within much larger and much more unified communities. They retained a common ethnic root and the relation of dialect variations of the same language, but were otherwise isolated from each other. Finally there were the very many ethnic groups which were still at the clan or tribe level, with primitive social organizations and a low level of economic development. These included the small peoples of the Far North, Siberia, and the Far East, and some of the remoter peoples of the North Caucusus. There were in addition to these four well recognized categories a small number of ethnic groups which, being unrelated in the true sense to any of the main ethnic classifications of the USSR, formed a collection of peoples with little prospect of independent development – the Gipsies, Arabs and Aisons for instance (Gardanov et al., 1961, passim).

In addition to the differences existing between the various nationalities and Republics there were differences of development within nearly all but the most primitive peoples. In some cases, for instance Azerbaydzhan with its great oil field and refineries as well as an undeveloped agriculture, the economic development of the country was far from uniform. In others the level of literacy varied between the areas occupied by the people, especially between the towns and the countryside: this was very true within Russia itself. Nor did the levels of development correspond, either within or between the Republics, to any consistent geographical division, and instances of similar levels of development were spread from Eastern Europe to the Pacific, and from the Arctic to the Black Sea.

The present linguistic situation, however much it may be affected by novel political and cultural considerations is overwhelmingly the consequence of what people have made of their geographical conditions, their history and their long standing language and ethnic contacts over many centuries. Isolation whether because of high and rugged contours as in the Daghestan highlands, in the Zeravshanskiy and Darvazskiy khrebets, and the whole complex of highlands surrounding Dushanbe in Tadzhikstan, or the sometimes desolate nomadic areas below the Kara Sea and between the lower reaches of Irtysh and Yenisey rivers and on the Kalyma plain help to preserve the local languages. Yagnobi, for instance, has survived because its speakers moved to the high mountain valleys; the Ossetes in the North Caucusus, and speakers of the Pamiri dialects of Tadzhikstan did the same in their own locations. The Uzbek 'language-divide' in the Ferghana valley shows many and considerable indentations into Tadzhik and Kirgiz areas, as well as creating small enclaves of speakers of Uygur. The Caucusus, 'the modern Tower of Babel', is the home of some 50 different language groups, and one of the reasons for the perpetuation of this complex situation is the existence of remote but not unpopulated areas, frequently above 10,000 feet and averaging 6,000, stretching from Krasnod at the foothills to the North West, almost to Baku on the Caspian to the South East, and north from Orjonikidze to beyond Erevan and Mount Ararat into Turkey and Iran. The area mainly to the north of the Vostochno-Kazakhstanskaya oblast in the North East corner of Kazakhstan, and Gorno-Altayskaya, west of the Altai range, are not unlike the Caucusus in some respects, but are much less complex linguistically.

On the other hand, areas like the neighbourhood of Tashkent, Samarkand, Ashkabad, Ferghana, Frunze, Dzhambul, because their relative lowland character facilitates communications between people of different language groups, possess conditions conducive to the spread of multi-lingualism. An area like Pavlodar, at the junction of the railway from the west and the river Irtysh, and of five important roads branching into the Altayskiy kray and Kulundinskaya steppe, has a considerable mixed language population. Good communications in such areas are a factor in bringing about language contact, and the same is true of centres like Chimkent, on the junction of a tributary of the Arys, with railways running from Tashkent and Dzhambul down along the Arys from the Aral sea, as well as important roads. Frunze, and especially Dushanbe are similar cases – the latter situated on the crossing of four major roads and the junction of two railways from the south. Ashkabad, at the foot of an extension of the Alborz mountains and on the border with Iran, has good road and river communications, as well as railways in several directions. A good example of the influence of lines of communication upon the languages spoken in an area is the completion of the Northern Pechora Line which brought into the Komi ASSR, and into contact with each other, speakers of Russian and other languages not native to the area. All the centres we have named are remarkable for their polyglot character, a consequence, in the main of a long history of social intermingling.

ii. *Quantitative Differences*

TABLE 1

National composition of the USSR 1926-1970 in thousands[a]

Nationality	1926 Totals	1959 Totals	Percentage of 1926	1970 Totals	Percentage of 1959
Russian	77,791	114,114	146	129,015	113
Ukrainian	31,194	37,253	119	40,753	109
Uzbek	3,904	6,015	150	9,195	150
Belorussian	4,738	7,913	160	9,052	113
Tatar	2,916	4,968	160	5,931	120
Kazakh	3,968	3,622	92	5,299	140
Azerbaydzhan	1,706	2,940	175	4,380	146
Armenian	1,567	2,787	178	3,559	128
Georgian	1,820	2,692	149	3,245	121

[a] Sources: 1926, and 1959 Census and *Izvestiya* April 1971 for 1970. Census Changes in status of some nationalities, e.g. Moldavian make 1926-1959 comparison unprofitable.

Nationality	1926 Totals	1959 Totals	1959 Percentage of 1926	1970 Totals	1970 Percentage of 1959
Moldavian	278	2,214	—	2,698	123
Lithuanian	41	2,326	—	2,665	115
Jew	2,680	2,268	85	2,151	94
Tadzhik	978	1,397	138	2,136	160
German	1,238	1,620	132	1,846	114
Chuvash	1,117	1,470	133	1,694	115
Turkmens	763	1,002	130	1,525	150
Kirgiz	762	969	122	1,452	150
Latvian	141	1,400	—	1,430	102
Daghestanis comprising	619	945	153	1,365	144
Avar	158	270	171	396	148
Lezgin	134	223	166	324	148
Dargin		158	—	231	146
Kumyk	94	135	142	189	140
Lak	—	64	—	86	134
Tabasaran	94	35	112	55	157
Nogai	46	39	90	52	133
Rutyl	—	6.7	—	12	179
Tsukhurs	—	7.3	—	11	150
Aguls	—	6.7	—	8.8	133
Mordvin	1,340	1,285	95	1,263	98
Bashkir	713	989	140	1,240	125
Poles	762	1,380	—	1,167	84
Estonian	154	989	—	1,007	102
Udmurts	504	625	125	704	112
Chechens	318	419	133	613	148
Mari	428	504	120	599	119
Ossetians	272	413	148	488	119
Komi	226	287	128	322	117
Permyak	149	144	97	153	106
Korean	86	314	—	357	112
Bulgarians	111	324	—	351	107
Greek	253	309	120	337	109
Buryat	237	253	106	315	124
Yakut	240	293	97	296	127
Kabardinian	139	204	148	280	138
Karakalpak	146	173	120	236	136
Gipsies	61	132	210	175	130
Uygurs	42	95	220	173	179
Hungarians	—	155	—	166	108
Ingush	74	106	143	158	151
Gagauz	—	124	—	157	126
Peoples of the North, of which	—	130	—	151	116
Nenets	—	23	—	29	126

Nationality	1926 Totals	1959 Totals	1959 Percentage of 1926	1970 Totals	1970 Percentage of 1959
Evenki	37	25	70	25	100
Khanty	22	19	88	21	111
Chukchi	13	12	92	14	116
Even	—	9.1	—	12	130
Nanais	5	8.0	160	10	125
Mansi	5	6.4	130	7.7	120
Koryak	—	6.3	—	7.5	120
Dolgan	0.6	3.9	600	4.9	125
Nivkh	4	3.7	93	4.4	118
Selkup	15	3.8	25	4.3	113
Ulchi	—	2.1	—	2.4	114
Saami	19	1.8	10	1.9	105
Udegeis	—	1.4	—	1.5	107
Itelmen	4	1.1	30	1.3	119
Keti	—	1.0	—	1.2	120
Orochi	—	0.8	—	1.1	136
Nganasans	—	0.75	—	1.0	133
Yukagirs	—	0.4	—	0.6	150
Kareli	248	167	66	146	87
Tuvin	—	100	—	139	139
Kalmyk	128	106	83	137	129
Rumanian	4	106	—	119	111
Karachai	55	81	148	113	140
Adygeis	65	80	122	100	125
Kurds	54	59	116	89	150
Finns	115	93	—	85	91
Abkhaz	56	65	116	93	128
Turki	—	35	—	79	225
Khakass	45	57	126	67	117
Balkar	33	42	127	60	143
Altai	39	45	115	56	125
Cherkess	65	30	47	40	133
Dungan	14	22	156	39	178
Iranian	43	21	50	28	133
Abazin	13	20	155	25	125
Aisors	9	22	242	24	104
Czechs	30	25	84	21	84
Tats	28	11	40	17	154
Shortsi	12	15	125	16	165
Slovak	—	15	—	12	80
Others	1,221	108	—	126	—
U.S.S.R.	147,027	208,827	142	241,720	115

Apart from the kinds of difference in development to which we have referred Table 1 emphasizes at least two other major dimensions of difficul-

ty which the new regime had to face in the attempt to move towards a planned economy and culture, including the planning of language development. The language communities are not only numerous but vary enormously in size. One has a population of over 114 millions; there is one with a total of 37 millions, three with totals between 5 and 10 millions, six between 2 and 5 millions, eight between 1 and 2 millions, five between half a million and a million, eight between a quarter and half a million, thirteen between 100 and 250 thousands, ten between 50 and 100 thousand, nineteen between 10 and 50 thousands, fourteen between 5 and 10 thousand, thirteen between 1 and 5 thousands, and three below a thousand. The degree of uniformity of the distribution of the population in relation to geographical area, and the differences in general population density varies between the extremely sparsely populated Yakutia on the one hand and the far more concentrated Armenia with an average population density at present of over 54.4 per square kilometer.

All these represent a vast complex of greatly differing ethnic and language communities. In 1949 (*Izvestiya* 5.5.1949) the number of nationalities was claimed to be 70 though in 1927 it had been reckoned at upward of 169 (*Sovetskaya Strana* Aug. 1929 p. 110). The Census of 1970 has been conducted on the basis of 122 recognized nationalities (Podiachickh 1969, 638 et seq.). The disparity in numbers is due partly to a change in the definition of what constitutes a nation in the Union, a complex legal issue, which although it is a factor of influence in promoting the existence of multilingualism and is a vital factor in language planning at certain levels, need not at this stage concern us, since the official ethnic status or designation of the group does not, save indirectly, determine who actually speaks what language. The disparity is also due to the changes which are observed in specific ethnic affiliation, so that in consequence some very small tribes cease to be significant for census returns. In 1917, 42 thousand persons in the Ferghana Oblast and 1,627 elsewhere regarded themselves as Kypshaks. In 1926 the total was 33.5 thousands. In the 1926 Census such ethnic (clan or tribal) groups of the Uzbeks as the Tyurks (60 thousand), and Kuramas (50 thousand) listed themselves as separate entities though they were all Uzbek speaking bilinguals at that time. In the 1959 Census the Kuramas do not figure at all – they have merged with the Uzbeks. Only about 100 Kypshaks of the lower Ferghana Valley called themselves by their clan name in 1959, while slightly over 4,000 people called themselves Tyurks. The same is true to a lesser extent of the Kara-Kalpaks of the Ferghana Valley in relation to the Uzbeks. In the 1939 Census many of the Pamiri tribal groups listed themselves independently of the Tadzhiks among whom they lived. In the 1959 Census these groups no longer appear, and it is assumed they now regard themselves as Tadzhiks.

Such a continuing process is regarded with favour in the USSR. In a comment on the Census preliminary returns an economist has noted that a "progressive process of drawing together of nationalities and the cohesion of peoples is taking place in the USSR", and after referring to the part played by the diffusion of the Russian language in this process he continues: "The changes in the size of individual nationalities indicate a process of consolidation of individual peoples, in which small ethnic groups unite to form larger related groups of peoples. Along with this consolidation the assimilation of the peoples of the USSR is also taking place; in the latter process persons of one nationality adopt the culture and customs of another. This is accompanied by increases in the size of the population of some nationalities and decreases in the size of others. Examples of nationalities that are being assimilated are the Mordvinians (-22,000), the Karelians (-21,000), and of particular interest in the light of current official antagonisms, the Jews are singled out for mention as one of the peoples who are being assimilated (-117,000, or 6%)." (*Izvestiya*, 17-4-1971).

Finally, changes have been introduced in the criteria for judging what constitutes one's ethnic group. In the 1926 Census an individual was required to state this in objective terms – his actual national origin, *narodnost*. In 1939 a subjective criterion was substituted – namely ethnic preference or chosen affiliation – *nationalnost*. The 1970 Census attempted to elicit information not only concerning the nationality and national language of each person but also the more general multilingual competence of each person, since it required him to name any other language in which he might be fluent. The number of nationalities does not bear any really exact relationship to the number of languages which are spoken in the Union, since many languages are used by groups which are not granted the status of nation. In 1926, 150 languages were officially recognized; since then the number has been considerably reduced. At present newspapers are printed in well over 122 indigenous and foreign languages.

B. CATEGORIES OF LANGUAGES

i. *Indo-European*

a. *East Slavic*

What makes the linguistic situation even more interesting and complex is the fact that many of the languages belong to widely different families of languages; there are several generic types, all making for a great diversity of contact patterns within an equally great variety of cultural and economic levels of development. (Matthews 1947, 1951). The first group of languages, the Indo-European, eight in number, are not the largest group but they are without question historically, demographically and politically the most influential. The group is represented by the East Slavic branch comprising Russian, Ukrainian and Belorussian. The demographic importance of East Slavic depends very largely on the influence of Russian, the speakers of which have played a leading role over many centuries, militarily, politically and latterly ideologically. In addition to consolidating their own national integrity in Russia itself they expanded into the far north and the eastern parts of Asia, into the South Uralian Steppes and along the Volga and Don into the Caucusus and surrounding areas. Although the Russian language has penetrated into the most remote areas, and is doing so ever more extensively, the very great majority of its speakers still live within the immense RSFSR, which has international boundaries with Norway, Finland, Poland, China, Korea; and internally with Kazakhstan, Azerbaydzhan, Georgia, Estonia, Latvia, Belorussia, and the Ukraine. In addition to these external ethnic and linguistic contacts there are within the RSFSR well over 50 different linguistic groups. It is not surprising that the Russian language has such a pervasive linguistic (apart from literary and cultural) influence, and enters into so many bilingual complexes. This natural, almost inevitable situation, has been steadfastly reinforced with considerable calculation and by economic and ideological manipulation.

Of the other East Slavic representatives the Ukrainians inhabit the rich land to the S.W. of the RSFSR and share common frontiers with Poland to the West, Moldavia to the S.W., and with Belorussia to the North. They occupy a somewhat anomalous position historically: until the middle of the 18th century they were not usually regarded as a separate people; and most Central Asians, for instance, still regard them as an indistinguishable element in the Russian majority. Nevertheless Ukrainians themselves are intensely conscious of their separate ethnic identity, and take every opportunity to assert it culturally and politically, at home and abroad. The Belorussians who also speak an East Slavic language are a compact and relatively homogenous ethnic group, though they have had a long history of contact and conflict not only with Russians but with Lithuanians and later Polish invaders. Belorussia has close geographical contacts with Latvia to the north, Poland and Lithuania. There is considerable bilingualism along those borders. Belorussians do not have the same sharp awareness of national and linguistic identity as the Ukrainians and other Soviet peoples, and are regarded by non-Slavs as even more intimately identified with the Russian majority than the Ukrainians.

The South East Baltic area is inhabited by two nations who speak a Slavonic language – Lithuanians and Latvians. With the non – Slavic

Estonians and Karelians, who speak varieties of West Finnic they represent a group of tribes who, although they have settled the land since the third millenium B.C., have formed identifiable and cohesive nations only in the 13th, 15th and 19th centuries respectively, mainly in response to the military challenge of the German Knights and the Swedes. They are relatively advanced and developed, formerly independent countries. Lithuania has considerable numbers of Russian immigrants in the towns, Belorussians on the borders with that Republic, Latvians and Poles with whom they were associated for nearly 500 years until the end of the 18th century. Even today the Polish style of life is not unrecognizable in Lithuania. Nevertheless it is very conscious of its own particular way of life, especially vis-a-vis the Russians. Latvia has similar infiltrations of Russians, together with Lithuanians, and a very large Jewish community which contributed greatly to its development, especially in Riga. Latvians, probably more than all the other Baltic countries, find themselves adversely affected by Russian influences during the last fifty years.

There are other Slavic languages represented by fairly large national groups in the USSR, though not strictly speaking indigenous to it. Among these are the Polish, Slovak, Bulgarian and some smaller groups speaking Serbian.

b. *Iranian*

The Indo-European languages include an important family of non-Slavic languages, the Iranian, in the Southern USSR and in Central Asian Republics. The most interesting, and perhaps the most important in the USSR is Tadzhik, spoken in what is probably the most mountainous area of the Soviet Union, on the borders with Iran and Afghanistan. Plains Tadzhik, the north-west dialect, embraces literary Tadzhik and has been considerably influenced because of contact with Uzbek, Kirgiz and Kazakh. The Soviets make the dubious claim for this language and its classical literature as the most directly representative of the ancient Iranic. "It should be pointed out that the peoples of Central Asia exercised a great influence on the cultural development of the western Persians of the Sassanid state. Thus for example, silk production came to Persia from Central Asia. The epics of the various Persian peoples consciously absorbed the works of the peoples of Central Asia, especially those of Khorezm and Sogdiana. The culture of the period of the Sassanids as well as that of Achaemenids, was thus indebted to the activities of the Central Asian peoples." (Quoted in Tillet, 1969, 104).

The Tadzhiks are traditionally Muslims, retentive of their faith and reputed to be clannish, but they have not been as opposed as other Central Asians to the process of linguistic and cultural penetration, and they have always had close contact with Uzbeks. Thus the Chust and

Kassansai (Uzbek) rayony at the foot of the Kuramanskiy range, with a combination of moderately good communications together with areas which are somewhat isolated, are characterized by intense bilingualism. These are smaller and less important centres of centuries old contact than those we have described before. Their communications are restricted, compared with those of Dushanbe and Frunze for instance. In consequence, in spite of the large number of people who have moved into the areas, the native population have preserved not only the national languages but the dialectal characteristics of those languages supremely well, though mainly among the older generations and in the rural area.

Inhabitants of the Rayony know both Uzbek and Tadzhik languages equally well from childhood, and in conversation they regularly switch back and forth. In local offices correspondence is carried on in both languages, and the office workers, most of whom are Tadzhik, address the different language groups in the appropriate language. In schools all the lessons are usually in Tadzhik, but teachers often prepare their lessons with the aid of Uzbek texts. At home, Tadzhiks will immediately switch language on the arrival of an Uzbek visitor. Women belonging to the two different language groups, in conversation, will each speak only her native language and carry on the discussion for any length of time without any feeling of awkwardness (Rastorgueva, 1952, passim). Radloff found that the inhabitants of Samarkand, in 1868, spoke more often than not the Tadzhik language. Within less than half a century Bartold during his visits to the city at the end of the first decade of this century heard very little Tadzhik and found that the large majority spoke Uzbek. The inhabitants of the village of Urgut, not far from Samarkand, used to regret that though they themselves were traditionally Tadzhik speakers their children had switched languages and had become Uzbeks.

It is not surprising, therefore, that there has been and continues to be considerable linguistic interference mainly of Uzbek with Tadzhik (Rastorgueva, 1952-1961 Vol. III, passim). So far as vocabulary is concerned, borrowed words do not always replace native Tadzhik terms, and examples of parallel existence have been cited such as:

Uzbek	Tadzhik	Meaning
ichki	booz	'goat'
iuldooz	sitora	'star'
iil	sol	'year'
av	shikor	'hunting'
sal	amad	'fruit'

Occasionally words from both languages are combined to form a new compound word – for example *kejin(U)* and *bad(T)* have produced *bad-kejin* with the same meaning – 'after' or 'afterwards'. And at times a sentence will correspond to one language in its basic structure and consist of a vocabulary which is almost entirely derived from the other language. The following has been cited:

mooshooka kovla koonam, teraka uchashba booromda biraft
'I was chasing the cat but it climbed to the very top of a poplar'

where *mooshook kovla terak* and *uch* are Uzbek and the structure is Tadzhik.

In the Chust dialect of Tadzhik bilingualism has produced the following changes:

(i)   in the formation of the comparative degree the Tadzhik suffix *tar* and the Uzbek *rok* are combined – *chukurtarrok*
(ii)   in the numerals from one to a hundred Tadzhik forms such as *um* and Uzbek *nchi* are both used.
(iii)   the Uzbek affix to express likeness *dak* has also been incorporated, e.g. *Saiddak budas* 'he was like Said'.
(iv)   Uzbek verbs are very often conjugated according to the Tadzhik paradigm – examples of such verbal stems being *tik* 'to insert' *chok* 'to smoke', *ich* 'to drink', and *chol* 'to play an instrument'.

There have also been some changes in the sound system of Tadzhik so that the Tadzhik /a/ is now a front vowel; Tadzhik /o/ is nearer to the Uzbek.

Other Iranian speaking groups, but possessing languages which are different in important respects from Tadzhik, are the Yagnobi and Pamiri, inhabiting almost inaccessible areas of the Gorno-Badakhsanskay mountainous region. Because of their location these tribes have been remarkably successful until recently in preserving their native tongue. Yagnobi is the only living representative of the ancient Sogdian language. The Pamiri dialects differ so much from each other that in conditions of intensified communication requirements Tadzhik has come to be used as a lingua franca (Rastorgueva, 1952, 78).

Other Iranian languages are Ossetian spoken in that ASSR situated between the Black Sea and the Caspian; Tat and Talysh, on both sides of the border with Iran, to the South of the Caspian – mainly in Azerbaydzhan and the Daghestan ASSR. Kurdish belongs to the same group, though those who speak it within the USSR, mainly in small enclaves in Georgia, Armenia, Turkmenia and Azerbaydzhan are bilingual to a considerable degree, using the local languages for the main purposes of communication. The Kurdish and the Turkmen population in contact are bilingual and even trilingual in some instances, speaking Turkmen

and Russian in addition to Kurdish. Instruction in the schools is in
Turkmen and in several villages such as Firyuza near Ashkabad, it may
be in Russian. The medium of communication between Kurds and
Turkmen is generally Turkmen. Conversation within the Kurdish home
will be in the mother tongue usually, but the younger children, especially,
have come to prefer Turkmen. In 1959 out of 2,263 who claimed they
were of Kurd nationality nearly 33% claimed Turkmen as their mother
tongue. It is not surprising therefore that Turkmen and Russian are
exercising an ever increasing influence on Kurdish. From the Turkmen
the Kurds have taken for instance *komek* 'help', *pichag* 'knife', *yerkume*
'mud hut', *down* 'gown', *koynek* 'dress', and *charykh* 'shoes'. From
Russian they have borrowed *akyshke* 'window', *ystakan* 'glass', *stol*
'table', *panjak* 'jacket', etc., but the main areas of influence are in agricultural terms and the vocabulary of domestic, social and political discourse.

Beludzhi is perhaps one of the most interesting of Iranian languages
from the standpoint of the sociology of contact. It is spoken in two
different contact areas and the history of the fate of the language varies
between the two areas. Generally speaking the Beludzhi have a strong
sense of national identity which appears to be intensified as the number of
the speakers of the language declines – a not unusual phenomenon. This
is true particularly of those living within the area of influence of Turkmen.
There the process of assimilation is relatively slow because there are
historical conflicts which help still to perpetuate differences (Graffeberg,
1969, 236). In Tadzhikstan on the other hand the Beludzhi have assimilated almost completely: they have adopted the Tadzhik language and
have merged culturally. As with the Kurds there are considerable borrowings from both Russian and Turkmen – from the former in the vocabulary
of domestic architecture, and from the latter in the vocabulary concerned
with farming and dress (Graffeberg, 236 239).

c.   *Other Indo-European Languages*

Apart from the two branches of Indo-European we have referred to
(Slavic and Iranian) there are several more of the same family, though in
most instances only single representatives of any sub-group. Armenian is
one of these, spoken by one of the oldest peoples of the Soviet Union. The
Armenian Republic in which the large majority of the speakers of the
language live is a developing industrial country though the land is generally barren. It has almost equal proportions of rural and urban populations, with admixtures of Kurds, Azerbaydzhanis and Russians, the last
mainly in the towns and cities. The Armenians have been Christians since
the 5th century and are a highly literate people, the language having been
given its written form in a variant of the Greek alphabet as far back as the
6th century. The existence of two major contemporary dialects together

with the survival of Church Armenian raises some problems in education and in literary publications. The Armenian language used in the USSR differs from the older dialect spoken elsewhere, in Turkey for instance. Old Armenian, a strictly formal literary dialect, differs a good deal from the simpler and less regular Middle Armenian on which the contemporary dialects are based. The Armenian people, next perhaps to the Ukrainians are among the most widely dispersed, with nearly a quarter of a million in North America, and half that number, again, in various European countries, as well as a considerable number in the Middle East. But they are nevertheless intensely conscious of their national identity on account of which they are not renowned for good relations with either their Georgian neighbours or the Muslims of the Caucusus.

Moldavian, a Romance language with heavy Slavic influences, is a European language spoken in the former Bessarabia, now incorporated with the Moldavian ASSR to form the present Union Republic. The Moldavians have close ties with the Ukraine and of course with Romania. Along the shores of the Black Sea and the Sea of Azov, as well as in parts of Moldavia, are spoken other Indo-European languages – Albanian, Greek and Yiddish, the last being the most important demographically. It is based on Middle High German with heavy Slavic and Hebrew influences. The language has had periods of extreme adversity one of which is enduring at present, since in the view of most competent observers, the prevailing political attitude is to discourage its use and to promote its discontinuance. The widely dispersed Gipsies of the Soviet speak an Indo-European dialect related to old Prakrit, though in their wanderings they have developed several Romance variants, especially in the Western areas of the USSR. Other Gipsies, for instance those living in Tadzhikstan, have been brought up to speak the local languages only.

ii. *Altaic Languages*

a. *Turkic*

The most numerous of the non Indo-European languages in the Soviet Union are the Turkic group, usually grouped with the Mongol and Tungisic languages to constitute the Altaic family of languages. Most of the Turkic languages have had centuries of contact with the Indo-European Iranic languages and dialects, and this has resulted in the adoption of elements of Iranic vocabularies and some of the sound patterns of those languages as well. Arabic influences are also fairly pronounced in several Soviet Turkic languages, and these were a matter of concern on political grounds to the language planners of the Soviet Union in its early days. Most of the Central Asian speakers of Turkic languages derive from the ancient Sogdian and Bactrian tribes, the nomadic Iranic-speaking tribes of the Steppes like the Sacae, and the later nomadic Turkic speaking groups and smaller infiltrations of Mongols, including those of Genghis Khan. The area in which the languages are spoken has always been the meeting point of several cultures, different ethnic groups with different characteristics, and different languages. It is not unlikely, in view of the considerable shifts of populations which are revealed in the 1970 Census, mainly but not exclusively from the Slavic West to the South and to Central Asia, that these contact features will be enormously intensified, and because of the development of universal literacy, the character of such contacts will be changed radically.

Uzbek, belonging to the South East Turkic Group is spoken mainly in the long corridor stretching from West of the Aral Sea to the Afghan border, and running between Turkmenistan and Kazakhstan. A long, almost detached tongue of Uzbekistan runs into the mountainous area of Kirgizia towards Ferghana and Andizhan. Uzbekistan includes among its centres of population some with the most historically evocative names in the world – Tashkent, Samarkand and Bukhara. The greatest population density and not unnaturally, therefore, of ethnic and linguistic complexity is found in the Ferghana Valley, Tashkent and Khorezm. No one attempts to deny the fact that the Russians and Uzbeks do not normally favour each other. For a long time before the present accelerated processes of immigration the Uzbek cities were divided into separate Russian and native Uzbek quarters; the former tended to be critical of the Uzbek way of life, and especially the devotion of Uzbeks to their Muslim faith. In addition to the Uzbeks themselves there are considerable numbers of Russians, Tadzhiks, Kazakhs, Tatars and Kirgiz in Uzbekistan.

The Ferghana group of Uzbek dialects are on the Turkic-Iranic language divide, especially around Namangan. Consequently there are in Uzbek a large number of words borrowed from Tadzhik, for instance, used with words similar in meaning to Uzbek items, and serving to reduce the polysemy of the Uzbek terms. Thus the Tadzhik word *sel* 'a heavy shower' is retained with Uzbek *kin* which means both 'a downpour' and a 'stream'. Tadzhik wordforming elements also play a significant part in the Uzbek language, such suffixes being Tadzhik – *zor, ston, don*. Specialists in Uzbek and Tadzhik claim the presence of Tadzhik elements in the vocabulary of Uzbek dating back to the 12th and 13th centuries. Uzbek has been influenced by other languages, over the centuries, Turkmen, Karakalpak and Kazakh especially. Uzbek has also been influenced by Uygur in parts of the Ferghana valley. The speakers of Karakalpak, also a Turkic language but belonging to the North Western Group, live mainly in their own ASSR as part of the Uzbek SSR, though Karakalpaks have closer affinities with Kirgiz and Kazakhs. The Iranian influence on Uzbek is reflected in the loss of sound harmony and, so far as syntax is concerned, in the development of subordinating structures.

Azerbaydzhan, to the east of Armenia, apart from the cosmopolitan city of Baku, the centre of the massive oil field and terminally situated on the Caspian, is not nearly so complicated linguistically as several other areas of the South East and South USSR. They are probably the most westernized of all the Turkic peoples though they remain Muslims. The Turkic language of Uzbekistan, which was given its literary form in the 14th century, is used in many parts of the Caucusus and across the international frontier in Iran. An instance of historical contact of Azerbaydzhani involves the Tat people. They have always been a divided and dispersed small group and their main language of communication with the numerous small groups surrounding them, such as Lezgin and Budhuz, is Azerbaydzhan. It is seldom possible to meet a Tat who is not bilingual, and near the highways this is invariably the case. Only Tat children under school age, and the very old in remote mountain settlements, know no Azerbaydzhani. It is becoming increasingly the case that children who are bilingual gradually lose their command of Tat, and the language is now, among most families, used only on the hearth. The traditions of the Azerbaydzhani and Tats are so intermingled that the Tats sing their songs in Azerbaydzhani, and the tales told to the children and their legends are related in the same language. Consequent on this considerable intermingling the Tat phonetic and grammatical systems are now considerably changed. The Tat language has basically five vowel phonemes: /u/ /a/ (labialized) both of them back vowels; three front vowels: /ae/, /i/, and /ii/, as well as three diphthongs: /ei/, /eu/, /ou/. Azerbaydzhani, on the other hand, has four back vowels and five front vowels. A number of Azerbaydzhani vowels have been introduced into Tat; for example, the vowel /e/, through a change in the character of the diphthong /ei/. The vowel /o/ has also developed in Tat through a similar change in the character of the diphthong /ou/. Similar influences have led to a change in the tense system of Tat to allow of the development of something akin to the Azerbaydzhan Future Tense. Unlike the Uzbek-Tadzhik bilingual contact situation, the influence of the Tat and Azerbaydzhan languages is almost entirely in the direction of Tat.

Turkmen, a sister language to Uzbek is spoken on the opposite shores of the Caspian from Azerbaydzhan, between the sea and Uzbekistan. Many, quite primitive, tribal vestiges can be observed still in some of the remoter Turkmen villages, which provide a strong support for the native language against the penetration of Russian and the less heavy but quite noticeable pressure of Uzbek and Kazakh. The nomadic Turkmen tribes have gradually become permanently centred on the oases and settled communities, such as those of the city of Ashkabad and towns along the Amu Darya (Oxus), which are becoming increasingly cosmopolitan.

This has considerable implications for the Turkmen language. Even as late as 1935 there was some conflict between those in Turkmenistan who wished to maintain external contacts by promoting Anatolian Turkish as the literary dialect and others who pressed the claims of the local dialects as the base for a standardized Turkmen literary language.

Two other Central Asian Republics, the Kirgiz SSR and the Kazakh SSR contain large concentrations of speakers of a variety of Turkic languages. The former territory is situated between Tadzhikstan in the south and Kazakhstan in the North, and the contact here of large numbers of Iranian Tadzhik speakers and those of the Turkic languages of Kirgizia has produced interesting patterns of 'radical' bilingualism and not simply bilingualism produced by the contact of dialects or languages within the same close language group. Kazakhs are close in physical appearance, culture and language to the Kirgiz, who were not inclined before the Revolution to regard themselves as different peoples, and they form an exceedingly numerous Turkic speaking group next in size to the Uzbeks. They inhabit an area over twice the size of that occupied by all other Central Asians, and they form an important geographical, linguistic and ethnic buffer between the RSFSR to the North and the more southerly Turkic and Iranian languages and ethnic groups. The population of Kazakhstan contains large minority groups of Russians, Ukrainians, as well as non-Slavs such as Uzbeks, Uygurs, Dungans, Tatars and Bashkirs (speaking a closely related language to Kazakh).

Other Turkic languages spoken in the Soviet Union are Karachai and Balkarian in the Caucusus, Nogai in Daghestan, Kumyk in the North Caucusus and Chuvash spoken in the south of the area, inhabited by speakers of Mari along the shores of the Volga. The Chuvash are isolated from Turkic culture since they are Christians by tradition and have had a long history of contact with and influence from Russia. Karaim is spoken by very small numbers in Lithuania. Gagauz, the language of a Christian group who fled originally from Bulgaria, is spoken in the Moldavian SSR and along the Azov coast. The Crimean Tatars, victims of the Stalinist deportations of the 1940's, also speak a Turkic language.

The group of Turanian Turkic languages which we have referred to form only one branch of the Altaic family. One of the members of this group, Yakut, the language spoken by a scattered population in the basin of the Lena and along the Aldan and Kolyma Rivers in an area which is the size of India, is so anomalous in the view of many linguists, that they have found it difficult to decide whether it forms, with western Chuvash, an independent group, or should be classified with Uygur, Khakass and Kazakh. The Yakut have remained the most advanced minority group in North Eastern Siberia. They are very conscious of their ethnic identity and appear to have resisted with some success the cultural domination, if not the political suzerainty of the Russians. The anomalous position of Yakut, like that of so many other languages in the Soviet Union, is due to its very long, almost uninterrupted history of contact with languages belonging to very diverse families, and to its migration from the S. Siberian steppeland to its present location. The 19th century Turkologist Radlov maintained that the language was not originally a Turkic language at all, but had acquired its Turkic characteristics before it began its long treck from the south to the banks of the Lena. Okladnikov (1968) came to the conclusion that it was a Turkic language from the beginning while Ubryatova has argued more recently that it is the result of the merging of several languages – Turkic, Buryat and Tungus. She found 33% of the Yakut lexicon to be Mongol or Buryat. Yakut folklore and linguistic features show the ancestors of Yakuts must have known about lions, tigers and leopards. They possessed terms in Turkic and Mongol for basic food stuffs, and there are other terms for weapons, wine and silk connecting them in some way with peoples with contact with distant countries in Asia, Iran and China. When they arrived on the Lena their relatively high level of culture helped them to dominate and subdue the local tribes, who were eventually assimilated and absorbed, and who adopted the Yakut language.

b. *Mongolian*

The second group of Altaic languages is the Mongolian, which has closer affinities to Turkic than either has with the third, Manchurian-Tungisic group of Altaic languages. The Mongolian branch includes four major dialect groups – Mongolian itself, spoken in the Mongolian People's Republic, Buryat spoken in the Autonomous Republic of that name below Lake Baykal, as well as in the region around Irkutsk; and Kalmyk in the Autonomous Republic east of the Lower Volga. Of these only the last two are indigenous to the USSR; they are closely related though widely separated geographically, and they have been considerably influenced by Russian. The Buryats are settled agriculturalists and to a lesser extent herdsmen. Their religious affiliations are diverse – some are Orthodox Christians, most are Buddhists and some even, until quite recently, were Shamanists. The Kalmyks of the Lower Volga are also traditionally Buddhists.

c. *Manchurian*

The third group of Altaic languages, Manchurian, includes the languages of the small eastern-most Soviet nationalities – the Oroches, Dakhurs and the stronger Orok and Ulcha of the Sakhalin area and the Central Kamachatka Peninsula, as well as the Eveni. There are other representatives of the same group, for instance the Evenki who live at

various points on the Pacific coast and the Arctic Ocean from the Yenisey
to Sakhalin. However, most speakers of these languages inhabit the
Krasnoyar Region, the rivers Yenisey and Amur being the most easily
recognizable of their linguistic boundaries. Evenk-Yakut contact has
produced another interesting example of long standing bilingualism. The
former belongs to the Northern branch of Tungisic languages, while the
latter is a branch of the North Eastern Turkic languages. During the last
three centuries Yakut has spread widely among the Siberian peoples of
diverse language groups. This process has been accelerated by the creation
of the Yakut Autonomous region and the creation of a written language
used in their own national schools, press, radio and theatres. One observer (Ubryatova, 1956) of the incidence of Yakut and Evenk in the
Taimir National District and in Krasnoyar territory reported the relatively rapid decline of Evenk in the face of Yakut influence. This decline takes one of two forms. In the first place in areas where Evenk is not
particularly stable the language disappears from the linguistic repertoire
of the people. For instance Ubryatova reports the story of a family, the
head of which, an Evenk named Siryagin, was 70 when she met him in
1932. He spoke no Dolgan, the local dialect of Yakut, though he understood it. His son, aged 40, was bilingual and spoke to his father in one
and to his sister, who had married a Dolgan and spoke no Evenk, in the
other. This daughter of Siryagin spoke to her father in Dolgan and could
barely understand his Evenk. Her son was a completely monoglot Yakut.
In the space of, at the most, two generations, the Evenk language was
being lost to one family, a typical instance. In areas where the Evenk
language is more stable, the decline takes another form. A special dialect
comes into being in which the phonetic, lexical and grammatical characteristics of Evenk are carried over into Yakut: in consequence in many
areas Yakut has lost some long vowels and shows a tendency to abandon
its characteristic feature of vowel harmony, as is revealed for instance
when it borrows from Russian. Dolgan, itself, to which we have referred,
is a Yakut dialect created under very early Evenk influence, for Dolgan
has preserved many features of Yakut which in other areas had disappeared by the 19th century. Generally speaking the main influence of
Evenk on Yakut is in the establishment of alien cases – the 'partial case'
and the 'mutual case' and the introduction of a personal attribute to the
verbal phrase.

iii.   *Uralian Languages*

a.   *Finnic*
Another largea nd dominant family of languages entirely separate from
both the Indo-European and Altaic is the Uralian, spoken by nationali-

ties inhabiting areas stretching across tundra and taiga from the Baltic in the West to Yakuta in the East. Attempts which have been made to relate the Uralian and Altaic families have not carried conviction with scholars. Like the Altaic, Uralian has three branches – Finnic, Ugrian, and Samoyedic, the first two very often being included within one Finno-Ugrian group. The Finnic languages themselves belong to three separate subgroups – West Somian represented in the USSR by Karelian spoken by about 25% of the population of the Republic of that name as well as in the area south east of Leningrad. It is the language of the Finnish epic Kalavela and of much of the traditional folk lore of the Karelians and Finns. Karelian has been heavily influenced by Russian vocabulary and phonology. Vespian is a language of the same group spoken by a diminished number of that nationality living east of Moscow and south of Lake Onega. They were known to historians in the 6th century and were mentioned by Arab travellers in the 9th. Vodian is related to it, but this language is now almost extinct. A variant of Lappish, sometimes classed with West Finnic languages, is still spoken in the USSR mainly in the Kola tundra. However the most important of this group of West Finnic languages is Estonian, which, during the twenty years of the independence of that nation was to all intents and purposes first standardized and 'purified' of German and Russian loanwords. The Russian element has returned and its influence is now greater than ever because of considerable immigration of Estonians to the West, prior to incorporation in the Soviet Union, and deportation first by the Germans and later by the Russians during the Second World War. The Estonians have been a highly literate people for many decades and were always anxious to maintain their close cultural and economic ties with Finland. Their religious affiliation is traditionally Lutheran.

A second group of Finnic languages includes Mari, spoken north of the Middle Volga in the Mari and Bashkir ASSR's, Komi and Komi-Permyak in the basins of the Dvina and Pechora rivers west of the Urals. Mordvin dialects are spoken by numerous scattered groups along the same rivers, a few hundred miles east of Moscow. The Mari have shown far greater tenacity linguistically than the Mordvins in spite of the ruinous influence of the Russian language and Russian immigration. Nevertheless they now constitute only a minority in the ASSR which takes its name from them. Their tenacity has expressed itself in a rather turbulent religious history – including adherence to the Orthodox Christian church and the Muslim faith, recent practice of animism, and in the 19th century promotion of a strange nationalistic anti-Tsarist religion, Kugu-Sorta. The Mordvins are the closest of all minority groups to Moscow, but a large proportion of the speakers of the language are scattered widely over the surrounding areas. The Russian pressure has driven them steadily eastwards, and made nearly all the population bilingual. Some interesting though tentative literary excursions have been attempted in both Mordvin and Mari, but it is dubious whether these have any future.

The third Finnic subgroup, Permian, includes Komian, spoken in several dialects in that ASSR and neighbouring areas, and ranking only slightly after Hungarian as the earliest Finnic literary language, its alphabet having been devised by St. Stefan of Perm in the 14th century. Another member of the same group is Udmurt, spoken east of Kazhan by nearly half a million people, though nearly all of them are bilingual speakers of Russian. The latter language is acquiring greater status among most Udmurts, who claim it as their native language in increasing numbers.

b. *Ugrian*

The second major branch of Uralian, namely Ugrian, is chiefly important for the inclusion of Hungarian, which, though it is not indigenous to the USSR is represented by over 150 thousand, 60% of whom claim it as their native tongue. However there are several indigenous Ugrian languages in the Soviet Union, some of which like Ostyak (Khanti) and Vogul (Mansi) spoken around Osmk in Western Siberia are the languages of fishing, herding and hunting tribesmen who have only recently taken to some sort of more settled agricultural economy. They have had, in their wanderings, over 1,000 years of contact with Russian, since the time when, like the Komi and Komi-Permyak, they were attacked and subdued by the Novgorod princes. The influence of the several Tatar dialects has also been pronounced. A large proportion of the younger age groups of these linguistic communities have become, in the main, Russian speaking, though preserving a rudimentary knowledge of their native tongue.

c. *Samoyed*

Samoyed is the third branch of Uralian languages, spoken in three National Okrugi scattered along the Arctic shore from the White Sea well to the east of the mouth of the river Yenisey. The four main Samoyed dialects have not seen any significant development during the Soviet period: they include Nenets in the Kola Peninsula and the Novaya Zemlya islands, as well as the Khanti-Mansi Region. The other dialectal groups are Taugi (Nganasan), Enets (Yenisey) and Ostyak-Samoyed (Selkup), all spoken by very small nomadic nationalities traversing an area from the Khatanga estuary to the White Sea, and meeting the land of Lappish peoples at its extreme point – a vast, cold, inhospitable desert.

iv. *Paleoasiatic Languages*

It is the kind of land occupied also by the disparate collection or conglomerate of nationalities and languages who are brought together, not because of any strictly scientific reason, in the so called Paleoasiatic group. These languages are spoken in the Ultima Thule of the USSR, and each of the languages has had considerable though varying degrees of Russian, as well as of Altaic (Yakut and Tungus) influence. The one which has been most affected is probably Yenisey-Ostyak in Central Siberia. Other members of the group are the 'reindeer' and 'fishing' languages, Chuckcha (Lurovetlan), Koryak, Itelman (Kamchadal), an exceedingly small and declining language. These are related languages and differ considerably from Yenisey, which is included in the same convenient category, and Gilyak (Nivkh). Eskimo, Aleut (cognate languages spoken in the Commander Islands), as well as Chuvan and Yuakir, belong to the same group and are spoken by a few hundred in remote Arctic lands. The first of these, Eskimo, has become a literary language of some modest pretensions. Books have been prepared for elementary school teaching and translations produced from Russian and some foreign language classics.

Kamchadal or Itel'man spoken in 1970 by less than 500 inhabitants of the Kamchadal peninsula, illustrates the history of Russian contact with a local language. At the end of the 17th century access to the peninsula was established by Russian traders and from that time onwards the population, which was at one time numbered in tens of thousands has been assimilated culturally and especially linguistically to Russian, though there has also been convergence with the related Koryak and Chukchi. Russian vocabulary concerned with material culture, household goods, animals and foodstuffs has been well represented in the borrowings, and Russian kinship terms have entered the language with the breakdown of the traditional kinship system. There has been considerable phonetic interference with both Kamchadal and the Russian that is spoken by the local inhabitants, resulting, for instance, in the loss of voiced/voiceless opposition. While stressed vowel phonemes are retained in Kamchadal the unstressed undergo radical changes. Consonant clusters are simplified but not eliminated, because this is a feature of the local language. There are instances of grammatical influences affecting, for example, the use of Russian pronominal adjectives and conjunctions. Russian loan words were adapted to take Kamchadal case suffixes and the adjectival ending -*n*, used to form substantives, is one way of forming Russian substantive loans from adjectives. Finally, there has been fundamental structural influence, such as the use of the absolute case in Kamchadal as both subject and object, parallel to the Russian nominative and accusative (Hammerich, 1954 and Worth, 1960).

v. *Caucasian Languages*

Finally there is that most linguistically complex area of all the USSR, the Caucusus. We have already seen that the area has representatives of Indo-European and Turkic-Turanian; and in addition to these the area is the home land of three major Caucasian groups, two of which, the North West (Abkhaz-Adygei) and the North East (Vakh or Checheno-Ingush) are generally regarded as cognate groups. The Kartvelian (Iverian) or South Caucasian group consists of Kartli, Iverian, Zan, Migrel, Laz and Svan. The tendency, certainly among Soviet scholars, is to regard these as so many dialects of Georgian. This is not surprising since of all the Iverian languages Georgian is the only one which has developed a long and rich literary tradition, which in this case goes back to the 5th century. Its original alphabets, one ecclesiastical and the other civil, were closely related to the traditional Armenian style.

The North West group consists in the main of Abkhaz, Abazin, spoken in a chain of villages along the Kuban and Zelencheck rivers, Kabardinian, Cherkess and Adygei, most of the speakers of which inhabit the Kabardinian-Balkar, and Abkhaz ASSR's, and the Karachaevo-Cherkess Autonomous Regions. The North East group of more than twenty languages including the large number of speakers of Chechen-Ingush are located in the Daghestan ASSR. These languages are usually regarded as identifying themselves according to 5 main written languages with a number of satelite languages. The five written languages, Lak, Tabasaran, which are close to Chechen and Ingush; Avar, which is spoken by fairly large numbers in Azerbaydzhan as well; Dargin, to which are related such languages as Kailag (15,000); and finally Lezgin, to which are related Tabasaran as well as smaller languages like Agul and Udi. To Lezgin is related also an interesting group of dialects, Shakhdag, spoken by about 3,000 people. The existence of so many different languages though clustered in the way we have indicated has posed a complex problem from the beginning of the Soviet administration. A language reform programme was proposed following the 1927-1928 language commission. This programme identified the five main languages to be used for the purposes of education, together with Tat and Kumyk. But the Russian language has made considerable advances at the expense not only of the local languages but also of Turkic and Arabic, each of which had been used for many years previously as a lingua franca. So far as Arabic is concerned the lingua franca was also a main literary language. In fact the tradition of Arabic culture is still strong in the area.

The Batsbi language is an instance of long contact within the Caucusus serving to establish important language changes (Desheriev, 1952). The Batsbi, 2,500 in 1959, became neighbours of the Georgians as far back as the 6th century and adopted Christianity from them. They speak a language within the Vakh Caucasian group. By the 19th century they had become a bilingual people and gradually came to use Georgian as the language of communication outside their own community. The language become more and more restricted in its usage, and in time a special dialect of the Batsbi language – the Tsiva-Tush dialect of Georgian – superseded the original language among a good proportion of the Batsbi. The same process is occurring among the Shakhdag group because of the influence of Azerbaydzhani, especially in the villages occupied by such tribes as Hinalug, and Kriz. There are now Georgian dialects of the Shakhdag language spoken by these groups. Similarly, contact of Abazin and Circassian in the northern Caucusus has resulted in the introduction of Circassian phonemes into the already complex consonantal system of Abazin. Since the Abazins had always been subservient to the Circassians, the Abazin Princes having had to acknowledge the Circassians as their overlords, the influence is entirely in the direction of Abazin.

Generally speaking the Caucasians adhere to the Muslim religion and are fiercely independent, with a long tradition of resistance to Russian penetration. The economy of the area varies according to the nature of the terrain and the climate, which ranges from clemency and mildness to the rigours of extreme highland conditions. The most important group in the area, the Georgians are Christian and they have inhabited their present homeland from the beginning of recorded history. Their hospitality is apt to be overpowering, but they are in my experience humorously tolerant of the failures of others to maintain their standards of conviviality. They are an open and gregarious people, conscious not only of their separation from the Russians but of an immensely valuable national tradition of civilized living, which they are passionately intent on preserving.

vi. *Exotic Soviet Languages*

The languages already referred to are spoken by autochthonous Soviet peoples, sometimes represented on either side of the international frontiers, or exclusively Soviet in their provenance. There are languages, however, which are spoken by non-native nomads such as Gipsies living mainly in Moldavia, the Ukraine, and parts of Central Asia, or non-indigenous peoples without common frontiers with the Soviets. For the sake of convenience their languages may be regarded as exotic to the USSR. There is, for instance, a small group speaking Semitic dialects in Armenia, the so-called Aisors (Assyrians, 24 thousand). Another Semitic language, Arabic, is spoken in Ordzhonikidze, not far from Tashkent. Although there were said to be over 21 thousand Arabs in Uzbekistan, Tadzhikstan and the Turkmen SSR., most have been assimilated, though there is considerable Arabic-Uzbek bilingualism. Others belonging to the non-indigenous group are Korean (357 thousand) and Japanese (1 thousand). These languages, spoken in Eastern Siberia, are not recognized in the USSR: and this is the case also of Chinese, except for Dungan, the language of Chinese speaking Moslems in Central Asia. But in this connection perhaps the most interesting, certainly from the standpoint of education and administrative policy, are German and Yiddish.

Speakers of Yiddish accounted for nearly 7 million in the old Tsarist Empire, but after the Revolution, with the separation of Poland, Lithuania and Bessarabia their numbers were halved. With the re-absorption of these territories after the beginning of the 1940-1945 war the Soviets had over 5 million Jews, not all of whom, of course, were equally proficient in or claimed Yiddish. For obvious, but nevertheless regrettable and tragic reasons, the number of potential speakers of Yiddish has declined by half since then. Since 1959 it is estimated that the number of those claiming to be Jews has declined by 117,000, from 2,268,000 to 2,151,000 – a reduction of 6%. Because of the unfavorable official attitude towards Yiddish it cannot but be the case that many actual speakers of the language do not declare their competence, and any official figure must be erroneous.

Although Jewish agricultural colonies had existed under Tsarist rule in Kherson and Dniepropetrovsk, and in 1934 a prospective Jewish administrative region (Birobidzhan) was planned and inaugurated in the far eastern territories as an autonomous oblast, the Jews never possessed an identifiable single Soviet land. They were dispersed throughout the Union and for that reason while exercising a profound and constructive influence on the life of the USSR they have constituted minorities in the areas where they lived.

Though they were almost invariably a minority, the size of that minority reached 25% of the population in some cases. In spite of the undeniable fact that the Jews satisfy all Stalin's criteria, save that of possessing a territorial base, they have never been recognized as other nationalities, considerably smaller and less influential than they have been. In 1961 the only Jewish Community, though not Yiddish speaking, which was recognized as a nationality, possessing its own literary language (Judeo-Tat) were the Mountain Jews of Azerbaydzhan. The other Jews, particularly the great mass of Yiddish speaking Ashkenazim have not been allowed a national press. The Buckharis Jews of Central Asia who speak a modified form of Persian, though not recognized as a nation had a press at one time. There are many strong Jewish communities in the USSR, especially in the Western Republics, for instance in the Crimea (See Chapter 5, p. 139). The traditional dispersal of the Jews, though this would never have operated so adversely but for the harsh political conditions to which they are subjected, accounts for the decline of their language, and for their gradual linguistic assimilation. In great urban centres like Kiev, the Jews very early spoke Russian and many lost their linguistic identity. However, in several large cities and small towns, as well as in some rural areas, the Jews continued to speak Yiddish and created educational institutions including Universities, where education was available to them in their own language. There are now to the best of my knowledge no Yiddish or Hebrew schools in the Soviet Union (Gitelman, 1967, 92-101). The case of the Yiddish language in the Soviet Union is a special one, partly because of its dimensions, but partly also because of the profoundly religious and almost metaphysical considerations which are involved. Its fate, tragic though it is, does not serve to illuminate the general issues of multilingualism in Soviet society and education, however interesting in itself, and however significant a part of the history of the Jewish people as a whole.

The German language, though similar in some ways in its vicissitudes to Yiddish, is different in one respect. The German-speaking people of the Union did not disperse very widely; and to all intents they occupied compact areas with considerable populations. Organized German immigration began in the second half of the 18th Century when, in consequence of the decrees of 1762-1763 promulgated by Catherine the Great, inviting foreigners to settle in the lands from which the Khans had been expelled, about 25 thousand migrated eastwards and settled on the Volga Steppe. Slightly later another group of immigrants settled in Russia to be followed in the 19th Century by much larger numbers, still in concentrated groups. In the Odessa district of Bessarabia they were especially important economically, culturally and linguistically. By the beginning of the 1940-1945 war, which sealed the fate of these immigrant communities, outside the Volga German Republic there were 17 German National Districts, including six in the Russian Republic itself, one in Georgia and one in Azerbaydzhan, with their own national schools and press (Hans, 1959). The story of the German language in the Soviet Union is not unlike the story of any other national minority and is radically different from that of Yiddish.

C. THE EXTENT OF SOVIET TRADITIONAL BILINGUALISM

TABLE 2

Percentage of each nationality able to speak a second Soviet language other than Russian[a]

Nationality	% Bilinguals	Nationality	% Bilinguals	Nationality	% Bilinguals
Russian	3.0	Tabasaran	10.2	Hungarians	9.8
Ukrainian	6.0	Nogai	1.1	Ingush	0.9
Uzbek	3.3	Rutyl	18.8	Gagauz	8.6
Belorussian	7.3	Tsukhurs	43.5	Peoples of	7.1
Tatar	5.8	Aguls	9.6	the North	
Kazakh	1.8	Mordvin	8.1	Nenets	3.3
Azerbaydzhan	2.5	Bashkir	2.6	Evenki	7.5
Armenian	6.0	Poles	12.7	Khanty	7.3
Georgian	1.0	Estonian	2.0	Chukchi	4.8
Moldavian	3.6	Udmurts	6.9	Even	17.6
Lithuanian	1.9	Chechens	1.0	Nanais	9.4
Jew	28.8	Mari	6.2	Mansi	5.4
Tadzhik	12.0	Ossetians	10.7	Koryak	5.5
Cerman	1.1	Komi	5.4	Dolgan	3.2
Chuvash	5.5	Permyak	4.6	Nivkh	5.6
Turkmens	1.3	Korean	1.7	Selkup	8.6
Kirgiz	2.3	Bulgarians	7.9	Ulchi	7.0
Latvian	2.4	Greek	14.5	Saami	9.3
Daghestanis	8.9	Buryat	2.7	Udegeis	10.1
comprising					
Avar	5.7	Yakut	1.1	Itelmen	4.3
Lezgin	22.3	Kabardinian	0.8	Keti	2.0
Dargin	2.8	Karakalpak	3.6	Orochi	6.6
Kumyk	1.2	Gipsies	16.4	Nganasans	15.7
Lak	3.5	Uygurs	9.5	Yukagirs	32.8
Kareli	15.1	Abkhaz	2.8	Abazin	6.1
Tuvin	0.4	Turki	31.2	Aisors	14.7
Kalmyk	1.5	Khakass	3.4	Czechs	21.4
Rumanian	16.3	Balkar	2.5	Tats	15.3
Karachai	1.2	Altai	3.2	Shortsi	5.9
Adygeis	1.4	Cherkess	2.5	Slovak	31.3
Kurds	36.2	Dungan	5.7	Others	12.8
Finns	8.5	Iranian	12.7		

[a] Source: 1970 Census reported in *Izvestiya* April 1971, Table 14.

The Census returns for 1970, for the first time, provide information about the degree of bilingualism prevalent in the whole of the Soviet Union and for each nationality separately. This bilingualism, though it reflects recent migrations and other equally important trends and processes in the

USSR, to which we shall refer during this study, must be assumed to relate preponderantly to the historical and traditional pattern of language contact in the country. It reflects far more the pattern of primary, that is fortuitous bilingualism than of secondary, that is induced or planned bilingualism. An analysis of the figures certainly appears to suggest that this is the case. The figures substantiate statistically the description we have already provided of the contacts of the different languages. From that point of view though the information is highly relevant and significant, it only confirms what is already known, and it contains few surprises. In one sense, too, the figures may not present an absolutely fair picture, though there is no way of providing such a picture without extensive field work in many sample areas. This arises from the fact that many people may have listed the native language of their nationality as their second language, because they have already switched to another language or are in process of doing so. For many people their second language is a vestigial mother tongue. This phenomenon is endemic in other bilingual countries where the social pattern is also fluid and it is unlikely that the Soviet Union is an exception. It is likely to occur most frequently among the members of nationalities where the degree of language maintenance is low, and for that reason the figures may very well exaggerate the degree of bilingualism (interpreted as the acquisition of an additional indigenous language) because the additional language is already accounted for in reduced language maintenance.

What is perhaps least surprising is that the speakers of the major national languages, and nationalities with a million or more members do not require and do not in fact extend themselves to learn a second language other than Russian. Apart from speakers of Belorussian, Armenian and Ukrainian none of the other major language groups have more than a five per cent level of non-Russian bilingualism, and most are in the 2% range. In this context it is noteworthy that the Russians, who are normally regarded as the most exclusive nationality so far as language affiliation and acquisition go, have a higher level than Kazakhs, Azerbaydzhanis, Georgians and the natives of the Baltic Republics. However, this is due partly to the fact that large numbers of Russians cannot fail to learn the language of one or other of the large minority groups constituting the Russian Republic. It should also be remembered that the nationalities who compare unfavourably with the Russians on the score of bilingualism have usually quite a high level of knowledge of Russian as a second language. When all has been said the Russians, like the English, are confirmed in their aversion for other languages, and for the same reason.

There are some exceptions to the generalization that major nationalities are not concerned to learn a second language. Poles with 12.7% and Jews with 28.8% bilingualism are instances. Their level of bilingualism is accounted for by their traditional dispersal among other major nationalities, and the fact that their own language is not recognized officially. The non-indigenous, whatever the size of the population and the status of the language, are apt to have high levels of bilingualism. If they are scattered the index of their bilingualism rises considerably. This is the case with the Gipsies (16.4%), who occupy parts of Moldavia, the Ukraine and the Central Asian Republics. The Tadzhiks (12.0%), too, are an exception but for a different reason. As we have already seen the Tadzhik language has always experienced considerable Uzbek influence: Tadzhikstan has a large Uzbek minority, 23% of the total population of the Republic. In addition, apart from Russians Tadzhikstan is the home of over a quarter a million people belonging to minority groups, constituting 11% of the population, including traditional minorities such as Tatars and Kazakhs. In such circumstances it is not surprising that the Tadzhiks in spite of their possessing an ancient and important language find it convenient to acquire one or other of the languages of the minorities.

High levels of bilingualism characterize the small national groups, especially if they are minorities within larger linguistic communities. This is the case of the Gagauz in Moldavia (8.6%) and of the Tats in Azerbaydzhan (15.3%). It is also the situation of non-indigenous but relatively stable minorities (unlike the Gipsies) such as the Kurds and Aisors of Azerbaydzhan and Armenia (36.2% and 14.7% respectively), the Slovaks (31.3%), the Greeks living in various Ukrainian villages and in Georgia (14.5%), Irani (12.7%) and the Bulgarians of the Ukraine (7.9%).

Nationalities whose numbers are small, their territories isolated and extensive, and who are therefore apt to be scattered and in contact with several similar groups naturally tend to become bilingual. This is true of the Evenki of N. E. Siberia with a population of twenty five thousand and a percentage bilingualism of over 7. The Mordvin who, although a very large national group, are scattered to the extent of 63% of the population among other national groups near and far, have a percentage of bilingualism above 8. To a somewhat less extent the same is true of the Tatars (5.3%) who are scattered throughout the RSFSR, Uzbekistan, Kazakhstan, Kirgizstan, Tadzhikstan and Turkmenistan. That the size of the scattered group is usually important is clear from the linguistic fate of the Yukagir where a very high level of bilingualism (32%) is combined with a very low level of native language maintenance (46.8%): their language is being rapidly replaced by the languages of those with whom they are in contact, and mainly the Russian language. They must exemplify the situation where, for many, the original native tongue has become a second language and to that extent the degree of bilingualism recorded in the Census figures overlaps very considerably with the high degree of language switching (53.2%) recorded in the figure for language maintenance.

Sometimes a normally scattered and mobile nationality like the Nanai of N. Siberia become settled, according to deliberate policy, either in collective farms or as part of the industrial labour force of cities such as Komsomolosk. This process of settlement has tended to inflate their traditional degree of bilingualism (9.4%), and the same is true of the Even (17.6%).

The most important factor in producing bilingualism is the existence of long and stable contact between communities of comparable size and status. This is the case of the relationship of the Kareli and Finns (15.1% and 8.5% respectively); the Khanty and Mansi (7.3% and 9.4%); the Nganasans in contact with a number of other Samoyedic languages and dialects (15.7%) and the Selkups (8.6%). The Udmurt (6.9%) have been in contact with Tatars and Bashkirs (who are sometimes barely distinguishable) for a long time and have a fairly high percentage of bilingualism. But as always, in this context we come back to the North Caucusus, and to the contact situations in which the Daghestani peoples are and have been involved for centuries. Among the most significant from this point of view are the Lezgin (22.3%), Tabasaran (10.2%), Rutyl (18.8%), Agul (9.6%) and above all the Tsakhurs (43.5%).

Because of the new dimension of Russian influence in producing planned bilingualism one tends sometimes to forget the Russian element in historical and fortuitous bilingualism. In fact the Russian element was always very strong and the separation of the figures for Russian as a second language from non-Russian indigenous bilingualism tends to oversimplify the picture. Large numbers who know a second language other than Russian will also know Russian, though this is not necessarily the case. Then again for large numbers bilingualism is limited to a knowledge of Russian and their native tongue. It is not surprising that contrary to the case of the Jews who are high on both indices of bilingualism the Germans who know Russian do not seem to have learned an additional language and rank very low on the non-Russian bilingual index. This is the case also of a very different kind of people, the Yakut. As we have described earlier the Yakuts have very long historical contact with the Russian language and since their arrival on the Lena, their relationship with their neighbours has been in the direction of assimilating them because of Yakut superior culture. The Yakuts do not learn the language of their neighbours – the reverse is the case, as it has also been with the superior Circassians in their relations with the Abazins (6.1%). It is also only natural and to be expected that the Chuvash lean to Russian in preference to any other language when they need to supplement their own – Russian 58.4%, non-Russian 5.5%. The same is true of the Kabardin people (71.4% and 0.8%), Kumyk (57.4% and 1.2%), Lak (56% and 3.5%)

and Nogai (58.5% and 1.1%). All these peoples have close contacts with the Russians and have had for many centuries.

D.   CONCLUSION

There always has been an exceedingly complex pattern of contact among scores of languages in the USSR. Some patterns of contact are more complex than others, and this is the consequence of physical and geographical conditions reinforced by economic and social intercourse, and the normal processes of historical development. The very small sample of evidence adduced in this Chapter indicates the extent of the bilingualism which has led to linguistic change, and the length of time it has taken for such changes to take root. It is just as well to bear this in mind when we come to consider the influence of more recent factors, which, though having some identifiable influence already, will take very many years and possibly centuries before they really bring about significant and widespread linguistic change. This is a long process and there is no real way of knowing how the conditions which conduce to such change actually will operate, whether to promote the survival of one language and the decline of another, or to create a new dialect which comes to supersede both, or simply to enrich both languages without fundamentally changing either. All these alternatives have materialized in the USSR before, and in the various contexts of the USSR the changes which are being facilitated along the way we have described can take any one or all of these forms. Only one thing is certain, the most optimistic of the assimilationists need to be cautious about believing that major languages like those of Central Asia will lose their identity. No matter how much they may come under the influence of languages other than those with which they have been accustomed to have historical contact, they are likely to survive at least within any extent of time which can be of interest to us. The languages, if they change through contact, will do so slowly; and as we shall have occasion to establish, the degree of culture-retentiveness and of language-maintenance is still so high that radical change in the demographic status of the major languages is also likely to be a long process.

Chapter 3

POLITICAL CONFLICT AND LINGUISTIC POLICY

"The idea that we can have a policy without conflict is false" (Aron, 1968)

A. PRELIMINARIES

Broadly speaking there are two sets of factors which have helped to determine the extent and character of multilingualism in the U.S.S.R. – demographic and physical factors on the one hand, and social, political, historical and cultural factors on the other. Making a definite distinction between the two sets, or between the several factors within the same set is difficult and perhaps impossible. But in so far as it offers a device for bringing order into the discussion the distinction will serve. The basic, though not the most important set is the physical and demographic, since the size and movement of the population, like their physical contiguity and contact, are the preconditions of the historical, social and cultural relation of the languages, and provide the framework within which all the other factors operate. For this reason the demographic factors should be our first concern: nevertheless, a consideration of Soviet policy for, and the official attitude to the great number of languages must be introduced early. "In so far as the economy and the demographic factors which conduce to the working of the economy are planned, there are long term aims, and a picture of the goals which the regime has set itself. The main features of the Soviet economy derive at least in part from the party and its ideology." (Aron, 1968, 8). The policy for languages is part of the expression of this ideology. An early consideration will also enable us to elucidate the aims and point the direction which multilingualism is taking in the Union, as well as to set out the historical plan of such progress as may have already occurred. Furthermore, an analysis of the development of the social theory guiding multilingualism in society and education will enable us to judge the consistency or inconsistency of theory and practice, about which there is considerable debate.

There is one consideration which is immensely important in ensuring that the inevitable contact of peoples and their languages is at least potentially beneficial. The peoples of the Soviet Union do not display any of the racial prejudices which complicate linguistic problems in other multinational states, for instance South Africa. And however much their traditional political aims may cut across other national susceptibilities this is as true of the Russians, it is claimed, as of other nations of the USSR.[1] Consequently with few exceptions contact has almost invariably led to assimilation rather than to segregation. This is true historically just as it is in contemporary life. Thus, a recent study of nationality interests and attitudes, and of the relationship of elements of national and international culture, traditions and innovations has been undertaken among the several ethnic groups in the Tatar ASSR, and the relations between the Tatars and the Russians especially have been analysed (Arutiunian, 1968). This shows that the acceptance of ethnic diversity has not been affected adversely by closer contact, and attitude is to some extent even more favourable than before. It is true, as one would expect, that members of different nationalities have a more favourable attitude towards their own nationality. There is also a steady increase in the number of those who favour Russian, and a greater intensity of interest in that language. But all levels of society have a high degree of tolerance of other nationalities, expressed in their acceptance of superiors from other national groups in their professions and occupations, and of ethnically mixed marriages (Arutiunian, 1968, Table 3).

There are however two considerations which a study of attitudes to different languages and nationalities has to take into account. Politically language is recognized as the main criterion of nationality in the USSR, and for this reason the administrative boundaries, whether those of Union Republics, or, within such republics, of Autonomous Republics, Oblasti (national provinces), Okrugi (national areas), or Rayony (national districts), reflect broad linguistic divides. The problems of language are tied to those of ethnicity, and language loyalty is a symbol of an attachment to, and is a criterion for determining membership of such groups. At the same time, it is an instrument for preserving the integrity

[1]   Many observers within and outside the U.S.S.R. would dispute this claim so far as the Jewish nation is concerned.

of the group. Attitude to language whether it is regarded symbolically, or as a criterion, or as a cohesive factor can range along a continuum from aversion to favour. At the same time, particular languages in particular local situations in the USSR are necessary to satisfy the demand for at least minimum literacy, and they can very often be used to provide the whole range of education, whatever attitude may be adopted towards them, favorable or otherwise. Language can be useful irrespective of any ethnic affiliation or emotional associations. This is what Stalin had in mind (Stalin, 1950b, 14) in arguing that "culture and language are two different things. Culture may be bourgeois or socialist, but language as a means of intercourse, is always a language common to the whole people, and can serve both bourgeois, (presumably the traditional culture of a nationality) and socialist culture". The difficulty in studying language policy in the Soviet Union during the last fifty years is to identify at any time the exact target of a policy statement or expression of attitude, whether it is directed to language as ethnic symbol, to be favoured in periods of stability and attacked during times of external threat; or language as the instrument of proletariat advancement and so to be distinguished at all times from its traditional 'nationalist' cultural associations. Language policy in the USSR is apt to oscillate because of the attraction of these two poles of influence. Writers seldom make any clear distinction between them and more often than not, confuse them.

A second difficulty is to estimate the reliability of the evidence offered from within or by outsiders, often emigrés of the Union. Nothing arouses the passions like concern for a language, and the more a language becomes an area for the operation of apparently ineluctable social forces the more extreme the passions become. Writers within the Union and critics elsewhere are often equally suspect. For instance, there is no reason to dismiss the claim made by an eminent linguist (Baskakov, 1960, 32), that "the relation between the languages before and after the victory of socialism is quite different". So much is obvious. However, he goes on to argue that "under capitalist conditions where intermixing of languages takes place, there may be a conflict for the supremacy of one or other language, but in our country, after the victory of socialism, languages can now develop in perfect freedom". To claim that language conflict is a function or an aspect of capitalism is patently erroneous, since it has not been abolished in socialist countries like Yugoslavia (Magner, 1967, 333), nor, for that matter, is it less acute now than it was in the Soviet Union. In fact, such conflict has been accentuated by steps taken by the socialist regime itself. Attitude may have been modified but conflict itself has not been ameliorated. Language conflict is the consequence of more than economic and political influence or policy, and to attempt to maintain otherwise is to fall into the very error for which Marr was criticized (Stalin, 1950b, 5).

Just as "the structure of a language, its grammatical system and basic word stock are the product of a number of epochs", so is attitude to language more than the result of immediate political affiliation, or simply the reflection of a current ideology, which as we shall see undergoes shifts of emphasis.

External critics of the USSR are similarly apt to arrive at superficial or facile conclusions. For instance, Barghoorn (1956, 69), in comparing it to that of the United States criticizes Soviet policy not for its tendency towards forcible assimilation, on which score the USSR is no different from other political systems, like the French in Africa, the British in areas as far apart as India and the Celtic areas of Britian, or the United States with its non-English indigenous peoples, are equally blameworthy. But he maintains that "the important considerations are the content of what is assimilated and the means by which it is effected". Assimilation in the U.S., he continues, "is voluntary and spontaneous", a conclusion which might surprise the American-Indian population, as well as the Spanish-speaking populations who have no choice but to assimilate. Nor is the comparison any more valid if the criterion of judgment is the nature of what is assimilated, since it is doubtful whether the moral or intellectual consequences for the Central Asian peoples are much more reprehensible than the moral and intellectual consequence of assimilating many of the cultural features of western civilisation has been for the American Indians. This is not to argue that either the means used for assimilation in the USSR or the content are not open to many criticisms, but simply to state, what is perhaps only too obvious, that comparisons between language policies adopted in different multilingual countries need to be instituted with more circumspection than is often the case, if we are to arrive at any useful conclusions. It is better to avoid interjecting moral judgments if our aim is to make an objective analysis, however much our emotions may be engaged.

Similarly, Kolarz (1967, 76) while pointing to the "impressive numbers of books published since 1917 in the native languages", criticizes the progress because of the quality and nature of the content of the literature. Unfortunately, just the same kind of argument could be advanced to-day against the growth of literacy in Britain, the U.S. or any other country for that matter. Those who promoted mass education in the 19th Century would be unhappy about some of the opportunities which literacy affords; and the fact that a system of education offers the means of enlightenment must not be discounted because the use to which the means are put are open to criticism. On that score no system of education would emerge guiltless. Kolarz is reinforcing the views expressed by Barghoorn, and the same caveat has to be entered.

However, perhaps the main problem arises from the tendency within

and outside the USSR to oversimplify the interpretation of official attitudes to language – to regard any statement regarding policy, favourable
or unfavourable as absolute, no intermediate shades or implicit qualifications being permitted. When consideration is given to large scale socio-
linguistic phenomena, it is sometimes necessary, and certainly easier to
think in simple terms rather than to tease out the strands in the tangle we
call attitude. But any language policy has ultimately to work through individuals, even in a highly centralized and authoritarian society, for
languages are spoken not by ethnic groups but by single persons within
each group. Though the weight of 'ethnic-group attitude' helps to determine the individual's use of the language the attitude of the group is an
abstraction, albeit for purposes of discussion a necessary one. Individuals,
because they cannot be the immediate targets of official statements concerning language tend to be disregarded. But individuals have their own
personal, sometimes idiosyncratic attitudes, which often cut across the
attitude of the group to which otherwise they are closely attached. No
interpretation of policy succeeds which works along the single, simple
dimension of favorable or unfavorable group attitude, for the individual
will always react in a way which reflects the balance of several separate
and incommensurate individual needs. There is the need for new knowledge, which one language rather than another can best serve. A person
has a need to satisfy hunger and thirst, to earn a living; and though more
often than not the same language will satisfy the demand for knowledge
and for a living, this is not always the case, especially in highly localized
industrial development. There is also the need, which most men feel, to
exert influence, to participate in decision making and exercise leadership.
And, finally, there is the need for congenial companionship. In most
multilingual communities no one language satisfies all four needs to the
same degree, so that attitude to a combination or a selection of languages
as it might be Georgian, Russian, Armenian or Azerbaydzhan in the
complex linguistic area of Tbilisi, will never be simple even over a short
period of time, but consist a complex of various degrees of positive and
negative attitudes.

It is unsatisfactory to base an interpretation of reaction within the
USSR to language policy as reflecting a homogenous attitude, conscious
or unconscious, capable of being discussed along one dimension. A
person will be willing to accept one language for some purposes, and
find it no hardship to give it precedence in some situations, though in
other circumstances he may have a firm negative attitude towards it.
Conflict can occur in the same person, between his individual needs and
capacities on the one hand, and on the other the demands of the group or
society to which he has affiliated. Attitude to language or reaction to
statements of policy is a cluster of related attitudes or motives, possessing

varying kinds of patterns or degrees of inter-relatedness to one another. At different times official policy takes into account one element in the cluster more than another, but the stresses between the elements are never absent. There is a 'structural strain', dissonance, within language attitude. In spite of the authoritarian character of the regime and the categorical manner of making known official policy, any interpretation needs to consider this shifting though not necessarily fortuitous combination of attitudes, or elements in the reaction of peoples. For, no matter how much official pronouncements emphasize the equality of all languages in the multilingual state, not all languages are equally competent to fulfil a particular individual's diverse needs at any one time, when several languages are available. This factor is conclusive in the development of bilingualism in the Soviet Union and elsewhere.

B. CENTRALISM AND PLURALISM IN LANGUAGE POLICY[2]

Like other bilingual and multilingual countries which possess at least one language of immense prestige, possible world stature, and with a considerable head start over most of the others, the problem facing the Soviet Union is to reconcile the almost inevitable tendency to assimilate, and the existence of intermediate or transitional as well as, in some instances, long term bilingualism. For instance, the position of the USSR is not at any point analagous to a federated system such as the Swiss where the only languages that really matter, German, French and Italian, have considerable reservoirs of support outside Switzerland and where the three languages are equal in most important respects (Mayer, 1956, 480 ff). In the conditions of contemporary Soviet society, whatever the policy might be, one language predominates. Consequently there is an inevitable oscillation between centripetal and centrifugal socio-linguistic policies, and this is related to the changing emphasis upon linguistic assimilation, and the intermediate, transitional policies for linguistic co-existence, pluralism and bilingualism. The ultimate aim of social and linguistic policy was stated by Stalin as early as the XVIth Congress – "the fusion of nations, languages and cultures", and this ultimate objective has never been abandoned or even modified except to the extent that what was originally set out as a declaration of intent is now progressively articulated as a maturing programme.

---

[2] Pluralism, in language policy, so far as this study is concerned is interpreted as reflecting the acceptance of a "society which is characterised by cultural sections, where each displays its own relatively distinct pattern of socio-cultural integration" (Despres, 1967, 12). In the U.S.S.R. the *society* is the whole Union, the *sections* being the nationalities and nations – for our purposes.

i. *Factors Favouring Non-Russian National Languages*

Several factors affect the balance between the centrifugal and centripetal processes. These factors are always at work but at varying levels of intensity at different times. Some of them favour the national languages and some the greater use and teaching of Russian. One of the factors favouring the national languages is just simply cultural inertia, especially among the rural population, as well as the nomads and the dispersed peoples in large areas of the Union. A political revolution, effective though it may be in promoting a new political concept, cannot of itself revolutionize the way people feel, particularly about social institutions and activities which are intimately related to their forms of expression, whether it is dance or music or art or language. A system of law may be changed without necessarily affecting deep-seated emotions, but language as Stalin stressed (Stalin, 1950b) defies political changes, and for that reason attitude to language survives changes in the political climate. Cultural inertia, the habit of clinging tenaciously to something simply because it is there, is one of the factors affecting the retention of national languages. As a key article in *Kommunist* stated: "national languages need to be encouraged because they will continue to exist [...] The literary languages of the nations show no tendency to merge". Therefore, the article continues, "the problems which most urgently require attention are those of the interaction and mutual enrichment of the languages of the USSR, bilingualism, the cultivation of the native languages and of the Russian language", rather than the possibility of replacing any of the languages by another (Desheriev, et al., 1966, 55-56).

Another factor within the category of forces working towards the retention of the national languages is their value in promoting proletariat literacy. At a time when the overwhelming majority of the population still have no very great knowledge of Russian, the use of the native language facilitates the realization of universal primary and then of seven and ten year school education, as well as the elimination of adult illiteracy. This in turn has made it possible to raise the level of vocational, technical and general education of the masses quickly (Galazov, 1965, 46). Partly for this reason many of the languages, spoken in some cases by very large numbers, which had hitherto not been put into writing, were in a relatively short time given alphabets. As a result their very significant oral traditions have been recorded and made generally available in teaching. In this way not only has individual literacy been promoted but the languages themselves have been given a greater guarantee of survival, and the ethnic group has received an additional dimension of dignity and self awareness. In some nationalities, even before the Revolution, the vernacular had become progressively important because, among other things, of increasing secularization following more frequent contacts with the Western world. In Armenia, for instance, this led to the greater use of Eastern Armenian instead of classic Armenian, between which two variants during a period of 1,500 years a cleavage had developed which made the latter virtually incomprehensible save to members of the clergy. In 1867 the vernacular was sanctioned for use in preaching, and this led to a considerable expansion of its use for teaching in the schools which then existed.

The importance of the national languages as a base for establishing literacy is particularly apparent in the case of the Muslim populations, who up to the middle of the 19th Century had only three 'literacy languages' in the USSR – Arabic, Persian and Chagatai. Only a very small minority of the privileged had any acquaintance with any of these, and the working population remained illiterate. Their general backwardness, which Naisiri, the Kazan scholar acknowledged, was attributable to ignorance of the vernaculars, even such important languages as Uzbek and Turkmen, their promotion as literary languages having long been frustrated. The Khakass are an outstanding example of a renascent people consequent on the creation of a literary language. Before their unification they were divided into several widely divergent dialect groups, Sagay, Kachin, Koybal, Beltire and Kuzyl, and without a unifying medium. The dialects are now merging to form the base for a strong literary language. The first Khakass alphabet, created between 1922 and 1928, was based first on Cyrillic and later Latin, finally reverting to Cyrillic but with considerable concessions to the characteristics of the native dialects (Baskakov, 1960, 7). The success of Soviet language policy during the half century of its existence can be measured partly by this kind of contribution – the number of new literary languages; the transforming of tribal, 'small nation' dialects into fully fledged national languages; the provision of written forms for languages, belonging sometimes to large populations, where the tradition had been hitherto entirely oral or preserved in another language; the enriching of the vocabularies of most national languages to accommodate contemporary needs, and to some extent developing their grammatical structures to ensure greater flexibility in dealing with more complex social demands. Such linguistic developments have affected not only the internal structure of the particular linguistic communities but have enabled them to enter into richer contacts with neighbouring languages, as has been the case with the Khakass, Altai and Tuvin language groups (Baskakov, 1960, 7).[3]

This campaign to develop the vernaculars as literary and teaching languages was waged from the beginning of the Soviet regime, but was accelerated from 1930 onwards, so that about fifty minority languages

[3] See Chapter 6 for further discussion of the creation of alphabets and growth of literacy.

acquired an alphabet for the first time.[4] Of course, literacy was already fairly widespread among some nationalities, for instance, the Azerbaydzhani, the Volga Tatars, and the Uzbeks. The Chuvash and the so-called baptized Tatars of the Volga basin were Christians and used Russian characters in writing, as did the Oirots in the Altai, the Abkhazians, Kabardinians and Ossetes. Among the Finno-Ugrian groups of the Volga basin literacy had appeared with Christianity, very early in the 14th Century; and because of the long tradition and the work of such pioneers as N.I. Ilminsky (1822-1891), by the end of the 19th Century there was a fair degree of literacy. The campaign among the Peoples of the Far North was a much later phenomenon. It began in 1927 with the establishment of *kultbazy* 'culture bases' in the Evenki okrug, at the junction of the river Tuva and the Lower Tunguzka. On 25th June, 1930, compulsory school attendance for the whole of the Soviet Union helped to maintain and to develop an interest in the use of the languages of the Far North (Terletsky, 1935).

Between 1914-1915 and 1938 literacy in the Central Asian Republics increased enormously. The most favorable estimates show that the highest literacy rate among Central Asian nationalities in 1926 (Census returns) was among the Kazakh, at 7%. By 1959 as the Census reveals this figure had risen to 52%. Comparable figures for other Central Asian groups are:

TABLE 3

Growth of literacy among selected nationalities.[a]

	Karakal-pak	Kazakh	Kirgiz	Tadzhik	Turkmen	Uygur	Uzbek
1926	1.3	7.0	4.5	2.2	2.0	4.5	3.8
1959	51.0	52.1	52.4	52.3	51.9	54.5	51.0

[a] Source: 1926 and 1959 Censuses.

It is estimated that during one year of the literacy campaign in the Republic of Azerbaydzhan, the number of literates increased from 25 thousands to 60 thousands. Overall figures for the USSR show that even by 1940 the percentage of literacy among men had risen to 20 and among women to 10. At present it is unlikely that illiteracy runs at more than 2%, and even among the Yakuts according to the 1959 Census there was a

[4] These are Abazin, Abkhazian, Adygei, Aleut, Altai, Avar, Balkar, Bashkir, Chechen, Cherkes, Chukchi, Dargin, Eskimo, Even, Evenk, Ingush, Itel (Kamchadal), Izhor, Kabardin, Kalmyk, Karachai, Karakalpak, Khakass, Khanty, Kirgiz, Koryak, Kumyk, Kurdish, Lak, Lezgin, Mansi, Mordvin, Nanai, Saami, Selkup, Shor, Tabasaran, Tat, Tuvin, Udi, Udmurt, Vepsian, Yenisei-Ostyak (Ket) etc.

literacy rate of 96.3%. Corresponding to this rise in literacy there has been a considerable development of publishing in the national languages. Whereas in 1913 only 10% of the 859 newspapers were published in the national languages, in 1940 there were ten times as many newspapers, of which 25% were in the 'national languages'. In 1964 this development had reached the point where, for example in Tadzhikstan over 3½ million books were printed and 24 newspapers with a total annual circulation of 65 million copies. Literature is now published in a large number of languages many of them with fewer than 100 thousand speakers, like Abazin, Abkhaz, Adygei, Altai, Balkar, Evenki, Ingush, Khakass, Khanty, Kalmyk, Lak, Nogai, Tabasaran, Tuvin and Uygur. Other languages now publishing a literature have fewer than 12 thousand speakers, like Chukchi and Tat; some fewer than 8 thousands, like Nanai, Even, Kalmyk and Mansi; and Eskimo with fewer than a thousand. At present each republican capital city has two daily newspapers, one Russian and one in the major local language, and most oblasts and many rayons have their weekly or bi-weekly papers in the local language. Nor has the scholarly bases for these developments been neglected as is shown by studies on Karakalpak (Baskakov, 1951-1952), Batsbi (Desheriev, 1952), Bashkir and Kumyk (Dmitriev, 1948, 1940), Abazin (Genko, 1955), Uzbek (Kononov, 1948), Talysh (Miller, 1953), Tadzhik (Rastorgueva, 1954), Avar and Dargin (Zhirkov, 1924, 1926) and the Paleo-asiatic languages (Vdovin, 1954).

It is doubtful however, whether the non-Russian national languages could have advanced as they have done, or have become so instrumental in promoting the cultural development of the nationalities but for an important political act taken in 1925, namely to concentrate national and ethnic groups within eponymous territories, bringing together as many as possible of the Uzbeks, for instance, in one administrative area or Republic. In consequence, whereas before this decision 66.5% of the total Uzbek population of Central Asia lived within the Turkestan ASSR, 22.2% and 11.3% within the Republics of Bukhara and Khorezm respectively, after the delimitation of 1925 over 82% of all Uzbeks in Central Asia were concentrated in Uzbekistan. The Turkmen population were originally even more dispersed, only 43% living within the Turkestan Republic, 27% and 29.8% in the Bukhara and Khorezm Republics respectively. After delimitation of territories over 94% of all Turkmen were brought together. The same process helped Tadzhiks, Kirgiz, Karakalpaks and Kazakhs of whom 75%, 86%, 79% and 61% respectively were brought together. Naturally the concentration helped to ensure, which was equally important, the greater linguistic homogeneity of the various republics. The Uzbeks came to constitute nearly 75% of the population of that Republic, Turkmen over 70% of the population of the Turkmen

SSR, and in the case of Tadzhikstan and Kirgistan the national group in each constituted over 74% and 66% respectively. Such unification and increased homogeneity made the task of providing vernacular education and literature much easier, and so promoted the non-Russian national languages.

Another consideration which, at least temporarily, favoured the teaching of national languages, is their alleged usefulness in facilitating the acquisition of Russian as a second language. This argument is encountered in most bilingual countries at the commencement of any campaign to promote or safeguard the teaching of minority languages. Officials, administrators and teachers who would be unwilling, or at the least embarrassed to be thought to support the teaching of a minority language for its own sake, seek to disguise their real attitude by claiming that the value and intention of teaching the native language was to prepare the way for a major language. It has occurred in Africa, and it was one of the main arguments deployed to secure the introduction of Welsh into the schools of Wales at the end of the last century (Lewis, 1952). Whether the argument is tenable is beside the point: the fact is that it has been used by influential educationists in the USSR. It is claimed that "well organised teaching of the national language promotes a deeper mastery of the Russian language and consequently all the subjects of the curriculum taught through the Russian language" (Galazov, 1965, 53).

Furthermore, some languages within the Soviet Union are spoken also over the international border, and there is plenty of evidence, first of all, that advocates of the centripetal policy were aware of the support some of the nationalities were hoping to foster by orienting their attention to cousins outside the Union. The fact that the nationalities of the eastern republics were turning to Persian, Arabic and Turkish was regarded as a sign "that they wished to be alienated from the Russian language" (Mordvinov, 1950, 78). The same tendency to seek support among other than Slavic languages, especially Russian, is expressed in the determination of some of the national leaders that their languages should not be absorbed or dominated by Russian, and "since all the peoples of the Turkic speech belong to the same family it is necessary to keep close touch with our brothers living outside Tatarstan [...] and with other Turkic peoples" (Bennigsen and Quelquejay, 1961, 154).

Though, as we suggested, extreme centralists look with suspicion upon these developments towards maintaining outside contacts there is evidence of official encouragement of good relations with non-Soviet but linguistically closely related communities over the border. For example, the Tadzhiks have been encouraged to maintain their contacts and their affinity with certain historical aspects of Persian culture. Consequently the Tadzhiks have come to claim at least some of the early Persian poets as part of their own literary heritage. Contacts in any case exist and cannot be avoided, as is the case with Turkmen which is in contact with Pushtu, and has permanent contacts with Persian in all major towns. Similarly, further north, the claim that the Finnish epic Kalevala belongs to Soviet Karelia ensures that the sentiments and part of the cultural life of the Karelians is not directed exclusively towards Moscow. However, Soviet leaders take care to neutralise or render innocuous any latent, and certainly all overt reflections of separatist nationalism which such traditional classics may express, "the expurgation being conducted on strictly scientific principles." (*Literaturnaya Gazeta* May 1952). National languages which are represented outside the Union by strong and enduring literary traditions, and which for whatever reason are in contact with such traditions, are unlikely to wither away within the Union, or be merged, at whatever distant future, in a common language.

To conclude, one permanent element in language policy in the USSR, in theory, is to preserve the two steams, *dva potoka*. At all times to maintain a delicate if unstable equilibrium between promoting the modernizing, technological and centralizing functions of Russian, as well as simultaneously taking account of the intractable fact of the practical necessity of the native languages for the vast majority, and their emotional adherence to them. The general policy is guided by the expediency of taking advantage of this emotional force rather than simply frustrating it.

Stalin's criteria for constituting a nation[5] were that it should be an "historically evolved stable community of people which is characterized by the following features: a common language, a shared and identifiable territory, its own economic life pursued in common, and a common culture based on distinctive psychological characteristics." (Stalin, 1950a, 16). Some of these criteria are, if not vague, certainly imponderable, but the possession of a common language is clear and invariably stressed. Nevertheless the weight attaching to the linguistic criterion has varied with the needs of the time; and support for it, or the lack of support, appears to be a matter of political expediency. Stalin's early commitment to linguistic distinctiveness has been held to be cynical, not without reason, in the light of his statement that "a minority is discontented not because there is no national union, but because it does not enjoy the right to use its language. Permit it to use its national language and the discontent will pass of itself." (Stalin, 1949-1952, Vol. II, 376). Language is regarded as the "opiate of the nations"; the use of the symbol is worth

[5]   The Soviets maintain a very precise distinction between the various strata of national development. The lowest is the clan or tribe (*narod*) – a primitive communal society. The intermediate level, identified historically with the emergence of a class society is the nationality (*narodnost*). This prepares for the third level, the nation (*natsiya*), usually interpreted in the Stalinist terms referred to above.

permitting so long as the substance is not affected. Such an attitude has been described as a respect for the nationality's right to say what the Kremlin wants said in the people's own language. Nevertheless whatever the motivation there are recurrent periods when the national languages have been strongly supported.

Stalin recognized the force of emotional attachment to national languages and the need to direct it in the case of the 1926 unrest in the Ukraine. He conceded the existence of a widespread movement of support for a Ukrainian culture, and he criticized those who had failed to understand its meaning and significance. The solution, he saw, at the time at least, would not be to ignore or suppress it but gain control of it (Stalin, 1949-1952, IV, 24). In line with such an attitude the 22nd Party Congress stipulated for the "free development of the language of the peoples of the USSR and the complete freedom of the citizens to speak and to rear and educate their children in any language".

Like the formula which encapsulates the theory of linguistic unification, attitudes favorable to the pluralist and centrifugal tendencies within the total theory, though they may be played down from time to time, have never been abandoned or even changed. In 1967 it is reiterated that "the policy continues to consist of furthering the development of national languages within the needs of every nationality; as well as the broadening and use of Russian as a means of international communication". Distinctive national statehood with all that implies linguistically is still "an integral element in the concept of the nation, which determines the nation's essence and true character". The same writer continues – "minimizing the role of the nationalities cannot promote the friendship of all the peoples" (Mnatsakanyan, 1966, 30). Furthermore, whatever the future may hold for the nations there cannot be any "artificial forcing of the coming together of the national cultures", including their languages, "and only stupid people suppose that the time is now ripe for de-accelerating national cultural and linguistic differences" (Dzhunosov, 1966, 43). Consequently, the operational as distinct from the long term theoretical and ideological aim is an "acceleration of the development of bilingualism and trilingualism (for instance in the national republics, provinces and regions), to begin with in the areas of child upbringing and education and social and political life" (Dzhunosov, 42).

ii. *Factors Favouring Russian*

Other factors however favour the expansion of Russian and to that extent are inimical to the retention of the 'national languages'. In the first place the very existence of multilingual communities, especially of the more urban kind favours the use of a lingua franca. Of course it is not necessary that the lingua franca should be Russian. Historically there have been more than one lingua franca in parts of the countries now incorporated within the Union, depending on the linguistic complexity of the area and upon the existence within that area of a dominant or at least a major language. Thus up to the beginning of this century Arabic was used in the Caucusus not only as the language of all men of letters, but as an inter-tribal language in parts of Daghestan even, and the Chechen country, where it was also a spoken lingua franca. There was similar use of Persian in the towns of Central Asia, for instance Kazan and Baku. Nogai was a trade language among the Cherkess, Georgians, Armenians, Ossetes and foothill communities. Avar and Kabardin had fairly wide use in Daghe-stan, as did Lezgin among the various linguistic communities of the Sumar Basin. But the writ of any one of these languages as a lingua franca was extremely limited geographically, as well as in range of usefulness.

The case of Russian is different. No other language in the USSR can satisfy so well the demands which have to be met in a multilingual so-ciety; and the fact that polemicists exaggerate the superiority in range of usefulness is no reason for not recognizing this objectively. To disregard the undoubted socio-linguistic advantages possessed by Russian would be to indulge in the 'fetichism' which Lenin for different reasons criticized in those who accepted uncritically the concept of the equality of all languages. In specific situations and for particular purposes some langu-ages are more appropriate than others, and Russian commands a greater degree of usefulness over a wider range of purposes and situations than the other indigenous languages of the Union. This purely pragmatic consideration is reinforced by ideological factors. All mass democratic systems whether in North America, Britain or the rest of Europe, have an inescapable tendency to work towards centralization. This is aggravated in the USSR by the emphasis on the controlling functions of the 'Party', and by the concept of the 'Party' as a unitary rather than a federal or conglomerate organization. The all embracing functions of this central organisation makes possible interchange of cadres among all the nations, and this interchange, in turn, justifies the further centralizing agency, the use of Russian.

Nevertheless the case for Russian might not appear so strong but for the operation of other factors. In the first place, Russian possesses an undisputed and overwhelming numerical advantage. It is already the language of more than half the total population of the Union.[6] Ukrainians, and Bellorussians who constitute another 25% of that population have linguistic kinship with Russian, while large numbers of them speak the language. In addition, to this demographic advantage and the fact that

---

[6]　Population trends, however, suggest that the status of Russian in this respect will depend increasingly on those who acquire it as a second language (See Chapter 4).

the geographic spread of Russian is so vast that it is in close contact with a far greater number of languages than any other, the cultural and political leadership of Russia is unquestionable and is stressed. Russian, it is said, is "the language of a people who played an outstanding part in the overthrow of oppression". It is also the means of communicating the "historically established tradition and the historical role of Russian Culture and science" (Desheriev, et al., 1966, 55). For this reason the language appeals to the intelligentsia and the writers of other nationalities. An example is the Avar poet Rasul Gamzatov (Quoted in Galazov, 1965, 46), who wrote:

> I love the language of those lullabies
> And tales that I heard in childhood
> For it told of boundless distances and all.
> A fellow citizen gave to me in friendship,
> Another language.
> I went across the mountain with him
> To perceive the grandeur of the Motherland.
> Then was the language mighty, in which
> Il'ich wrote and spoke.
> With all my heart, son of a mountaineer, I came
> To consider that great language as my own.

Then again, because of the numbers of those who speak it, its role as the language of political leadership over several centuries, the association of Russian with a rich cultural and literary heritage (though not the only Soviet language to have such associations), Russian is recognized as one of the four or five major world languages,[7] and therefore a possible means to enable all those of whatever nationality, educated within the Soviet Union, to participate in developments in all aspects of international scholarship, as well as to take advantage of international industry and technology. A revolutionary society which has embarked upon vast developments in traditional industries, like agriculture and cotton growing, or new extracting and heavy industries, as well as in the field of electronics is dedicated to modernization. Russian is the most likely language to satisfy the demands which the urge to modernize makes upon Soviet society, and for this and other reasons it has come to symbolize as well as to cater for "the deep processes which lead to the creation of a technological society. It would be wrong" it is argued "not to see that the study of the Russian language is progressive, that it must be encouraged

[7] The emergence, consolidation and decline of 'world languages' has been related to phases of economic and political development, by Soviet theorists. Latin is related to 'antique economy', French to Feudalism, English to Capitalism, while Russian emerges as the world language of a socialist era (Zaslavsky, 1949).

and supported as the seedling of innovation. This tendency is conditioned not by accidental or artificial means, but by deep processes which are occurring in the life of a society building socialism: the creation of a materialist technical base for communism..." (Rogachev and Sverdlin, 1963, 15). Only a year later the Secretary of the Daghestan Committee of the Communist Party argued for the promotion of Russian in the following terms: "A soldier when he goes into battle chooses from all the types of weapon the most accurate and the one with the greatest range. The Russian language is one of the sharpest types of ideological weapon, and the better the non-Russian peoples know it, the more successfully will they be able to develop their economy and culture, their exchange of spiritual values." (Abilov, 1964).

Nevertheless, although there are, as we have described, several historical forces which favour Russian, it is wrong to deny, as it is frequently in the USSR, that the tendency is to a considerable extent reinforced and accelerated by "accidental and artificial means", that is, politically. Although other national languages too have been deliberately promoted in several ways, it is undeniable that Russian has been the subject of a campaign to extend its influence beyond the range of its normal or historical milieu. For instance, because it is claimed that knowledge of Russian ensures the development of the national languages, the borrowing by these languages of scientific, technical, literary and artistic terms from Russian is fostered intensively, as a means of "enriching the languages of all the peoples" (Mordvinov, 1950, 78). The increasing influence or interference of Russian with national languages is deliberately contrived, lexically, morphologically and phonetically, to say nothing of the way in which the languages are written. The press, education, the language arts as well as high level linguistic scholarship all contribute to a process of 'linguistic engineering'.

This deliberate promotion of Russian influence is part of an ideological vision of the coming together (*Sblizheniye*) leading to the ultimate merging (*Sliyaniye*) of the nations. The 1961 Party Program for instance spoke of the "actual growing together of the nations of the Soviet Union and the achievement of their complete unity" (Programme 1961),[8] a view reflected not only in the attitude of those directly concerned with language policy but of such specialists as jurists, who see "the mutual relations of nationalities of the USSR in the light of the final prospect of complete coalescence. Therefore, whereas formerly [...] the juridical maintenance of national and state borders meant a guarantee of national freedom, now in essence they have no such meaning. Already one can say with confidence that in this respect national statehood and the federal system have ful-

[8] The theoretical articulation of this official statement of policy was undertaken by Gardanov, et al (1961).

filled their historical function". (Quoted in Avtorkhanov, 1964, 84). Already, it is maintained, the mutual assimilation of nations denationalizes the peoples of even Union Republics, bringing Soviet Society towards the forseeable political, social and legal merging of the nations (Semenov, 1966, 25). This ultimate fusion presupposes the emergence of a single language for all the peoples (Gafurov, 1959, 16-17), a view shared and promoted by a linguist who was concerned that the schools in the systems of the various nationalities were burdened with far too many languages (Desheriev, 1958, 333). Similar views about the desirability of fusion were expressed a little later in Azerbaydzhan (Gadzhiyev), though the consummation he envisaged might be somewhat delayed. The writer describes the ways in which the national cultures are coming together through translations, films, concerts, etc. In the future it is not unlikely that "fewer and fewer signs will remain which distinguish one nation from others." The old national forms are bound to go through an intensive process of refinement, he thinks, so that new characteristics will emerge capable of conveying Soviet content in the most appropriate way, though the old national framework will be retained. The process whereby the borrowing of Russian words is said to enrich the national languages reflects, in his view, not so much an intensification of Russianization as the internationalization of cultures and languages, and this process is unlikely, he thinks, to deprive the traditional arts of their national distinctiveness.

The movement towards mutual assimilation is accentuated by such cultural changes as accompany industrialization, urbanization and intensified contact of languages, irrespective of any ideological promotion, and these conditions naturally affect attitudes towards particular languages. Those who "view national characteristics, traditions and ethnic differences as unchanging" are the exception. "Archaic national characteristics and traditions [...] are inconsistent with twentieth century technique and cultural progress". (*Kommunistas Vilnius*, Nov. 1963). In fact, "the historical experience of national development shows that national forms do not ossify, but change, improve and grow closer together" (*Pravda*, 6-6-1965). But a relevant consideration in the USSR is that these changes are sought, engineered and induced by such agencies as the educational system, among others, and in consequence the process is accelerated.

Nevertheless, however much it might be desired in the USSR that changes in national consciousness might lead to the disappearance of national languages other than Russian, strong national partialities and preferences, not to say prejudice, ensure that this is not necessarily and invariably the case. The Director of the Ethnographic section of the Academy of Sciences, following a survey of relations between Russians and Tatars in a fairly rural area of the Tatar SSR found that though the traditional national-cultural prejudices persist only among the older and less well qualified members of society, national prejudices of another sort have taken their place among the intelligentsia and better qualified adults. This is reflected in a form of nationalist suspicion concerning job opportunities, and prospects of promotion among members of the different national groups (Arutiunian, 1968, 3-13 ff).

Of the place of language in this change towards the merging of nations there are several conflicting views, but most of them tend to stress the diminishing importance of national languages, and their increasing identification. Baskakov is representative of this school for he recognizes and welcomes a gradual merging of the important languages, since "a historical review of the development of literary languages among the peoples of the USSR in the socialist epoch does show up certain tendencies which are common in the development of those languages" (Baskakov, 1960, 9). He refers to vocabulary as the linguistic level which most clearly manifests this growing together. "The universal socialist character of the economy of all the peoples of the USSR and the general socialist content of their culture combine to form in the vocabulary of a number of languages a considerable common section relating principally to socio-political, scientific and professional terminology, that is to say that part of the vocabulary which relates to the post-revolutionary period". A second argument takes the line that since language is one of the most important elements of the national culture "the process of bringing together the languages of the socialist nations is one of the most conspicuous indices of the merging of national culture" (Mordvinov, 1950, 78). The basic assumption of this second argument is that merging affects language and culture simultaneously. A third argument, while conceding the importance of language, emphasises that the culture and especially "the emotional imagery of the people, its perception of the world, are not materialized in language alone" (Oskotsky, 1965, 256). Consequently even if very different national cultures continue to thrive there is no reason to believe that the importance at present attached to national languages will remain undiminished. Conversely, on the basis of this proposition, even if national cultures merge, there is no reason for maintaining that the associated languages will do so. It is this conclusion which Stalin maintained in the discussions relating to the theories of N.Y. Marr (Stalin, 1950b).

C. THE FOUR STAGES OF POLICY IMPLEMENTATION

"Marxist doctrine lends itself to many interpretations. It includes many elements. According to circumstances the doctrine expands and contracts" (Aron, 1968, 182). There is no area of Soviet life which illustrates this better than language policy. In the Soviet Union, though, there may be shifts of emphasis language policy does not develop or evolve, it expands, or contracts. And though it is customary nowadays to identify several stages in the implementation of this policy,[9] these correspond only to different relations between or temporary readjustments of the same elements. There is, of course, a pre-history of the language policy which consists of the theoretical discussion of the nationality question, and there is clear development towards the ultimate policy; but subsequently there are only shifts of position. The first phase of policy implementation lasts from the beginning of the Revolution to the end of the 1920's or early 30's. The second ends, to all intents and purposes, with the death of Stalin. The third phase extended to the deposition of Khruschchev, or to 1967 approximately. At the time of writing we are in the fourth phase. This is a highly schematic formula and though it is convenient for organizing the data it tends to disguise the struggle within any one of the phases. The tensions between the centrifugal and centripetal tendencies are always present and the differences in periodic and temporary resolution of these tensions are as great within any one phase as are the differences between the phases themselves.

i. *Phase One*

There are important ideas about national relations and the tasks of each 'national proletariat' in the works of Marx and Engels, especially their correspondence. Lenin stresses that "Marx's theoretical work is far from ignoring the problems of national movements." (Lenin, 1929-1935, Vol. XX, 436). The Bolsheviks had been concerned for many years with problems created by the existence of national minorities and their languages, and had accepted as early as 1903 the "theory of self-determination of all nations which enter into the composition of the state", a resolution which dates back to the International Socialist Congress of London in 1896. After 1912 Lenin made the meaning of this resolution explicit – the right to secede (Lenin, 1956, 450). So far as people like the Finns, the Ukrainians, Belorussians and Muslims were concerned they could, they were told in 1917, organize their national life freely, and their national and cultural institutions, including languages, were inviolable (Lenin 1956, 259). Inspired by these promises demands were made in the early 1920's for the creation of schools teaching the minority languages. A number of such schools came into being, and institutions of higher and scientific educa-

---

[9] For instance Ablin (1970) organizes his Documentary History of Decision Making in four phases: Part I – Early Years; Part II Stalin – Centralization and Order; Part III – Khruschchev and Experimentation; and Part IV (beginning with 1966) – Seeking An Acceptable Balance.

tion in the national languages were established. All this simply attempted
to put into practice the views also expressed by Stalin at the XVIth Congress, in his attack on Great Russian Chauvinism – the Russian tendency
to ignore if not to suppress national differences of language, culture and
daily life. "The proletarian culture, socialist in content, assumes a variety
of forms and is expressed differently among the different peoples who
contribute to the creation of socialism and this arises out of differences in
language. It does not change these national characteristics but gives them
content." (Stalin 1950b, 43).

This first phase, and the previous preparation for it before the beginning of the Revolution, is a reflection of the pluralist concept of Soviet
culture; but there was even during this period, which was favorable to the
nationalities, never any doubt that this was only one of two related forces,
or that it could ever be regarded in isolation or without a consideration of
its dialectically opposed tendency. Thus it is interesting to note among the
resolutions of the Tenth Congress in 1921 (*Resolutions*, Vol. I, p. 559)
that three stress the recognition of the claims of the non-Russian peoples.
However, these follow a resolution in which both the 'national' and
'centralist' elements in language policy are equally stressed, thus setting
the interpretation to be given to the remainder:

a. to develop and consolidate their *Soviet* statehood in forms approp-
    riate to the conditions of national way of life of the various peoples,
b. to develop and consolidate in the native language, justice, administra-
    tion economic and governmental bodies composed of local peoples
    who know the way of life and psychology of the local population,
c. to develop the press, theatre, clubs and educational establishments
    generally, in the native tongue,
d. to establish and develop a wide network of courses and schools,
    general as well as professional and technical, in the native language.

As far back as the 1923 Congress the two opposing points of view had
been given equal opportunities for expression. The first, represented by
Stalin and Ordzhonikidze advocated centralism; the second view was
supported by the leaders from Georgia, the Ukraine and other areas, who
pressed for a more federal approach. Lenin took no part in the discussions
in 1923 but he let it be known that each Republic should be granted extensive rights of its own, apart from those concerned with military and
foreign policy. He spoke in private in favour of giving all the languages of
the USSR equal rights with Russian (*Kommunist*, 9. 1956, 26). The
Ukrainian Mykola Skrypnic attacked the Russification of the Ukrainians
living in the RSFSR who had been denied their own newspaper and were
not allowed to have their children taught in Ukrainian. The conclusion of

the Congress saw a resolution attacking Russian nationalism; but even so, within two years the opposite tendency found expression in attacks on the leaders of non-Russian minorities in the RSFSR. In other words even in this first phase, when the general tendency was to favour a more liberal approach to nationalities and their languages the conflict between the two tendencies was joined in theory and practice. Thus Stalin at the same 1923 Congress as witnessed his attack on "Great Russian Chauvinism", spoke of the need to "struggle on two fronts" in seeking to promote the Communist Nationalities theory; and he "disavowed any adherence to the concept of national culture" as traditionally formulated. "I do not understand National culture". In this he was only reinforcing Lenin's view that "the slogan of national culture is false, and expresses only a bourgeois, narrow-minded understanding of the national question" (Lenin, 1956, 88).

There is nothing inherently contradictory in these apparently conflicting standpoints, once they are conceived within the framework of a class-analysis of the concept of national culture, wherein the traditional cultures are seen as expressions of the single bourgeois class. For "there is no point in speaking seriously of the cultural community of a nation when employers and workers have ceased to understand each other" (Stalin, 1949-1952). There is not the slightest reason to doubt the interest of Lenin or Stalin in the continuing existence of nations, and less reason to doubt their interest in the national languages, but this interest is determined precisely and absolutely by their conception of national characteristics as synonymous not with the historically developed 'state' nationalism of the 19th century, but with the aspirations of the working populations, the proletariat; so that "the propagation of the full equality of and the rights of nations and languages distinguishes in each nation only the consistent democratic elements" (Lenin, 1956, 136). These democratic elements or components of the national groups were motivated as much by international as national ideas and emotions, and for that reason they promote not only the languages in which alone it is possible for the large masses to become literate, but at the same time "everything that binds nations closer together, everything that leads to the merging of nations" (Lenin, 1956, 130). While it is perfectly possible to dispute the desirability of proceeding along these lines, there is nothing inconsistent about the two postulates, nor is there any basic, theoretical inconsistency in the language policy which is based on both.

Nationalism, then, during this first phase was identified with submerged elements in society as opposed to the traditionally developed cultures. For instance a decree was promulgated forbidding further Russian settlement in the territory of the Kalmyks, which was granted the status of Autonomous Republic in Nov. 1920, with considerable independence in so far as education and language were concerned. It is for this reason, as much as for the political expediency of dividing the opposition, that the national language policy expressed support for the most backward national languages against the most highly developed, historically speaking; and led to an almost feverish interest in the languages of the very scattered small groups, as well as an unrealistic attempt to provide all with alphabets and literatures. Within ten or fifteen years of the creation of the Soviet Union, and of the development of national schools in the Soviet education system, good materials in national languages which had only recently acquired a script were being demanded. Complaints were made that a satisfactory range of books was not available, for instance in the languages of the Peoples of the North, such as Nenets. Several other very small nationalities were handled in the same way. Under a decree issued by the Central Executive Council of the RSFSR Dec. 10, 1930, national areas were set up for the following peoples – Ostyak-Vogul, Yamal, Taimyr, Evenki, Chukot, Koryak and Okhotsk.

The Peoples of the North were not alone in experiencing this development. As early as February 1921 under special decrees on the use of Russian and Kazakh in state institutions the Kazakhstan authorities instituted universal bilingualism in the republic. In 1923 a Central Commission for the 'indiginization' of the State apparatus of Kazakhstan, and for the introduction of the Kazakh language for the conduct of business, was set up. At the same time it was laid down that the administrative languages should be Kazakh in districts and regions with predominantly Kazakh populations, and Russian together with Kazakh in mixed population areas.

In the Ukraine, too, the same steps were taken. As a result, "in view of the elimination of a government language and the decision to make all languages equal, the local population have the right to determine the languages used in schools, so long as the minority interests are safeguarded" (Weinstein, 1942, 129). The extent to which this latter proviso was respected is indicated by the fact that in 1927 2.8% of those attending general education schools were in separate Jewish schools, 1.4% in German and 9% in Polish schools. Schools using one or other of the following languages were also established – Bulgarian, Czech, Hungarian, Tatar, Swedish, Greek, Assyrian and Moldavian. In all, those attending such schools constituted about half the minority population of school age. At the same time if Russian was the medium of instruction for a school the local population had the right to have a second language included in the curriculum. In spite of the difficulties in recruiting teachers for such schools the percentage of the school population attending them increased from 42% in 1923 to 76% in 1927. A considerable number of schools in the urban areas of the Ukraine used Russian and many others used Russian and Ukrainian. In Kharkov 20% of the schools were Russian and 49% Ukrainian medium schools in 1924 (Weinstein, 1942, 130). However, the tendency even at this time of linguistic pluralism in education stopped short of providing entirely separate schools. The national language, and minority languages, if they were asked for, were usually included together in the curriculum of a single school and this embraced the policy for the teaching of Russian as well.

The Chairman of the Supreme Soviet of the Republic of Azerbaydzhan reflecting on the shifts in language policy implementation commented that during the "first ten years of the Soviet regime there was respect for national languages at all times". The *korenizatsiya* 'local-rooting' whereby greater demands were made on and greater responsibilities given to local cadres in administration affected the employment of teachers, in Armenia for instance. There, during 1925 the elementary school staff consisted of 80% Armenians and nearly all the secondary staffs were recruited locally. (Matossian, 1962, 83). Even in 1938 77% of all pupils were receiving instruction in Armenian language schools; 12% were in bilingual schools with Azerbaydzhan as the second language, and 2.8% were in Russian language classes. (Matossian, 1962, 190).

ii. *Phase Two*

If, as between promoting either the centralizing or pluralist aspects of Soviet language policy the first phase favoured pluralism, the next two decades, constituting the most important part of the second phase of policy implementation, saw a sharp readjustment of equilibrium, a shift towards a centripetal movement and a diminution of the approval given to national and minority languages. It was a period of contraction. Late in 1927 the Central Committee of the Communist party in the various Republics drew attention to what they conceived as the danger of "petty bourgeois nationalism". In 1930 Stalin while emphasizing the need to "advance on both fronts" repeated his attack on Great Russian Chauvinism, but on this occasion directed his most blistering invective against "deviation towards local nationalism, including the exaggerated respect for national languages" (Stalin, 1961). In line with this shift of emphasis towards 'centralism' large numbers of the creative intelligentsia who had encouraged the study of national languages were expelled from the party and many were 'eliminated'. (*Pravda*, 20.11. 1961). The policy of *korenizatsiya* was abandoned. This affected the favorable attitude towards the local languages severely, especially in Turkestan, the Caucusus, Tartaria, the Ukraine and Belorussia. However this negative attitude was not absolute. In the case of Armenia for instance, until as late as 1944 many concessions were allowed to Armenian national susceptibilities. In

1940 the new uniform orthography was modified in favour of Armenian traditional practice (Matossian, 1962, 164). Ancient Armenian place names were substituted for newer forms, and the republication of the works of the respected Armenian novelist, Ruffi, was permitted. In 1941 Armenian soldiers were organized in territorial units, while in 1943 a considerable degree of national autonomy was granted, first to the Armenian Academy of Sciences, associated with the central Academy, and later the Armenian Ministries of Defence and Foreign Affairs. (*Kommunist*, Nov. 12, 1943).

The creeping shadow of the European war, and the growing fear of separatism worked in two opposing directions. Because of suspicion of the loyalty of elements within some nationalities Soviet authorities made quite considerable concessions, and at the same time the emphasis on nationalism and patriotism became more pronounced. The historical traditions, even those which might in other circumstances be attacked as promoting separatism, were favourably noticed. Nevertheless the compromise with the basic tenets of centralism was never allowed to get out of hand. There was, therefore, an opposing tendency based on the fear of a nationalist backlash which became apparent in 1943. Warnings were administered to Bashkirs and Tatars. Publications which had previously been promoted, advancing the claims of the national traditions of Buryats and Kazakhs alike, were attacked; and rather than the praise which had previously been profferred to Georgian national leaders it was now the custom to favour those who had, in the past encouraged close relations with Russia. History and historical writing were distorted so that the advantages to the nationalities of their incorporation within Russia should be emphasized. The most publicized example of this periodic shift in attitude from favour to disfavour is the Caucasian leader Shamil,[10] whose fate in the history textbooks is a very useful barometer of the acceptability of national traditions within Soviet policy. After a considerable relaxation of the attacks upon him, in the early forties the onslaught was resumed in 1947 and continued into the fifties.[11]

During this period of centralist propaganda it was customary first to stress the need to develop a *Soviet* patriotism, and then by an almost imperceptible switch to identify Soviet with Russian patriotism. The case for Soviet patriotism was promoted in the Russian language. Even prerevolutionary Russian influences on education were stressed. The work of

[10]   He was the elected Imam in 1834 and led the Caucasian Wars of the 1830's and 40's. He was a native of Daghestan and after coming into power he reorganised the civil and military administration of the area efficiently. He surrendered in 1859 and died in 1870.
[11]   The problems of 'national', Russian and Soviet historiography, and the vicissitudes of the Shamil theme are treated authoritatively in Tillet (1969).

the Orthodox missionaries, which would normally have been the occasion for denigration was praised. In view of these tendencies in propaganda it is not surprising that the Russian language became more and more prominent in the national schools. For instance before 1938 Russian was little favoured in the non-Russian schools of Armenia. In 1937 there were only 470 teachers of Russian compared with 1,295 three years later in these same schools. In 1940 the Russian Pedagogical Institute was founded in Leninakan (*Kommunist*, Erevan 3-7-1943). The promotion of Russian, of course, was statewide and not confined to isolated republics. In 1938 the Central Committee of the Party decreed the compulsory teaching of Russian and at the same time further promoted the language by beginning the processes of successive changes of the national languages' scripts, first to Latin and then to Cyrillic. What were alleged to be "archaic and dialect expressions" reflecting the unique character of the several languages were eradicated, and borrowings from Russian were encouraged. In 1935 at the Samarkand Conference of Central Asian Historians the traditional affinities of Turkestan peoples, which up to that time embraced Uzbeks, Tadzhiks, Kirgiz and Turkmens, were attacked, and the concept condemned (Barghoorn, 1956, 75). The danger inherent in the existence of a focal point or unifying idea which might, in those areas, compete and possibly conflict with the influence of the Russian language was recognized by the 'centralists' and quickly neutralized. Pluralism was one thing but a polarizing of group-national and Russian interests was entirely different.

The second phase, especially after 1945, was a lean period for the national languages. One administrator who had reflected nostalgically on the first comparatively ten fat years regretted that "for fifteen to twenty years the position of the languages has been endangered. They have not been used in schools or elsewhere and documents have been ignored because they have been written in the national language". His concern was with Azerbayzhan, but what had happened there was the case in other areas also. For instance, in Daghestan in 1928 a special commission had recommended the use of the indigenous languages of Daghestan for use in schools, and 12 such languages were recognized for this purpose – Russian, Kumyk, Azeri, Avar, Lak, Dargin, Lezgin, Tabasaran, Chechen, Tat, Adkvakh and Nogai. Towards the end of the 1940's the number had been almost halved (Bennigsen and Quelquejay, 1961, 23). In June 1950 the plenary session of the Union of Writers of Armenia condemned 'nationalist isolation' in language and literature.

iii. *Phase Three*

The third phase reveals a new readjustment of the language policy, a compensatory shift, following the repressive centralizing bias of Stalin. Here again, it must be stressed, both aspects of the programme, though with different weights, are attended to. This duality of approach is evident from the fact that there was considerable lattitude to express opposing views concerning national problems at the two conferences held in 1956, the first at Makhachkala and the second in Moscow. In 1962 conferences on nationalities policy affecting Central Asia were held in Tashkent and a month later in June at Dushanbe. In both conferences there was vigorous expression of opposing views. These discussions were continued from 1963 to the end of 1969 beginning with a major conference in Frunze sponsored by the USSR Ministry of Higher Education and sections of the Academy of Sciences. This was followed by regional conferences in the Ukraine and Uzbekistan in 1964 and 1965. A follow up conference was convened in Tirasol, Moldavia and very many of the participants of the conferences contributed to a great debate, which was extremely open, in journals like *Kommunist, Voprosy filosofii* and *Voprosy istorii KPSS*.

Meanwhile within the Party itself similar conflicts were evident. In 1960, while the Party Programme gives prominence to the "growing together of the nations of the Union and the achievement of their complete unity" (1961 Programme CPSU) the Party Congress emphasized the separate identities of the several nations and nationalities. During the first discussion at official level concerned with the same problems, following Stalin's death, Khrushchev maintained that a denial of the contribution which nationalities and national loyalties can make to the advancement to socialism is regrettable. Those who believed that "love for one's country contradicts the international solidarity of the workers" and internationalism (which are the basic arguments for centralism) were, he thought, quite wrong. "Only a great attentiveness to the interests of the various nations removes the grounds for conflicts and removes mutual distrust." (*Pravda*, 15-2-1956). At this time the deported nationalities began to reappear, and some were allowed to return to their former territories. Historical figures in nationalist struggles were, albeit grudgingly, rehabilitated; including, as was predictable, Shamil.

At about the same time the conflict appears in divergent views about the expression of national feeling in, and a national base for literature. The Daghestan writer Aagayev had attempted to maintain in articles in *Izvestiya* (Dec. 1961) and in *Literaturnaya Zhizn* (Nov. 1961) that it was the writer's function to create "works of an international character [...] so as to produce a single international culture." The opposing standpoint was expressed by the poet Soloukhin (*Literaturnaya Gazeta*, Feb. 1962). "A writer is interesting to other people and expresses international (*internatsional'nyy*) attitudes and the solidarity of the working classes (*mezhdunarodnyy*) only in so far as he expresses the soul and character above all of his own people [...] The formation of a single international culture should not take the path of levelling and promoting the disappearance of national traditions, national peculiarities [...] Taking this view we would slip into the most rudimentary and vulgar cosmopolitanism rather than true internationalism."

These two strands in the nationalities policy, especially as that affected the languages, received perhaps their most thorough discussion in the arguments concerning Khrushchev's proposal for the reform of Education, and for the rationalization of the place of the several languages in the curriculum. These discussions, whatever the actual consequences, were aimed to create or to establish a new equilibrium between centralist and pluralist dogmas. The discussions centre on Khrushchev's Thesis 19, concerning the position of languages in schools. This became the basis for part of the subsequent Law on the Strengthening of the Relationship of the School and Life and on Further Development of the System in Education in the USSR (*Pravda* 25-12-1958). The proposal is the distillation of the experience of several years and an attempt not only to establish a balance between the two main forces in the languages policy, but at the same time to safeguard the general intellectual and psychological development of individual children.[12] Khrushchev's motives for proposing his Theses have been questioned and there is no doubt that if an analysis is directed exclusively at their political implications such criticism may be justified. The motivation was however only partly political, and there was ample evidence in the files of schools inspectors and day to day administrators of schools to justify the attempt to rationalize the situation (Lewis, 1962c and later personal discussions).

Many educationists had regularly complained that the school curriculum was not simply overloaded but also seriously unbalanced on account of the linguistic bias. This imbalance had serious detrimental effects particularly on the teaching of the sciences. Consequently, it was argued, the parents must be allowed to retain the right to select the language of instruction, as well as the language the child should learn as a class subject, wherever a choice was possible or necessary. Thesis 19 begins by restating that "instruction in the Soviet school is carried on in the native language." It then draws attention to the importance of Russian in the curriculum – "the powerful means of international communication, of strengthening friendship among the peoples of the USSR and bringing

[12]   The discussions which took place, admirably summarised by Bilinsky (1962) did not, and perhaps could not in the oppressive political atmosphere which the Soviet Union seems able to create at will, do justice to the considerations affecting the psychological development of individual children. The Theses were, it appears to have been agreed, a *political* instrument and for that reason invited only a *political* discussion. This was a pity: they deserved better.

them into contact with the wealth of Russian and world culture." Having made these predictable points Khrushchev takes up the problem that some children in the "nationality schools study three languages – their national language, Russian and one foreign language". These, so it is implied, are in addition to the language of instruction if it differs from Russian or the national language – as it might be, for instance for Armenian children in Tbilisi, who would, if they chose to be educated in Armenian, be required to learn Georgian (the national language), Russian (the compulsory lingua franca) and a foreign language (Lewis, 1962c).

The thesis then proposes that the number of languages should be limited according to the parent's wishes. Khrushchev proposed that a parent should have the right to ask that a child should not be taught Russian if he attended a nationality school. If he attended a Russian medium school the child should have the option of omitting the native language. It is these proposals which were discussed at some length and with some considerable acrimony at Conferences and in the press in nearly all the Republics, Autonomous Republics and in professional journals. During the Moscow conference to finalize the discussion the President of the Academy of Pedagogical Sciences, Kairov referred to the fact that some of those who took part had proposed that "in schools of the Union and Autonomous Republics, the study of Russian and the native language should be obligatory on all pupils". (*Izvestiya* 24-12-1958). This certainly reflected the mood of Armenian educationists, who argued that by far the greater proportion of all students remained to work in the Republic, making the fullest command of the national language necessary (Bilinsky, 1962, 14). Similarly, voices were raised in the Azerbaydzhan press in support of the national language, often in preference to Russian. In fact so intense was the expression of support for the language that the First Secretary, Mustafaev, was dismissed, together with several key men, including the Central Committee Secretary (Bilinsky, 1962, 142). However, the dominant mood was more moderate, reflecting the realization of a need to maintain a balance of forces. Such an attitude was expressed by Simonyan, Director of the School Administration of the Armenian S.R. He argued that Russian should remain a compulsory language for all, while the study of Armenian was made compulsory for all Armenians, irrespective of whether they attended Russian or other medium schools (*Pravda* 12-12-1958).

The First Secretary of the Communist Party of Georgia, Mzhavanadze, having emphasized predictably the importance of continuing the existing policy so far as it made Russian compulsory went on to support "the obligatory study of the language of the Republic in which a young boy or girl will be living and working". This would make, he maintained, "a positive contribution to the international upbringing of the new generation", and not simply reinforce their local affiliations (*Pravda*, 2-12-1958). Mzhavanadze was supported by his own Minister of Education, Professor Dzhiblidze, who pressed that the study of Georgian was of considerable importance and deserved encouragement. Almost identical views were expressed in Azerbaydzhan S.R., where a proposal was made to delay the introduction of Russian until the Fifth Grade, so as to safeguard the national language. In the Baltic Republics too, the debate revealed considerable support for the national languages; Lithuanian, Estonian, but especially Latvian. In the case of the last, the Prime Minister of the Republic insisted that whatever the importance of Russian, the native language was necessary to everyone in the republic. He asserted that any change unfavorable to Latvian in the schools would be detrimental to the friendship of the Latvian and the Russian people. As happened in Azerbaydzhan, the intensity of the support for the national language, threatening any possibility of linguistic-educational equilibrium, caused considerable perturbation at the centre, and the Deputy Prime Minister of Latvia, Berklov, was dismissed with the First Secretary and the Second Secretary of the Party.[13]

iv. *Phase Four*

The record of the third phase does not accord with what is usually regarded as the normal concept of Soviet totalitarian politics, according to which monolithic political solidarity was the aim. Partly because the cost of such an achievement came to appear as exorbitant, and partly because it was felt that the aim itself was perhaps illusory readjustments of emphasis between the centre and the periphery were attempted. The monolithic structure of Phase 2 even when it was most emphatically approved was a myth – factions and groupings of particular interests always exerted quite perceptible influences and these groupings grew in importance with increased specialisation in industrial management, in aspects of the military and in political bureaucracy. Khrushchev's strategy was an attempt to balance such groups against each other and against the persistent hard core centralist dogmatists. Consequently tendencies towards pluralism were supported by legal enactments. In 1956 the 20th Party Congress produced several laws transferring powers from the

[13] The present position of the languages taught in schools is laid down in the Statutes of the General Education Schools, USSR Council of Ministers Resolution of September 8th, 1970: Pupils are given the opportunity to receive instruction in their Native Language. Their parents or guardians have the right to select for their children a school of their choice with the appropriate language of instruction. In addition to the language in which instruction is conducted the pupils may choose to study the language of another people of the USSR (*Uchitelskaya Gazeta* Sept. 15th, 1970).

centre to individual Republics. For instance, in May 1956 a number of enterprising sectors of the economy, excepting heavy industries, were transferred from the authority of the Union to the Republics. At the same time, the All Union Ministry of Justice was ordered to transfer its function to the Ministries of Justice in each Republic. In February, 1957, the Republics were empowered to issue their own laws concerning their judicial system and procedures. They were also given the right to establish new *krais* and *oblasts*. Up to the beginning of the 1960's it may be seen then that attempts were made to abandon the centre-periphery model which Stalin had operated ruthlessly, and to create, instead, a network system whereby the Republics co-operated without having to refer everything to the centre.

But there was a decreasing conviction of success and of even the justification of the strategy. One observer (Lepeshkin, 1962, 827) wrote of the "experiment in setting up inter-republic economic bodies", but claimed that it had not succeeded. Kosygin (1965, 3), about the same time, posed the choice between a co-operative network system, feeding back to each unit and so creating in the long run, out of the related units, a total organism resulting from largely independent but complementary activities; or on the other hand a centre-periphery model where the national units were little more than branches of the central organization. Before the State Planning Committee he asked whether the plans should be drawn up in the centre or in the localities. "Some feel", he maintained "that the plan must be drawn up in the centre and be sent to the localities and that the function of the localities is no more than to administer this plan. Others feel that the plan can best be prepared and implemented if it is drawn up in the dispersed areas" and that the Central Planning Organisation should simply co-ordinate these independently prepared plans. But, in line with the intensifying centralist tendencies of the present fourth phase, having posed the alternatives, he concluded that "the Central Planning Committee should decide on the basic questions of development [...] and must determine the appropriate trend of development for the economy in the various localities". Such a decision also lies at the root of the Party's reversion to the old practice of having a Central Asian bureau to which Uzbeks, Turkmens, Tadzhiks and Kirgiz are subordinated as branches. In 1966 were set up a central organisation to control Higher and Specialist Education and a Central Union Republics Planning Committee for Education.

The current centralist point of view is reinforced even more in the areas of literature and culture generally. What is stressed in these areas is the virtue of uniformity. Some ritual acknowledgment is made of the existence of the pluralist point of view, and "the diversity of to-day's Soviet reality" is mentioned. But the problems created by such diversities, it is claimed have been solved and have been "irrevocably consigned to the past" (Brezhnev, *Pravda*, 11-4-1971). Henceforth the aim is to ensure a general uniformity. The Party, with its monolithic structure, as usual is identified with the people as a whole; and literature is expected to reflect not only the unity of the people but the kind of uniformity which the Party necessarily seeks to create. "In this country, the people and the Party are one. If you write for the people you write for the Party; if you write for the Party you write for the people." (Brezhnev, *Pravda*).

The centralist bias of the present period is well exemplified by the publication of an article, written by a Daghestan teacher in 1970 (Garunov). The article is important not for any substantial contribution it makes to the discussion of the problem of multilingual education but as an indication that the weight of authorized opinion at present favours the centralist and Russophile approach. The writer seeks to make two points: first, that the linguistic situation of the villages and schools of Daghestan is complex and therefore difficult to administer satisfactorily. For instance in one class alone in a small school more than six nationalities and languages are represented. Consequently "schools with a multi-national intake of students and using Russian as the language of instruction, have become widespread in our multinational and socialist country, and this is a progressive phenomenon", compared with the provision of separate "national schools" (Garunov, 1970, 14).

The second intention is to emphasize that the only acceptable policy, since it conforms with Lenin's views, is the denial of separate schools for language minorities. This intention the writer fulfills by selecting for quotation only those pronouncements of Lenin which favour such a policy, though in point of fact a review of Lenin's 'nationalities theory' would show considerable ambivalence, and at best a support for the *dva potoka* 'two paths'. Garunov quotes Lenin to the effect that "we must strive for a merging of children of all nationalities into one school in a given area. We must decisively oppose any movement whatsoever to divide the school in terms of nationalities." (Garunov, 7). Such separation along national divisions in education will only exacerbate latent community conflicts. The article refers to the supporting Resolution of the Central Committee in 1913, to the effect that "separation of schools by nationality within any one country is unquestionably harmful from the point of view of democracy in general and the interests of the class struggle of the proletariat in particular." (Garunov, 11). The whole intention is to remind us of the centralist standpoint, and its respectability.

The centralist line is very apparent in all the reports of the recent 24th Congress, also. In a Congress which more than any other since that of 1923 gave considerable attention to the nationalities question the 'Brezhnev line' is repeated time out of number. The General Secretary himself emphasized the diligence and selflessness of the Russians which had enabled them to offer such outstanding leadership to other nationalities, and only in perfunctory and almost mechanical fashion referred to the policy of friendship between peoples. He was most emphatic, however, in stating that there would be implacable opposition to all manifestations of nationalism. But the clearest evidence of the current primacy of centralisation is found in the speeches at the Congress, of the leaders of the nationalities themselves. Their subservience to Russia, and its language is most striking. Kunaev of Kazakhstan for instance takes occasion to praise the leadership of the Russians, while the Uzbekistan Communist Party Secretary, Rashidov, said: "The Russian people is the elder brother and true friend of all Soviet peoples. The ardent love and respect of all people is due to them. The people of Uzbekistan are inseparable from and in one sacred tie with the Russian people." (*Pravda*, Ap. 2, 1971). Of course such statements are not unexpected nor are they new; but what is interesting is that they are not in any way balanced by an assertion of the individuality of the nationalities these leaders represent. In other words the centralist line is so firm at present that it is unwise to attempt any qualification of even its most extreme developments.

D. THE ADJUSTMENT OF *CIVIC* AND *GROUP CULTURE* LINGUISTIC ROLES

The adoption of either pluralist or centralist models does not involve any change in the importance attached in the USSR to conscious adjustment and planning – the operation of any strategy is not to be left to chance, for "the drawing together and flourishing of nations on the basis of socialist communist construction is proceeding not spontaneously but according to [...] a process of state planning." (*Voprosy filosofii*, 1961, 9, 31). The question is whether planning is to be operated from a centre, or whether it is to be characterised by a network of centres. In this process the position of the languages is only one aspect of broad political planning in an area of social conflict. The broad question is one of determining the principles for apportioning jurisdiction between the Soviet State, the Union Republics, and subordinate units, the study of which it is maintained would have to embrace more general questions of economic, language and social planning. It is because "the experiment in setting up separate major economic regions and forming inter-republic institutions has broken down and because the network of inter-republic co-operative agencies have been abolished" that it is now thought a broad theoretical strategy for the future of the nationalities has to be produced (Lepeshkin, 1962, 8). The study of the demographical and linguistic viability of the languages and of their relationships is only one aspect of that larger study of political planning.

In a large and culturally heterogenous country the need in purely pragmatic terms, for a powerful centre, which is not simply a territorial but also an ideological focus cannot easily be discounted. Nor, unless the ideological centre is not to become alienated from those it is meant to serve, can the usefulness of a substantial number of intermediate centres reflecting local cultural affiliations and characteristics be denied. This being the case, the effectiveness of a language policy must depend on how the administrative, political and ideological centre, in this case Moscow, relates to the 'group culture' centres in this case represented by each significant nationality, and how the latter relate not only to the centre but to each other. This has been suggested as the model for the political, cultural and linguistic development of other heterogenous linguistic states, like India; it is certainly a possible model for use in interpreting the shifts in language policy in the Soviet Union, the history of which is of attempts to adjust the relations of the demands of the ideological centre and the 'national periphery', sometimes in terms of linear and sometimes in terms of reticular communication patterns.

Pluralism has not been advocated at any time by any recognized Soviet theoretician as a concept which is acceptable in the USSR for the *permanent* solution of the inevitable difficulties arising from diversities of ethnic characteristics and national languages. Nevertheless 'pluralism' and not simply diversity is a fact of contemporary life: periodically the concept of the co-existence of nationalities for as long as it matters informs the views or at least the public expressions of politicians. This is likely to remain a feature of the Soviet cultural scene. The tendency, therefore, is to make, by implication a distinction between a *civic culture* and a *group culture*.[14]

The civic culture distinguishes itself in certain formal, as well as substantial ways from the traditional or group culture. Formally, it is an abstraction from the interaction of political as distinct from more personal or group processes. It involves the adoption, or at least the recognition, of roles concerned with the use and justification of authority and power. Civic culture involves an awareness of political affiliations. This formal characteristic determines the substance of the civic culture. In the first place compared with traditional culture it is supra-national; and because of this, in the Soviet Union it is oriented to the centre and involves a recognition and evaluation of the status and operation of centre

[14] Interesting material concerning the retention of aspects of traditional group culture, especially religion and the relation of the local to the Soviet (civic) culture, is available in the report of the Minsk Conference (1965) and Ostapenko (reference in Pravda, 2 April 1971).

ideology; while group culture is limited to the recognition and evaluation of the periphery, and especially the non-Russian national languages and their roles. For this reason the civic culture is identified with the Russian language which is its main instrument of communication and its symbol.

Secondly, the civic culture in the USSR (and this would not necessarily be the case in the civic cultures of some democratic systems) is focused on the ideological character of a dominant political party, the most important features of which serve to accentuate the differences between the centre and the periphery, especially as these are represented in religious commitments whether these are Christian, or Muslim or Jew. Furthermore because of this identification with the Party the civic culture of the Soviet Union tends to have élitist rather than folk connotations. There is no conceptual overlap between the élitist and traditional group cultures in the Soviet Union, since they belong to separate and different dimensions. This means that adherents of Soviet civic culture look to the state to provide what the group cultures had sought in local community or religious institutions, especially the provision of education and the dissemination of literature and the arts. Finally, it is a culture devoted to modernization, to scientific and technological change, to an urban way of life and to industrial expansion. Fundamentally it is a culture which promotes processes of understanding and application derived from knowledge acquired theoretically.

Everybody in the Soviet Union, in varying degrees, participates in the two cultures: all possess as part of their total human inheritance a particular national or local culture constituting the distinctive achievement of a particular group, the essential core of which consists of traditional ideas and their attached values, expressed in the language with which those values have been associated down the centuries. To the degree that they are aware of belonging, in the Soviet Union, to an overarching political system (no matter what the strength of their adherence might be) all Soviet citizens possess, potentially at least, a different kind of culture altogether. Both cultures are aspects of the total culture available to those living in the Soviet Union, but because the differences between the two cultures are not only matters of substance but formal differences, in varying degrees they offer themselves as alternatives to each other. For some, namely the élite, the civic culture is increasingly an attractive alternative. For others the two cultures are complementary, while for others their main affiliation is to the local group culture.

All aspects of life are politicized in a socialist society, and the civic culture embraces the political and ideological allegiances and affiliations of all people, irrespective of ethnic or national origins. The group culture concerns the local traditions and 'allegiances'. This difference involves the creation of 'structural strains' where some class or classes of roles have very different and possibly conflicting expectations from others. The populations of the nationalities can only with difficulty cope with such strains. The problem they face has two dimensions – the identification of roles which belong to either civic or group cultures, and the establishment of an equilibrium between their demands. Language is crucial in both contexts and the conflict of Russian and the other national languages is one reflection of the search for some kind of accommodation between the two cultures. The alternative outcomes are 'rapprochement' (*sblizheniye*) on the one hand or 'fusion' (*sliyaniye*) of nations. The nations can grow together, in the sense that they continue to co-exist but with increasing identity of views, without losing their necessary and defining characteristics, especially languages. It is true that "rapprochement of the Soviet nationalities at the contemporary stage will undoubtedly contain elements of fusion", but this does not mean that there is no difference between the processes of growing together and merging. "Elimination of national differences [...] is not the main and basic feature of the development of Soviet nations at the present time." (*Voprosy filosofii*, 1964. 2-158-161).

So far as languages are concerned this pluralist concept of *sblizheniye* implies that membership of each group prepares for, enriches and is compatible with, simultaneous membership of the language group having the next widest range of social relevance. There is every evidence to support the claim that small nations do continue to use their own languages and to maintain their cultures while at the same time reaching outward to other areas of social life, including learning the other languages made necessary by such a larger context of living (*Voprosy filosofic*, 1961 No. 9, 40). So, the argument goes, it is incorrect to maintain as the assimilationists have done that to preserve "one's love for one's people and its language [...] makes it difficult to participate in creating an international community." (Novichenko, 1967, 260). Languages complement each other, according to this view, and the aim is to maintain the stable relationship of their social functions. Those who are committed to this hierarchical model of national and socio-linguistic development are committed also to the acceptance of the fact that different languages in the USSR have different roles to play. They are committed to the creation not of an ultimately monolingual state, but one with enduring systems of bilingualisms (cf. Fishman, 1964, 19), with Russian, admittedly, as a predominant element because of its wider diffusion.

Sliyaniye, the alternative, centralist concept of political, social and linguistic development, seeks to justify one of two alternative strategies. In the first place there is the strategy of 'assimilation' which differs from the strategy of 'fusion' in that the latter conceives of the need not so much of growing together and of mutual enrichment, but of essentially denationalizing nationally autonomous units, so that they lose their identity even to the extent of being disregarded as separate administrative units. (Semenov, 1966, 25). So far as languages are concerned, instead of their having complementary roles in ever widening social contexts, according to this direct-incorporative concept, one language is envisaged as offering all the advantages the others possess, it encourages the substitution of one language for others, the substituted language having increasingly overlapping roles with all other languages rather than being complementary to them. Such linguistic incorporation and substitution is facilitated by transfer of cultural affiliation. It is claimed for instance that voluntary exposure to educational mass media, such as the cinema, television, books, clubs, theatres and places of culture, is determined not according to membership of the national group but according to more general, impersonal, civic interests (Mansurov, 1969).

As the present Party Programme indicates these developments towards a uniform civic culture expressed in the media, as we have described, are promoted by the "appearance of new industrial centres, Virgin Lands development, the increase of mobility because of new modes of transport". The people of the Soviet Union are assimilated uniformly and directly as *citizens*, their political and *civic* behaviour is determined by factors which are independent of their national allegiances and this direct incorporation at the level of citizenship or within the several *civic* domains, facilitates and encourages their direct incorporation from other group-culture spheres, including local language.

E.   UNIFICATION LEADS TO FRAGMENTATION

The strategy of direct incorporation has another set of consequences which, though they are not explicitly discussed to any great extent within the Soviet Union are nevertheless recognised as having an important consequence for the maintenance of national and especially national language affiliations. A direct incorporative or assimilative strategy leads to fragmentation of the close community life of small ethnic groups and even of larger nationalities and nations. Most of the peoples at the present moment are at a transitional stage, literate in their own languages but not yet brought to the point where they can participate meaningfully in wider civic transactions, or, for that matter, where they can recognize their significance. It is at this stage that linguistic unification is most divisive. Whatever may be the ultimate achievement of the Soviet Union, the strategy of direct incorporation as opposed to complementarity, or the hierarchical approach, has already produced to some extent and in fact necessitates, the decomposition of the fundamental constituent units of the Union – the ethnic groups and nations. And it is because the Jewish people are the most vulnerable in this respect that they are at present the main victims of the fourth phase of policy. This stage of relative disarray in the national structures leads to significant instabilities in personal attitudes, including attitudes to languages. It leads to the collapse of the corporate unit – the clan, small ethnic organisations and village life, or the family, the disintegration of the old primary group ties. In consequence of his isolation the individual is violated, and this is not compensated for by his ability to play a meaningful 'civic' role in newer and larger organisations founded on the new ideology, the state and the party. Compared with the hierarchical strategy, this is a radically revolutionary procedure – it is concerned not only to exploit but to create a situation of crisis and to encourage discontinuity, often traumatic, between the traditional and the newly created organisms – it is deliberately meant to promote severe structural strains. New status groups tend to close their ranks by using the new language as a symbolic and distinguishing feature. The introduction of the new language affects relations between the different age groups and generations of the same family. (Lewis, 1962c, 93). In such circumstances a loosening of traditional attachments to ethnic languages and the substitution, usually of Russian, is inevitable.

This is the more extreme of the two aspects of a basically centralizing concept of society, and of language relationships. It is the one which at the present moment is in the ascendancy, the one which is most characteristic of the fourth phase. But even within the centralizing concept there is an alternative approach aimed at ameliorating the harsher consequences of the process of centralized control and ultimate uniformation. This might be styled the strategy of mutual accommodation. It was cogently argued at the first and second Frunze conferences, but perhaps most explicitly at the Ukraine and Uzbek regional conferences reported in *Kommunist* in 1967. It was pointed out that the normal course of development had already ensured that the languages of the various nationalities, especially their vocabularies, were becoming more international in character, not only because of specific Russian influence but because of the genuinely international or universal influences of science and industry, and the quality of life in urban areas. In turn this kind of development makes it possible to envisage the use of an international language, such as Russian, which is bound consequently to increase and to accelerate its influence within the USSR generally without envisaging its exclusive use. There are deep processes of social development which make the mutual accommodation of the languages inevitable, but this does not imply abrogating the theoretically orthodox position of "continuing to promote the free development of the languages of the peoples of the USSR and the complete freedom of every citizen to speak and to bring up and educate his children in any language". The difference between the two aspects of the centralizing strategy is that the first, the incorporative strategy is concerned to plan deliberately for assimilation, while the second, the accommodative strategy relies, more optimistically, on the inexorable, and guided rather than promoted social and industrial change to produce ultimate uniformity. The first envisages immediate substitution of one language for another; the second envisages, for a very long time to come, the continuing existence of the separate languages which nevertheless, are converging to create one new language.

Finally there is the conflict, which has emerged over time, and which more than any other aspect instantiates whatever *development* in policy may be said to have occurred between the first phase we have described and the present. This affects the policy of separating linguistic and national communities which had not hitherto regarded themselves as constituting separate ethnic and language groups. The degree of mutual comprehensibility of Kazakh, Kirgiz and Karakalpak is high. Their common origin is recognized and they share the same folk traditions, yet Karakalpakia was included in Uzbekistan. In the 1920's there was considerable support among local communists for the establishment of the Central Asian Federation. The delimitation of national territories and the concentration of ethnic and language groups was seen as "the first step to the international unification of the toiling masses of Central Asia." (*Turkestanskaya Pravda*, Aug. 24, 1924). In 1924 the dream was shattered – "the higher organs of the Party decided that its formation was premature." (*Turkestanskaya Pravda*, Sept. 1924). The present policy reverses this development and as part of the general centralising policy the historical and cultural unity of regions, hitherto regarded as exemplifying sometimes extreme diversities of culture, is now stressed. In the past it was the *divergencies* of the Caucusus that were identified; and there was always plenty of evidence to support this claim. For instance the music (to say nothing of the languages of Daghestan) has taken very many forms in different ethnic groups. Most songs in Daghestan are in the couplet form, and the melody is usually two-part. Those sung by the Avars are three part. Throughout Daghestan the Aeolian mode is the most characteristic, while among the mountain peoples the Doric mode is most popular, and in the South the Phrygian is preferred. There is a similar diversity in the instruments which are preferred – in some localities it is three stringed (*agach-kumus*) and in others a kind of flat violin played on the knee; and in the N. Caucusus for instance it is not a stringed or wind instrument which enjoys favour with the people but the drum, or the accordion. (Riza, 1971, 67). However, at the present time the policy is to stress the traditional cultural unity of the whole area of the Caucusus. One must recognize, it is stressed, "the presence and persistence of common traditions in the mode of life of the Caucasian *gortsy*. Types of dwelling have much in common as do methods of house construction, furniture, tools, clothing, decoration and ornamentation. Experts in different fields – archeologists, ethnographers, sociologists, historians – establish a definite continuity of cultural forms among all the peoples of the Caucusus from antiquity to the present day. The amity and the mutual under-standing of the mountain peoples, whose roots reach back into the mists of time were forged in the joint struggle against a foreign enemy." (Badal-bayan, 1968, 191).

So far as languages, specifically, are concerned, it is stressed repeatedly that internal subdivisions have lost their former significance and have almost completely disappeared. Although the Svans, Mingrelians and Laz still, to some extent preserve their languages as means of domestic communication, the social and political life, the civic culture, it is empha-sized, is based on the use of Georgian. In the 1959 census approximately 800 people claimed Svan, Mingrelian and Laz as their native languages. The case of the Batsbi is very similar, having almost completely merged with Georgian, and their language, especially on the level of vocabulary having been submerged under the overwhelming influence of Georgian. It is doubtful whether during the last few years there remain any but the very old who regard Batsbi as their native language. This situation is not confined to the Caucusus, and the Udins, Tats and Talysh of Azerbaydzhan have incorporated culturally and linguistically into the major ethnic group.

In view of the great pains that were taken during the early years of the regime to exaggerate the differences between even small communities and to separate peoples who had for centuries regarded themselves as sharing a common tradition, it is disconcerting to find in recent years that the reverse tendency is promoted and encouraged. "Under the socialist system the regional ties of peoples who live in areas with historical and ethnographic close relations are becoming stronger and firmer. In such areas, which in fact never were characterized by any very great differences of language, friendship and economic complementariness are bringing the peoples into single regional bonds." (Gardanov, et al. 1961). This serves only to emphasize one of the inherent contradictions within Soviet national and linguistic policy, and bears out Raymond Aron's conclusion that the characteristic mode of behaviour for Soviet ideology is not so much progression or development as contraction and expansion of per-manent and immutable elements. It is difficult to avoid the conclusion that so far as language policy is concerned all that has happened over fifty years is a series of periodic shufflings and re-shufflings of the same pack of ideas, or elements of the original prescription, formulated before the Revolution even began. Nothing is being said at present that was not debated during the pre-history of the Revolution.

F.   CONCLUSION

Language policy in the Soviet Union and the theoretical considerations
which led to its formulation were well established before the Revolution.
These considerations all enter into a general plan for social engineering in
which language figures prominently, and which is inspired by a long term
vision. The ingredients of the policy have not changed, though the relative
importance attached to either of its two main elements or forces – the
centrifugal, pluralist aspects on the one hand, and on the other the
centripetal, Russian oriented aspects, have varied. We can recognize four
main phases between which the variations are pronounced, though within
each phase there are the same tensions no less pronounced, as exist between the four phases themselves. Furthermore it is possible to identify
two aspects of the centralizing tendency itself: first, there is the concept of
a uniform Soviet culture which is the result of mutual accommodation,
based on the flourishing of individual nations (*rastsvet*), and in which all
languages of the Soviet Union play their part and to which they make
their contribution. In this view Russian is only *primum inter pares*. Then,
there is the second concept where assimilation is in terms of the dominance of Russian and its substitution for all other languages. This is part
of the theory of merging (*sliyaniye*). As has been argued, the centralist
attitude, of which both these concepts are aspects, is not inactive even
during the pluralist phases of language policy; but whereas during the
pluralist phases centralism expresses itself in terms of mutual accommodation (*sblizheniye*), during the predominantly centralist phases it is the
concept of substitution and assimilation to Russian (*sliyaniye*) which
prevails, as it is doing at present.

To conclude, during the progress of history, in order to safeguard the
promotion of a particular language three language policies have been
pursued by the rulers of multilingual states, and each of them has found
favour in Russia or in the Soviet Union at one time or another. In the
first place the language of the most powerful nationality has been imposed
deliberately and consciously upon all the other nationalities and their
languages, and the use of these has been prohibited. This was the Tsarist
policy, as it was also the policy pursued in Hungary after 1867, when
Magyar replaced Latin. Stalin favoured this policy. Secondly, a supra-
national legitimacy derived sometimes from religious, cultural or ideological presumptions, has been attributed to a particular language. This has
been the major effect of Soviet Policy, and it is not unlike that of the
Ottoman, the Habsburg, and the British imperialist position in India and
Africa. A third policy has also been pursued – namely virtually to create

new languages by the elevation of local dialects or by developing two or more variants of the same language in different regions so as to ensure that the supremacy of a favoured language is not threatened. This has been attempted by the British in Africa, for instance in Nigeria where separate orthographies were originally proposed for a large number of local dialects. In Yugoslavia attempts have been made to create anew a Macedonian language as a political device to balance the competing claims of Serbians and Bulgarians on the Macedonians. The policy has been pursued in the USSR also where Kazakhs, Turkmens, Kirgiz, Uzbeks and Karakalpaks have been encouraged to develop their languages as a means of ensuring the separate development of related Central Asian languages and the continuance of a centralist trend and a Russian hegemony. Apart then from the fact that language policy has shown such extreme opposing centralist and pluralist tendencies at all times, it is doubtful whether the Soviet policy for language can claim convincingly to safeguard the non-Russian languages when it represents at different times three such attempts to ensure the continuing supremacy of one language, namely Russian.

Chapter 4

DEMOGRAPHIC FACTORS

A. CHANGES IN THE RELATIVE STRENGTH OF LANGUAGE GROUPS

One of the most significant novel factors in the language situation of the USSR is the change which has occurred in the size and distribution of the populations of the various nationalities. Changes of this kind are not in themselves new, since fluctuations in the rate of growth and movement of populations have always been a feature of large aggregations of people such as we find in the constituent members of the Soviet Union. However, the rate of change, the combination of a large number of different kinds of change all operating simultaneously, the size of the population on the move and the fact that these movements are to a very large extent part of a general plan affecting nations, some of which are near and others at vast distances from each other, make the problem of population change in the USSR as it affects the languages, if not a new one, at least one with several added dimensions.

Table 1 shows that a few nationalities with large populations such as the Kalmyks, Mordvins and Jews tended to decline between 1926 and 1959, a tendency which has continued into the 1970's. The first of these recorded a population of 128,700 in 1926 but by 1970 their number had increased to only 137,000, an insignificant increase of 7% compared with the enormous growth of over 100% in the total USSR population. Between 1959 and 1970 the Mordvins actually dropped 2% from 1,285,000 to 1,263,000, the Poles 16% from 1,380,000 to 1,167,000, the Karelians 13% from 167,000 to 146,000. The Jewish population declined from 2,680,000 in 1926 to 2,268,000 in 1959 and to 2,151,000 in 1970, a total decline of over 20%. Apart from these losses and the 900,000 Kazakhs who drop out of the records between 1926 and 1939 thus virtually stabilizing the population of the Kazakhs until 1959,[1] the major nationalities and language groups increased between 1926 and 1959 and have continued to do so, the Kazakhs being among the most prolific. Among the major nationalities the highest growth rates between 1926-1959 was among Armenians, Uzbeks, Belorussians Aberbaydzhans, Tatars and Georgians. Between 1959-1970 the Tadzhiks made the front running followed by Kirgiz, Uzbeks, Turkmens, Azerbaydzhanis. The Georgians and Armenians are still increasing fast but have dropped behind the others in the expansion rate. It is noteworthy that 8 of the first 10 places among major nationalities are taken by Central Asian or Eastern nationalities and the Daghestanis. By 1970 the Europeans, and especially the Slavs, though they had continued to increase their total populations had declined in relative positions. Between the 1959 and 1970 Censuses the growth of the Central Asian nationalities, Kazakhs and Armenians has continued to be far ahead of most of the others, with percentage increases of 44% on average for the Central Asian nations, 40% for Kazakhs, and 41% for Armenians, compared with 11% for the whole of the USSR.[2]

The fate of the smaller nationalities appears to be related directly to their size. For instance the peoples of Daghestan, 669,000 in 1926 had increased 53% by 1959 and by 44% in 1970. The largest among them, Avar had a population of 158,000 in 1926 and the Lezgins 134,000. These grew by 71% and 66% respectively during the period up to 1959 and by 48% each between that date and 1970. The same is true of the Bashkir (713,000 in 1926) which grew by 40% and 25% between 1926 and 1959 and between that date and 1970. During the two periods 1926-1959, 1959-1970 the Ossetians (272,000 in 1926) grew by 48% and 19%, the Kabardinian (139,000) grew by 50% and 38%. The smaller nationalities fare very much worse: between 1926 and 1970 Nogai (46,000 in 1926) increased by only 13% in 44 years. This situation is most characteristic of the peoples of the North: though all have increased their populations between 1959 and 1970, yet compared with 1926 they have with only one or two exceptions declined very considerably – Evenki by 30%, Khanty by 9%, Selkup by 31%, Saami by 90% and Itelmen by 33%. The exceptions are Mansi who

---

[1] Lorimer, 1946, (140) accounted for the Kazakh losses in terms of extreme economic stringency and the depletion of their cattle. This explanation is supported by Soviet economists. "While the total population of the USSR rose by 16% between 1926 and 1939 the increase was only 1.2% in Kazakhstan. In Kazakhstan the intensification of the class struggle coincided with the break-up of the previously dominant herding economy: this led to the loss of much livestock and a temporary decline in living standards. Some of the former nomads settled on neighbouring lands in Uzbekistan." (Pokshishevskii, 1966, 5).

[2] Sources: *Narodnoye khozaistvo SSSR v 1964*, Moscow 1965; *Izvestiya*, April 17th, 1971 (Table 1).

have increased by 54% since 1926 and Nanai who doubled their population in the same period.

This process of rapid expansion of the major nationalities has enabled the populations remaining within their home territories to expand, while allowing an accelerated rate of dispersal or outmigration. In a few cases, however, although the ethnic group has grown the total, and more especially the proportion of the population remaining within its own territory or Union Republic has declined (Table 17). For instance, between 1926 and 1939 the Uzbek SSR grew by 37%, Azerbaydzhan by 39%, Kirgiztan by 40%, Tadzhikstan by 40%, Armenia by 45% and Georgia by 34%. These are much higher than the rate at which the population of the whole of the USSR was growing – 15%, in the same period. During the next period, 1939-1959, the growth rate for the USSR declined, but some Republics, especially the Central Asian and Caucasian groups had high levels of growth – Uzbekistan 25%, Kazakhstan 50%, Kirgiztan 33%, Tadzhikstan 30% (Table 4). The great differences between the growth levels of the Asian and Trans-Caucasian groups compared with the Slavs has continued after the differential effects of the war have been phased out. Thus between 1959 and 1970 compared with an increase in the USSR, as a whole of 16%, the level of increase for the Central Asian Reps. as a whole has been 44% and for Kazakh SSR 40%, and Trans-Caucusus 29%. The population growth in the European part of the Russian Republic on the other hand has dropped considerably – the Central Economic Region recorded only 8%, the Urals Economic Region 7%, the Central-Black Earth 3% and the Volga Vyatka no more than 1% (*Izvestiya* Ap. 17, 1971).

B. EFFECTS OF DIFFERENTIAL GROWTH RATES

The rate of growth, whether high or low in different areas is, of course, attributable to many causes, one of which is migration. But we need to consider the other factors before we assess the consequences of migration on the language pattern of the USSR. Changes in international boundaries have meant additions to some of the territories within the USSR, but these are mainly in the European areas of the Union. War losses to some extent have neutralised the gains in these areas. By 1970 persecution had altered the relative importance of some linguistic groups such as Germans, and Jews, but this factor does not seem to have affected the deported Ingushi, who grew by over 50% or the Tatars who grew by 20% between 1959 and 1970. But apart from migration the main cause of changes in the pattern of populations has been a differential birth rate. Between 1900 and 1950, the birth rate for the whole Union declined from

TABLE 4

Populations of the USSR (present Republic boundaries) 1913-1970

Totals in thousands[a]

Republic	1913 Total population	1926 Total population	% of 1913	1939 Total population	% of 1926	1959 Total population	% of 1939	1970 Total population	% of 1959
U.S.S.R.	139,153	165,000	105	190,678	115	208,872	110	241,748	116
R.S.F.S.R.	89,903	93,000	106	108,379	110	117,534	108	130,090	111
Ukraine	35,210	36,000	103	40,464	111	41,869	103	47,136	113
Belorussia	6,899	7,100	104	8,910	120	8,055	95	9,003	112
Georgia	2,600	2,677	103	3,540	134	4,044	111	4,688	116
Armenia	1,000	881	88.1	1,282	145	1,762	138	2,493	141
Azerbaydzhan	2,339	2,314	98.9	3,205	138	3,698	115	5,111	138
Uzbekistan	4,331	4,609	106.4	6,336	137	8,106	125	11,963	145
Tadzhikistan	1,034	1,032	99.8	1,484	140	1,980	130	2,900	146
Turkmenia	1,042	998	99.5	1,525	150	1,516	100	2,158	142
Kirgizia	864	1,002	116	1,458	140	2,066	133	2,933	142
Kazakhstan	5,600	6,037	107.8	6,094	100	9,310	150	12,850	140
Moldavia	2,056	—	—	2,452	—	2,885	116	3,752	124
Lithuania	2,828	—	—	2,880	—	2,711	98	3,129	115
Latvia	2,493	—	—	1,885	—	2,093	106	2,365	113
Estonia	959	—	—	1,052	—	1,197	104	1,357	113

[a] *Sources:* 1913 and 1926: *Itogi vsesoyuznaya perepisi naseleniya*, 1926 g. Moscow; 1939: *Izvestiya* June 2 1939 and additional material 1959 Census; 1959: *Itogi vsesoyuznaya perepisi naseleniya* 1959 g. Moscow, 1962-1964; 1970: *Izvestiya* April 17 1971.

4.4% to 1.8%. By 1965 it was 1.85%. This decline was compensated for by a similar decline in the death rate, from 2.03% in 1950 to 0.73% in 1965. Within this overall pattern, however, the several ethnic groups have varied greatly especially where the birth rate is concerned.

TABLE 5

1959. Birth rates per cent of populations[a]

Republic	Rate	Republic	Rate	Republic	Rate
Russia	2.3	Estonia	1.7	Kazakhstan	3.7
Ukraine	2.0	Moldavia	2.9	Uzbek	3.8
Belorussia	2.4	Georgia	2.5	Kirgiz	3.5
Lithuania	2.1	Armenia	3.9	Turkmen	4.1
Latvia	1.6	Azerbaydzhan	4.2	Tadzhik	3.3

a   Source: *SSSR v tsifrakh v 1959* Moscow 1960 (Statistical handbook).

The birth rate is especially low in European regions. In 1967 the reproduction index for the Baltic Republics was less than 1. In Latvia the birth rate was as low as 1.4% and the natural rate of growth 0.34%. In certain areas of N. W. Russia the population was declining. The Muslims of the Central Asian Republics have very high rates – 3.7% on the average, Tadzhiks for instance, being at the mean of 3.73% 2½ times greater than Russia. The birth rate of the rural areas has been consistently higher than that of the urban areas – in 1926 it was 4.6% and 3.4% and in 1964 it was 2.2% and 1.7% respectively. Apart from the period of the war the differential of rural/urban rates has been of that order. Partly because of the raw differences between Central Asian and European areas and the rural/urban difference, which works in favour of the Central Asian territories in the main, natural population-growth rates have been six or seven times greater in the Asian areas, and this has tended to increase with time. Thus in 1950 the differences between Estonia and Latvia on the one hand and Azerbaydzhan and Turkmenia on the other was nearly 600%. In 1963 it was well over 600%.

TABLE 6

Percentage natural growth in two European and two Central Asian Republics 1950 & 1963[a]

Year	1950-1963			
	Estonia	Latvia	Azerbaydzhan	Turkmenia
1950	4.0	4.6	21.6	28.0
1963	4.8	5.1	33.6	33.2

a   Source: *Vestnik statistiki* 1965. No. 1, 90-91.

That migration alone cannot account for the large population changes is illustrated by the case of the Andizhan Oblast, where in spite of the fact that little industrial development occurred to attract new settlers, its annual growth rate has increased from 0.8% between 1939 and 1959 to 6% by 1964. This subordinate, though important effect of migration compared with natural processes of population growth is borne out in Table 7. It will be apparent that in no single area did the net result of

TABLE 7

Calculation of net population movement, 1959-1963
(Thousands of persons)[a]

Area	Population		Increase of Population		
	1st January, 1964	15th January, 1959	Gross	Natural	Net results of migration
RSFSR	124,700	117,534	7,166	8,395	—1,229
Ukraine	44,636	41,869	2,767	2,625	+ 142
Belorussia	8,455	8,055	400	663	— 263
Azerbaydzhan	4,382	3,698	684	690	— 6
Georgia	4,415	4,044	371	362	+ 9
Armenia	2,069	1,763	306	290	+ 16
Kirgizia	2,492	2,066	426	317	+ 109
Uzbekistan	9.818	8,262	1,556	1,421	+ 135
Tadzhikistan	2,346	1,980	366	300	+ 66
Turkmenia	1,803	1,516	287	278	+ 9
Kazakhstan	11,511	9,154	2,357	1,437	+ 920
Moldavia	3,242	2,885	357	320	+ 37
Latvia	2,217	2,093	124	63	+ 61
Lithuania	2,908	2,711	197	186	+ 11
Estonia	1,259	1,197	62	34	+ 28
USSR	226,253	208,827	17,426	17,426	0

[a]   Source: Perevedentsev 1966 (b), Part I, table 7.

population influx and outflow exceed natural increase. In three areas only, Russia, Belorussia and Azerbaydzhan did outflow exceed influx and in their cases the net result of population movement amounted to 17%, 40% and 9% respectively. In each case natural growth more than compensated for loss by movement. Only in Latvia did the net migration figure approach parity with natural growth. Population movement in Kazakhstan was 60% of the size of the natural growth, the figure for Kirgizia being 34%. All the other territories experienced population movements which ranged from 5% to 17% of their natural growth. While migration undoubtedly contributes to the *redistribution* of populations within the USSR, and ensures a considerably greater variety of ethnic and language contact than existed before this century, it is important to stress that natural growth, far exceeding in nearly all cases the net result of movement, tends to maintain the size of the ethnic groups, though not always their proportion of the total Soviet population. Consequently while migration ensures contact, an ever higher rate of natural growth helps to ensure that the national language survives.

C. MIGRATION[3]

i. *Preliminary Considerations*

Whatever concessions are made concerning the effect of differential natural growth rates in maintaining strong ethnic and linguistic non-Russian groups, it cannot be denied that one of the major causes of the *redistribution* of ethnic groups and their relative strengths in specified areas is migration. A good deal of migration occurred during the period immediately following the Emancipation of the Serfs, mainly from European Central Russian areas to the frontier lands, to urban areas and to more literate communities. The Steppe and the southern parts of Siberia were the areas of highest in-migration, where the increase was sometimes of the order of 33% of the native population. The Transcaucusus and the Central Asian lands were not greatly affected; but where they were the large majority of the immigrants came from neighbouring areas. This is true also of the Polish lands of the Russian Empire, where 68% of the immigrants moved into other Polish areas. 66% of the immigrants in the Transcaucusus moved to immediately neighbouring areas, while about 50% of the Central Asian immigrants did so. During this period therefore though migration tended to be mainly over long distances, which was contrary to the general pattern of population movements in the rest of the world, the ethnic factors in such movements were not very much involved (Leasure and Lewis, 1968, 376-380).

Soviet economists have given the following estimates of the principal inter-regional population flows between 1863 and 1913, and the net balance in each case (in millions): Siberia, $+4$; Far East, $+0.7$; Urals, mostly Southern Urals, $+0.8$; Central Asia, $+1.3$; Steppes of New Russia, $+3.6$; Northern Caucasus, $+1.5$; Chernozem, -4.5; Ukrainian Wooded Steppe, -3.2; Volga, -0.8; European North, -0.5. Migration from the Baltic and Polish territories occurred to other countries. (*Ekonomicheskaya geografiya SSSR*, No. 5, 1960). By 1926 there was a

[3] It is generally agreed among Soviet and non-Soviet observers that the study of internal migration in the USSR has been neglected (R. A. Lewis, 1969 and Perevedentsev, 1967). Almost nothing has been done to relate internal migration to culture and language maintenance.

net population increase due to migration to West Siberia alone of nearly 3 millions, and of 1.5 millions to Central Siberia. The point of importance is that these movements were mainly from homogeneous linguistic areas to areas of linguistic diversity. Kazakhstan had a net migrational increment of 186,000. Consequent on these movements over 6% of the population of the Ural Oblast' in 1926 was born in some other part of the Union, 12% of the population of the Caucasian Krai and 10% of the Siberian Krai. The whole of the land from Belorussia and the Ukraine to the Pacific tended increasingly to be populated by people of Slav origin. (Lorimer, 1946, 53 ff).

ii. *Questions of Interpretation*

There are several problems which affect the interpretation of the statistics which are available for the period following the Revolution, when migration was accelerated and expanded. Reference has already been made to the effect of changes in international boundaries and absorption of populations upon the size of ethnic groups within the USSR. The changes which have occurred in the boundaries between constituent republics are relatively insignificant, so far as we are concerned, because the boundaries generally are drawn according to 'national' and linguistic criteria.[4] Changes have also occurred in the limits of urban and rural areas, however, and these do affect the estimate of the relationship of urbanization and maintenance of native languages. Some rural areas have been reclassified and the boundaries of cities have been extended. But an examination of these changes separately would hardly justify the modest degree of refinement in the data on language maintenance which might result.

There are other changes which affect the content of the Censuses and which introduce significant new variables. For instance it is estimated that World War I, the Revolution of 1917, the subsequent Civil War and its consequences reduced the population by over 4%. Collectivization in the 1930's accounted for only a slightly lower percentage loss, while actual and presumable, projected losses attributable to the political uncertainties of the late 30's cannot be estimated precisely but must be calculated in millions. World War II meant a loss of over 15 million people. The spread of these losses, the differential effect on nationalities and age groups especially, can be assessed only with great difficulty, but the indirect consequences of such losses, varying from nation to nation, on the extent and direction of migration are obvious. Not only are we obliged to take into account these cataclysmic events but we must also make some adjustments

[4] This is not always the case. For example the strong case for maintaining Karakalpakia within Kazakhstan, which are close ethnically and linguistically, was ignored and the Karakalpaks were incorporated in Uzbekistan.

on account of the irregular appearance of authoritative statistics, especially the Censuses. Following the Revolution the number of years between
each Census following the first in 1920 has been 6, years (1926 Census),
11 years (though the figures for the 1937 Census were never issued), 2
years (1939 Census), 20 years (1959 Census) and 11 years (1970 Census).[5]

Second, while it is possible to obtain a fairly accurate picture of changes
in population which have resulted from migration between Census dates,
intercensal figures are open to many misinterpretations. In the first place
annual figures are based, in the main, on police registration of persons
arriving and leaving.[6] Such movements may have to do with any number
of occasional and casual visits of more than a month's duration. Then
again, it is difficult, if not impossible, to measure the permanence of the
movements which are registered. A study of three typical settlements in
the Krasnoiarskiy Krai indicated that migrants were exceedingly mobile,
and the degree of permanence of a migrant's settlement rather low. Between 23% and 31% of the migrants left at the end of the first year and the
average mobility during each of the first three years was 53%. About 80%
of all those who left the three settlements during the period of the investigation were people who had moved there during the previous five
years (Zaionchkouskaia and Perevedentsev, 1964, passim). However
this, though of considerable importance to students of migration as a
general phenomenon, is of less significance to students of the relationship
of migration to cultural change and particularly the maintenance of
native languages. While the permanence of the consequences of mobility
is one part of the interest of the students of cultural change, the phenomenon of mobility itself must be their fundamental consideration.

Mobility, no matter how short the stay at any one place, is bound to
have a disruptive influence on the traditional pattern of life. There is no
doubt that changes in the socio-cultural patterns of both the out-migration and in-migration areas are among the most important consequences
of population movement. This is certainly a factor in the thinking of
those in the USSR who are promoting and planning migration. For them
Lenin's insistence on the value of mobility in creating a sophisticated
proletariat remains a basic proposition – "like the attraction of people
away from agriculture to the cities, temporary departure is a *progressive*

---

[5]   The following questions on migration were incorporated in the 1970 Census:
Q.16 How long have you resided continuously in this place? Q17. If less than 2 years
state your previous permanent place of residence (Repub., oblast, rayon, etc.) Q.18
Reason for changing your place of residence.
[6]   Statistical registration of migration is based on tear off stubs of address sheets
completed on arrival and departure. These are filled out for arrivals in respect of
permanent or seasonal employment, prolonged study or business journey and for all
family members who arrive for joint residence with an existing resident. The information covers date and place of birth, sex, ethnic affiliation, reason for arrival etc.

phenomenon [...]. It raises people's literacy and consciousness and imbues them with new cultural habits and needs. This raises the personality of the peasant to a higher level of awareness, and releases him from long established personal relations which are apt to ensnare" (Lenin, 1929, Vol. II, 63). Language loyalty, which is a significant aspect of the cultural pattern, is bound to be affected by the disruption, however short it may be, if that disruption affects a large enough number of people.

A third complexity in interpreting the statistics is the existence of migrational cross-currents. The figures obtained from censuses and registrations are in the last resort the net results of a large number of movements in varying and conflicting directions. In order to establish with any degree of confidence the relationship between migration and language affiliation, one would have to know not only the net figure but also the group identity of those who left compared with those who arrived. Between 1956-1960 for every 100 departures from the Ukraine for Siberia, 143 moved from Siberia to the Ukraine. Out of every 100 persons who moved into Siberian cities, 16 represented additions to the urban population; the rest, 84%, filled the gaps created by immigrants who had left (Perevedentsev, 1966b Part V, p. 115). What is true of Siberia is equally the case elsewhere for "most factors in population movement operate more or less identically everywhere." (Perevedentsev, 116). Most areas of the USSR gain from some and lose to other areas. The most interesting of these is Central Asia. Table 8 indicates that irrespective of total losses or gains, Central Asia collects and distributes its immigrants almost impartially. Part of the reason for this near equality of gains and losses from and to specified areas is the return of immigrants; but the complexity of movement is not thereby diminished.

The population of Siberia gains from the Far East territories and from European Russia, but loses to nearly all the Union Republics other than Russia. In the five years 1959-1963, the number of people who left Siberia exceeded the number who arrived by a quarter of a million, while half-a-million more people arrived in the North Caucusus than left, and this in spite of the fact that the North Caucusus was a major resource area for Siberia (Perevedentsev 1966b, 106).

According to Table 9 Kazakhstan gains from nearly every area and loses to the North Caucusus, and the North West Region. In fact Kazakhstan compares with Siberia in the complexity of its in and out migratory movements. After the unprecedented developments of the 40's and 50's Kazakhstan cities began to lose on the net-migration scale, but not because of a decline in arrivals but because of an increase in departures. In 1955 44.1% of new arrivals settled down; in 1963 the figure was only 18.5%. The following Table 9 indicates the origin of new arrivals between 1960-1962, and the percentages who actually remained in each case.

TABLE 8

Central Asia 1962 – Percentage of inward and outward immigrants from and to specified areas[a]

Economic Area or Territory	From named area to Central Asia	To named area from Central Asia
Baltic Republics	2.6	0.7
Moldavia	2.6	0.3
Kazakhstan	13.5	19.5
Trans-Caucusus	9.3	3.2
Belorussia	2.1	1.2
Ukraine	4.0	7.5
Far East	3.9	3.4
Eastern Siberia	5.2	5.6
Western Siberia	8.2	10.1
Urals	9.8	16.4
N. Caucasus	6.7	7.6
Volga Valley	9.6	10.6
Volga Viatka	3.1	3.2
Central Black Earth	2.5	2.4
Central	3.3	4.8
North West	2.6	2.4
North	1.8	1.1

[a] Source: Perevedentsev 1966b, Part III, Table 30 (Extracted).

TABLE 9

Permanency of immigrants in Kazakhstan – 1960-1962[a]

Area of Origin	% from area of origin	% of permanent settlers	
		Urban	Rural
RSFSR	51.6	30	23
Ukraine	28.3	38	42
Belorussia	9.7	42	50
Moldavia	1.9	17	51
Others	8.5	—	—

[a] Source: Pokshishevskiy (1964, 13).

The complexity of the pattern of movements and the difficulty of establishing, without intensive local studies, the composition of the groups who leave, makes it well nigh impossible to establish the ethnic or linguistic character of the migrational residuum. The decennial Census returns are the only sources for a reliable estimate of the changes. However, ten years is sufficiently long for non-migrants and migrants, especially the young, to shift language loyalty and for this reason it is impossible to apportion the responsibility for language change as between the direct effects of migration on the composition of the population, and the attraction for the native of a new language brought by the migrant, or of the local language for the immigrant.

The figures for existing populations and for migration are apt to be seriously deceptive for an important reason – they cannot take into account the natural processes of assimilation which have occurred over a period of time. Statistics on changes in the size and nationality structure of the population of various areas over a period do not give a full picture of the actual territorial redistribution of the population of the different nationalities. Thus the analysis of migration into Siberia over a long period might lead one to expect a sharp increase in the proportion of Belorussians and Volga peoples in the Siberian population since 1926. In reality the statistics fail to reveal such effect; the migrants have been assimilated and no longer appear as Belorussians, etc. Table 10 shows the changes which have occurred:

TABLE 10

Ethnic composition of the population of Siberia in 1926 and 1959

People	Percentage of people in Siberia	
	1926	1959
Russian	75.5	83.7
Ukrainian	8.3	3.9
Belorussian	3.2	0.7
Bashkir, Mordvin, Mari, Tatar, Udmurt, Chuvash – Volga people	2.8	2.8
Latvian and Estonian – Baltic	0.7	0.6
Buryat, Altai, Khakass and other minor Siberian peoples	6.2	3.6
Other	3.3	4.7

The Russians alone increased their overt representation substantially, the overt representation of others either remained stable like the Volga peoples, or declined like the Ukrainians and Belorussians, apparently because of assimilation; or increased slightly from very low bases. Over any length of time the comparisons of population sizes and movements are apt to be distorted by the concealed factor of assimilation (Perevedentsev, 1965a, 515).

Fourth, any discussion of the relationship of population movement and the maintenance of language and ethnicity has to give some prominence to the fact that the effect of this relationship is reciprocal. Many factors conduce to population movement and consequent culture modifications, and it is generally agreed that economic factors take priority of importance. At the same time broadly ethnic and specifically linguistic characteristics serve either to influence the direction of the migration of a particular ethnic and language group or to inhibit them from making any migratory move at all. The rate of population migration into Siberian cities from the Ukraine and Belorussia is approximately one half that from the Northwest and the North Caucusus, while from the Transcaucusus, the Baltic area and Moldavia it is only one third to one sixth as high. It is therefore possible to conclude that "ethnic factors play a significant role in these differences [...]. The relative rate of migration of the indigenous population of ethnic republics into areas with a predominantly Russian population is higher the more nearly the language, daily customs and culture of that population resemble those of the Russians." (Perevedentsev, 1966b, 134-135, Part V). It is not unlikely that this same principle will be found to obtain in respect of other national population movements, as we know is the case among Central Asians.

We have referred so far to methodological problems of interpretation, but there is one consideration which, though it presents few difficulties of interpretation, should, nevertheless, be raised at this point. Migration is a selective process in all countries; and where the relationship of migration to culture change and the maintenance of language is concerned, the two most vital characteristics of this bias are age and sex. The pattern of population distribution of in-migrants according to both criteria is radically different from that in the total population. So far as age goes there is always a higher proportion of young adolescents and young employable men than of young children and the middle aged and elderly. Among Soviet immigrants the employable young account for about 85%, while they constitute only about 55% of the total population.[7] Among the Nanai, Ulchi and Russians in the Lower Amur Valley who wish to move to towns nearly 60% are between 14 and 29 while only 22% are between 35 and 49. The elderly group is quite insignificant – 3.8%. Of those between 24 and 34 who wish to move most have other, if larger villages in mind. (Boiko, 1970, 59-60).

Since most of the immigrants were originally members of rural communities the migrational bias in favour of the young results in the rural populations becoming progressively older with a consequent threat to local languages, over the long term. Furthermore, the higher fertility of the migrant age-groups means that there is an indirect increment in immigration. These considerations affect the position of languages in both the source and host areas. In the first place because the stable rural population comes to consist mainly of the old (who are bound to one language) and the very young, (who have had no opportunity to acquire a

---

[7] Half the net in-migration into cities is in the 15-24 age group almost ⅔ in the 15-29 group. (Perevedentsev, 1967,89).

second language) the local languages appear to be reinforced, but only temporarily. In the host areas the greater adaptability of the employable young ensures support for bilingualism, and later so far as their children are concerned, the likelihood of a complete shift of language loyalty. A study of the age distribution of bilinguals in Central Asia bears this out. Tables 11 and 12 suggest first, that beyond age 10 the younger the population the more likely it is to be bilingual; and secondly, the incidence of bilingualism, irrespective of age grouping, is greater in the Urban areas, and here again beyond age 10 the younger the group the greater the incidence of bilingualism. If we compare the percentages of urbanized non-Russian nationalities of *all ages* with the *10-19 age group* of the same urbanized nationality, we find on average that twice as many of the 10-19 age group have learned Russian as of the older groups. The figures for a small sample of such nationalities illustrates this point.

TABLE 11

Percentage of native population who claim another language as their native language, according to age group and Urban/Rural location (1959)[a]

Nationality	Rural and Urban population		Urban population only	
	Age Groups		Age Groups	
	25-29	10-19	25-29	10-19
Kazakhs	1.0	2.5	1.7	4.4
Georgians	0.3	0.8	0.6	2.0
Uzbeks	1.3	2.0	2.3	4.3
Kirgiz	1.0	1.8	1.0	3.4
Azerbaydzhanis	1.4	2.7	1.4	2.9
Tadzhiks	1.6	2.3	2.3	4.6
Armenians	6.8	10.7	9.9	17.9
Turkmens	0.3	1.0	0.8	3.7

[a] Source: Perevedenstev 1965b, Table VIII and Perevedentsev, 1965a, 518.

TABLE 12

Comparison of age groups choosing Russian in small urban communities (1959)[a]

Urban population	Chuvash	Mari	Mordvin	Udmurt
All ages	16	16	22	23
10-19	34	28	58	36

[a] Source: Census 1959, RSFSR, Table 54.

Of the Tats of Azerbaydzhan the same is true. There are frequent cases when the old people speak only Tat among themselves but address children in Azerbaydzhani. In such families the young people usually have a poor command of Tat, if they know it at all. One can come across families where only the Azerbaydzhan language is used, though parents, who had only recently passed away, used to speak the Tat language (Grunberg). We have also referred to the case of the Evenk family of Siryagin which had switched language loyalty in the progress of only 15 years (Ubryatova), and to the changes of language affiliation among Tadzhiks, reported at the beginning of this century (Chapter 1).

The disparity between proportions of male and female immigrants is also significant. In 1964 men accounted for 56% and women 44% of arrivals and departures from Soviet Cities, though women predominate in the total population. (*Vestnik statistiki*, 1967, 7, 20). Of the age groups 15-19, 20-24 and 25-29 in the urban areas, the male component of the population was 53.7%, 54.3% and 52.5% respectively, an average of nearly 8% more men than women. This disparity again affects both the host (urban) areas as well as the rural (source) areas, since in the rural areas the preponderance of women tends to ensure greater attachment to the local language, on account of the traditional conservative linguistic attitude of women in such close knit communities.

iii.   *Types of movement*

Study of migrations has to take into account the existence of several types – migration within rural areas (from smaller to larger units); migration from rural areas to towns in the same region; migration between urban places within the region (from smaller to larger units). These are relatively short distance migrations, and might on the face of it appear not to involve different language groups. This is not the case. Intra-oblast, short distance migration, in so far as it is to larger and more populated areas, even rural areas, may mean that those who are involved come into contact with people from different nationalities, even if the representatives of these are few. A lingua franca is usually adopted. Furthermore these intra-oblast movements are usually preparatory to longer migrations, which is the fourth type of migration – inter-oblast, or inter-region.[8]

But to whatever type it conforms, migration is the consequence of two complementary forces; on the one hand a push exerted by uncongenial conditions, or political and other types of pressure – ranging from propaganda to forcible removal and deportation; and on the other, the pull of

---

[8]   It has been established for example that places occupying intermediate positions between large cities and small rural places, small towns, and rural rayony also perform an intermediate role in migration as 'trans-shipment points' in the movement of rural populations to cities.

the availability of new job opportunities, or new challenges, the incentives offered (for instance in the USSR the prospect of less collectivization and greater opportunity for limited individual interprise) as well as possibly more congenial physical and climatic conditions. The 1970 Census shows a continuous belt of climatically and topographically congenial country stretching from Moldavia in the West across the Southern Ukraine, the North Caucusus, Trans-Caucasia, Central Asia and Kazakhstan where the influx of population is very much greater than to the climatically far less hospitable north. These forces operate, whether migration is confined to fairly closely related neighbourhoods or takes place over vast distances. The two forms of migration, short distance, usually restricted to processes of urbanization of the immediate rural area, or long distance, which so far as the USSR is concerned is also mainly an aspect of urbanization, are closely linked but distinguishable processes. It should also be emphasized that 'long distance' is a relative description, and in fact the amount of movement of populations between contiguous political units is always much greater than that between units which are far apart. Nevertheless the migration distance may still be very great.

a. *Long-distance migration*

Long distance migration takes several forms in the USSR and arises from the operation of two sets of motives – punitive, and economic or strategic. Among the former which existed also in Tsarist Russia[9] may be included mass deportations of peasants during the forcible collectivization of agriculture. Russians, Ukrainians, Poles and Jews were the groups mainly affected by forcible migrations, but considering their size among the most profoundly affected have been the Baltic republics. Lithuania in 1948, Latvia between 1949-1951 and Estonia in 1949 saw the deportation of what has been estimated at over half-a-million people. Elsewhere, however, whole nationalities and ethnic-linguistic groups were deported over vast distances – in 1941 the deportation of Volga Germans was decreed; and of these the numbers in Soviet Asia were estimated at one time to be one million, located in Altayaskiy Krai, Kazakhstan, and in Novosibirskaya and Omskaya Oblasts (Roof 1960, 2). Between 1942-1944, Kalmyks (134th), Karachai (75th), Chechens and Ingushi (500th) and Balkars (42th) were deported to North Kazakhstan and Kirgizia, the Karachai and Balkars to areas between Dzhambul and the Kirgiz border. The Kalmyks were also deported into Kazakhstan and Kirgizia. Chechen and Ingushi often intermixed with the indigenous population of the deportation areas, for instance beyond Frunze and in the Petropavlovsk regions. These reception areas undoubtedly felt the influence of the deportees,

[9] For instance the Tsar gave his consent to a decree issued in 1854, to ensure that Muslims of the Crimea living along the coastal strip should be deported inland.

especially following the 'thaw'. It is true that Chechens in the Kalininskoye area complained of the lack of any interest in their cultural welfare (*Sovetskiy Kirgiz* Feb. 11, 1956), but talks in the Ingush language and publication by the Kirgiz State Publishing House of works by Karachai-Balkar writers were announced in 1956. The Germans, too, received some attention in spite of their deportation, and a newspaper in their language appeared in the Altai Territory in 1958, and only slightly later German radio programmes were broadcast from Alma-Ata. It is also true that a million and a half of those who were deported were allowed to return (Roof, 1960, 1) but the return of the Chechen, Ingushi and Kalmyks, particularly, only served to exacerbate the problems of ethnic identity and language maintenance. To make room for the rehabilitated nationalities Avar and Dargin families had to be moved into other areas of Daghestan, thus creating new patterns of heterogeneity.

Unemployment is an aspect of the economic motivation for migration. The apparent high level of employment in the USSR serves to disguise the situation in some areas. Kosygin (*Pravda*, Sept. 28th, 1965) during an address to the Central Committee referred to "considerable manpower reserves in the small towns of the Ukraine, the Western regions and Belorussia as well as Transcaucasia".[10] The existence of this 'reserve of manpower' is the reality behind the deployment of labour resources frequently mentioned in the discussion of Soviet demographic processes. The movement of formerly unemployed persons to new industrial areas is significant from the standpoint of language maintenance because, whereas new technological and industrial developments in the host areas pull and select the best educated, the existence of an 'unemployment pool' ensures that selectivity is not a significant factor – or if it is, it tends to be contrary to the selective pulls exerted by industrial and technological development elsewhere. These two tendencies, selection exerted from the host, and non-selection from the source areas, do not neutralize each other when it comes to language maintenance. The unselected mass who emigrate are likely to be monoglot at home, but unretentive of their native language in a new mixed industrial centre. The non-Russian national language suffers a loss. At the same time the loss of a selected educated population from any area tends to ensure that the status of the non-Russian language declines in the area of origin. This is true not only of the Soviet Union but of other areas, like Ireland and Wales where unemploy-

---

[10]   This statement seems to contradict the views expressed by Pokshishevskii (1964, 4) that "driving forces of the migration process in the USSR are not related to unemployment and over-population in the areas of origin [...] but to the positive aims of resource development ... etc." Perevedentsev (1967, 104) agrees with this view: "the results of inter-regional migration are not related to the availability of labour in particular regions."

ment leads to emigration, and consequent decline of the native language.

Nor should we under-estimate the dimensions and the strength of the impact of temporary war-time evacuation to the East of millions from the occupied territories. Between June 1941 and February 1942 10.4 million were moved into the Volga, Urals, Western and Eastern Siberian oblasts (6 millions) and Kazakhstan, Central Asia and Transcaucasia (3.5 million). Although it was temporary in theory, large numbers settled permanently in their new homes. Three years after the end of the war 15% of the evacuees still remained in Irkutsk (Pokshisheviskii, ct al., 1964, 5).

One characteristic punitive and forced migrations on the one hand, and economically motivated migrations have in common is the fact that they are part of a planned and deliberately executed programme.[11] In the 1920's, shortly after the Revolution, a special state Colonization Institute was set up which did a great deal to rationalize migration. In 1940 for instance labour for some areas of the Far East could be obtained only from the Tatar, Bashkir and Chuvash ASSR's. Other areas had to depend exclusively on the North Caucusus. In this way the problem of language maintenance among immigrant groups was affected favorably, since the migrants did not become entirely lost as ethnic groups through fragmentation and dispersal to several new habitats, and they could at one time claim the right to have separate schools. In 1956 most problems relating to migration were brought under the control of the Main Administration for Organised Recruitment and Resettlement. In 1966 State Committees for the Utilization of Labour Resources were set up in all Union Republics. Among the duties of such Committees are organised recruitment of groups and their resettlement. The Young Communist League is very active in this respect among its own members. During the years prior to 1962 planned resettlement of Ukrainian families accounted for 810,000 workers, and in the relatively short period between 1946 and 1962, 88,000 peasant families were involved. As late as 1965 the Draft Directions of the Twenty Third Party Congress emphasised the need to ensure rational and planned deployment of immigrant labour resources.

This continues to be the case. In one respect, however, the character of planned and rationalized migration has changed. Government hiring for work in distant places, planned rural resettlement etc. now account for only about 15% or slightly more, and the remainder is accounted for by the initiative of individuals though still operating within the overall plan – the planned development of specific industries and the "guided" training

[11] Perevedenstev and his associates tend to deprecate the attachment of any particular importance to the part played by planned population movement (Zayonchouskaya and Perevedentsev, 1967, 178). I suspect that this attitude is not unrelated to Perevedentsev's campaign for greater rationalization of labour supply in the USSR.

of personnel, and other measures (Pokshishevskii, et al., 1964, 11). This change means that there are even fewer safeguards for the language of the immigrant because he is no longer a member of a cohesive group with group ties and group associations with a common area, and a common language of origin.

Family resettlement and some other forms of migration were voluntary. The people were recruited on contract, on the expiry of which they could return home if they wished. The same is true of the student immigrant populations. The compulsory labour draft of students was abandoned and placed on a voluntary basis in 1955. Thereafter volunteers, on graduation, were subject to four year assignments, and some to three. Shortly after 1955 the number involved was not less than one and a half million. Even after the completion of their assignment, the students were liable to a continuance of their service. Similarly, the Komsomol (Communist Youth Organisation) has been used to recruit immigrants, especially to the Far East, which has been described as Komsomol Territory. Large numbers of such volunteer immigrants have become members of the Soviet Army and there is no doubt that the latter has played an important part in promoting bilingual communities like the Roman Armies in Gaul and Britain. Since the 1930's normally no military units in the Soviet Union have been recruited on a territorial basis. Ethnic groups are fragmented.[12] Such a procedure helps to break down ethnic insularity no matter how short the duration of the military service may be (Bennigsen and Quelquejay, 1961, 194). Whatever proportion of the immigrant population returned to their original habitats, the effect of even a temporary concentration of immigrants upon the local population would be difficult to remove. Though the tide of immigrants might recede temporarily and slightly, there still remain permanent marks upon the life and languages of the local populations. Similarly the effect of even temporary dispersal upon the resource area and on the immigrants themselves is permanent and adverse to the continuity of the traditional cultures and languages. This is what Lenin envisaged.

Between 1926-1939 about 3 millions moved to Siberia and the Far East and more than 1.7 millions to Central Asia and Kazakhstan, which are the most important areas to be affected by long distant migration (*Trudovyye resursy SSSR*, 1961, 209). Between 1913 and 1964 the population centre of the RSFSR shifted to the south-east. Between 1913 and 1964 there was a decline in the proportion contributed by the European Republics to the total Soviet population, from 80% to 68.2% and a rise in the Asian Republics from 11.8% to 17.1%. This rise in the latter areas corresponded to the losses in the other Union republics of the USSR

[12]   Concessions, as in the case of Armenia, were sometimes made to avoid the exacerbation of political conflict.

together with a decline of nearly 1.5% in the Russian Republic itself (Perevedentsev 1966b, part I, Table 6). Between the 1959 and 1970 Censuses the proportion contributed by the Western Economic Areas has declined from 68% to 65%, that of the East has dropped from 11% to 10%, and that of the South East has increased from 21% to 25% (Perevedentsev 1970b, 41). This sharp rise must be seen against the prior comparative closedness of the Central Asian territories up to the period in question. Between 1926 and 1939 the official estimate of migration into Central Asia was 1.7 million, though Lorimer (1946, 137-140) favours a figure lower by 16%. Between 1959-1970 the net gain by immigration to Central Asia was 1,200,000. While some of this movement has taken the form of a redistribution among the five Republics – for instance Kazakhs migrating from the inhospitable steppe – a major part was played by the migration of Slavs. During 1913-1968, the annual growth rate in these areas accelerated from 0.5% between 1913-1926, to 1.6% between 1926-1939, and 1.9% during the next 20 years, reaching 3.6% in 1968. Even when account has been taken of the high level of natural growth a considerable element of this total growth must be left at the door of immigration.

The growth and immigration rates vary between the several Asian Republics. For instance, during the early periods Kazakhstan and Turkmenia showed an overall decline and Uzbekistan and Kirgizia increased by twice the rate of the Asian Republics as a whole.

During the second period, 1926-1939, Kazakhstan declined with a loss of 869,000 as against an expected or projected increase of 631,000, largely because the economic stringency to which reference has been made produced a lower natural growth rate, and a considerable movement of population into Republics neighbouring to it. Possibly there was movement out of the USSR altogether. Between 1959-1967, 1.8 millions of the Republic's growth of 3.5 millions were immigrants, the great majority from the European areas of the Union. Since, simultaneously with this immigration, there was a cross current of South Kazakhs migrating into neigh-

TABLE 13

Increase in total population and in number of immigrants in Central Asian Republics.
1959-1967[a]

	Kazakhstan	Turkmenia	Uzbekistan	Kirgizia	Tadzhikistan
Total population increase (thous.)	3,500	500	3,000	766	750
Increase in number of immigrants (thous.)	1,800	100	800	255	250

[a] Source: Mirenenko, 1967, 23-25 (Extracted).

bouring Asian Republics, the total of 1.8 million immigrants is an exceedingly conservative estimate. In Turkmenia during the same period
immigration has been less pronounced. Between 1959-1968, migration
accounted for approximately 20% of the half-million population increase. In Uzbekistan the proportion of the total increase due to migration was approximately 27%, and in Kirgizia, it was approximately 33%,
as it was also in Tadzhikstan.
Between 1913 and 1968 immigration into the Central Asian Republics
must account for approximately 12.5 millions. Even in the 8 years between 1959 and 1967, 3.3 millions moved from the European areas to the
Central Asian Republics (Mirenenko, 17).

b. *Industrialization*

A factor which is common to the processes of long and short distance
migration in the USSR is the rapid growth of industry in hitherto undeveloped areas. "The springing up of new industrial centres, the discovery
and exploitation of natural wealth, the cultivation of virgin lands and
the development of all types of communication systems needed by these
processes, intensify the mobility of the population and contacts between
nations. Frequently the indigenous population of a republic is incapable
of making full and rational use of natural wealth. In such cases the interests of the indigenous nationality and the entire Soviet people demand
labour assistance from fraternal republics [...] The objective processes
taking place in the country are having the result that the boundaries between republics are more and more losing their former significance"
(Rogachev and Sverdlin, 1963, 15). This argument, which was deployed
in the discussion on the problems of merging nationalities and cultures
points to one of the most important causes of migration. It is true that
the local rural populations are ill equipped for the frequently skilled requirements of new large industrial complexes. This is supplied from traditional industrial areas in the West, and facilitated by the pool of unemployed labour to which reference has been made.

However, it is not their general *inability* so much as the *reluctance* of
the local rural population to undertake industrial work which makes long
distance migration necessary. While there is an acknowledged intention to
encourage migration from the west for social and ideological reasons,
new industrial employment attracts the Russians and Ukrainians frequently because of the reluctance of the neighbouring rural population to
move into an alien industrial environment and away from their attachment to the village way of life, together with their inability or reluctance to
learn a new language which industrial employment among a mixed population might make necessary.[13] Of course, industrial development is not a

[13]   "Experience shows that a poor knowledge of Russian among a substantial part

new phenomenon even in the more remote parts of the Union. At the beginning of this century, when it was fairly isolated, shepherds left their flocks at various times during the year to work in Baku. In 1875, even though Azerbaydzhanis contributed 90% of the city population, Russians and Armenians each claimed a 5% share. However, by 1905, the number of Russians exceeded the number of Azerbaydzhanis, and 39 other nationalities were represented there. In 1949 the school population of the city consisted of an almost equal proportion of Azeri and Russians, with Armenians accounting for a little more than 19,000 of the population, about 20% of the combined Azeri and Russian total (Kolarz, 1958, 240).

The Kazakh Republic is a good example of the influence of new industrial development upon population changes. Even before the revolution, the vast, sparsely populated lands of Kazakhstan were among the principal areas of mass settlement of peasants, mainly from the Chernozem Center, the Volga, the Ukraine and Belorussia. This migration flow has continued in Soviet times, varying in intensity at different stages under the influence of changing factors. As the industrialization of Kazakhstan proceeded in the 1930's, demand was greatest for industrial workers and trained personnel at construction projects of the republic, which lacked its own industrial labor force. There was also some planned settlement of peasants, especially in northern Kazakhstan. Cities grew rapidly. From 1926 to 1939, urban population increased from 519,000 to 1,690,000. (In this period, many large villages, rayon seats, and railroad settlements were transformed into urban places.) More than 321,000 people moved to the cities of Kazakhstan in 1939-1940. During World War II, when Kazakhstan became one of the arsenals in the eastern part of the Soviet Union and received many evacuated industrial plants with their labor forces, the population of the republic's cities increased by 30 per cent (by the beginning of 1945) despite mobilization into the armed forces and a low rate of natural increase.

Toward the end of the war, starting in 1944, re-evacuation resulted in out-migration from Kazakhstan. A large in-migration in 1946-1947 and a high rate of settlement of the arrivals (48 to 51.6 per cent of them remained in Kazakhstan) were related to mass demobilization. Subsequently the movement to Kazakhstan cities remained high until the opening up of the virgin lands (for example, in 1950, more than 100,000 people moved to the cities).

In 1955 a stage began of unprecedented intensive migration processes related to the opening up of the virgin lands and an increased rate of in-

---

of the non-Russian population is one of the principal reasons for the low rate of migration of the indigenous rural population to the cities of their Republics" (Perevedentsev, 1967, 116).

dustrial development. A chronic manpower-deficit region, Kazakhstan would have been unable with its own human resources to plow up 22 million hectares of virgin and idle lands and at the same time to develop its extractive industries and other branches of the economy and culture. (Pokshishevskii, et al., 1964, 12).

That it is actually industrial development which accounts for this influx of heterogeneous ethnic groups can be demonstrated by an analysis of two specific projects, the Nurek GES Textile Combine construction project and the Dushanbe Textile Combine.

TABLE 14

Composition of the labour force of two industrial projects by nationalities – September,
1964[a]

Nationality	Nurek GES %	Dushanbe Combine %
Tadzhiks	27.8	15.2
Uzbeks	1.7	10.1
Russians	51.8	55.7
Ukrainians	7.3	2.3
Belorussians	1.9	1.0
Tatars	4.2	7.4
Mordvins	1.0	2.4
Others	4.3	5.9

[a]   Source: Perevedentsev 1966b, Part V, Table 69.

The Nurek Combine is near a new town in the heart of the rural area of Tadzhikstan, which is remarkably homogenous linguistically. The Dushanbe Combine is the largest industrial enterprise in the Tadzhik capital, and the heterogeneity of the industrial plant is a reflection of the general urban position. With such a large number of different linguistic groups on one site, and such a preponderance of Russians, it is only natural that the language of the latter should become a lingua franca, and several varieties of Russian-related bilingualism emerge. "The overwhelming majority of the indigenous townfolk of Central Asia, Kazakhstan and Azerbaydzhan speak Russian fluently" (Perevedentsev 1966a, 52).

Other areas exemplify the same increasing tendency towards mixed populations. For instance, the urban population of the Irkutsk area of the RSFSR in 1959 consisted of 86.5% Russians, 4.9% Ukrainians and a little more than 1% Belorussians, the remaining 7.5% being distributed among several other nationalities. With the building of the Bratsk hydroelectric station in the region there has been a great increase in the diversity of the population involved in the work. Only 70.3% of the work force is Russian while the Ukrainians have increased to 13.3% and Belorussians to 6.7%. The remaining ten per cent are distributed among a larger selection of nationalities including Tatar (1.4%), Chuvash (1.4%), Mordvin (1%), Buryat (0.8%), Bashkir (0.8%) and Baltic peoples (0.7%). In many state farms in the virgin territory of the Kazakh SSR, fifteen to twenty-five nationalities are often represented among the work force. The inhabitants of Nebit-Dag on the line from Ashkabad to Krasnovodsk on the Caspian represent more than 50 different nationalities, while in Tashkent, in addition to the Uzbeks and Russians who constitute among them 80% of the population, there are nearly 100 other different national groups. Needless to say these international migrations still continue. The population of Western Yakutia, for instance, has become the centre of diamond mining, and the industry demands a work force larger and more skilled than the hitherto sparsely populated locality and its environs can supply. Similarly, the migratory movements into Sakhalin has assumed classic characteristics according to Soviet observers (*Voprosy trudovykh resursov v rayonakh Sibiri*, 1961, 157). In 1939 the population of the area was 100,000, but by 1959 it had reached 650,000, and of this increase all but 30,000, i.e. 520,000 were new settlers, and their children, who arrived in the main between 1946-1954. A survey of eight enterprises in southern Sakhalin, in 1960 indicated that only 3% of the labour force was indigenous. (*Vopr. trud.* 159).

c. *Urbanization*

If industrialization calls for manpower from distant republics, it also makes demands upon localities where the industries are situated, and draws rural populations over relatively short distances into the urban scene. Once a new industry is located in an area the city develops its own momentum. A single enterprise attracts associated undertakings, and at the same time institutions have to be created and manned to serve the influx of new workers. These institutions become the centres of regional services: new educational establishments, for instance, tend to draw upon areas well outside the city itself. For this reason an urban area exerts a pull over great distances, and a town may be the focal point for populations living within a radius of much more than a hundred miles. In 1927 the rural population of the USSR constituted 82% of the total but in the last few decades while the total population has increased by nearly 70 millions the rural population has declined to less than half the overall total. In the 11 year period from 1959 to 1970 the number of urban residents has increased by 36 millions (36%) while the rural population decreased by 3,100,000 (2.8%). The main source for the growth in the number of urban residents has been the local rural population. Two thirds of the new urban populations come from the rural areas in the immediate vicinities of the cities, if we include in that category people who became urban residents through the expansion of city boundaries etc. (Pereve-dentsev, 1970b, 34).

In comparison with the shift to the cities, the movement of populations across the Soviet Union from West to East has played only a moderate part in the general growth of urban centres. Nevertheless it has to be remembered that long distance migration is almost exclusively directed towards the cities and towns, whether the immigrants were originally urban residents or part of rural communities.

TABLE 15

Growth of urban population in the USSR 1897-1970[a]

Year	1897	1914	1923	1926	1939	1959	1962	1968	1970
Urban Total Millions	15.8	24.6	21.4	26.3	60.4	99.9	113.4	131.1	136.0
Urban % of Total	14.8	17.7	16.0	20.5	32.0	48.3	51.0	55.0	56.0

[a]   Sources: (a) 1897-1962: Pisarev, 1962, 74; (b) 1968: *SSSR v tsifrakh* 1968; (c) 1970 *Literaturnaya gazeta* 29-4-1970.

Whereas in 1914 there was only one Republic (Latvia) with an urban population of more than 30% of the total, in 1965 there was only one Republic lower than 30%. In the same year two Republics had over 60% and four others between 50% and 60%. Between 1959 and 1970, in the fifteen Union Republics the total as well as the proportion of rural residents declined in only six, most of the decline being reported from the RSFSR (12.2%), Belorussia (8.6%), Estonia (8.9%), Lithuania (6.5%), the Ukraine (4.6%) and Latvia (3.4%). In Georgia and Moldavia there was an increase of 5% and 8.9% respectively, and in Armenia one of 11.8%. Apart from Russia and Estonia the greatest proportional changes between the beginning of the century and 1970 have occurred in Armenia, Turkmenia and Kazakhstan. Considerable urban development has occurred in the Central Asian Republics rising between 1926-1968 from 25% to 43% of the total: at the same time the rural population of the same Republics increased between 1959-1970 by 32% in Azerbaydzhan and 34% in Uzbekistan. In Kazakhstan the rural population rose by 26%, from 5.1 millions, to 6.4 millions, while the urban population also rose by 57%. In Uzbekistan the urban population increased by 45% (1.25 millions) and the rural population by 32% (1.75 million). Of this total increase of over 3 millions, 2.2 millions can be accounted for by natural growth. The remaining 800 thousands must have been assimilated entirely by the urban areas. The same is true of Kirgizia, where the population increased from 2.06 millions in 1959 to 2.82 millions in 1967 – an increase of 766 thousands. Of this, 500 thousands can be accounted for by natural increase, with an immigrant increase of 266 thousands. The urban population, however, increased by 400 thousands, leaving 134 thousands to be accounted for by movement from the surrounding rural areas. In other words the urbanization of Kirgizia during the last 10 years has been due almost equally to long distance immigrants, mainly Russians, Ukrainians and Belorussians and the indigenous rural population.[14] Nevertheless, by 1970, in Uzbekistan the rural outflow was only 10% of the natural rural increase, which seems to suggest an increasing reliance on international migration to the growing cities, and a growing rural reservoir for local languages.

The same is true of some of the smaller Autonomous Republics. For instance, between 1926 and 1964, the Buryat ASSR increased its urban population from 339 to 429 thousands, the Khakass Oblast from 115 to 189 thousands and the Gorno-Altai Oblast from 101 to 133 thousands. Their urban populations increased at such a rate that only a large measure of international migration could have accounted for it. It has been calculated that a half of the urban population of the USSR has been born and partly bred in the rural areas. This fact has a profound implication for the maintenance of ethnicity and language.

This phenomenal growth in the urban population of nearly all the Republics has meant the creation and growth of large towns and cities, and nowhere has the development of towns been more remarkable than in the Central Asian Republics. Tashkent has nearly trebled its size since 1926. Alma-Ata is ten times the size it was in 1926, and Dushanbe has grown from being a small town of 5,000 to a large city of over a quarter of a million. Frunze has added over 180 thousands to its population in thirty years and Chimkent has added over 120 thousand. The North Caucusus has over 20 cities with a population greater than 50,000, the Urals over 30, West Siberia 20, Kazahakstan 20 and Central Asia 16.[15]

It is important to note that there is a tendency for the larger cities to grow more rapidly than the smaller and medium-sized towns. This tendency towards megalopolitic communities has accelerated. Between 1959-1970 while those living in cities under 50 thousand had increased by only 17% those living in cities between 100 and 500 thousand had increased by 78%. Those in cities of intermediate sizes grew by 18% and 57%. (Perevedentsev 1970b, 38). The larger the city the greater the likelihood of its having to depend upon long distance migration to ensure its growth and consequently the greater the degree of heterogeneity. At the same time there is a tendency in such cities for large migrant communities

[14] Sources: *SSSR v tsifrakh v 1967 goda* (The USSR in Figures) Moscow 1968, 6, et seq.
[15] Sources: The 1926 and 1959 All Union Censuses, and *Narodnoye khozaistvo SSSR v 1958 g.* Moscow 1959.

to cohere in national enclaves, and so to preserve their national peculiarities, especially when it comes to having their national language used as the medium of instruction, and in marriage as is clear from the example of Tashkent below.

D. MIXED MARRIAGES

The processes we have already described, migration, industrialization and urbanization, all lead to contact of peoples, and one such contact which itself intensifies the processes of change in language maintenance is the marriage of partners who belong to different cultural and linguistic communities. It has been stated, for instance, that the diffusion of the Azerbaydzhan language among the Tats is promoted by mixed marriages – the marriage of a Tat to an Azeri girl. In this way the Azerbaydzhan language becomes firmly rooted in Tat families. Similarly the use of the Circassian language was undoubtedly promoted by the Circassian women who married into Abazin families and taught their children Circassian. The tendency of these two groups to inter-marry has continued so that they represent the highest percentage of mixed marriages in the Caucusus – 24.6% Circassian males and 26% females enter into mixed marriages, the percentages for the Abazin being 36.3% and 25% respectively. Of these mixed marriages well over a half of the Circassians marry Abazins and nearly two-thirds of the Abazin mixed marriages are to Circassians (Smirnova 1967, 140).

Before the Revolution marriages even between different nationalities, even between Muslims, in such areas as the Caucusus, Central Asia and particularly Turkestan, was extremely limited. It is true that occasionally Tatar immigrants married into local families, but there was little contact between the various peoples at this level of intimacy and little linguistic significance derived from the marriage. Inter-marriage between Ibero-Caucasians and Turkic men and women occurred only between the most élite families. Even in towns, where it might be thought such exclusiveness might have been eroded, little inter-marriage occurred. New settlements might be built, but adjacent to older cities and immigrants would gravitate there: there was little contact, and marriages between Russians and the others were rare. From 1871 to 1917 there was only one instance of a marriage recorded as taking place between a Turkmen man and a Russian woman. It is true that in certain areas, for instance the coastal regions of Khorezm, the Karakalpaks had a long tradition of such marriages with Kazakhs, but the latter had very close linguistic and ethnic affinities with the Karakalpaks, in any case. In Ferghana the tradition among Karakalpaks was not so liberal for while the men could marry girls from other nationalities, preferably Uzbeks, the marriage of Karakalpak girls outside their own ethnic group was discouraged. However, things began to change among many nationalities after the Revolution; and even before the Revolution, in fact, cases were being reported of Russian girls marrying Kirgiz. The Revolution only accelerated the process and intermarriage became more popular in the period between the Revolution and World War II. There are no figures for the larger nationalities but it is known that the Arabs rapidly lost their revulsion of such marriages. Out of 487 families investigated between 1936-1938 nearly one sixth were mixed, involving Arab males and Uzbek or Tadzhik women. The same tendency was noticeable among the more well-established Central Asian nationalities also.

The war brought such areas as Turkestan much closer to Europeans and to other Asian nationalities. Of the 5.2 million householders in the USSR in 1959 10.4% consisted of partners belonging to different nationalities – 15% of these were in urban areas and 6% in towns and cities. The comparable figures for Central Asia alone were 11.6% overall, 8% rural and 17% urban. (Isupov, 1964, 38). In the city of Ashkabad the war brought the rate of mixed marriages up to 34.5%. The settlement of nomads facilitated stable contact between groups who had previously been isolated or had only the most fleeting contacts, though the process had begun before extensive urbanization got under way, and involving more particularly the larger villages. Perhaps the importance of the war lay not so much in increasing the number of these marriages but in promoting relations between groups who belonged to vastly different cultural and linguistic traditions, so that the individuals involved were, for instance, not Muslims of different nationalities but Muslims and non-Muslims, such as Ukrainians, Belorussians and Russians. These marriages took place during the war or soon afterwards between Central Asian soldiers and Slav girls whom they met during their war service. Students from Central Asian countries, too, have brought back Slav wives after periods of study outside their own Republics. Mixed marriages became more frequent among very isolated groups such as the Kurds among whom there are increasing numbers of marriages with Russian, Tatar and Turkmen wives, or with Azerbaydzhan husbands. (Aristova and Vasilyena, 1965).

In the cities the rate of intermarriages increased rapidly. In Ashkabad, of the 381 marriages registered there in 1920, 81 (21%) were contracted between different nationals. In 1940 the percentage had increased to 31, and the number had grown to 400. Following the steep rise during the war the percentage dropped between 1951-1965 to 29%. The same process is evident in other cities. In Tashkent, a town of more than a million inhabitants in 1959, there was a considerable degree of ethnic heterogeneity – Russians constituting 43%, Uzbeks 33%, and other nationalities including Tatars, Ukrainians, Jews, Armenians, Kazakhs, Tadzhiks, Mordvins, Uygurs, Belorussians, Azerbaydzhanis, Bashkirs, Chuvash and Poles. Among these nationalities, within two districts of Tashkent intermarriage increased from 19% to 22% between 1926 and 1963. But interestingly enough there were nearly four times the number of such marriages in the new district of Tashkent as in the old town. Furthermore there was a tendency for a greater number of nationalities to be involved in such marriages – in the new town the number rose from 26 nationalities in 1926 to 33 in 1963, and in the old town from 9 to 26. An analysis of the figures also shows that mixed marriages were far more popular among members of nationalities which were represented by only small numbers within the city. Where nationalities had fairly cohesive representation they tended to maintain their ethnic independence far more. (*Pravda Vostoke*, 1963; and Khanazarov, 1963).

Such marriages have become more and more frequent in the Slav areas also, for in 1965 the figures for Leningrad district amounted to 17% of all marriages (*Trud*, June 1965). In the town of Brask near Irkutsk where, as we have noted already, there has been built an important hydro-electric plant employing representatives of well over a dozen nationalities, the number of children born in mixed marriages constituted 21% of all the children born between 1960 and 1962. Nevertheless it is important to maintain our estimate of the contribution of mixed marriages to establishing bilingualism at a realistic level. Mixed marriages occur, in the main, in areas where there is already a considerable degree of linguistic contact. For this reason the function of such marriages is to reinforce and possibly accelerate the process of developing bilingualism rather than initiate it.

Attitude to mixed marriages is an important factor in determining how popular they become as well as how successful they are, both of which are important in determining the contribution of such marriages to the development of bilingualism. Attitude varies according to the disparity between the cultural backgrounds or ethnic distance of the partners. On the whole it is favorable and this promotes the intensification of the influence of this factor – acceptance of the mixed marriage leads to acceptance of its consequences in the form of bilingualism among children in a hitherto monoglot community. A study conducted in Tataria not so long ago showed that between 60 and 80 per cent of those surveyed were not opposed to mixed marriages. More would have been favorable if they could be assured that there was a reciprocal learning of the relevant languages within the family. Nevertheless, in spite of a favorable official attitude, prejudice is still very strong in some areas. *Komsomolskaya Pravda* reported on September 5th, 1970 that "while today there are many happy mixed marriages it is also true that dissolution because of national prejudice is not rare." And in January the same publication quoted a correspondent who asked: "What is good about the fact that after being discharged from the army members of small peoples settle far from their native land, marry and forget their native tongue, culture and parents? [...] I am first and foremost a Kabardinian, vitally interested in the development of my people's language and culture and in increasing their numbers." Needless to say the editorial comment was disapproving: it was regarded as "a vulgar interpretation of the process of internationalization."

The differences between urban and rural areas in respect of inter-marriage is illuminated by the figures for some of the nationalities of the North Caucusus. In the urban areas 16.0% of the male Karachais and 6.8% of the women entered into mixed marriages but the figures for the rural areas were 4.2 and 2.6. For the Cherkess the comparable figures are Urban 45% (M) and 53% (F) and Rural 22% for men and women. For Abazin: Urban, 56% (M) and 41% (F) and Rural 34% (M) and 23% (F), while for the Nogais the figures were: Urban 44% (M) and 28% (F), Rural 6.3% for men and women. It will be seen from these figures, too, that the percentage of men entering into mixed marriages is greater than the percentage of women (Smirnova 1967, 140). In the Central Asian Republics the comparable figures for Urban and Rural marriages are Kazakh, 17.5% and 12%, Uzbek, 14.7% and 4%, Kirgiz, 15.1% and 9.2%, Tadzhik, 16.7% and 5.5% and finally Turkmen, 14% and 2.5% (Benningsen and Quelquejay, 1961, 144). This heavy preponderance of urban as compared with rural mixed marriages not only reflects the greater conservatism and isolation, ethnically and linguistically, of the rural areas, it also reinforces such conservatism, leading to what has been observed previously, as the maintenance in the rural areas of a deep reservoir of attachment to local languages.

That this is the case cannot be doubted, for, as has been estimated, the reduction in the number of Kazakhs maintaining their own language in their Republic can be attributed in part to mixed marriages. There, we find 14.4% mixed marriages, 18% in urban and 12% in rural areas, the offspring of which sooner or later pass through a stage of bilingualism to a switch of language loyalty (Taskin, 1964, 4). Whether or not such marriages are encouraged as a matter of policy by the central government the fact remains that they are increasing and are a powerful agent in the assimilation of nationalities and in producing bilingual children. "Marriages with women of other nationalities is becoming quite commonplace. Even in remote villages, marriages are arranged, primarily with girls and women of Slav stock: Russians, Ukrainians and Belorussians" (Abramson, 1962, 31). The children of the mixed marriages tend to enrol at Russian schools rather than in one or other of the 'nationality schools';

normally the father has acquired a command of Russian in the course of his education and work; and Russian is spoken increasingly in the home, especially in the urban districts. From the time they go to school, or even to kindergarten, the children are known by Russian names. Some of the parents may be teachers or engaged in other occupations which bring them into close contact with the local population. In some such families there is usually a form of functional or complementary bilingualism, one language being employed for some purposes and another for the remainder. However the families in the urban areas pass rapidly through a bilingual stage and become completely Russian. Very complex and sometimes strange results ensue. For instance, there is the case of a Korean teacher who married a Kirgiz pupil (Abramson, 33). His Korean speaking mother, who lived with them, had no knowledge of Kirgiz and only a little Russian. His wife knew no Korean and only a little Russian. The husband spoke all three languages and Russian became a halting lingua franca.

An analysis has been made of the consequences, for the language of the children of such mixed marriages. In the town of Karasuk, the centre of an ancient culture in Novosibirskaya, marriages among Ukrainians and Russians were found to be common, and the overwhelming majority of the children of such marriages were regarded as Russians. Table 16 shows the correlation between the nationality and mother tongue of the parents on the one hand and the nationality and mother tongue of the children on the other.

TABLE 16

Distribution of children by nationality and native language in mixed Russian-Ukrainian families[a]

Parents				Children %		
Father		Mother		Language and nationality Russian	UKR nationality and Russian language	Language and nationality Ukr.
Nationality	Language	Nationality	Language			
Russian	Russian	Ukrainian	Ukrainian	100	—	—
Ukrainian	Russian	Russian	Russian	97	3	—
Russian	Ukrainian	Ukrainian	Ukrainian	82	15	3
Ukrainian	Ukrainian	Russian	Russian	88	7	5
Russian	Russian	Ukrainian	Russian	49	51	—

[a]   Source: Perevedentsev 1965a, 516.

Frequently parents who are both of Ukrainian stock and regard Ukrainian as their native language bring up their children to regard Russian as their native language and often to identify themselves as Russian in general ethnic character. The same process has been observed in the two districts of Tashkent to which reference has been made earlier. There in 1963 marriages between non-Russian speaking people where Russian became the common language constituted 10.5% of the total of intermarriages in one district and 7.9% in the other. Where Russian was already the language of one partner the percentage of marriages in which that language became the normal means of communication with the children was 79% and 47% in the two districts. All in all during 1963 in the old and the new towns of Tashkent over 54% and 86% respectively of the mixed marriages saw Russian adopted as the native language of the children.

Mixed marriage is not the only familial consequence of migration with a significance for language maintenance. Irrespective of its ethnic composition and possible linguistic complexity, a migrant family, as a primal social unit, faces considerable problems of integration. Several alternatives are open to it in its dilemmas; the family may disintegrate, the members of the different age groups tending to respond to the new challenges in radically different ways. This process we have already documented. Secondly, it may isolate itself from the host community as far as possible, and this tends to be the case when the family is one of a large number from the same source area or belonging to the same ethnic group. It is most apparent among Russian and Ukrainian immigrant families, and it tends to reinforce an already strong tendency to preserve their mother tongue. Or, thirdly, the whole family may integrate quickly: this appears to be the case with non-Russian migrant families, especially in determining the rate if not the final outcome of language and cultural assimilation, and in determining also whether the bilingualism of the younger children is acquired in a favorable or unfavorable setting.

E. CONCLUSION

Several conclusions are suggested by the facts adduced in this chapter. In the first place there is a considerable shift of populations from West to East and South East, together with infiltration of mainly Slavic elements. Second, the disproportionate natural growth rates (of the Central Asian Republics, more especially) ensures that in spite of the Slavic penetration and outmigration of native populations of those Republics, there remains a considerable reservoir of local interests, linguistic and otherwise; and this reservoir shows every sign of being extended and deepened. Third this reserve of native population though it is being fed increasingly into towns, exists in the main in the rural areas where the comparative isolation is again a factor favorable to local languages. Fourth, this maintenance of local languages is being reinforced over the short term by the age and sex bias of the migration processes, though in the long term this bias will operate in the reverse and adverse direction. Fifth, in the towns and cities, the same bias so far as age is concerned, is working even now in a direction adverse to the native languages through immediate bilingualism among the male young, and fairly rapid movement to the adoption of Russian. Sixth, industrialization, urbanization and consequent greater numbers of mixed marriages are important factors in creating multilingual communities. So far as industrialization is concerned it will be interesting to observe in the future how population mobility and therefore, linguistic heterogeneity will be affected by the present policy of making each national republic a *specialized* economic component of the complete economic structure of the USSR. This should mean that each such specialized unit will tend to develop its own internal system of recruitment and any population movement will be within any one unit rather than across the board. It will tend to retard international mobility, and if this stabilization occurs soon enough, whatever the economic consequences may be, it could be of advantage to the major, though perhaps not the smaller national languages.

So far as urbanization is concerned there is no question but that this process will undoubtedly continue to accelerate and that its effect on the contact of languages will also intensify. Because the city is a diffusion centre, and because life there is less tightly controlled the close personal ties of the village give way to greater anonymity: even brief stays in urban surroundings or very casual visits have a disproportionately great influence. Migrants, no matter how fleeting the stay, carry home new ideas and attitudes. They are stimulated by novel experiences and contact with new skills; and these innovations in conjunction with the changes which the rural areas would in any case undergo, especially as they affect family life and leading to the questioning of religious beliefs or traditional *mores*, stimulate a rapid enfranchisement from customary ways of life and local affiliations. These changes cannot but affect the strength of will required to maintain a local language when the economic influences are adverse. When everything else is the object of comparison or questioning attitude to language cannot be isolated from challenge.

So far as intermarriages are concerned though they must be regarded as an important factor it is difficult to estimate the weight of that importance. They are frequent only in areas of existing considerable ethnic heterogeneity, and it is impossible to tell how far they are a correlative or a causal index of bilingual development. There is no doubt but that the root processes are economic and political and that these processes are being engineered and planned meticulously. Nevertheless the promotion of the *sblizheniye* and *sliyaniye* of the nations so far as concerns the quality of the new life that is envisaged will depend not so much on the demo-graphic and economic aspects of planning as on the organization of educational and other cultural facilities, directing their efforts to the maintenance of the vernaculars as more than the mere 'languages of the hearth', or 'kitchen dialects' which they otherwise inevitably become.

Chapter 5

LANGUAGE MAINTENANCE – CONSEQUENCES OF POPULATION CHANGES

A. CHANGES IN THE ETHNIC STRUCTURE AND LINGUISTIC CHARACTER OF REPUBLICS

Migration results in the dispersal of nationalities and produces consequent changes in the ethnic composition of the various Union Republics, and their constituent areas – Autonomous Republics and Regions. Such changes affect the problem of language maintenance since the position of the language depends very much on the compactness as well as on the size of the linguistic group in question. There are two aspects of such demographic changes as they affect language. In the first place there is the degree to which the ethnic group, native to a particular republic, is dispersed – the number of those who emigrate compared to those who remain at home. And second, the extent to which members of other nationalities become immigrants of a particular republic. Both processes co-operate to change the balance of native and non-native populations, as well as to distort the historical relationship of languages to each other. Table 17 shows the percentage of each of the major nationalities and of some smaller ones, distributed among the various Union Republics. It provides an 'index of distribution'.

Most resistant to the pull of other areas are the Georgians, only 4% of whom live outside their own land. The Baltic Republics in 1970 had a mean emigration index of only 7%. Generally speaking the nations with low proportions of indigenous peoples, e.g. Kazakhs, Tatars, Mordvinians and Bashkirs, have high emigration indices. The reverse is the case of the Baltic peoples and Georgians. On the other hand some peoples, Russians, Belorussians and especially Armenians, are able to combine high level emigration with high proportions of indigenous populations. However, these are usually the very large nationalities upon whom very high rates of emigration have not made a significant impact yet. Therefore their language is not threatened at home, nor are they likely to be assimil-

TABLE 17

Distribution of major nationalities in Union Republics – 1959 and 1970[a]

Nationality	Percentage of Ethnic group in native Union Republic		Native ethnic group as percentage of total population of Republic	
	1959	1970	1959	1970
Russians	86.0	82.0	83.0	82.8
Ukrainians	86.0	88.0	77.0	75.9
Belorussians	83.0	80.0	81.0	81.0
Uzbeks	84.0	85.0	62.0	64.7
Kazakhs	77.0	79.0	30.0	32.4
Georgians	97.0	96.0	64.0	66.8
Azerbaydzhanis	85.0	81.0	67.0	73.8
Lithuanians	92.0	94.0	79.0	81.1
Moldavians	85.0	85.0	65.0	64.6
Latvians	93.0	94.0	62.0	56.8
Kirgiz	86.0	85.0	40.5	43.8
Tadzhiks	75.0	76.0	53.1	56.2
Armenians	56.0	62.0	88.0	88.6
Turkmens	92.0	92.0	60.9	65.6
Estonians	90.0	91.8	74.6	68.2

[a] Sources: 1959 Census, and 1970 Census reported in *Izvestiya* April 17, 1971.

ated easily abroad, because their dispersed populations constitute such large minorities in their new homes that they can withstand the pressures of local languages. It is hardly necessary to state that a low dispersal rate combined with a high percentage of indigenous population does not constitute a threat to the national language, and this is the case with the Baltic peoples, Georgians, and Turkmen.

On the other hand a combination of high levels of immigration of non-native and emigration of native populations has been generally adverse to the latter. In the Ukraine while the total population increased by 13% between 1959 and 1970 the increase in the indigenous population, constituting 74.9% of the republic total, was only 9%. The indigenous proportion in 1959 was 76.8% and in 1926, 80%. The number of Latvians living in Latvia in 1970 increased by only 3% (1,298,000 to 1,342,000) compared with a total population increase of 13% (Izvestiya, Ap. 17, 1971) – 56.8% of the total population. In the Central Asian Republics the changes have meant that some nationalities have become minorities in their own Republics. Taking the Central Asian group as a whole the proportion of the indigenous population dropped from 76% to 70% between 1926 and 1934; in 1959 the figure was 60% and by 1970 it had dropped even further, to 54%. Even in 1939 the Kazakhs were a minority (43%), and by 1959 they constituted less than a third of the population of the Republic. By 1970 they had increased their representation to 32.4%. By 1959 the Kirgiz had become a minority in their own Republic (40.5%) though their position had improved by 1970 to 43.8%. By 1970 the Tadzhiks had raised their proportion of the population of the Republic, but only from 53.1% in 1959 to 56.2% in 1970 (1959 and 1970 Census).

In the case of the smaller nationalities such as Mari and Udmurts this process has been proceeding for a considerable time. For instance, between 1926 and 1959 the native population of the Mari Oblast declined from 51% to 43%. In the Altay ASSR during the same period the decline was from 36% to 25%. While the total population increased by 100% between 1926 and 1946, the native population declined by 10%, and by 1956 the native component amounted to no more than 19%. The Buryat people declined in their own Autonomous Republic by 10%, from 44% in 1926, while the total population rose by 100%. An identical rise in the total population of the Yakut ASSR was accompanied by increase of only 18% in the native population. In the Khakass Autonomous Oblast the position of the native population became even more precarious, for though the Khakass themselves increased by 25%, the total population of the Oblast increased fifteen times that amount. (Census 1959). Other small nationalities which are now minorities in their own territories are Udmurt (35%) and Kalmyks (35%). North Caucusus exemplifies this process very well. Up to the outbreak of World War II the native population was everywhere in the majority in the autonomous republics of that area. Nowhere did it constitute less than 60-70% of the totals: the Chechens accounted for 80% of their own territory, and in Daghestan the indigenous peoples were 90% of the total. By 1959 this last figure had dropped to 69.3%. The native Chechen now account for only 41%. Only 53% of the Kabardin – Balkar ASSR are natives, 48% of the N. Ossetian ASSR are natives. The Adygei Autonomous Oblast has only 20% indigenous population (1959 and 1970 Census).

It is the peoples who are high on both the inward and outward migration scale who are at risk; and if, in addition, they are relatively small nationalities their position is extremely precarious. This is the case with Udmurts, Bashkirs, Mari and Mordvinians. The Central Asian Republics, it is interesting to note, differ among themselves in the pattern of their outward migration, and this fact may affect the maintenance of their cultural integrity in ways which are different from the maintenance of their languages. For instance, only 10% of Kirgiz migrants, 6% of the Tadzhiks and 3% of Uzbeks, move out of Central Asia altogether, so that relatively few move into different cultural areas, though they live in different language communities. Azerbaydzhanis have a similar reluctance to move into a novel cultural setting – only 2.4% emigrate to the RSFSR, 0.2% into the Ukraine. Naturally enough Georgia with 5.2%, and Armenia with 3.7% are the most attractive to the Central Asian emigrants. (*Azerbaydzhan tsifrakh* 1964, 23, Baku). On the other hand, of Turkmen emigrants 30% (and even more Kazahks – 47% of the migrants) have left Central Asia altogether. It is not improbable that, for them, a movement outside the traditional culture will accentuate the risk to language. It is noticeable, in this context that Tatars, who have a high dispersal index, tend to maintain their language in the areas which, though linguistically disparate, have close cultural affinities with them. Whereas the extent of language maintenance among Tatars who do not emigrate was 92% in 1959, it was only 1% less among Tatars in Kirgizia (91%), Tadzhikstan Tatars 91%, Kazakhstan Tatars 85%, and Turkmen Tatars 84%, suggesting that the adverse effect of emigration is modified by cultural affinities of a more general character.[1]

B. COMPLEX AND HETEROGENEOUS POPULATIONS

TABLE 18

Ethnic composition of Union Republics and percentage contribution of each nationality 1959 and 1970[a]

Union Republic	Nationalities and percentage contribution in 1959 and 1970
Russian SSR	Russians (83.3, 82,8), Ukrainians (2.9, 2.6), Belorussians (0.7, 0.7), Tatars (3.5, 3.7), Kazakhs (0.3, 0.4), Azerbaydzhan (0.1, 0.1), Georgians (0.05, 0.1), Moldavians (0.05, 0.1), Jews (0.7, 0.6), Chuvash (1.2, 1.3), Peoples of Daghestan (0.7, 0.9), Mordvin (1.0, 0.9), Bashkir (0.8, 0.9), Udmurt (0.5, 0.5), Chechen (0.2, 0.4), Mari (0.4, 0,4), Ossetes (0.2, 0.4), Komi-Permyak (0.4, 0.4), Buryat (0.2, 0.2), Yakut (0.2, 0.2), Kabardinian (0.2, 0.2), Karakalpak (0.2, 0.2), Armenians (0.2, 0.2), Peoples of the North (0.1, 0.1), Karelians (0.1, 0.1), Tuvin (0.1, 0.1), Ingush (0.05, 0.1), Kalmyk (0.1, 0.1), Karachai (0.1, 0.1), Adygeis (0.1, 0.1), Khakass (0.05, 0.05), Altai (0.04, 0.04), Balkar (0.03, 0.04), Cherkess (0.02, 0.03), 20 other nationalities (1.4, 1.3).
Ukraine SSR	Ukrainians (76.15, 74.9), Russians (16.9, 19.4), Belorussians (0.7, 0.8), Moldavians (0.6, 0.6), Jews (2.0, 1.6), Poles (0.9, 0.6), Bulgars (0.5, 0.5), 10 other nationalities (1.6, 1.6).

[a] Sources: 1970 Census – Reported in *Izvestiya* 17-4-1971.
[1] Sources: *Itogi vsesoyuznaya perepisi naseleniya* 1959, Moscow: the volumes for the Uzbek, Kazakh, Turkmen, Kirgiz and Tadzhik Republics.

Union Republic	Nationalities and percentage contribution in 1959 and 1970
Belorussian SSR	Belorussians (81.1, 81.0), Russians (8.2, 10.8), Poles (6.7, 4.3), Ukrainians (1.7, 2.1), Jews (1.9, 1.6), 8 other nationalities (0.4, 0.6).
Uzbek SSR	Uzbeks (61.1, 64.7), Karakalpak (2.0, 1.9), Russians (13.5, 12.5), Tatars (5.4, 4.8), Kazakhs (4.9, 4.6), Tadzhiks (3.8, 3.8), Koreans (1.7, 1.3), Ukrainians (1.1, 1.0), Kirgiz (1.1, 0.9), Jews (1.2, 0.9), Turkmen (0.7, 0.6), 18 other nationalities (3.4, 3.0).
Kazakh SSR	Kazakhs (29.8, 32.4), Russians (43.2, 42.8), Ukrainians (8.3, 7.2), Tatar (2.1, 2.2), Uzbek (1.4, 1.6), Belorussians (1.2, 1.5), Uygur (0.7, 0.9), Korean (0.8, 0.6), Dungan (0.1, 0.1), 20 other nationalities (12.4, 10.7).
Georgian SSR	Georgians (64.3, 66.8), Ossetes (3.5, 3.2), Abkhaz (1.6, 1.7), Armenians (11.0, 9.7), Russians (10.1, 8.5), Azerbaydzhanis (3.8, 4.6), Greeks (1.8, 1.9), Jews (1.3, 1.2), Ukrainians (1.3, 1.1), Kurds (0.4, 0.4), 19 other nationalities (0.9, 0.9).
Azerbaydzhan SSR	Azerbaydzhanis (67.5, 73.8), Russians (13.6, 10.0), Armenians (12.0, 9.4), Lezgin (2.7, 2.7), 12 other nationalities (4.2, 4.1).
Lithuanian SSR	Lithuanians (79.3, 90.1), Russians (8.5, 8.6), Poles (8.5, 7.7), Belorussians (1.1, 1.5), Ukrainians (0.7, 0.8), Jews (0.9, 0.8), 6 other nationalities (1.0, 0.5).
Moldavian SSR	Moldavians (65.4, 64.6), Ukrainians (14.6, 14.2), Russians (10.2, 11.6), Gagauz (3.3, 3.5), Jews (3.3, 2.7), Bulgars (2.1, 2.1), 7 other nationalities (1.1, 1.3).
Latvian SSR	Latvians (62.0, 56.8), Russians (26.6, 29.8), Belorussians (2.9, 4.0), Poles (2.9, 2.7), Ukrainians (1.4, 2.3), Lithuanians (1.5, 1.7), Jews (1.7, 1.6), 8 other nationalities (1.0, 1.1).
Kirgiz SSR	Kirgiz (40.5, 43.8), Russians (30.2, 29.2), Uzbeks (10.6, 11.3), Ukrainians (6.6, 4.1), Tatars (2.7, 2.4), Uygur (0.7, 0.8), Kazakhs (1.0, 0.8), Tadzhiks (0.7, 0.7), 14 other nationalities (7.0, 6.9).
Tadzhik SSR	Tadzhiks (53.1, 56.2), Uzbeks (23.0, 23.0), Russians (13.3, 11.9), Tatars (2.9, 2.4), Kirgiz (1.3, 1.2), Ukrainians (1.4, 1.1), Kazakhs
Armenian SSR	Armenians (88.0, 88.6), Azerbaydzhanis (6.1, 5.9), Russians (3.2, 2.7), Kurds (1.5, 1.5), 9 other nationalities (1.2, 1.3).
Turkmen SSR	Turkmens (60.9, 65.6), Russians (17.3, 14.5), Uzbeks (8.3, 8.3), Kazakhs (4.6, 3.2), Tatars (2.0, 1.7), Ukrainians (1.4, 1.6), Armenians (1.3, 1.1), 12 other nationalities (4.2, 4.0).
Estonian SSR	Estonians (74.6, 68.2), Russians (20.1, 24.7), Ukrainians (1.3, 2.1), Finns (1.4, 1.4), Belorussians (0.9, 1.4), Jews (0.5, 0.4), 7 other nationalities (1.2, 1.8).

The second consequence of demographic change for ethnic and language loyalty is the increased linguistic heterogeneity of the various republics. (Table 18) As a consequence of the complex of migration tendencies, the number of nationalities within many republics has increased considerably so that single republics are becoming images of the heterogenity of the Federation. This is 'secondary level heterogeneity', since the territorial

TABLE 19

Distribution of the national language groups of the Turkestan ASSR
1920 Census

Nationality	Number in Thousands & Percentage of nationality in each Oblast											
	Amu-Daria		Semirechie		Samarkand		Syr-Daria		Turkmen		Fergana	
	No.	%	No.	%	No.	%	No.	%	No.	%	No.	%
Uzbeks	48.7	30.4	15.0	1.6	472.0	59.5	370.0	28.4	1.3	0.4	1440.0	68.0
Kazakhs	35.0	22.1	430.0	44.8	22.4	2.8	606.0	46.0	3.2	1.0	—	—
Kirgiz	—	—	172.0	18.0	14.0	1.8	57.0	4.4	—	—	362.0	17.2
Tadzhiks	0.5	0.3	0.09	0.01	234.0	29.6	15.3	1.2	—	—	187.0	8.9
Turkmens	5.6	3.5	—	—	—	—	—	—	261.0	78.0	—	—
Karakalpaks	62.7	39.1	—	—	—	—	4.3	0.3	—	—	10.7	0.5
Kurama	—	—	—	—	—	—	49.7	3.8	—	—	—	—
Taranchi	—	—	44.9	4.7	—	—	—	—	—	—	—	—
Kipchaks	—	—	—	—	—	—	—	—	—	—	42.3	2.0
Jews	5.7	3.6	—	—	8.4	0.1	2.3	0.2	0.8	0.2	3.9	0.2
Russians	0.8	0.5	268.8	28.0	21.0	2.7	167.0	12.8	30.0	9.0	48.0	2.3
Persians	0.5	0.3	—	—	12.2	1.5	1.3	0.1	18.4	5.5	2.3	0.1
Tatars	—	—	10.5	1.1	—	—	8.0	0.6	—	—	2.6	0.1
Armenians	—	—	—	—	2.6	0.3	3.1	0.2	—	—	—	—
Dungans	—	—	10.3	1.1	—	—	0.68	0.1	—	—	—	—
Others	0.13	0.2	6.8	0.7	5.2	0.7	19.8	1.5	7.8	2.3	48.3	0.8

units when first created, already combined several different nationalities. Daghestan, for instance, at present contains over thirty different nationalities and this is not the consequence of recent migration only. Nor is the heterogeneity of other areas entirely due to migration within the period with which we are concerned. What recent migration has done is to superimpose a new level of ethnic and linguistic heterogeneity upon a historically complex situation.

For instance the Turkestan Republic of 1920, before territorial delimitation of nationalities and the formation of the Central Asian Republics in their present form, consisted of more than twenty different linguistic groups, which were, to add to the heterogeneity, dispersed widely in eash case, and not limited to their respective enclaves. (Table 19)

Recent migration then has not created our problem, but it has added a new dimension to it, especially in the 'gaining republics' of Central Asia. The Tadzhik SSR now has at least 16 minority groups of significant size. In 1929 the Tadzhiks accounted for 78.4% of the population, the remainder consisting of Uzbeks 17.94%, Kirgiz and Kazakhs 1.98%, Turkmen 1.43% and others including Russians and Ukrainians, accounting for no more than 0.27%. In 1939 the proportion of the native population declined to 59.5% and in 1959 it was reduced to 53.1%. The 16 minority groups at present include Uzbeks (23%), Russians (11.9%), Ukrainians (1.1%), Kirgiz (1.2%), Kazakh (0.3%) Turkmen (0.4%), Tatars (2.4%), German (1.4%), Jews (0.6%), Mordvin (0.3%), Ossetes (0.2%), Bashkir (0.2%), Armenian (0.1%), Belorussian (0.1%), Korean (0.1%).[2]

The other Central Asian Republics are equally complex in their linguistic constitutions. The population of Azerbaydzhan now includes over 510 thousand Russians (10.0%), 484 thousand Armenians (9.4%), 40 thousand Jews (1.1%), 29 thousand Tatars (0.8%), 26 thousand Ukrainians (0.7%), 9 thousand Georgians (0.3%), and many smaller groups of Daghestan – 121 thousand (3.3%), as well as ten other groups 33 thousand (0.9%). Small Volga-Ural Autonomous Republics like Tatar, Chuvash and Bashkir, include among their populations Belorussians (21,000), Jews (17,000), Russians (2,993,000), Udmurts (48,000) and Ukrainians (103,000) (1959 and 1970 Censuses).

The minorities within some of these areas have grown enormously in number and in size during the last 40 years. The Kazakh SSR is a good example of this. (Table 20)

Not only have the Kazakhs become a minority within their own territory, but by 1959 they had become in fact less than 75% of the immigrant Russian group, though this disproportion has been eased slightly by 1970.

[2]   Source: A. M. Briskin, *Strana Tadzhikov*, Moscow 1930; *Bolshaya Sovetskaya Entsyklopediya* 1946, XLI, 471; *Narodnoye khozaistvo* 1961, 15; 1970 Census: *Izvestiya* April 17, 1971.

The important Pavlodar Oblast' with a population of half a million is a reflection in miniature of the general Kazakh picture. There, the proportions of the various linguistic groups in 1961 were as follows: Kazakhs, 25%; Russians, 40%; Ukrainians, 15%; and six other groups making up

TABLE 20[a]

National composition of the population of the Kazakh SSR – 1926-1970

	Kazakh		Russians		Ukrainians		Others (10 ethnic groups)	
	No. of (thous.)	% of pop-ulation	No. of (thous.)	% of pop-ulation	No. of (thous.)	% of pop-ulation	No. of (thous.)	% of pop-ulation
1926	3,713	56	1,280	20	860	13	646	10
1959	2,795	30	3,924	42	762	8	1,779	19
1970	4,161	32.4	5,500	42.8	930	7.2	1,849	18

[a] Source: For 1926: *Itogi vsesoyuznaya perepisi naseleniya* 1926 *goda* Moscow 1928, vol. VIII; For 1959: *Vestnik statistiki*, 1960, No. 2, 18; For 1970: *Izvestiya* April 1971.

the remaining 20%. The non-Kazakh population had increased from 60% to 74% and most interestingly the proportion of the population speaking the several smaller languages had nearly trebled, representing a higher rate of growth than either the Russians or Ukrainians (Taskin, 1964), in spite of the fact that other important areas such as the Kaliningrad Oblast had shown a rise of 20% in the Russian population. In 1959 six languages were used in the schools of Kazakhstan, the languages being Uzbek, Uygur, Dungan and Tadzhik, in addition to the major languages referred to (*Kulturnoye stroiteltsvo SSR* 1956. 186-187).

Similar changes have occurred in the Baltic Republics (*Itogi Vsesoyuznaya perepisi* 1959, 202-208). Since 1923 Lithuania has trebled its Russian minority, now 8.6% of the population and added a large number of Ukrainians and Belorussians constituting 0.8% and 1.5% respectively. While the Jews have been decimated from 7.6% to 0.9% of the total population, the Poles have increased in number and constitute 8.5%. In Latvia the number of Russians has more than doubled to 29.8% and Lithuanians, Belorussians and Ukrainians have increased to 1.7%, 4.0% and 3.3% respectively. The Germans have very largely gone, and the Jews are only slightly more than a third of their former strength, 1.6% of the population. In Estonia the Russians have increased their proportion from 8.6% to 20.7% in 1959 and 24.7% in 1970, while other minorities, including Jews, had improved their position in 1959 (0.5%) but have declined since (0.4%).

This process of intensifying the intermingling of linguistic groups is universal in the Soviet Union and involves even small villages such as those of the Balkar region, where it was stated in 1966 that it was rare to find a village where representatives of two or three nationalities might not be found. However, the effect of such population movements on the composition of cities is greater still. In 1959 the indigenous population of Frunze amounted to no more than 17% of the total, while 68% were Russians or Russianized immigrants, and 15% were made up of five other nationalities. In Ashkabad the ratio of the indigenous to the immigrant population of Alma Ata was even more adverse, in that only 13% of the population was indigenous, over 75% were Russians, the remaining 12% consisting of Ukrainians, Jews and Belorussians. Even in Tashkent over 65% of the population were Russians, 9% came from twelve other nationalities and only 24% of the population were native Uzbeks. Similarly, Dushanbe had less than 20% native Tadzhiks. In the case of this last city, we have already referred to the composition of its most important industrial combine (Perevedentsev, 1966b, 33 et seq.). We have already referred also to the historical bases of language contact in Daghestan, but in the towns and cities of that area there is intensifying heterogeneity. For instance in 1824 only 3 nationalities were represented in Derbent. Now there are 47.

C. CHANGES IN DEMOGRAPHIC STATUS OF LANGUAGES

TABLE 21

Maintenance of national languages

% of nationalities claiming national language as native tongue – 1926 to 1970[a]

Nationality	1926	1959	1970
USSR		94.3	93.9
Russian	99.7	99.8	99.8
Ukrainian	87.1	87.7	85.7
Uzbek	99.1	98.4	98.6
Belorussian	71.9	84.2	80.6
Tatar	98.9	92.1	89.2
Kazakh	99.6	98.4	98.0
Azerbaydzhan	93.8	96.7	98.2
Armenian	92.4	89.9	91.4
Georgian	96.5	98.6	93.4

[a]   Sources: 1926 and 1959 Censuses: 1970 Census figures in *Izvestiya* April 17, 1971. Figures refer to the population of an ethnic group claiming the ethnic language as their native tongue. In effect this is a conservative estimate since some members of the ethnic group will be able to speak the language though they have switched their primary language; and more members of the ethnic group may have learned it as a second language. Members of other groups may speak it as a first or second tongue.

Nationality	1926	1959	1970
Moldavian	92.3	95.2	95.0
Lithuanian	46.9	97.8	97.9
Jew	71.9	21.5	17.7
Tadzhik	98.3	98.1	98.5
German	94.9	75.0	66.8
Chuvash	91.3	90.8	88.9
Turkmen	97.3	98.9	98.8
Kirgiz	99.0	98.7	98.8
Latvian	78.3	95.1	95.2
Daghestanis	96.4	96.2	96.5
of which			
Avar	99.3	97.2	97.2
Lezgin	97.4	92.7	93.9
Dargin		98.6	98.4
Kumyk	99.2	98.0	98.4
Lak		95.8	95.6
Tabasaran	92.9	99.2	98.9
Nogai	97.2	90.0	89.8
Rutul		99.9	98.9
Tsakhur		99.2	96.5
Agul		99.4	99.4
Mordvinian	94.0	78.1	77.8
Bashkir	53.8	61.9	66.2
Pole	42.9	45.2	32.5
Estonian	88.4	95.2	95.5
Udmurt	98.9	89.1	82.6
Chechen	99.7	98.8	98.7
Mari	99.3	95.1	91.2
Ossetian	97.9	89.1	88.6
Komi	96.5	89.3	82.7
Komi-Permyak	93.9	87.6	85.8
Korean	98.9	79.3	68.6
Bulgarian	92.4	79.4	73.1
Greek	72.7	41.5	39.3
Buryat	98.1	94.9	92.6
Yakut	99.7	97.6	96.3
Kabardinian	99.3	97.9	98.0
Karakalpak	87.5	95.0	96.6
Gipsies	64.2	59.3	70.8
Uygur	52.7	85.0	88.5
Hungarian		97.2	96.6
Ingush	99.5	97.9	97.4
Gagauz		94.0	93.6
Peoples of the North	82.1	75.9	67.4
of which Nenets	76.2	84.7	83.4
Evenki	63.8	85.9	51.3
Khanty	83.5	77.0	68.9
Chuckchi	99.3	93.9	82.6
Even	97.0	81.4	56.0
Nanai	96.7	86.3	69.1

Nationality	1926	1959	1970
Mansi	88.9	59.2	52.5
Koryak	95.3	90.5	81.1
Dolgan	99.5	93.9	89.8
Nivkh	97.0	76.3	49.5
Selkup	88.9	50.6	51.1
Ulchi	86.0	84.9	60.8
Saami	85.0	69.9	56.2
Udegei	85.0	73.7	55.1
Itelmen	20.4	36.0	35.7
Keti	83.5	77.1	74.9
Orochi		68.4	48.6
Nganasan		94.3	75.4
Yukagir		52.5	46.8
Kareli	95.5	71.3	63.0
Tuvin		99.1	98.7
Kalmyk	99.3	91.0	91.7
Romanian	51.9	83.3	63.9
Karachai	99.5	96.8	98.1
Adygei	98.4	96.8	96.5
Kurd	34.4	89.9	87.6
Finn		59.5	51.0
Abkhaz	83.9	95.0	95.9
Turki		82.2	92.3
Khakass	89.9	86.0	83.7
Balkar	99.6	97.0	97.2
Altai	79.4	88.5	87.2
Cherkess	98.4	89.7	92.0
Dungan	99.2	95.1	94.3
Iranian	67.8	44.7	36.9
Abazin	94.4	94.8	96.1
Aisor	91.1	64.3	64.5
Czech	79.5	49.0	42.9
Tats	86.6	70.9	72.6
Shortsi	87.9	83.7	73.5
Slovak		61.2	52.0
Other nationalities		61.6	69.4

The redistribution of populations has had and is likely to continue to have a notable influence on the relations of the great variety of national cultures and languages. This influence has been reinforced by the predictable but nevertheless potentially great effects of mixed marriages. Education also, as we hope to show, has reflected and reinforced these changes. The consequence has been to create conditions where an enfeebled, if not actual loss of attachment to national languages can ensue. Nevertheless, what is most striking to any observer is the extraordinary resilience of the various national languages, a fact which on the face of it appears to make nonsense of the claim that nationalities are actually merging, or that it is possible in the foreseeable future to envisage a merging of languages or the creation of a common language (Table 21). In 32 of the 101 nationalities with more than a thousand members listed in the 1970 Census, 95% or more of the population in each case claimed the national language as their native tongue. Eleven nationalities had percentages ranging from 90% to 95%, seventeen nationalities had percentages between 80% and 90%, seven between 70% and 80% and only nine had percentages lower than 50%. Twenty six nationalities improved their positions slightly between 1959 and 1970. It is worth noting that while those with 60% maintenance and above in 1959 were in 1970 evenly distributed among gainers and losers, all but one of those below 60% in 1959 were losers by 1970 – the process of switching is apt to accelerate. At the present time, among Armenians and Tatars, who have considerable dispersed populations, there are losses of 8.6% and 10.8% in attachment to national languages compared with 10.1% and 7.9% in 1959 – a gain. Among the Ukrainians and Belorussians who also have widely dispersed populations in large numbers, but in addition have close affinities with the Russians and so assimilate more easily, the percentage loss of language maintenance is 15.3% and 19.4% respectively compared with 12.3% and 15.8% in 1959 – a decline. Apart from these, the percentage loss is very low – and lowest of all among the Georgians, Turkmens, Kirgiz and Uzbeks. The Baltic countries are very retentive considering the pressures to which they are exposed. The relatively high level of retentiveness, almost uniform among the larger nationalities, is emphasized when we take into account what occurred during the war and afterwards, in the way of disruption of family life and the insecurity of society generally. Bearing these facts in mind, it is remarkable, even after allowing for some changes in the criteria employed for assessing language loyalty, that the percentage losses among some nationalities, Ukrainians, Belorussians, Azerbaydzhanis, Georgians, Moldavians and Turkmen, is less in 1970 than in 1926. The most serious decline during the period 1926-70 has been among the Tatars (10.3%). On the other hand the Azerbaydzhanis improved by 4.5%, Belorussians by 8.7% and Turkmen by 1.5% between 1926 and 1970.

The nationalities in the middle population ranges, those of a quarter to half a million, seem to be able to hold their own, much as the larger language groups do. For instance, Bashkir, the largest of these, has improved since 1926, moving from a percentage maintenance of 53.8% to 66.2% in 1970. The degree of language maintenance among Avars fell by 2.1% between 1926 and 1970; Chechens have declined by 1.0%. Of the intermediate nationalities included in Table 21 the average erosion of language maintenance is approximately 3% over 40 years, the greatest decline occurring among Ossetes (9.3%) and Lezgins (3.5)%. Dargins have continued to retain a high maintenance level, as have the Chechens.

Among the others, Buryats have had a loss of 5.5% and Yakuts a loss of 3.4% between 1926 and 1970.

The smaller nationalities irrespective of the proportion of their population which is dispersed, tend to be less retentive than the larger. Those which are under greatest pressure, e.g. Mansi (4.5th) have considerable rates of decline from a maintenance level of 88.9% in 1926 to 59.8% in 1959, and 52.5% in 1970. Similarly, the Nivkh-speaking people (4.4th) had an enormously increased rate of linguistic assimilation – from 3% to 24% between 1926 and 1959, and to 50.5% in 1970. Other small nations, Tats (17 thous.) and Evenki (25 thous.) also show a great decline in language maintenance – in the first case from 86.6% to 70.9% in 1959, but improving to 72% in 1970. And in the second case from 63.8% to 55.9% in 1959 and 51.3% in 1970. The very small nations, those not much exceeding a thousand, like the Itelmen, have at the present moment very low levels of maintenance (35%) and Yukagirs (46.8%) (Isupov, 1964, 34 et seq., and Izvestiya April 1971).

TABLE 22

Percentage of persons among the main peoples of the Union Republics, migrant, urban and rural, regarding the language of their nationality as their mother tongue, in 1959.
(1959 Census)

| Republic | Percentage claiming their native tongue as that of their stated nationality | | | | | |
	Total pop.	Total Urban pop.	Total Rural pop.	Migrant pop.	Migrant Urban pop.	Migrant Rural pop.
Russian	99.8	99.9	99.7	96.4	98.0	99.0
Ukrainian	87.7	77.2	94.5	51.2	45.9	57.8
Belorussian	84.2	63.5	94.2	41.9	37.7	49.8
Uzbek	98.4	96.7	98.9	97.4	94.9	95.5
Kazakh	98.4	96.7	98.9	95.6	91.6	97.8
Georgian	98.6	96.8	99.7	73.4	68.3	86.3
Azerbaydzhan	97.6	96.4	98.2	95.2	87.0	98.1
Lithuanian	97.8	96.6	98.4	80.3	75.0	86.4
Moldavian	95.2	78.4	97.7	77.7	57.7	87.2
Latvian	95.1	93.1	96.9	53.2	43.7	66.0
Kirgiz	98.7	97.4	9.89	93.3	89.6	92.5
Tadzhik	98.1	96.4	98.6	94.6	92.7	95.1
Armenian	89.9	84.4	97.1	78.1	69.3	92.5
Turkmen	98.9	97.3	99.4	92.0	81.6	93.8
Estonian	95.2	93.1	97.0	56.6	43.2	69.5

The losses we have discussed above relate to the total of those who claim to belong to a particular nationality, wherever they may be living within the Soviet Union. It is to be expected that the loss of the national or native language is greater among dispersed members of a nationality than among those who remain within their own territory, where, whatever extraneous inimical influences they may be subjected to, they are at least operating within the framework of the native language group. The loss of

TABLE 23

Language maintenance among migrants and non-migrants of some smaller nationalities: 1959 compared with 1926[a]

Nationality	1959		Nationality	1959	
	Non-migrants	Migrants		Non-migrants	Migrants
Avar	97.2	78.8	Chechen	98.8	84.1
Lezgin	92.5	68.6	Ossetes	89.7	52.7
Dargin	98.6	88.1	Kabardin	94.2	79.6
Kumyk	98.0	78.2	Ingush	97.9	78.9
Lak	95.8	79.9	Adygei	96.8	71.9
Nogai	84.3	65.3	Karachai	96.6	65.2

[a] Source: (a) *Itogi vsesoyuznaya perepisi naseleniya* 1959 Moscow 1962; (b) Isupov, 34 et seq.

a supporting background means that the degree of detachment fiom or loss of the native language is apt to be severe. (Tables 22, 23) For instance, in 1959 while the general level of Ukrainian linguistic assimilation was 12.3%, dispersed Ukrainians assimilated more easily – 48.8%. Of the total number of Belorussians 27.8% forsook their native tongue, while 58.1% of the migrant Belorussians did so. Other nationalities who show considerable differences between the levels of linguistic assimilation among non-migrants and migrants, are Latvia (4.9% and 46.8%), Estonia (4.8% and 43.4%), Moldavia (4.8% and 22.3%), Georgia (1.4% and 26.6%), Armenia (10.1% and 21.9%). Immigrant Russians do not, any more than non-migrant Russians, show any inclination to adopt another language (1.2% and 3.6%). Nor do the nationalities of Central Asia (average of 1.3% and 5.6%).

However, again as one would expect, the difference between retentiveness of migrants and non-migrants, is greatest among the medium and small ethnic and language groups. There does not appear to be any significant correlation between the difference between retentiveness among migrant and non-migrant populations on the one hand and on the other the general level of retentiveness among the total ethnic group. Sometimes high general retentiveness is related to great differences between migrants and non-migrants, and sometimes a low general retentiveness is related to a similar large difference between the mobile and non-mobile groups.

For instance Ingush have a very high degree of retentiveness 97.9% and a wide disparity of 19½% between the two sections of the same ethnic group, while Bashkir who have a very low retentiveness, 62% have a disparity not very different in extent from Ingush between the two sections – non-migrants 68% and migrants 43%, a difference of 23%.

It is also significant that when migrants move into rural areas their rate of linguistic assimilation is very much lower than that of the urbanized migrants.[3] The greatest differences occur among the Western nationalities – Moldavians have a difference between rural and urban migrant retentiveness of 29.5%, Estonians 26.3%, Armenians 23.2%, Latvians 22.3%, Georgians 18%, Lithuanians 14%, Belorussians 12.1%, and Ukrainians 12.2%. The differences between urban and rural assimilation rates among the Central Asians is significantly less – Uzbeks 0.6%, Kazakhs 5.2%, Kirgiz 3.9% and Tadzhiks 2.4%. The fact of the difference between urban and rural migrant assimilation is in line with the differences between the levels of assimilation among indigenous populations in rural and urban areas. The differences between the urban and rural migrants is not very much greater than the differences between the two groups of the stable population. For instance in Latvia the *non-migrant* urban/rural disparity is 18.5%, in Armenia 21% and in Estonia 24%, which are not very different from the *migrant* urban/rural disparities in each case. This would seem to indicate that while migration is, as we have seen, an important factor influencing language maintenance, urbanization may be an even more influential factor.

One of the most illuminating, as well as theoretically intriguing instances of the effect of dispersal, as opposed to normal or historical language contact within a particular territory, upon the maintenance of national languages is afforded by the situation of the several Jewish languages – Yiddish, Judeo-Georgian, Judeo-Tadzhik, Judeo-Tat, and Judeo-Crimean Tatar. The position of the Jews is unique because while they resemble other nationalities in many respects, and constitute without doubt a 'Soviet nationality' they are distinguished from others by the absence of a single territorial base. They are not only a highly intellectualized and urbanized people, but so far as they are a 'Soviet nationality' they may be said to belong to several distinct Soviet nationalities. If it is true that, as a distinguished Jewish scholar argues "the Jew, unlike the Mordvin or the Yakut, is as often as not *not* a foreigner living in Russia, but a Russian ..." (Schapiro, 1970) it is equally the case that he is not a foreigner in other areas either, e.g. Georgia, or Armenia, or Azerbaydzhan. The

---

[3]   One would expect, in view of the strength and stability of the local language in rural areas, that assimilation of immigrants would be high in such a context. The reason for low assimilation may be the higher prestige of the immigrant language. This is borne out in the case of migrant Central Asians.

Jews, compared with other nationalities, have very sizeable minorities in most of the capitals of the Union Republics and in many other large towns and cities as well, for instance Kishinev 21%; Odessa 15.5%; Makhachkala 14%; Kiev 14%; Kharkov 12%; Samarkand 8.6%; Vilnius 8%; Minsk 7.5%; Tashkent and Riga 5%; Dushanbe 4%; Frunze 3%; Baku 3%; Tbilisi 2.5%; Alma Ata 2% (1959 Census). Unlike other nationalities within the USSR therefore the Jews are, though small minorities, still *natives* of several Union Republics. They are not a dispersed single 'Soviet nationality' but rather representatives of several nationalities secondary to their original, historical and primary nationality – Jewish. The complex of factors which operate to determine the nature of their linguistic affiliation, and its extent is exceedingly more intricate than is the case with other nationalities, involving as it does diverse 'secondary national' affiliations, a national language (Yiddish) several Jewish dialects corresponding to the several 'secondary national' affiliations, an almost exclusively urban population, a far more intensely intellectualized population than the average, etc. While it is difficult to distinguish and estimate the extent of the influence of any one of these several factors it is not difficult to understand how, operating in conjunction with an extremely adverse official attitude which compels large numbers to disavow their actual competence in their national language, the degree of language maintenance among them should have declined so very greatly. In 1926 71.9% claimed Yiddish as their native tongue; in 1959 only 21.5% claimed Yiddish, and by 1970 this figure has been reduced to 17.7%. Compared with the Germans who also suffered deportation but were never involved in such a tangle of influential variables, the Jews have fared very badly. Among the Germans the decline in linguistic affiliation between 1926 and 1959 was 19% – from 94.4% to 75%, but by 1970 this fell to 66.8%.

D. RUSSIAN LANGUAGE PENETRATION

i. *Demographic Status of Russian*

The extent of the penetration of the Russian language and the consequent linguistic disaffiliation of speakers of various other national languages depends upon the operation of several factors, all of them forming in some way or other a pattern of complex inter-relationships. There is first of all the fact that this penetration has a very long history, and the present position is the result of an accelerating historical process, not a novel phenomenon. For instance in the Turkestan Kray of 1897 there were 200,000 Russians (3% of the population). In 1911 this figure had doubled constituting nearly 7% of the population. There is a long standing history of the Russian penetration of the Steppe Kray – 20% of the total population in 1897, which rose within 15 years (1911) to 75%. (1926 Census). There is in the second place the difference between the effect of Russian on members of a linguistic group who remain within their own national confines, and the effect on those who emigrate to other parts of the USSR. A third consideration is the size of the nationality, whether it is comparable to Armenian or Georgian on the one hand, or on the other, one of a large number of moderately sized groups like Avars, or again a very small nationality like Aleut. Fourth, irrespective of size, there is the relative 'distance' not in geographical but ethnographic terms, of one culture from another. This has relevance to the differences in the influence of Russian on Georgians and Armenians and especially the Central Asian nationalities on the one hand, and on the other hand the group of western and European nationalities. Fifth, is the comparative isolation of the nations, whether they are isolated geographically, inhabiting highland territories but forming close knit communities like some of the Caucasian nations, or by their way of life like the nomads. Sixth, the size of the Russian immigrant group, though not decisive, is an important factor, especially if, as in parts of the Ukraine, this influence has occurred over a long period. Seventh, one of the most important factors is the character of the area of Russian influence, whether urban or rural. And, finally, for our purposes at least, there is the kind of relationship that has existed between the local languages and each other, the kind of historical contact system we have described, against which Russian has to compete, as is the case in the Caucusus. No doubt there are several other factors which should be taken into account and the working of some of those we have mentioned must be so complex that anything we say is bound to distort the picture of their operation. Without going into a repetitous account of the working of each of these factors, it is impossible to disentangle them absolutely, and we have to rely to a considerable extent on a descriptive rather than on an exclusively or exhaustively analytical account.

The fate of the Mordvin language well illustrates the effect of the joint operation of the several factors we have described – the birth rate, the scattered settlements, migration, urbanisation of the emigrants, etc. In 1926 there were just over 1.340 million Mordvinians. By 1939 they had declined by 12% to 1.184 million, one of the very few nationalities to have done so. In 1959 the figure was 1.285 million, and by 1970 it had declined to 1.263 million. Over the same period their neighbouring Volga nationalities grew because of a high rate of natural growth. The Mordvinians are probably the most scattered peoples of the Volga republics, and they have also among the highest rate of emigration, mainly to Siberia, the Urals and the Far East. Furthermore of those who have left, the vast majority have settled in towns and cities. Consequently during the period 1926-1970 the level of language maintenance has dropped from 94% to 77.8% and even more precipitously among the young. According to the 1959 Census only 39% of those between 9 years and under retained the language; and only three percent more, 42% of the age group 10-19 living in urban areas. A considerable proportion have not only ceased to claim Mordvin as their native tongue, but identify themselves completely with other nationalities, mainly Russian. This appears to be a classic instance of the combined operation of the relevant factors that operate to alter adversely attitude to language, and against the maintenance of the native tongue.

The Republics where Russian demographic penetration is greatest are Latvia, Estonia, Ukraine, Kazakhstan, Uzbekistan, Kirgizia, Turkmenia and Tadzhikstan, more or less in that order. In the case of the Baltic countries, though the pressure of Russian immigration between 1926 and 1970 has been about the same as in the Central Asian Republics, the difference in the present potential of Russian influence in the Baltic, with the possible exception of Latvia, where there has been a long history of considerable Russian influence, is nothing like as great as it is in the Central Asian Republics. In these Central Asian Republics the increase in the percentage of Russians in the total populations was, according to the 1926, 1939, 1959 and 1970 Censuses, as follows: Kazakhstan 23.5, 37, 43.2 and 42.8%; Kirgizia 11.7, 25, 30 and 29.2%; Tadzhikstan 6.8, 9, 13.3 and 11.9%; Turkmenia 7.5, 18, 17.3 and 14.5%; Uzbekistan 5.5, 11.6, 13.6 and 12.5%. It is interesting to note that Republics, with large indigenous populations, but more important still, with strong independent and different cultures, such as Georgia, are able to continue to resist heavy Russian influence, unlike, for instance, the Ukraine. Apart from the latter, resistance to Russian language influence is still very strong in nearly all Union Republics.

ii. *Influence of Non-demographic Factors*

The greater importance of factors other than the degree of actual Russian immigration is suggested by the fact that the intensity of such immigration does not correlate positively or directly with the degree of Russian language influence. In the case of the Kazakhs demographic penetration is of the order of 42%; linguistic penetration is 1.2%. In Azerbaydzhan the number of Russians is fairly high – 10.0%, but the switch to the Russian language is low – 1.2%. The respective figures for other nationalities are – Latvia – 29.8% and 1.4%; Kirgizistan – 29.2% and 0.3%. In other Republics the reverse is the case. In Armenia the percentage of Russians is only 2.7 but the loss of language is 8.6%. This would suggest that factors like geographical contiguity and cultural affinity (Belorussia), or a relatively not unfavorable acceptance of the political system (Armenia)[4] are as important as the actual presence of Russians. The slightly smaller group, Eveni (12,000), Nanai (10,000) and Chukchi (14,000), have lower degrees of Russian penetration – 5.7%, 13.3% and 8.9% respectively.

It will be seen (Table 24) that these small nationalities vary considerably in their attachment to the national language, and though the Russian influence is considerably less in the North Caucusus, the same variability is discernible there too. In Daghestan the use of Russian is increasing as a lingua franca in an area of great linguistic complexity. In 1897 2.8% of the population spoke Russian; in 1926 it was 12.5%, in 1939 19%, in 1959 44.7 and in 1970 41.7%. (1926, 1959 and 1970 Censuses). Even so, all but one of the Siberian nationalities have a lower degree of attachment to their national language than the lowest among the North Caucasians. The second most retentive among the Siberian nationalities is the Koryaki, with 9.5% loss of national language in 1959, and 18.1% in 1970; and the worst among the Caucasians are the Nogais with 9.4% in 1959 and 10.2% in 1970. The latter are an agricultural people, less isolated in highland areas and open to Russian influence. However, when it comes to the question of which language takes the place of the national tongue, as the latter gives way to another language, there is very little difference between the two groups – Siberian and Caucasian – Russian is the almost inevitable choice, except for the Eveni and Evenki. The probable explanation for this exception is that these two peoples, closely related and relatively large for Siberian nationalities, occupy extensive territories and are extremely self-conscious groups. They have given their name to a national okrug and have withstood attempts to collectivize their reindeer herding. They are remarkably independent. However, it is probably their nomadic way of life, making contact with Russian spasmodic and very intermittent, which is the decisive factor.

There is one other conclusion which suggests itself in comparing these two groups of nationalities. Among the North Caucasians who do not range over such vast territories, the opportunity for contact between the local languages is very much greater than among members of the Siberian nationalities. For the latter the probability of Russian contact compared with contact with other languages is greater than it is in the Caucusus. Consequently since such contacts as occur in the Caucusus are so various and of such long standing, and since the languages in contact have about the same kind and degree of prestige the bilingualism that eventuates does not lead to the replacement of the mother tongue. Contact with Russian among Siberian nationalities however, where it occurs, is apt to be decisive and to allow little chance of maintaining the mother tongue – Russian is

[4]   In comparison to their attitude to non-Russians, like Georgians or Azerbaydzhanis, or non-Soviets like Turks.

TABLE 24

National language retentiveness and Russian language penetration among Siberian and Caucasian nationalities – 1959[a]

Siberian and Far East	No. in thousands	% using non-native language	% using Russian	North Caucasian Nationalities	No. in thousands	Non-Migrant		Migrant	
						% using non-native language	% using Russian	% using non-native language	% using Russian
Aleuts	.4	77.7	77.2	Avars	270	1.0	.4	21.2	14.2
Itelmen	1.1	64.0	63.1	Dargins	158	.8	.6	11.1	9.9
Selkup	3.8	49.4	48.4	Kumyks	135	1.1	.9	21.8	16.2
Yukagir	.4	47.5	34.4	Lezgins	223	1.8	.9	31.4	26.3
Evenki	24.5	44.1	8.7	Laks	64	1.5	1.3	20.9	14.2
Mansi	6.4	40.8	40.4	Chechens	419	.2	.2	15.9	15.0
Orochi	.8	31.6	29.7	Kabardins	204	.8	.8	10.4	18.3
Saami	1.8	30.1	28.6	Adyges	80	1.9	.19	28.1	27.6
Udegei	1.4	26.3	22.4	Ossetes	410	2.5	2.4	37.3	36.1
Nivkh	3.7	23.7	23.2	Karachays	181	1.0	.5	34.5	9.0
Khanty	19.4	23.0	22.3	Ingush	106	.6	.5	21.1	20.4
Keti	1.0	22.9	20.6	Nogais	41	9.4	1.1	34.7	30.0
Eveni	9.4	18.6	5.7						
Eskimos	1.1	16.0	13.0						
Ulchi	2.1	15.1	14.8						
Nentsi	23.0	15.3	5.5						
Nanai	8.0	13.7	13.3						
Koryaki	6.3	9.5	8.9						
Chukchi	11.7	6.1	5.7						

[a] Source: Isupov, 1964, 40 et seq.

an intrusive and not a neighbour language. However, though there may be these divergencies of pattern between areas of the USSR the overall extent of the penetration of Russian is increasing substantially. The 1970 Census shows that 3 millions of the non-Russian population have adopted Russian as their native language during the last 11 years making a total of 13 million. Those who speak Russian as their native language amount to 129 million, 53% of the Soviet population. Those who have adopted Russian are the equivalent of one tenth of those who speak it as their mother tongue. Furthermore the increase annually since 1959 if it continues at the same rate would indicate the possibility that well over 40% of the present non-Russian population would have switched to, or adopted Russian by the end of this century. According to present projections this means that over 69% of the population of the USSR will be Russian speaking.

iii.   *Russian and Urbanization*

Although the influence of Russian is felt among the rural populations (even the isolated and nomadic groups to some extent), it is the urbanized populations who feel the main force of the impact, for it is to the towns that the Russians gravitate. For instance in Uzbekistan Russians constitute 14% of the total population but 33% of the populations of the towns and cities. In Kazakhstan the figures are 43% and 48%, while in Latvia the respective percentages are 27 and 34. It is not unimportant therefore that in spite of considerably rapid and widespread migration from rural areas to the towns and cities the overall numbers of rural residents declined in the 11 years up to 1970 in only 6 Union Republics, all in the Western Soviet Union – the Baltic Republics, Russia, Belorussia and the Ukraine. In Georgia and Moldavia the rural population rose slightly, and quite considerably in the rest of the USSR. This increase in the size of the rural population means that in spite of the penetration of Russian in the urban areas there continues to be a very large reservoir of speakers of the local languages.

Nevertheless the fact cannot be ignored that the intellectual support for the local languages is often very modest, so far as concerns the rural areas. Among the Nanai of the Lower Amur, of those with 9-11th grade or specialized secondary education, more than half plan to move, while only a third of those with 5-8 years schooling plan to do so. More than half the teachers and specialist technologists intend to migrate, but among the collective farmers or state farmers only about 25-29% plan to move. The educational structure of potential migrants among the Nanai is distinctive and biased towards denuding the countryside of its ablest young people. (Boiko, 1970, 59-60). This is not surprising if one compares the standards of educational attainment in the rural and in the urban populations.[5] In 1959 while 17.3% of the urban population had university, or middle and higher specialised or a full secondary education only 6.5% of the rural population had attained the same standard. (Itogi, 1959 Table 35a extracted). By 1970 it is true the disparity had decreased so that while 75% of the city populations had secondary or higher education about 50% of the rural population had received comparable education. Nevertheless the gap of 25% is still very great, and accounts for the disillusionment of the best representatives of the rural young, among a small sample of whom only 6% proposed to return to the countryside after receiving a satisfactory education (Garin and Druzhenko). Moreover, the disparity is a distinctive feature of most societies, and there is no reason to believe that it will be eradicated in the USSR over the next few decades.

It is in the towns, too, that conditions are created which make the use of Russian as a lingua franca convenient to say the least. This is especially the case in the Ukraine, though Lenin had prophesied differently. He mistook the relative weight of urban and rural influences on language maintenance, for during the Xth Congress Lenin is reported by Stalin to have argued that "Ukrainian cities, then possessing a Russian character would be Ukrainized because cities grow at the expense of the villages which are the guardians of Ukrainian." (Stalin, 1953, 49). In 1959 the percentage of Ukrainians speaking Russian in the cities and more extensive urban areas was high, varying between 57% in the Crimea, 31% in Odessa, 28% in Kiev, 25% in Donets and 16% in Kherson, to 2% in the much newer area of Volhynia (1959 Census). Among the smaller nationalities the case is the same. For example among the Chuvash and Mari there are sixteen times more speakers of Russian among the indigenous urban population than among the rural workers. Among the Mordvin the difference in favour of the urban areas is 26 to 1, and among the Udmurts 12 to 1.

In some urban areas, for instance, in Kiubyshev Oblast, the percentage of those who have adopted Russian is as high as 47%. In the Bashkir ASSR four times as many migrant Tatars have adopted Russian in the urban as in the rural areas, while in the Perm Oblast the proportion of urban to rural Russian speaking Tatars is twelve to one (1959 Census RSFSR, Table 54). At the same time it is important to note that the extent of the present rate of Russian immigration does not entirely account for the extent of the Russian language penetration. Thus in the Ukraine it is those urban areas which have long traditions of Russian contact which produce the highest degree of Russian language penetra-

[5] Compare Ostapenko's description of the village of Gadyschi in the Kalinin Oblast. (*Sovetskaya Etnografiya*, 5. 102-111).

tion. In the Crimea this long process of contact has ensured that among the total population, 50% speak Russian, whereas in Lugansk only 53% of the total population are Russian, and in Lvov only 28% are Russians. In these two areas, compared with the 57% of the indigenous population who speak Russian in the Crimea, only 15% and 5% of the indigenous population speak Russian (1959 Census, Ukraine).

iv.   *Preference for Other Languages than Russian*

Urbanization affects the choice of other languages too. Immigrants to Turkmenia have adopted the native language in not inconsiderable numbers, but there are some differences between the rural and urban immigrants. For instance, while only 13% of the urbanized Kurds have adopted Turkmen, 67% of the rural Kurds have done so. Among the Karakalpaks there are 4 who have adopted Turkmen in the rural areas to 3 in the urban, and the comparable proportions for Uzbeks are 1.7% (urban) to 2.6% (rural); Tatars 1.2% (urban) to 7.4% (rural), and Azerbaydzhanis 1% (urban) to 16.7% (rural) (Newth, 1964). In Kazakhstan there were, in 1959, 9,200 immigrant Uygurs, Azerbaydzhanis, Bashkirs, Uzbeks and Kirgiz. Of these half lived in urban and half in rural areas. However, whereas twice as many Uygurs adopted Russian as adopted Kazakh in the urban areas, 3 times as many adopted Kazakh in the rural areas. The differences are even greater among the other immigrant groups. Among the Azerbaydzhanis the urban advantage of Russian was 4 to 1, and the rural advantage of Kazakh was 16 to one. Among the Bashkirs the figures are: Urban 5 to 2 for Russian, and rural 2 to 1 in favour of Kazakh; Kirgiz urban 2 to 1 in favour of Russian, and rural 13 to 1 in favour of Kazakh (Benningsen and Quelquejay, 1961, 233).

However, though urbanization strongly favours Russian, both in inducing nationalities in the first place to change their native tongue, and then to adopt Russian as opposed to a competing new language, it is not unknown for even an urban group of immigrants to transfer to a language other than Russian. This is the case in the Tashauz Oblast in Turkmenia. In the urban areas the Uzbeks form much the largest group – 47% of the population. That being the case, though Russian is adopted by a considerable number as their first language, and probably many more speak it in addition to another language, many Turkmen immigrants have adopted the non-native Uzbek (Newth, 1964, 461). Bashkirs, too, when they settle among Tatars in urban areas are apt to favour the Turkic language rather than Russian. In these cases the choice of a language other than Russian is not hard to explain. In the Tashauz Oblast the need for Russian is not immediately evident among the workers (those who are not concerned with school or higher education) because Uzbek provides the logical and convenient choice of lingua franca. In the case of the Bashkirs the dividing line between Bashkirs and Tatars is fluid, and it is virtually impossible to make a reliable distinction between individuals who are Bashkir and those who are Tatar. In fact it is accepted that a person who might call himself Tatar in one census might even shortly afterwards, for different registration purposes, call himself Bashkir. If the need arises to choose a language to replace one's native tongue, there are very many factors to take into account in addition to the pressure of Russian population flow.

The tendency in rural areas is not only for immigrants to adopt the native language in preference to Russian, as we have seen, but for members of some of the larger nationalities in exile to retain their own language. Of the Armenian immigrants to the rural areas of Azerbaydzhan, Georgia, Turkmenia and the RSFSR, the percentage who retain their own language is extraordinarily high – 99%, 91% and 86% respectively. And this is in spite of the fact that, naturally, they constitute a very small minority of any of the rural areas they inhabit – 9% in Georgia and Azerbaydzhan, 1.9% of the RSFSR areas with which we are concerned, and 20% in the Abkhazian ASSR. This retention of the native tongue in rural areas, though it is known to be the case with other immigrant nationalities, appears to be a particular consequence of the Armenian's intensity of loyalty to the native tongue, for it is exemplified also in urban areas of the same territories. Thus, though they constitute only 18% of the population of Baku, 69% of the Armenians retain their native tongue. In Tbilisi the Armenians form 21% of the total population and of this number 70% continue to claim Armenian as their native language. In Ashkabad where only 5% of the population is Armenian, over 67% of that number retain Armenian, while in some of the urban areas of the RSFSR, like Moscow, Krasnodar Oblast, Rostov Oblast and Stavropol Oblast, where the proportion of Armenians is very low, not more than between 0.4% and 3% of the total population, well over 50% continue to claim Armenian as their native tongue (1959 Census of various Republics, extracted).

E. RUSSIAN AS A SECOND LANGUAGE

The factors which have influenced the degree of language maintenance which we have analysed affect the acquisition of Russian as a second language no less. It would be difficult at present to assess objectively the relative weight to be attached to any one factor or to analyse the degree of interaction between them. All that is offered here is a series of suggestions. One of the most important factors is the degree of geographic isolation

TABLE 25

Percentage of those claiming a non-Russian language as their native tongue who have learned Russian as a second language, according to nationalities in 1970[a]

Nationality	%	Nationality	%	Nationality	%
Russian	0.1	Pole	37.0	Selkup	40.8
Ukrainian	36.3	Estonian	29.0	Ulchi	56.8
Uzbek	14.5	Udmurt	63.3	Saami	52.9
Bellorussian	49.0	Chechen	66.7	Udegei	46.0
Tatar	62.5	Mari	62.4	Itelmen	32.5
Kazakh	41.8	Ossetian	58.6	Keti	59.1
Azerbaydzhan	16.6	Komi	63.1	Orochi	44.4
Armenian	30.1	Permyak	68.5	Nganasan	40.0
Georgian	21.3	Korean	50.3	Yukagir	29.1
Moldavian	36.1	Bulgarian	58.8	Kareli	59.1
Lithuanian	35.9	Greek	35.4	Tuvin	38.9
Jew	16.3	Buryat	66.7	Kalmyk	81.1
Tadzhik	15.4	Yakut	41.7	Rumanian	28.5
German	59.6	Kabardinian	71.4	Karachai	67.6
Chuvash	58.4	Karakalpak	10.4	Adygei	67.9
Turkmen	15.4	Gipsy	53.0	Kurd	19.9
Kirgiz	19.1	Uygur	35.6	Finn	47.0
Latvian	45.2	Hungarian	25.8	Abkhaz	59.2
Daghestanis	41.7	Ingush	71.3	Turki	22.4
comprising		Gagauz	63.3	Khakass	66.5
Avar	37.8	Peoples of the North	52.5	Balkar	71.5
Lezgin	31.6	comprising		Altai	54.9
Dargin	43.0	Nenets	55.1	Cherkess	70.0
Kumyk	57.4	Evenki	54.9	Dungan	48.0
Lak	56.0	Khanty	48.1	Iranian	33.9
Tabasaran	31.9	Chukchi	58.7	Abazin	69.5
Nogai	68.5	Even	48.4	Aisor	46.2
Rutul	30.7	Nanai	58.0	Czech	35.6
Tsakhur	12.2	Mansi	38.6	Tats	57.7
Agul	39.8	Koryak	64.3	Shortzi	59.8
Mordvin	65.7	Dolgan	61.4	Slovak	39.3
Bashkir	53.3	Nivkh	43.8	Others	38.4

[a]   Source: 1970 Census account in *Izvestiya* April 17, 1971.

and consequent low economic development together with relatively poor educational provision. This accounts in part for the comparatively low level of Russian among, for instance, the Uygur, Mansi of N.W. Siberia, Itelmen, Yukagirs and Tuvin all of which are well below 40%. Others like the Yakut, although isolated are more advanced and their level of Russian acquisition is higher. A second factor is the nature and the length of the historical contact of the people with speakers of Russian, which tends to ensure a high level of Russian in the nationality. This is true of the Nogai, Cherkess and Adygei of the Caucusus, Udmurt, Komi-

Permyak, Mari within the RSFSR and the Ossetes and Chuvash who have mixed freely with the Russians. This has helped to ensure that they have levels of Russian acquisition in the ethnic group above 60%. A third factor is not unrelated to the second – namely the degree of Russian penetration by immigration. This has helped to bring about a high level of Russian among the Kazakhs, for instance.

The operation of a fourth factor, namely the level of mature language standardization, is related in turn very often to the size of the native population and it is undoubtedly related to the fact that the major language groups, the Ukrainians, Uzbeks, Armenians, Azerbaydzhanis, Georgians, Moldavian, Tadzhiks, Kirgiz and the Baltic Republics are all below the 40% level. One would have expected that, but for the self sufficiency of their native languages, the fact that they possess advanced educational provision and are well developed economically would have produced a higher level of Russian in each of these nationalities. Other language groups, like Kabardinians, Ingush, Kalmyk, and Balkar have a high level of Russian partly because they require that language to supplement their own, not particularly well developed historically. At the same time other nationalities, for instance Germans, have a high Russian rating in spite of their possession of a language of world currency. Their high Russian rating is due partly to the fact that they are mainly an urbanized community at present, partly because they have had nearly two centuries of very close contact with Russian and partly because like Gipsies, Assyrians, Bulgarians they speak a non-indigenous language.

Here again the position of the Jews is anomalous, for although like the Germans they possess an important language of international currency and are a scattered Soviet people, like some of the others we have referred to, they still rate among the lowest on an index of Russian within the community – no higher for instance than the Azerbaydzhanis. But these two cases are otherwise not comparable. Among the Jews the low level of Russian as a second language is combined with an equally low level of native language maintenance, whereas among the Azerbaydzhanis the low level of Russian is combined with a very high level of native language maintenance. One is drawn to the conclusion that the Jews who know Russian prefer for very obvious reasons to claim it as their native language rather than as a second language. There is no such compulsion on the Azerbaydzhanis. The Jewish case points to more general conclusions, however, for what characterizes them is true also of other nationalities with low levels of Russian as a second language – a knowledge of Russian prepares the way for a change of native language, as we know is the case outside the USSR. For instance the Bashkir have a relatively low maintenance and a low Russian index (66.2 and 37.5); Evenki (51.3, 54.9); Selkup (51.1, 40.8); Itelmen (35.7, 37.5); Orochi (48.6, 44.4) and

Yukagirs (46.8, 29.1). It may be assumed that the Russian these nationalities learn leads rapidly, for reasons we have suggested above, to an irreversible switch. In which case the idea of Russian as a second language in these nationalities does not reflect the true status of Russian in those communities: the degree of Russian penetration is very much greater than appears to be the case from a study of the Russian as a second language index alone. What will be interesting to observe is the future relationship between these two indices – language maintenance and Russian as a second language.

F. LINGUISTIC 'INTERFERENCE' OF RUSSIAN WITH OTHER
    LANGUAGES

Migration has not created but only intensified and extended the manifestation of the linguistic interference we have described earlier, (Ch. 1). The new element introduced by the acceleration of Russian immigration and the promotion of the Russian language in other ways is the contact of the Russian language, on a *popular* level with a great number of languages where previously such contact, if it had occurred at all would probably be limited to a few educated people and would even then have been occasional and restricted in range. The Russian language though it had always exerted some influence on the development of many of the national languages has now entered on an entirely new era of influence. This, as we have seen, is planned and actively promoted; strong resistance, it is urged, "should be put up against any tendencies to avoid borrowing from neighbouring and more highly developed languages and particularly from Russian, and to avoid drawing closer to the Russian language." (Baskakov 1960, 35).

It is recognized by some that the influence of Russian may become predominant, and occasion is taken to emphasize the need to maintain the contact influences among the non-Russian national languages themselves, as well as the normal autonomous development of each language. Baskakov, for instance, emphasizes the continuing contact-relationships of groups of languages such as the Turkic languages of the Volga area, the Caucasus and Central Asia, which have their own sources for borrowing (Baskakov, 15). It is claimed by several scholars that the Russian influence "does not retard the process of development of the national languages". Serdyuchenko, for example, maintained that Russian influence is "facilitating the development and enrichment of the national languages as well as their scientific investigation" (Serdyuchenko, personal communication).

The introduction of new Russian terms has not meant the disappearance of the native 'archaic' words. More often than not the availability of two words has meant a specialization of usage, so that, for instance, the Tadzhik *vuejils* is used for 'assembly of the people' and the Russian *Sovet* for 'official Council meetings'. But whatever the truth of this particular aspect of Russian influence may be, there is no denying the increasing influence of Russian on the national languages. The phonetic system of the Turkic languages has been enriched by new vowels and consonants and, as Baskakov maintains, there has been a greater Russian influence on the consonantal system. This is confirmed by Serdyuchenko, who writes; "new consonantal phonemes have been introduced into Turkic, Caucasian and other languages – previously unknown consonants such as /'-f'/, /'-v'/ and /'-ts'/ are now included because of the influence of Russian loan words." (personal communication). At the beginning speakers of non-Russian languages adapted the pronunciation of new Russian words to the native sound system and as far as the Central Asian languages were concerned this continues to be the case, except in respect of vowel harmony. Here, the influence of Russian has served to accelerate a process of attenuation which was already well under way in the urban areas and in the large oasis dialects under the influence of Persian.

One matter of interest should be mentioned at this point, though it is only indirectly related to the influence of Russian, namely the development of increasing diglossia within several of the non-Russian languages. Changes in orthography, which we refer to later, though they have modified the written form of several of the languages have not always led to phonetic changes. Long vowels are no longer identified in written Turkmen, but they persist in the spoken language. Then again, under Russian pressure Soviet linguists have often tended to create a literary standard on the base of urban dialects, which often bear only limited similarity in some important respects to rural dialects. Since the rural areas are the reservoirs of the living national speech there is increasing divergence between the literary and spoken language.

The grammar of the languages, likewise, has been influenced by Russian. But perhaps the level of language which is most clearly influenced is the vocabulary. The problem of lexical borrowing from Russian was very early recognized as being of exceptional importance for the national languages, and in the discussions of the 1926 Congress at Baku, it was to be expected that attention should be focussed first of all on the new scientific and political terms that would be required because of the need for translating the works of Marx, Engels and Lenin. The eradication of Arabisms and words of Persian origin, the development of the separate vocabulary of each national language or, on the other hand, where the Muslim languages were concerned, the desirability of developing a common Turkic vocabulary – all these questions were immediately given considerable attention, and participants in the discussions in conferences and in periodicals had to try to balance the dangers of what was conceived as linguistic nationalism, pan-Turkicism and, if Russian influences were allowed to predominate, the danger of "flooding a primitive vernacular with international expressions ... with the consequence of its becoming alien and incomprehensible to the masses". In the twenties there was little pressure to introduce Russian vocabulary. The non-Russian languages tended to make use of their own resources, partly by translating Russian into native equivalents. Sometimes the Soviet languages which had close relations with important languages possessing great literatures, outside the Soviet Union such as Persian, preferred to borrow from those languages the words they needed for new concepts – *inqilob* in preference to Russian *revolutsiya*, for instance.

But with the passing of the years the pressure became intense. Sometimes, in fact, Russian terms were introduced even where a national language possessed a satisfactory item, because the native word did not truly reflect the nuances of the Russian term. In the late thirties attempts were made (principally in the fields of social and political, scientific and general terms) to standardize native technical terms to conform to Russian models, or where Russian borrowed them, to the Russian form (Koutaisoff, 1951, 126). These if they are not borrowed directly from Russian, are transferred to the national languages from international sources through Russian. In many of the languages loans from Russian and non-Soviet languages are said to comprise 70% to 80% of the 'new concept' vocabulary (*Izvestiya Akademii Nauk. SSR* No. 4, 1959). There is no doubt that this influence will continue and increase. As universal, compulsory education, with the opportunities to learn Russian, becomes more and more the accepted way of life, the people will be exposed to the new vocabulary, as well as new grammatical structures and new sounds. New experiences will make demands for new linguistic means to communicate those experiences; and the reiteration of Russian in bulletins, in newsprint and in the speeches of officials will make it easy to use Russian terms. This is the official attitude towards the development of the influence of Russian. "The leading role of the Great Russian people and the leading role of its socialist culture relative to the cultures of all the peoples of the country produces a certain merging of the lexical composition of the national language and the lexical composition of the Russian language; and through this, and with its assistance – a certain merging of the lexicons of these languages among themselves. However, this merging does not retard the process of development of the national languages but on the contrary promotes their flourishing" (Mordvinov, 1950, 79).

G. CONCLUSION

Changes in the population structure of the USSR have not created the basic problems of language contact but simply added a new dimension to such problems – secondary levels of contact have emerged, especially (but not exclusively) in the urban areas. The changes in population structure threaten the position of several of the non-Russian national languages in their traditional geographical areas, and at the same time they have encouraged the dispersal of large numbers of speakers of those non-Russian languages. In consequence there has been a considerable degree of assimilation among non-Russian speakers, again in the urban areas mainly. Other factors than population movement have influenced both the nature and the extent of the secondary contacts – the size of the nationalities involved, their history of previous contacts with the same or other linguistic groups, and their geographical contiguity and cultural affinities with the areas from which they receive or to which they send migrant populations. The main beneficiary of the various changes has been the Russian language. The Russians have penetrated in three ways, first by actual movement of populations, second by the substitution of Russian for national languages among large numbers of people, mainly the young, living in urban areas, or in non-urban areas where a lingua franca is a convenience; and third, by influencing the actual languages spoken by non-Russians, especially the vocabulary. In spite of the changes in population structure the place of local languages in rural areas of the USSR remains in 1970 largely unchanged, and since it is here that the non-Russian languages have their stronghold there is considerable hope for the survival of these languages for as long as one needs to consider this problem. Nevertheless without a much stronger educational programme to give an intellectual support to the use of these languages their numerical strength will be irrelevant because standards will decline. Among all these considerations the case of the Jews and their languages is seen to be a-typical, and for that reason they need to be studied separately so far as concerns attitude to language. Finally, the most striking inference one is forced to make is that in spite of the very large number of changes, and the enormous effect of some of them the non-Russian languages in 1970 are still very strong, and claim a considerable degree of loyalty among the respective nationalities, except perhaps among the smallest linguistic communities, and especially those who have had long histories of involvement with Russian.

Chapter 6

THE BASES OF BILINGUALISM IN SOVIET EDUCATION

A. INTRODUCTION

The aims of education in the USSR have been stated explicitly and author-itatively, and apart from the increasing emphasis on science, they are not the subject of change. In 1962 the Minister of Education for the RSFSR maintained that the main task of the Soviet School was to "prepare the pupils for life and for socially useful work: to raise the level of their general and poly-technical education: to graduate educated people with a good knowledge of the fundamental sciences: to rear youth in a spirit of profound respect for labour and the ideas of Communism" (Afana-senko, 1962, 3). More recently the aims have been included in the 'General Provision', of the Statutes of the Secondary Education School, incorpor-ating a Resolution of the USSR Council of Ministers. (*Uchitelskaya Gazeta* 15-9-1970). There it is stated that the main aim of such schools is to give an education that corresponds "to the present day demands of social, scientific and technical progress, seeking to impart to the pupils a sound knowledge of the principles of science, and the ability to enlarge their knowledge on their own [...] to mould the Marxist-Leninist world view in the younger generation [...] Soviet patriotism, love for home land and for the Communist Party of the Soviet Union [...] to ensure the all round harmonious development of the pupils". Such a statement should help to do at least one thing, namely to help us maintain a sense of pro-portion in our treatment of languages in Soviet education. In spite of their importance in the curriculum and in the organisation and administra-tion of school systems in the USSR languages do not receive within the Statutes an extended treatment; and we should at the outset realize that

whatever controversies exist concerning language, and however they reflect far more deep seated issues in Soviet Society those controversies are
not central to the fulfilment of the broad aims of education as they are
conceived in the USSR.

Furthermore, there is nothing in the statement of aims which conflicts
fundamentally with the aims of education in the United Kingdom or the
United States, for instance. If we substitute 'Christianity' or 'Democracy'
for 'Communism', any country in Western Europe could adopt the series
of tasks as appropriate for their schools to pursue. Nor should this fact
perplex us. The two principles, and there are only two, on which any
system of education is based are universal. They are also essentially
irreconcilable, operating at all times in all systems of education in dialectic
opposition. Plutarch in his life of Lycurgus describes the Spartan belief:
"Nobody was free to live as he wished but as in a camp every one had his
way of life and his public duties fixed; and he held that he did not belong
to himself but to his country. In general", he continued, "Lycurgus
accustomed the citizens to have neither the will nor the ability to have a
private life". According to the second and opposing principle the aim of
education is the enthronement of the individual and the encouragement
of an attitude that, being critical of the 'idols of the tribe' may sooner or
later topple them from their preeminence. In this case the ideals are individual initiative, versatility and above all a ranging and exploring intellect. So it was in the other Greek city, Athens; and so it was, if we can
believe de Toqueville, in the heyday of democracy in America – "The
young were to be brought up to evade the bondage of system and habit,
of family maxims, class opinions and national prejudices [...] to seek the
reason of things for oneself and oneself alone". Just as it is important for
us to maintain a sense of proportion about the problem of languages in
education, so we should not ignore the fact that the elements which go to
make up the system of education in the USSR operate in all other systems
too. For good or ill the Soviet Union, in this respect, is not unique.

The differences between countries, and between different times in the
history of education in any one country, arise from the changing and the
shifting relative importance attached to these two principles. Every
system, and this is the case in the USSR as we have observed in an earlier
chapter, has to strike a balance between two equally necessary and equally true ideals. On the one hand the need to safeguard the mere existence
of the society and to ensure the continuity of its ethos – the emphasis on
this is the mark of the closed society or of the concept of closure within
any society. Its value cannot be denied. Without a certain element of
closure there is small hope of a fund of common convictions or a secure
set of agreed premises. Without these the child's upbringing is likely to be
unstable. Nevertheless, to the extent that a society is closed it is in danger

of stagnating. It inevitably happens that education, if it pursues the aims of a close society exclusively or excessively, becomes more and more identified with the 'secret transmission of a mystery, a treasure of arcane revelations within the closed circle of a ritual community', whether what is transmitted is dogmatic religion, a humanist philosophy of life or a political ideology.

Consequently, by promoting individual excellence and so enriching the quality of life in the society, the system of education attempts to ensure not simply the continuation of the society, but its protection against stagnation, irrelevance and triviality. To some degree the young in this kind of society are brought up to question revelation, dogma, and tradition. For them the truth lies with Charles Pierce: "the only thing that is really desirable without a reason for being so is to render ideas reasonable. One cannot demand a reason for reasonableness". This is the critical as opposed to the incorporative principle in education. It ensures a proper evaluation of the necessary contribution each individual has to make, while the first principle directs the individual's contribution where it can be maximally useful – its ultimate repository, the community. No system of education has escaped the tension of the operation of these two conflicting and complementary principles. They are as active in Britain and the United States as they are in the USSR, the difference lying in their relative weight within the three systems at any one time. In every country they have been adjusted differently at different times. In the USSR, just as the story of the implementation of a national language policy in respect of ethnic groups and nationalities has been adjusted and readjusted time and time again, so the implementation of an educational-language policy has shifted the relative weights periodically. A multilingual society such as that of the USSR reflects the tensions between the two forces more than a linguistic or ethnically homogenous society can do. So the tension is reflected in the educational system of the USSR and in the strains between the individual's allegiance to his 'civic' or to his 'group culture'; and between the great variety of local ethnic and linguistic communities on the one hand, ranging from the smallest minorities up to Union Republics, and on the other the Central Authority and its Party apparatus based on Moscow. More than any other aspect of a multilingual society the education system reflects the inevitable tensions on both levels.

Education in such a society has always been characterized by conflict between the demands of the centre and those of local cultural and linguistic interests. But the historical contingencies in culture and language have been very different in the widely separated parts of the USSR and for that reason considerations of the impact of 'centre-ideology' have produced and continue to promote and maintain different patterns and stages of linguistic and cultural assimilation. The educational systems of established nationalities such as the Baltic countries, the Ukraine, Armenia and Georgia, have operated to produce linguistic consequences among the students, which differ from those produced by the educational system of the group of small nationalities like those within the RSFSR for instance, and these in turn have been different from those produced in the Central Asian Republics. It was inevitable that historical antecedents and different levels of economic development, as well as the existence of different linguistic elements within these Republics would result in the different reactions to the centre-ideology stimulus we have examined. Then again, individual self-consciousness, often cutting across the more local group patterns generally, result in contradictions which are more apparent in the area of language and education than in other fields of social action, such as the economic. For instance, under pressure from the centre many individual writers have abandoned their native tongue in favour of Russian. On the other hand, it is from among representatives of the same class of the local intelligentsia that has emerged the leadership to retain local cultural and especially local linguistic loyalties. In fact it is against this group that the complaint is frequently made that they are persuading parents to place their children in national schools contrary to what is argued to be their best interests (*Partiinaya zhizn* 23, 1962). The two principles which govern the pattern of political action, the principles tending towards the open and the closed society are very active in the system of education; and in a multilingual society we have a unique opportunity to examine the tension between them.

B. THE BASES OF LITERATE BILINGUALISM – EXPANSION OF
   EDUCATIONAL PROVISION

i. *Introduction*

So far as the USSR is concerned advancement of a language policy either in society at large or in the education system presupposed the creation, almost from nothing in the case of many nationalities, of a system of education where such a policy could be put to work. In fact the system of education has reflected from the beginning the changes of general or political and social policy and has been the agent of such changes. In the end the pluralist element in the policy has offered the chance for the smallest languages to become viable in a literate civilization. Thus they have become languages of education. The centralist principle on the other hand has tended to ensure that these new literary languages do not simply contribute to the creation of individual excellence through education, but are directed towards safeguarding and consolidating a particular kind of society – Communism – and creating greater social and political homogeneity. The service of the new literary languages in promoting individual excellence is subordinated to the requirements of the centralist ideology.

The creation of individual excellence has been promoted in two ways, and these have had considerable implications for the development of the non-Russian languages. First, there has been the improvement of the standards of existing education, raising individual achievement through improved pedagogy. Second, there has been considerable pressure to equalize the opportunity for such education between and within the various Republics. This is sometimes stated as "helping the toiling masses of non-Great Russian peoples to catch up with Central Russia", enabling the less advanced nationalities to make good the differences. In this way the creation of a universal system of education and the adoption of a uniform language policy have served to create a more homogenous pattern of nationalities. At the same time because of the respect paid to the mother tongue in this system of education, and the support for linguistic engineering and standardization, these national languages have been able to overcome many of the problems which obstructed their emergence as languages of education. In this way increasing social homogeneity is enriched (almost against the State's will at times) by diverse arrangements of different relationships between the languages in school and society.

Education not only reflects major changes in the structure of Soviet society and the distribution of power, but it helps to direct such changes. For instance, the system of education has been a factor in regulating the rate at which different national, ethnic and language groups are assimilated; on the other hand, it has helped them to preserve, unassimilated, their national integrity. Soviet Arabs, for instance, are educated in either Uzbek or Tadzhik language schools; and partly, but only partly for this reason, the children of parents who have always described themselves as Arabs have lost even the recollection of their ethnic tongue. Similarly, education policies throughout Uzbekistan have meant the gradual secularization of a formerly largely theocratically oriented society, and consequently has tended to attenuate the relevance of their traditional language loyalty. On the other hand several small nationalities, among the Peoples of the North for instance, have acquired new strength because their languages have been able to develop a literature either for the first time, or much more satisfactorily than before. The Yakut is a case in point.

While much that is taught in Soviet Schools, the oral traditions of the nationalities, the native tongue and respect for native cultural traits, art, design and music, encourages the pluralist concept of Soviet Society, the administration of education is a main agent in promoting centralist tendencies. Administration has always developed, mainly in response to the planners' preference function. Ideological considerations alone would not account for the extreme reluctance until late in the 50's to accept the fact that diversified courses were necessitated by educational expansion. Then again, in 1966, there was set up in Moscow the Union Republics Ministry of Education, which has largely usurped the theoretical independence of the several Republic Ministries. Previously education was administered by the Council of Ministers of the Union Republics through the respective Ministries of Education. In 1966, also, the control of Higher and Specialist Education was centralized (*Pravda*, 9-7-1966).

But although these changes towards centralization appear to be very recent they only formalize a situation which has obtained for a considerable time, as was evidenced during the discussions of the proposals for the 1959 Education Laws. In the last resort, especially where Khrushchev's Theses concerning languages were concerned, whatever suggestions for modification might be advanced in an individual Republic, the ultimate decision lay with the Central Authority in Moscow. When the proposals were discussed there at the end of the time of open debate the laws, which had never received the general assent of several Republics (so far as concerned the place of their own languages in the curriculum), were adopted in almost identical terms with only two exceptions. In fact no Republic has been able either in general or particular to administer a language policy which was tailored to fit its own local requirements; all that a Republic is able to do is to implement the general formula. Again, although several of the Republics have their own publishing houses which issue text books, teaching aids, teaching manuals and literature connected with language teaching, they have always had to work, first, within the overall planning of the Soviet economy and the centrally controlled budgetary provision; second, according to the decisions and joint conclusions of the Central Committee of the Communist Party and the Council of Ministers of the USSR; and finally, they have been guided not so much by their own research institutes, but by the Scientific Research Institutes of the RSFSR Academy of Pedagogical Sciences, who largely direct the preparation of curricula and syllabuses in language as in other subjects, together with the production of materials in and outside the RSFSR.

ii. *The Story of Expansion*

The expansion of educational provision has by all standards been remarkable. Before the Revolution of 1917 the broad mass of the people had no opportunity of obtaining any kind of education, even at primary level. According to the census figures 76% of the population aged 9 and over were illiterate, with a figure of 88% in the case of women. It was said that in the central regions of Russia, and in what now constitute the

Central Asian Republics and Kazakhstan it would be rare to find a person who could read and write. There was no general access to secondary education; but for those who could afford it or were otherwise privileged there were *gymnasia* and *realschule* with a few technical and vocational establishments. Many restrictions on entry existed, based on nationality and religion. By the decree of 21st January 1918 the Church was disestablished and the existing schools were secularized. At the same time a radical reorganisation of the system of education began. In November 1917 'The Principles of the System of Public Education' was published, on the basis of which education was made available to the working masses. In 1919 the 8th Congress adopted a programme in which was laid down the aim of the schools to educate the children in Communism as well as to provide for their individual development – the two universal principles already identified. These aims were to be achieved through the establishment of compulsory general and polytechnical education for boys and girls up to the age of 17, and prepared for in pre-school co-educational classes.

The initial system of school education was based on the regulations governing the 'unified labour schools' set up in 1918 and took the following form: a primary school for children of 8 to 12, with a four year course (a seven year secondary course) and a nine year or complete secondary course with a two year course following the seven year school. Starting from 1931 the course at the secondary (complete) school was extended by a year so that the nine year normal-type school became a ten year school with three senior classes. At present (1970 Regulations) the period of instruction is still ten years (having reverted to that figure after an experimental 11 year school in Khrushchev's time). However 11 years is still the period of instruction in schools where the medium of teaching is not Russian. The instruction hours at present are 24 in the first four grades, 30 hours in grades 5-8, and 32 in grades 9-10 (11). In national schools in the RSFSR, for instance, and in 10 year schools in other Republics (i.e. Russian schools in the non-Russian Republics) an increase of 2-3 hours per grade per week is permitted. Furthermore in 10 year schools where instruction is not in Russian one week is added to the annual programme.

Table 26 indicates not only that the increase of educational provision laid down by these decrees has been rapid and comprehensive, but that the greatest advance has been in professional specialist and higher education. By 1969 the number of students in schools providing a general elementary and secondary education rose in the Soviet Union as a whole to five times the number in 1914. In the 5th to 11th classes the increase was forty fold that of 1918. On the eve of the Revolution Buryat-Mongolia had only 48 schools of all kinds, but even as early as 1932-1933, 700 schools were claimed for it, while the numbers enrolled increased from approximately 1,000 to 67,000. In Bashkira, prior to the Revolution the proportion of children enrolled was 3%, but by 1929-1930 the figure was nearly twice that. Just before 1914 only 16% of the school age children of Eastern Armenia attended school (Kalashnikov, 1927-1929, Vol. III,

TABLE 26

Expansion in the number of school places – 1914-1969
Number of pupils and students according to types of education (at the beginning of the academic year; thousands)[a];

	1914-1915	1940-1941	1945-1946	1960-1961	1968-1969
Total number including:	10,588	47,547	37,385	52,600	73,559
in general educational schools of all types	9,656	35,552	26,808	36,187	48,170
of whom					
in elementary, incomplete secondary and secondary schools	9,656	34,784	26,094	33,417	43,529
in schools for young people and schools for adults (including in correspondence departments)	—	768	714	2,770	4,641
in professional, vocational and trades schools	106	717	945	1,113	1,961
in specialised secondary educational establishments	54	975	1,008	2,060	3,994
in institutions of higher learning	127	812	730	2,396	4,123
those who learned new trades and took refresher courses at enterprises or training centres and attended other courses	645	9,491	7,894	10,844	15,311

[a] Source: *Strana Sovetov za 50 let.*, 278.

642), but by 1967 the number had multiplied by 15. The figure for all education enrolments in Uzbekistan rose from under 2% to 33% in the same period. In Tataria it was claimed in 1933 that enrolment had reached 90%, which is probably a highly inflated figure, but nevertheless an enormous improvement on anything that had gone before. In the Central Asian Republics as a whole total enrolment rose from 32,000 immediately prior to the Revolution to three and a half million in 1963, and in the top grades from 5,000 to 1.7 million. In Tadzhikstan while there were, at the beginning, no classes above grade 4, in 1963 the number was 213,000.

iii. *Differential Expansion in Primary and Secondary School*

It cannot be denied that a great deal has been done to extend educational opportunity wherever it is needed, but the process has not been straight-forward – it is not a matter simply of raising the level of achievement of individual pupils. If that alone had been accomplished the disparities between nationalities might still remain as great as ever, and the creation of a homogenous society not one step more advanced. The national differences in standards of education and in opportunities to profit from the availability of education had also to be removed.

TABLE 27

Number of students in all educational establishments according to Union Republics 1914-1967[a]

Republic	In Thousands				
	1914	1941	1946	1951	1967
USSR	10,588	47,547	37,385	52,600	73,559
RSFSR	5,684	20,633	15,421	19,399	26,187
Ukraine	2,607	6,830	5,151	7,134	8,469
Belorussia	489	1,737	1,358	1,555	1,769
Uzbekistan	18	1,325	948	1,347	2,592
Kazakhstan	105	1,148	794	1,349	2,866
Georgia	157	767	628	738	928
Azerbaydzhan	73	695	504	660	1,199
Lithuania	118	380	310	430	562
Moldavia	92	440	431	481	763
Latvia	172	242	223	295	343
Kirgizstan	7	343	228	343	657
Tadzhikstan	0.4	315	244	322	613
Armenia	35	333	261	319	553
Turkestan	7	253	181	224	455
Estonia	92	121	126	156	215

[a]   Source: *Strana sovetov za 50 let*. (Extracted 310-340).

Between 1914 and 1967, something slightly more than half a century, while the total USSR expansion was of the order of 700% some of the countries which now form the Central Asian Republics multiplied their educational provision by nearly twice that sum – Uzbekistan (1,300%), Tadzhikstan (1,000%). Kirgizstan multiplied its provision by ninety and Turkestan by sixty. Meanwhile the more advanced countries, those on the Western marches of the USSR moved forward more slowly, relatively speaking – the RSFSR by a figure of four, the Ukraine by three and the Baltic countries slightly more. (Table 27)

The same is true if we take only one aspect of that total provision, Secondary Education. During the crucial period beginning with the year which saw a main consolidating point in Secondary provision, 1939, and ending with satisfactory re-establishment of that provision following the

War and its aftermath, 1959, while there was an overall Soviet advance in secondary education, some of the hitherto less advanced Republics moved forward at over four times the general rate. (Table 28) Tadzhikstan improved its secondary provision by a ratio of 10.6, Kirgizstan by a

TABLE 28

Enrolments in secondary education – 1939-1959[a]

Republic	% with complete or incomp. sec. educ. 1959	Increase ratio 1939/59	Republic	% with complete or incomp. sec. educ. 1959	Increase ratio 1939/59
Tadzhik SRR	2.7	10.6	Azerbaydzhan	7.3	4.1
Kirgiz	3.2	9.9	RSFSR	7.6	3.7
Uzbek	3.9	7.7	Armenian	8.1	4.9
Moldavian	4.0	5.5	Ukrainian	9.0	3.3
Turkmen	4.6	6.7	Georgian	11.3	3.2
Kazakh	6.0	6.1	Estonian	12.9	2.7
Lithuanian	6.4	2.6	Latvian	14.0	2.7
Belorussian	6.7	3.0			

[a] Source: 1939 and 1959 Censuses for USSR and separate Republics.

ratio of 9.9, and Uzbekistan by a ratio of 7.7. At the other end of the scale the Baltic countries had improvement ratios of round about 2.7 and the RSFSR one of 3.7. During this critical period the Republics with undeveloped systems of secondary and other forms of education began to catch up with the more advanced countries of the USSR. While this would in any case be expected in the normal course of events, simply because those who begin with nothing register a phenomenal advance if they provide only a few schools, the kind of differential ratios we observe operating in the USSR can have come into existence only as the result of positive discrimination in favour of the Central Asian Republics and others similarly placed.

It is the levelling and equalization of opportunity just as much as the improvement in the average achievement of individuals who were given those opportunities which have characterized Soviet education during its existence. This has been the pre-condition of social mobilization and greater homogeneity based on the elimination of illiteracy through the use of the national languages in school. While Lorimer could say with absolute justification that in the early days of the regime "a large proportion of many minorities could not understand any other language nor read their own" (1946, 198) almost the reverse is now true – only an insignificant number cannot read their own language, and a vast number

are able to speak at least one other language and very many of them two
and more.

iv. *Differential Expansion of Higher Education*

Most educationists agree that while the provision of elementary and
secondary education is the presupposition of any successful advance in
national wellbeing the extent of that advance, and certainly the quality
of what is provided depends on the development of higher education. It is
the product of the higher education establishments which sets the pace,
and, even in authoritarian countries, helps to determine the direction of
the general advance. This is true of the non-Russian Republics of the
USSR in the same way that it is true of other hitherto educationally
underdeveloped countries, for instance in Africa or Asia.

TABLE 29

*Number of students of major nationalities of the Union Republics receiving higher
education – 1927-1967*[a]

Republics	Number of students in thousands		
	1927	1960	1967
USSR	168.5	2,396.1	4,123.2
RSFSR	94.5	1,480.1	2,494.7
Ukraine	24.6	343.6	590.2
Belorussia	4.9	63.7	122.6
Uzbekistan	0.5	57.5	112.4
Kazakhstan	0.3	40.8	75.9
Georgia	4.0	48.5	77.0
Azerbaydzhan	1.9	28.5	63.9
Lithuania	—	25.8	46.0
Latvia	—	16.5	22.7
Moldavia	0.2	12.0	26.4
Kirgizstan	0.1	9.8	18.7
Tadzhikstan	0.1	11.9	19.9
Armenia	3.4	36.7	67.7
Turkmenistan	0.1	9.5	17.8
Estonia	—	12.9	18.8

a   Source: *Strana Sovetov za 50 let.* – extracted.

Among the Uzbeks, Kirgiz, Tadzhiks and Turkmens between 1927 and
1967 the number of students increased by 225 times, 183 times, 199 times
and 178 times respectively, compared with an improvement in the USSR
as a whole of 25 times the 1927 figure, which is also the ratio for the
RSFSR, the Ukraine, and Belorussia. (Table 29) Relatively low rates of

increase are evident in the Baltic countries during the slightly later period 1939-1959 – an improvement ratio of 3.75. Between 1960 and 1967 the ratio for these same countries is of the order of 1.8, 1.4, and 1.4 for Lithuania, Latvia and Estonia in that order. (Maciuika, 1963, 346). But while the rate of growth is relatively slow in the Western and larger Republics, the small nationalities and those constituting Autonomous Republics and Autonomous Regions now have fairly large numbers of students in establishments of higher education, the most favoured in this respect being Buryats (4%), Abkhaz (3%), Balkars (3%), Adygei (3%), Khakass (2%), and Karakalpaks (2%). Even a very small nationality like the Karachai (81 thousands) have a 3% Higher Education intake. Of all the nationalities not granted Union Republic Status, however, the Jews have the highest percentage intake (5%) (*Strana Sovetov za 50 let*, 1969).

v. *Maintenance of Russian Preponderance*

However, although there has been considerable advance towards equalizing educational provision between the various nationalities the fact cannot be disguised that the Russian predominance continues to be extremely heavy, and this for two reasons. First, if we compare the various nationalities according to the relation between their share of the total population of the USSR and their take up of places in Institutes of Higher Education (the relation between what they might numerically be entitled to, and what they actually enjoy), the previously more advanced nationalities still have a disproportionate share, and the Russians especially (Table 30). The struggle of the non-Russian nationalities to achieve anything approaching parity with the Russians must continue to be arduous and long.
It is clear that apart from the Armenians, who have a very slight advantage, and the Georgians who break even, the only Republic where the proportion of higher education places is greater than the size of the population would indicate it ought to be is Russia.
   Second, it should be emphasized that the increase of the total enrolment in any Republic is a very crude yard-stick by which to measure the increased take up among the indigenous nationalities, so far as concerns Higher Education establishments. The use of Russian as a medium of instruction in these institutions, and especially at the Universities, means that non-native speakers of Russian are disadvantaged. In fact, Russian is used not only because of the benefits arising from the use of an international language of science and scholarship, but quite explicitly to facilitate the inclusion of non-native students in state universities. These non-native students are, it is true, sometimes permanent immigrants, but they are often exchange-students from other Republics (Binder, 1967, 349).

TABLE 30

Comparison of population and higher education places as proportions of total USSR figures (Population for 1970, Education for 1966)[a]

A	B	C	D
Union Republic	Proportion of population	Proportion of higher education places	Discrepancy between A & B
RSFSR	53.2	61.1	+ 7.9
Ukraine	19.5	14.4	— 5.1
Belorussia	3.7	2.9	— 0.8
Uzbek	4.8	2.4	— 2.4
Kazakh	5.1	1.8	— 3.3
Georgia	1.8	1.8	—
Azerbaydzhan	2.1	1.4	— 0.7
Lithuania	1.3	1.1	— 0.2
Latvia	0.92	0.67	— 0.2
Kirgizstan	1.2	0.46	— 0.7
Tadzhikstan	1.3	0.67	— 0.7
Armenia	1.0	1.33	+ 0.33
Turkmenstan	0.8	0.48	— 0.3
Estonia	0.6	0.47	— 0.2
Moldavia	1.4	1.06	— 0.3

[a]   Sources: Column B: *Izvestiya* 15-4-1970; Column C: *Narodnoye khozaistvo SSSR v* 1966.

Kazakhs and Kirgiz students, to take only two groups, have complained strongly because of the Russian examination for entrance to such Institutes.

For these reasons, although the improvement of the native population's take up of higher education places has been gratifying so far as the actual numbers of native or indigenous students of a Republic, there has been a very perceptible drift towards increased Russian predominance. The position of the Kirgiz and Tadzhik SSR may be taken as not untypical of the rest of the USSR. In Kirgizia, whereas there were in 1953 roughly twice as many places taken by Kirgiz compared with Russians (a ratio of 10 to 5), in 1963 the respective percentages were Kirgiz 43 and Russians 38 – a ratio of 10 to 9. In Tadzhikstan the ratio in 1965 was only 2 to 1 in favour of the native population, whereas in 1953 there is no indication of the presence of any Russian students at all. The predominance is even more marked if we compare the relative take up of places in higher education not in terms of the number of places available, but of the proportion of the respective ethnic groups in the general population. In 1953 in Kirgizia, for example, the index of Kirgiz student to total population was 12 and the Russian 9. In 1963 the index was 12 and 13 (Bilinsky, 1962, 430).

C. BASES OF LITERATE BILINGUALISM – STANDARDIZATION OF 'NATIONAL' LANGUAGES.

i. *Creating Literary Languages*

a. *Provision of Alphabets*

Increasing the provision for formal education is only one of several conditions for the implementation of a national language policy. Without schools of some sort and a predictable period of attendance, it is difficult to teach children to read their own language, to say nothing of learning a second, whether it is Russian or another language spoken normally within a Republic, or a foreign language. Nevertheless school attendance is only a precondition – the language itself, if it is to be taught and used for teaching subjects within the curriculum, must be in a satisfactory condition. Literacy, and the employment of languages in education at whatever level, require the standardization of the relevant languages. From this point of view it is possible, historically, to recognize three groups of nationalities and their languages in the USSR. The first consists of national literary languages like Russian, Ukrainian, Georgian, Armenian, etc. Among these there are considerable differences, however: some inherited Arabic scripts which were difficult to learn and ill adapted to the characteristics of the particular languages. Others, like the Chuvash, the Volga Tatars, groups in the Altai ranges, Abkhazian, Kabardinians and Ossetes, had been christianized and used variants of Cyrillic. The Georgians and Armenians possessed their own remarkably individual scripts. Others used a Latin script and others again, mainly members of the Finno-Ugrian group of the Volga Basin, like Mari and Komi, had been provided with an alphabet as far back as the 14th Century, mainly through the efforts of missionaries like St. Stephen of Perm. His was a highly personal alphabet, Abur, based on Church Slavonic and Greek. It must not be assumed, however, that it was the languages of the less advanced peoples alone which were influenced by the processes of standardization. Armenian has been considerably affected; the local dialects have tended to disappear partly, it is true, because of mass media and centralized administration and education, but also because of precise and specific linguistic planning.

The second group consisted of peoples whose vernaculars and dialects had not yet developed as national languages though some had been given, tentatively, a written form. Among this group should be included Kumyk, Nogai, Karakalpak, Kirgiz (which is closely related to Karakalpak) and Yakut. Finally there were the languages belonging to the Khakass, Karagas, Shors, Chulym and a number in the paleo-asiatic group, consisting of about sixteen representative languages spoken by approximately 120,000. Some of these languages became extinct and some of the alphabets of other languages in the same group have since been allowed to lapse; while others, like Itelmen, have developed to become members of the second group. The Khakass are an outstanding example of a renascent language (and people) consequent on the creation of a literary language. Before their unification they were divided into several widely divergent dialect groups – Sagay, Kachin, Koybal, Beltire and Kuzyl, and without a unifying medium. The dialects are now merging to form the base for a strong literary language. The first Khakass alphabet, created between 1922 and 1928, was based on Russian and later Latin, reverting to Cyrillic but with considerable concessions to the characteristics of the native dialects. (Baskakov, 1960, 7). Generally speaking the languages of the third group (and those of the second at one time) are conglomerates of several dialects, none of which has fully emerged to provide an acceptable base for standardization. They have too few common spoken forms, though some, like the Altai dialects, are emerging to provide a common means of communication. Within this group Karachai, Balkar, Gagauz and Tuvinian had experimental alphabets.

b. *Reform of Existing Alphabets*

With the Revolution, for ideological reasons, and because of the commitment to a process of rapid social and industrial mobilization, and a drive towards a system of mass education which had to rely on the exploitation of the vernacular, it became imperative that unsatisfactory or 'unsuitable' alphabets should be improved or replaced, and alphabets created which served in some way to unify the people. The problem, though perhaps not most acute there, was urgently pressed in the Central Asian Republics. Up to the middle of the 19th Century the Muslim populations of Central Asia had only three languages of literacy – Arabic, Persian and Chagatay. Only a small minority, of the privileged even, had any acquaintance with any of these and the working masses remained illiterate. Their general backwardness, which the Kazan scholar, Naisiri, acknowledged, was attributable to ignorance of the vernaculars, including such important languages as Uzbek and Turkmen. The promotion of these as literary languages had long been frustrated.

The movement for reform was not originated by the Soviets: as early as 1863 a reform of the Arabic script for the Turkic languages had been proposed and in 1870 it was generally accepted that the Arabic alphabet was not only "unfit but extremely harmful in purely altaic languages" (Koutaisoff, 1951, 117). It was decided to proceed with the development, if possible, of uniform scripts for at least the Central Asian area, rather than create a large number of different alphabets, though this latter policy might have better suited the needs of the different languages. The use of a reformed Arabic or a Russian alphabet was discounted, though Kazakhs, Uzbeks, and Tatars continued to be attracted to a reformed Arabic. (Winner, 1952, 135). Beginning in Azerbaydzhan, the movement for developing the use of the Latin alphabet as the base of the new scripts spread rapidly. In 1921 the Caucasian Highlands Republic adopted a Latin variant. But though 17 different varieties were already being used, it was not until 1923 that the Latin base was firmly established. In 1923 the Azerbaydzhan Republic gave equal status to the Latin and the Arabic alphabets, and a year later the Latin script was made official.

The justification of this policy of ensuring the adoption of a single unified base for the new alphabets rather than proceed with the creation of several independent scripts becomes clear when we recall that by 1930 a total of 36 nationalities were using the new alphabets. Newspapers were printing occasional columns in the new standard script, and by 1928 in Kazakhstan alone 6,300 people were reported to have learned to read. At the same time the schools of Kirgizstan were using the new alphabets. (Winner, 142). Meanwhile, the success in Central Asia led to similar approaches being made among the peoples of the North whose alphabets were either variants of Cyrillic, or, as in the case of the Komi, fairly idiosyncratic.

Even while the adoption of the Latin alphabet as the uniform base for prospective literacy was being consolidated, a movement was inaugurated to substitute a Cyrillic base. The first to adopt this were the Kabardinians in 1935. In 1937 when the 9th Session of the reconstituted All Union Committee on the alphabets was called, the movement to change to Cyrillic was well underway and its adoption was supported by the Secretary of the Soviet Nationalities of the USSR. In 1938 Daghestan adopted Cyrillic and by 1940 it had spread to most Republics, more than 68 languages having been supplied with scripts and over 25 million non-Russians able to use them. In these developments at least 5 different but related aspects have to be distinguished. In the first place, there was the creation of alphabets of any kind, and this, in the abstract, was the main contribution to literacy. Secondly, there was the decision to have a uniform base for the alphabets, whether this base was Latin or Cyrillic. This, again, in the abstract, has conduced to the development of a homogenous society through the processes of education, more than separate alphabets would have done. The third aspect is concerned with the choice of Latin, which meant severing connection with the written form of related languages outside the USSR. The fourth is the change from Latin to Cyrillic which was brought about not simply in order to improve the foundations for literacy, but to promote the easier learning of Russian, so ensuring to some extent that homogeneity should be in terms not entirely of mutual adjustment but of accommodation to Russian.

From recent discussions it is apparent that this is still an open question, and attempts are being made to improve the mutual intelligibility of the written languages, more particularly the Turkic group, both among themselves and between them and Russian, by eradicating the differences between the various Cyrillic-Turkic alphabets. These alphabets, which attempted to equate the conventions of Turkic and Russian orthography, have proved unsatisfactory in many respects and it is not surprising, therefore, that they have not succeeded in helping speakers of other languages to learn Russian. It seems that the creation of satisfactory scripts, as one aspect of the process of standardizing Soviet languages for the purposes of education is still very much a live issue. Finally, whatever base was used for the creation of literacy, Latin or Cyrillic, new alphabets meant that the national languages were, for the first time in many instances, able to begin to compete with Russian, could be used in the schools and could become the foundation for a different kind of bilingualism than had previously existed – literate bilingualism.

ii.   *Problems of Dialects*

In addition to improving existing alphabets or creating new ones the preparation of numerous Soviet languages for use in a system of mass education necessitated two other processes. In the first place there was the need in many instances to select for promotion the most useful or viable dialect. For example, as we have seen, before the unification of the Khakass there existed only several separate spoken dialects – Beltir, Sagay, Kachin, Koybal and Kyzyl. Only one of these tribal dialects, Sagay-Kachin, forms the base for the new written language used in schools. In this aspect of standardization the established Soviet practice has been first to ensure there is as little disparity as possible between the written and spoken forms, and that the written form reflects accurately the development of the language in all its aspects.

Uzbek is a good example of the problems facing language planners in the first few years of the Soviet regime. The literary language of the area before the Revolution was Chagatay and though a literary Uzbek has been traced back as far as the XVIIth century and the linguistic adumbrations of such a literary language have been identified as far back as the XIth – XIVth centuries the condition of Uzbek has been of a language characterized by a large number of very important and widely used dialects. These have been classified according to their locale – Central Uzbek spoken around Tashkent; and a variant of this dialect spoken in Samarkand and its environs. Another group of dialects is spoken in the Ferghana Valley and these are in close contact with dialects of the Andizhan area. Then there are the North Uzbek dialects spoken in Chimkent and north of Tashkent, and in the southern areas of Kazakhstan. There are also Kazakh dialects of the Uzbek language; and finally there are forms of a Turkmenized Uzbek spoken in the area surrounding Khiva. The first choice of dialect to serve as the basis for the new Uzbek literary language fell on the variant spoken in South Kazakhstan. It was generally regarded as a 'pure Uzbek' with full vowel harmony, and so its sound system was thought to commend it for valid transcription. This was in 1920; but only ten years later the urban dialect of Tashkent replaced it as the proposed standard. There remained the selection of a suitable orthography, and the problem posed by the increasing number of Russian loan words. Morphological and lexical features of the Ferghana valley dialects also have continued to have an increasing influence on the standard language. But to all intents and purposes the Uzbek language was stabilized.

Tadzhik, also, is usually regarded as possessing at least five groups of dialects. The first, the North Western, is the best known. It is spoken west of Ferghana, near Samarkand and Bukhara, its most northerly variant being found north east of Tashkent. The second group of dialects, the South West, are spoken by the Mountain Tadzhiks of the Badakhshan-Goron area. Farsi, the Central Asian form of Persian, and Yagnobi dialects are two other groups, and there is also a collection of dialects spoken by Beludzhi, Kurds and Afghans on the frontiers. The standard literary Tadzhik is based on the 'Plains Tadzhik' – the north western variant. It has had a continuous literary history for many centuries, and the lesser dialects like Yagnobi and the Pamiri now use the standard dialect as their language of literacy. One consequence of the standardization of these languages or of the adoption of a particular dialect as the base for standarization is, as is the case with Uzbek also, that there are considerable divergencies between the written language and the dialect spoken by the same people. The result is that literate Uzbek, and indeed literate Tadzhik bilingualism too, involves diglossia – not simply the acquisition of separate languages such as Tadzhik and Russian but two widely used variants of the same language. In the case of Uzbek this has given rise to the co-existence of a general standard (written) and a more restricted regional standard, not dissimilar in their relation to the two variants of German in Switzerland.

Other languages, like Turkmen and Uygur, have not raised the same problems of standardization since they have long literary traditions – in the case of the former reaching back to the XIVth century. Even after the adoption of Chagatay Turkmen continued to be a literary language in the XVIII and XIXth centuries. The problem in each of these cases was the adoption of an orthography considered to be suitable by the regime. Kirgiz, on the other hand and to a lesser extent Kazakh, presented more general problems of standardization since in neither case was there a tradition of literacy in the language extending for more than a century – and in the case of Kirgiz far less. The remaining problems of language stabilization are now, almost inevitably, considered within the context of the influence of the Russian language, partly because of the universality of the Cyrillic script, and partly because of the increasing number of loan words which help to influence systems of word formation within the recipient languages, and the sound systems as well.

iii. *Vocabulary and the Planned Penetration of Russian*

Standardization of the languages has involved a considerable effort in the area of terminology and vocabulary. In a society built on new political and ideological foundations, attempting to move rapidly into an area of sophisticated technology and industrialization, and starting, as many of the nationalities have done, from a nomadic and peasant economy and culture, the problem of vocabulary has been very urgent. The treatment of this problem has reflected the way in which linguistic policy has helped to create a more homogenous society. 'The creation of a common lexical stock for the languages of the USSR' which was one of the main concerns of the 1962 Alma-Ata Conference on the Development of Literary Languages, has meant in actual practice a consideration of the relation of the other national languages to Russian. The problem was illuminated at the Conference by a Komi scholar, who though she did not oppose the use of Russian loan words as a means of creating useable languages for education among the peoples of the north, criticised the general tendency to argue that the only way in which such languages could be made viable lexically was by bringing them as close as possible to Russian (*Voprosy razvitiya*, 18). Nevertheless, lexical innovation has been to an outstanding degree a matter of Russian influence. In Armenia by 1950 the special Terminology Commission had approved 18,000 medical terms, 13,000 legal terms and a large number of other specialized and learned items, most of them of Russian origin, or international terms derived through Russian. In Latvia 40,000 terms were approved in the space of 3 years between 1947 and 1949 (Mordvinov). The special Commission to which we have referred, and which was set up in 1933, dealt drastically with the Turkic languages. Archaisms, by which was meant the survival of Arabic and Persian influences, were discarded. The percentage of such words in a sample of Uzbek language periodicals declined between 1923 and 1940 from 37% to 25%, while Russian elements increased from 2% to 15% (Kari-Nyazov, 1968, 276). In 1950, 18% of the words in a Uzbek-Turkic dictionary were of Russian origin (*Kizil Uzbekistan*, 14th April, 1952). And in a Turkish-Tatar dictionary published in 1958 there were twice as many Russian loans as there were in the 1929 edition of the same dictionary (*East Turkic Review* 4. 1960, 38).

It is undoubtedly true that the influence of Russian on the development of the new literary languages and the enrichment of the more established ones has been exceptionally pervasive. It has led to "a merging of the lexical composition of the national languages and of the lexical content of the Russian language; and through this [...] a certain merging of the lexicons of these languages among themselves." (Baskakov, 1960, 50). But this process of uniformation has been part of the process of standardization without which the languages could not have operated satisfactorily in the area of education. It is therefore an important contribution to the development of a planned and literate bilingualism. Furthermore, whatever the impact of Russian on this process it has not prevented the various languages developing their own resources, and in fact it has been claimed, not unjustifiably, that the Russian influence has "not retarded the process of development of the national languages but on the contrary promoted their flourishing." (Baskakov, 1960, 50). This is exemplified by the case of Lithuanian, where the Russian influence has tended not simply to impose an undoubtedly excessive burden of loans, but equally to develop new ways of exploiting the native resources. It is hardly necessary to illustrate the former point since the privileged place of Russian, together with its undoubted international role, has resulted in what is agreed is a flood of special Soviet terms which are no different from those introduced into other Soviet languages. In consequence there is a Lithuanian conformity with the reiterated demand for a common core of lexical items among Soviet languages.

But Russian influence has also resulted in promoting innovations which are basically true to the character of the Lithuanian language. For instance, Lithuanian follows in its own way the useful Russian practice of forming abbreviations and contractions – acronyms. From *spec* the Russian abbreviation for 'specialist', the Lithuanian counterpart *specas* has created several forms such as *specsemeniras* 'special seminar', and *speckyrius* 'special division'. The Russian characteristic of prefixed and compound words has influenced the creation of similar words in Lithuanian. The Russian *soavtor* is the analogy for the Lithuanian creation of *bendrãautoris* 'joint author'. The same is true of the creation of new Lithuanian terms by means of productive suffixes such as *-ỹste*, to produce on the analogy of the Russian *naćetćik* the Lithuanian *prisiskaĩtelis*, 'well read'. Hybridization of Russian and Lithuanian terms has become a fruitful resource – for instance – *energotraukinys* (Russian: *energogopojezd* 'mobile track for railways'). Lithuanian words have developed, mainly because of Russian influence, new, more specialized meanings while retaining their traditional ones. For instance, the verb *užãstrinti* 'to sharpen', has come to acquire an abstract or metaphoric meaning on the lines of Russian *zaostrit* 'to refine or to stress an argument'. Finally, international words borrowed through Russian help towards greater discrimination of the meaning of native parallels. For instance, in addition to the native *pìlnatis* 'plenary session', there is now in use, to refer to special political meetings, the Russian-derived foreign word *plènumas*. In effect the interaction of Lithuanian and Russian, while clearly one-sided and, because of the excessive borrowing, liable to be disadvantageous to Lithuanian, has considerable advantages in terms of enriching and refining the native resources of the language, and so permitting it to play an even more advanced role in the education of Lithuanian children and adults in the context of contemporary civilization (Salys, 1967, 47).

What is true of Lithuanian is true, also, of other languages. Whatever the degree of Russian influence it cannot rival the importance of the native element in the vocabulary, which still reflects the characteristic way of life of the speakers of a language much more than it does the external relations and the international or cosmopolitan constituents of contemporary life. Furthermore, the more isolated peoples still depend for enrichment on the resources of the languages most closely related to them by linguistic or geographical affinity. Many of the languages of the peoples of the North borrow from Tungus, Finno-Ugrian and Chinese languages. At the present time the non-Russians probably depend far more on their traditional national resources than on Russian influences. Loan translations, extensions or restriction of the meaning of words native to the language, word composition, derivation and abbreviation, are the main processes on which national languages everywhere depend for their successful adaptation to the purposes of contemporary civilization and for educational uses. It is for this reason that diverse patterns of language contact and bilingualism in speech, rather than the 'merging' of languages or usurpation by Russian of the general means of communication, will continue to characterize the educational systems of the nationalities of the USSR for a long time to come.

D.   GROWTH OF LITERACY

The consequence of the general increase in educational provision, improvement in pedagogy, as well as planned programmes of linguistic engineering among the many vernaculars has been a remarkable rise in the level of fundamental literacy. The campaign to develop the vernaculars as literary, teaching languages, was waged from the beginning of the Soviet era. But it was accelerated from 1930 onwards so that about fifty minority languages acquired alphabets for the first time. Of course liter-

TABLE 31

Literacy of the population in the Union Republics 1968 (percentages of literates in the 9-49 age group)[a]

	Both sexes				Males				Females			
	1897	1926	1939	1959	1897	1926	1939	1959	1897	1926	1939	1959
U.S.S.R.	28.4	56.6	87.4	98.5	40.3	71.5	93.5	99.3	16.6	42.7	81.6	97.8
R.S.F.S.R.	29.6	60.9	89.7	98.5	44.4	77.1	96.0	99.3	15.4	46.4	83.9	97.7
Ukrainian S.S.R.	27.9	63.6	88.2	99.1	41.7	81.1	93.9	99.6	14.0	47.2	82.9	98.8
Belorussian S.S.R.	32.0	59.7	80.8	99.0	43.5	79.1	90.7	99.5	20.7	41.3	71.4	98.6
Uzbek S.S.R.	3.6	11.6	78.7	98.1	5.6	15.3	83.6	99.0	1.2	7.3	73.3	97.3
Kazakh S.S.R.	8.1	25.2	83.6	96.9	12.0	35.4	90.3	98.8	3.6	14.5	75.8	95.1
Georgian S.S.R.	23.6	53.0	89.3	99.0	29.1	61.2	93.4	99.4	17.1	44.6	85.2	98.6
Azerbaycžhan S.S.R.	9.2	28.2	82.8	97.3	13.1	36.1	88.8	98.8	4.2	19.2	76.1	96.0
Lithuanian S.S.R.	54.2	—	76.7	98.5	57.1	—	78.7	98.9	51.4	—	75.0	98.1
Moldavian S.S.R.	22.2	—	45.9	97.8	31.2	—	59.0	99.1	12.7	—	33.1	96.6
Latvian S.S.R.	79.7	—	92.7	99.0	80.5	—	94.6	99.4	78.9	—	91.0	98.8
Kirgiz S.S.R.	3.1	16.5	79.8	98.0	5.0	23.9	84.9	99.0	0.8	8.4	74.4	97.0
Tadzhik S.S.R.	2.3	3.8	82.8	96.2	3.9	6.4	87.4	98.0	0.3	0.9	77.5	94.6
Armenian S.S.R.	9.2	38.7	83.9	98.4	14.5	53.7	92.7	99.2	2.9	22.7	74.7	97.6
Turkmen S.S.R.	7.8	14.0	77.7	95.4	11.5	18.3	83.0	97.7	2.7	8.8	71.9	93.4
Estonian S.S.R.	96.2	—	98.6	99.6	96.0	—	98.9	99.7	96.3	—	98.3	99.5

[a] Source: *Strana Sovetov za 50 let.*, 1969, 278.

acy was already fairly evident among some nationalities – for instance the
Azerbaydzhanis and the Uzbeks. The Chuvash and the so-called baptized
Tatars of the Volga basin were Christians and used Russian alphabets, as
did the Oirots in the Altai, the Abkhazians, Kabardins and Ossetes.
Among the Finno-Ugrian groups of the Volga literacy had also appeared
with Christianity very early in the 14th Century; and because of the long
tradition and the work of pioneers like N. I. Ilminsky (1822-1891), by
the end of the 19th Century there was among these people relatively
widespread literacy. The campaign among the Peoples of the North was
a later phenomenon. It began in 1927 with the establishment of *kultbazy*
(culture bases) in the Evenki Okrug, at the junction of the Tuva and
lower Tunuzka. June 25th 1930 saw the introduction of compulsory
school attendance and this helped to maintain and to develop an interest
in the use of the languages of the Far North.

Nevertheless the general picture in the Soviet Union was dark with
illiteracy. In 1897 only 28% of the whole population of the Russian
Empire were able to read and write at all. By 1926 the general level for the
population between 9 and 49 years in the whole of the USSR including a
large population which had no previous pretensions to any degree of
literacy had risen to 56%. By 1939 87% literacy had been achieved and
1959 saw this figure rise to 98%. The 1970 Census figures give an estimate
of 99.7% literacy (*Izvestiya*, April 1970). The figures for some of the
language groups and nationalities which, prior to the Revolution had
used what the regime regarded as unsatisfactory alphabets, or had not
acquired a written language at all, were equally impressive. During the
twenty three years between the two census counts, 1897 and 1920 the
level of literacy was very slow to rise among these nationalities. In Semi-
rechie and the Syr-Daria oblast the Kazakh population did not reach
more than 3% literacy. In the Angren valley the proportion who were
literate was 1%, and the same was true of the Samarkand and Transcas-
pian oblasts. The Uzbeks of the Ferghana Valley shared with the Kypshaks and Tadzhiks a literacy level of 1% though in the same area the
Kirgiz reached 4.5% (*Turkestanskaya Pravda* February, 3, 1923). Reliable
estimates show that the highest overall literacy rate among Central
Asians in 1926 was among the Kazakhs at 7%; for those between the ages
of 9 and 49 it was 25%. By 1959 these figures had risen to 52% and 97%
respectively. Among Uzbeks between the ages of 9 and 49 the percentage
rose from 3.6 in 1897 to 98 in 1959, Tadzhik 2.3 to 96, Turkmen 7.8 to
95.4%. Among minorities within Union Republics the same degree of
improvement was registered. For all ages in their populations the following figures illustrate the growth of literacy:

TABLE 32[a]

Literacy of the population of the Union Republics 1968[a]

Year	Karakalpaks	Yakuts	Uygur	Chukchi
	%	%	%	%
1926	1.3	2.0	4.5	6
1959	51.0	96.3	54.5	54

[a] Sources: 1926 and 1959 Censuses.

E. PROVISION OF LITERATURE

Corresponding to this rise in literacy, and constituting a pre-condition for it, has been the development of publishing in the non-Russian national languages. Whereas in 1913 only 10% of the newspapers were published in those languages, in 1940 there were ten times as many newspapers in all languages, and of these 25% were published in languages other than Russian, together with a total of 372 new books. Literature is now issued in a large number of languages many of them with populations of fewer than a 100 thousand – like Abazin, Abkhaz, Adygei, Altai, Balkar, Evenki, Ingush, Khakass, Khanty, Kalmyk, Lak, Nogai, Tabasaran, Tuvin and Uygur. Other languages with fewer than 12 thousand speakers publish books and newspapers – for instance Chukchi and Tat; some fewer than 8 thousand speakers – Nanai, Even, and Mansi; and some, like Eskimo, have fewer than a thousand.

The greatest impact in publishing has been made upon the Turkic peoples, who prior to the Revolution had no publishing houses, or where publishing was severely restricted. For instance within the fifty years between 1913 and 1963 titles published in Kazakh rose from 40 to 187. By 1964 the number had increased to 500, and by 1966 to 557. No Kirgiz books were published in 1913, but in 1957 over 400 titles appeared and though by 1963 the number dropped, the figure was 382 in 1966. The record of Turkmen publishing is not unlike that of the Kirgiz – none in 1913, 392 titles in 1959, in 1963 a slight reduction to 365 and a final reduction in 1966 to 307 titles. On the other hand Uzbek publications rose from 37 in 1913 to 699 in 1957, and to over 794 in 1966. Perhaps the most interesting set of figures relates to the smaller nationalities like the Mari, Mordvin and Bashkir with 135 titles in 1966, and the smaller groups in Daghestan, many of which have developed a significant publication system, Lak and Dargin having 28 publications each in 1966. (Sources: *Strana Sovetov, za 50 let* 1969, 296; *SSSR v tsifrakh* 1958, 375, and *Narodnoye khozaistvo SSSR* 1963, 613). At the same time the scholarly bases for these developments in literacy and publishing in the non-Russian national languages have not been neglected, as is evidenced by the linguistic studies on Karakalpak (Baskakov, 1951-1952), Batsbi (Desheriev, 1952), Bashkir

TABLE 33

Publication of books in the national languages of the USSR[a]

Nationality	1913		1966	
	Number of titles	Printings ('000 copies)	Number of titles	Printings ('000 copies)
Russian	23,805	80,218	54,968	1,012,515
Ukrainian	228	686	3,026	80,059
Belorussian	2	4	336	7,716
Uzbek	37	86	794	18,373
Kazakh	40	161	557	8,998
Georgian	232	453	1,657	11,408
Azerbaydzhan	91	112	1,062	9,313
Lithuanian	—	—	1,541	11,873
Moldavian	none	none	564	7,337
Latvian	—	—	1,007	10,583
Kirgiz	none	none	382	2,710
Tadzhik	none	none	372	3,614
Armenian	257	349	846	6,584
Turkmen	none	none	307	2,982
Estonian	—	—	1,453	8,960
Bashkir	none	none	135	792
Buryat	none	none	55	232
Kabardinian and Balkar	none	none	70	176
Kalmyk	none	none	17	33
Komi and Komi-Permyak	2	1	34	124
Mari (Valley and Mountain)	18	28	78	274
Mordvin (Moksha and Erzya)	none	none	53	84
Languages of the peoples of Daghestan total	16	26	176	379
Avar	3	6	28	88
Dargin	1	1	28	72
Lak	12	19	27	39
Kumyk	none	none	34	63
Lezgin	none	none	43	99
Tabasaran	none	none	12	13
Tat	none	none	4	5
Ossetian	5	3	95	152
Tatar	340	1,671	252	3,966
Tuvinian	none	none	55	234
Udmurt	19	29	23	95
Chechen and Ingush	none	none	35	147
Chuvash	56	93	111	805
Yakut	1	2	85	578

[a]   Source: *Strana Sovetov za 50 let*, 1969, 269.

and Kumyk (Dmitriev, 1948, 1940), Abazin (Genko, 1955), Uzbek (Kononov, 1948), Talysh (Miller, 1953), Tadzhik (Rastorgueva, 1954),

Avar and Dargin (Zhirkov, 1924, 1926) and among the Paleo-asiatic languages (Vdovin, 1954).

However though the new literacy meant that the speakers of many of the minority languages were able to read in their native languages for the first time the tendency towards native language literacy has not been straightforward. In the first place the more 'advanced and literate nationalities other than Russian, whose languages were fairly well established already, continued to develop their national language publications, but relatively slowly. For instance, at the nadir of the Ukrainian language in 1950, less than 2,000 titles appeared and though this number increased to 4,000 in 1958, the position again deteriorated so that in 1963, a crucial point, only 3,200 publications appeared. Between 1960 and 1963 printing in Ukrainian comprised less than half the number of titles and slightly more than two thirds the number of copies printed. The percentage of copies published by the Ukrainian publishers fell from the 80% of 1959 to 66% in 1963 (*Narodnoye Khozaistvo* 1963). In 1968 only 39% of the total of titles published in the Ukraine were in that language. (*Pechat SSSR* 1968, 95). Meanwhile, the number of books in Russian in the Ukraine rose without interruption until in 1963, for the first time, more Russian than Ukrainian books were published in the Republic (*Pechat SSSR*, 1963, 90).

Among the similarly well established Baltic languages the position has been very similar. From 1950 to 1965 the relative standing of native language books, journals and newspapers has deteriorated; in Estonia Russian publications increased from 25% to 30% of the total; in Latvia from 25% to 35%; in Lithuania from 15% to 27% (*Narodnoye Khozaistvo SSSR*, 1966). Even among Turkic nationalities the spectacular increase in native language publications to which we have referred has been matched and in some cases overtaken by publications in Russian. In 1964 in Kazakhstan titles published in Russian were half as many again as the national language publications (763 and 518). In Kirgizia the native language publications failed to equalize the Russian (393 and 410). In Tadzhikstan and Turkmenia, Russian publications, though far fewer than those in the national languages, were still considerable – 231 and 175 respectively. Only in Uzbekistan did Russian compare unfavorably – 641 Russian to 1,039 Uzbek (*Narodnoye Khozaistvo SSSR*, 1963, 613). But perhaps the most interesting instance of the competing claims of the native and Russian languages is the case of Azerbaydzhan between 1940 and 1958. During that critical period the total of copies in all languages rose from 5 to 8.3 millions, an increase of 60%. The Azerbaydzhan contribution to this increase was also exactly 60%, a rise from 3.3 to 6.5 million copies. In 1968 the total of Soviet publications was 75,699 titles, of which 76% were in Russian, and 24% in non-Russian languages. In terms of copies the respective proportions were 79% and 21%.

What we have described so far has been the part played by the two most important partners in the contemporary Soviet multilingual situation – the national language of a particular Republic and Russian. So far as literate bilingualism is concerned, the growth of fundamental literacy has meant in the first instance the establishment of the vernacular, the national language. But as we have seen, it has meant, secondarily, the rapidly growing and planned impact of Russian, promoted by centralized control of the press and publishing houses and the system of education. However, the national languages and Russian are not the only ones to be considered in any Republic. For instance, books in some minority languages, such as Polish in Lithuania, have also been supported. However, it is doubtful whether those who are bilingual in Polish and Russian or Lithuanian are without a command of the third language. Nevertheless, in general there has been an almost total failure to meet the native language needs of immigrants or, for that matter, indigenous minorities. Their attachment to the native tongue is gradually undermined and the switch to another language, usually Russian, soon follows. One important factor in this process is the absence of what might be called a 'foreign language press' for such immigrants. The UNESCO Conference on the Cultural Integration of Immigrants, 1956, reported on the "potentiality of a foreign language press to operate in respect of the first generation [...] so as to retain association with the culture of the areas of origin". Researches in the United States, especially Park (1922) and, more recently, Fishman (1966), have drawn attention to the specifically linguistic associations which the foreign language press can foster. Its absence in the USSR cannot be entirely accidental, since other aspects of language policy are very well planned. But it is a fact that, for instance, no Ukrainian newspapers or periodicals are published outside the Ukraine, in spite of the large proportion of Ukrainians involved in the West-East population movement. Of the 3,320 Ukrainian books published in 1963, only 4 were published outside the Republic. The Tatars offer another example; in 1935 there were 208 Tatar newspapers of which 80 were published outside the area. The number declined to less than half in 1956, a figure which has remained relatively stable, mainly because of combining publication in Bashkira and the Lower and Middle Volga (Bennigsen and Quelquejay, 1961, 19). Not only is the immigrant or minority press ignored but attempts to obtain copies of native language publications by exiles from the home Republic is so frustrating as to kill off any remaining interest after a little time.

Chapter 7

TYPES OF BILINGUAL EDUCATION

A. INTRODUCTION

As with other aspects of the treatment of the 'nationalities question' the approach to the organization of schools providing for bilingualism among young children and adolescents has been guided by the pronouncements of Lenin, whose view it was "that the demarcation of ethnic groups within one country is harmful. Marxists should be striving to draw them closer together". Naturally this general philosophy determines the type of schools which are approved – "we must strive for a merging of children of all nationalities into one school in a given area [...] We must decisively oppose any movement whatsoever to divide the schools according to nationality." (Lenin, 1929-1935, Vol. II). These views, in turn, were the basis for the resolution of a Conference of the Central Committee in 1913, to the effect that "the separation of schools by nationality within one country is unquestionably harmful from the standpoint of democracy in general and the interests of the class struggle of the proletariat in particular." Taken in conjunction with the acceptance of the other postulate of Soviet language policy for schools, that the mother tongue should be the language of instruction, these statements lead directly to the policy of creating bilingual or multilingual schools, with more than one language of instruction where necessary, rather than separate schools with a single teaching language.

Though this main direction of school policy has been followed, from the beginning, without any significant deviation, one can identify five points of reference in its implementation. There is first of all the relationship of Russian and the 'national languages' of the various nationalities in each administrative area, a relationship which is rapidly promoting more varied patterns of Russian-related bilingualism, and more intensive cultivation of them, than could have been the case without the planned involvement of the schools. The relationship is reflected partly in the shifting over-all balance between the use of the 'national languages' or of Russian in teaching the subjects of the school cirriculum to non-native speakers of Russian, in separate or in bilingual schools. In some cases one but not the other of the languages may be employed – Russian or the native language; in other schools both, either to separated groups or tracks or streams within the same school unit, or to all the children whatever their mother tongue. It is the bilingual school using more than one language for teaching all children that is being advocated with increasing assurance of its appropriateness at the present time.

A further point of reference in school policy is the provision for minorities (other than Russian). These minorities may be native to the Republic as is the case with the smaller ethnic groups within the RSFSR, or they may be immigrants, representing the diaspora of very much larger and otherwise separate Union Republic populations, such as Armenians in Georgia. There is a third aspect, one which, though it would not normally be included in a study of bilingual education in the accepted sense of the term, is, for various reasons, becoming an integral part of Soviet-type bilingualism, namely the teaching of foreign languages.[1] Foreign languages affect the more limited concept of bilingual education in the USSR because their compulsory inclusion in the curriculum of all children affects the students by exaggerating what is already a bias towards a linguistic component of the curriculum. It is this consideration which Khrushchev emphasized to justify his controversial Theses, suggesting as they did a system of language options which would include Russian, the national language of the Union Republic, a minority language where relevant, and a foreign language. In addition to their compulsory teaching in the normal type school other factors have served to give a novel status to foreign languages in education. The first of these is the creation of special schools where the languages are not only taught more intensively but used as a medium of instruction. A second factor is the very early introduction of foreign languages to an increasing number of infants in pre-school. This ensures that the teaching of a language like English approximates to the treatment given to Russian in areas like the Central Asian Republics, where it is no less a foreign language to large numbers, especially those living in rural areas. Finally, there is the problem of teaching Russian as a second language, as distinct from the use of that language as a teaching medium in Russian schools to non-Russian child-

[1] This, of course, is not peculiar to the Soviet Union, but characterizes all existing bilingual countries embarking on very intensive foreign language teaching.

ren. One consequence of what is generally agreed to be the ineffectiveness of the teaching of Russian is that parents are ever more anxious to send their children to Russian schools to compensate for the failure of the teaching of the language as a class subject in 'national language' schools. Maximum contact with the language in Russian schools is meant as a substitute for effective second language pedagogy.

B. TYPES OF SCHOOLS

i. *'Nationality Schools'*

a. *Non-Russian Teaching Languages*

There are two aspects of the official language policy governing the relationship of Russian and non-Russian languages in schools – in the first place, so far as concerns the actual teaching of the individual child, he is to be educated in his mother tongue, unless his parents make a positive decision to the contrary. Nevertheless there is the proviso that this principle of parents' choice "... must in no circumstances be left to take care of itself. The press, radio, the public, must conduct insistent explanatory work among the parents", who, if left to themselves, would, by implication, opt for the native language. Regard for the mother tongue has always inspired Soviet pedagogy when it is not overpersuaded by political considerations. It was emphasized in the 19th Century by Ushenskii (Goncharov, 1964), and his philosophy still governs strictly pedagogic principles. The second consideration is that Russian should be taught as a second language to all pupils. Consequently, and in order that it should be able to function according to the role set out for it, Russian was made a compulsory subject for schools in 1938. These two aspects of school policy reflect the way in which the two languages are regarded as related functionally in Soviet society generally. "... the correct policy in the linguistic development of the Soviet multi-national state" it is argued, "should be to prompt the development of the national languages to meet the vital *internal* or *local* needs of each people, while the study of Russian should be extended so as to provide for all the wider, international communication demands." (Desheriev, et al., 1966, 81). This concept is bound to have a debilitating effect on the national languages and to depress their status, since it does not encourage or promote their competence to handle the whole range of contemporary usage, broadly social, technological and literary.

The consequence of the acceptance of the national languages as media of instruction has meant that at least in each Union Republic, several of these languages are regarded as official in the sphere of education.

TABLE 34

Languages of Instruction 1959[a]

Republic	Language used	Total
Russian SFSR	Russian, Tatar, Chuvash, Mordvin, Bashkir, Udmurt, Mari, Komi, Komi-Permyak, Avar, Buryat, Ossetian, Yakut, Lezgin, Kabardin, Dargin, Kumyk, Adygei, Azerbaydzhani, Lak, Khakas, Altai, Nenets, Evenki, Khanty, Chukchi, Koryak, Abazin, Nogai, Tabasaran, Balkar, Kalmyk, Karachai, Ingush, Mansi, Tuvinian, Finnish, Chechen and Even.	39
Ukrainian SSR	Ukrainian, Russian, Moldavian, Hungarian, Polish.	5
Belorussian	Belorussian, Russian.	2
Uzbek SSR	Uzbek, Russian, Kazakh, Tadzhik, Kirgiz, Karakalpak, Turkmen.	7
Kazakh SSR	Kazakh, Russian, Uzbek, Tadzhik, Uygur, Dungan.	6
Georgian SSR	Georgian, Russian, Armenian, Azerbaydzhani, Ossetian, Abkhaz.	6
Azerbaydzhan SSR	Azerbaydzhani, Russian, Armenian, Lezgin.	4
Lithuanian SSR	Lithuanian, Russian, Polish.	3
Moldavian SSR	Moldavian, Russian, Ukrainian.	3
Latvian SSR	Latvian, Russian.	2
Kirgiz SSR	Kirgiz, Russian, Uzbek, Tadzhik, Kazakh, Turkmen	5
Tadzhik SSR	Tadzhik, Russian, Uzbek, Kirgiz, Kazakh, Turkmen	6
Armenian SSR	Armenian, Russian, Azerbaydzhani	3
Turkmen SSR	Turkmen, Russian, Uzbek, Kazakh.	4
Estonian SSR	Estonian, Russian	2

[a]   Source: *Kulturnaya Strana SSSR* 1959, 186-190.

The official recognition of so many teaching languages stems from the policy pursued rigorously for many years after the Revolution. During the early period when concessions were made to the pluralist concept, the Ukraine, for instance, gradually substituted the national language for Russian as the teaching language of most of its schools, and the Commissariat of Education declared its intention to give the local population the right to determine the language in which the school should be taught (*Zbornik Uzakonen*, 1919, Sect. 260). It is not surprising, therefore, that by 1927 over 93% of Ukrainian speaking children received their elementary education in their mother tongue, and 83% in Secondary schools, amounting to 75% of the total child population (Bilinsky, 1968, 418). Up to 1935 this position was not only held but in some cases improved, so that the percentage of the child population in Ukrainian language schools corresponded very nearly to the proportion of Ukrainians in the Republic population: 83%. This was due partly to the extension of education into the rural areas, the main bastion of the national language (Weinstein, 1942, 142). Since that time the number of schools in which Ukrainian has been the teaching language has declined from 84% in 1959 to 82% in 1967-1968 (*Pravda Ukraini* Nov. 3, 1968, 2). When it comes to the urban areas and especially the cities the decline has been quite precipitous. Thus in 1965 there were only 56 Ukrainian schools in L'vov – 65% of the total. The position in Kiev in 1959 was even more discouraging: although the proportion of Ukrainians in the population was more than 60%, Ukrainian schools accounted for no more than 41% of the total, and even these were unsatisfactory from the point of view of the age range for which they catered (Bilinsky, 1968, 181).

The liberal policy of the first two decades of the regime is reflected in the high percentage of pupils taught in the national language schools of other Republics in the USSR. In 1927 90% of Belorussian speaking children were taught in their national language. The Armenians and Georgians competed for the highest provision: 98.5% and 98% respectively. In view of the accelerating tendency at present to transfer from the native language in elementary schools to Russian in the secondary schools, it is significant that some nationalities in the early years, during the period of *korenizatsiya*, had very high percentages of national language secondary school instruction. Nationalities, for which we have information, are Azerbaydzhanis (93.8%), Tatars (77%), Tadzhiks (54%). In Uzbekistan there were schools where tuition was conducted in Uzbek, Russian, Tadzhik, Kazakh, Tatar, Korean, Armenian, Yiddish and several others. This was in 1935. By 1960-1961 only Uzbek, Russian, Tadzhik, Kirgiz, Turkmen and Karakalpak were used.

The rate of decline in the schools of these different nationalities has not been uniform. For instance in the Ukraine during the 12 years following Stalin's death the decline in use of national languages in schools was not great – from 83.4% in 1953 to 82.6% in 1965 (*Narodnoye Khozaistvo SSSR*, v 1965 240-241). In Belorussia the fall was not much steeper: 90% in 1927 to 78% in 1955, and this during a period of more than average stringency for the language. Among the Azerbaydzhanis, however, there was a 27% fall to 71% in 1963. The same rapid decline is found among Tatar children; in 1927 77% attended national schools, by 1939 there was only provision for 46.8%; in 1956 this fell to 34% and to 31% in 1960, a decline of over 50% during 30 years. Among Turkmen children the percentage attending national schools actually rose from 61.5% in 1938 to 69.7% in 1958, though even among the Turkmen the proportion of Turkmen speakers living in urban areas, who were taught in Turkmen medium schools was very low: 13.7% of the Turkmen-speaking population, which was 29.7% of the total population of Turkmenia.

b. *Training of Teachers for Non-Russian Schools*

A major problem is the training of sufficient teachers of the various national languages, who are also competent in Russian, and of a sufficient number of teachers who are able to teach the subjects of the curriculum in a national language other than Russian. Naturally the difficulties are increased by the inaccessibility of the areas inhabited by the various nationalities and by the fact that the long history of poor educational provision makes it difficult to recruit students with satisfactory qualifications for entry to teacher Colleges. The vicissitudes of the Abkhaz language is much to the point here. It was the language of instruction until 1945, when it was replaced by Georgian. It regained its status in 1956, but owing to the lack of teachers competent to teach and use the language the restitution of status was far from complete (Bennigsen and Quelquejay 1961, 51). The extension of the statutory period of education first to 7 and in 1959 to 8 years, meant that there were relatively fewer competent teachers to handle education in non-Russian languages.

Again, it was reported in 1949 that 60% of the teachers in the schools of the far north had to be recruited from outside that vast area; to attract candidates, teachers in the far north were paid a bonus amounting to 20% to 50% of their basic salaries (*Nar. Obr.* Sept. 1966, 46). But this step, without the kind of preparation which the difficulties of these schools made necessary, could do nothing to make the teachers, attracted by such special conditions, suitable for teaching the languages. The huge Evenki area is a good example. In 1947 very few more teachers were available than the two native speaking teachers who were employed in its 19 schools over 12 years earlier. A training college existed, but it did little to alleviate what the local inspector of schools reported as "an acute shortage of national teaching cadres". The Institute of Peoples of the North, which developed from the Leningrad Institute of Geography, following the work of 'Committee for the Assistance and Protection of the Peoples of the North and Siberia', founded two years earlier, was of little immediate assistance, because the nationality schools did not produce students who were good enough to gain entry to the Leningrad Institute. It was no wonder, therefore, that the teachers of the Evenki were almost exclusively of Russian origin, with little command of the national language (Kolarz, 1967, 63).

The difficulties of these people had been realized during the very early days of the existence of the Union, and the Leningrad Institute, now incorporated administratively in the Herzen Institute had pioneered successfully, but mainly in the study of the history and structure of the languages. The first twelve specialists in Northern Languages graduated from the Leningrad Institute of Geography in 1926; they carried their theoretical knowledge from academic philology (promoted by the work of Stralenberg and later by Scandinavian, Russian and German scholars) into the field. 1926, too, saw the first group of young northerners enter the preparatory teacher courses of Leningrad University. By 1928 their number had risen to 200 and in 1930 the Institute of the Peoples of the North was set up as an independent establishment. It was both a research centre and a teacher training college. In collaboration with the Leningrad University Laboratory of Phonetics directed by Shcherba alphabets for 14 nationality languages were envisaged, but eventually those which were proposed for Itelmen, Keti and Saami did not materialize. In the languages which were provided with alphabets, text books for the two junior classes were written although, because the teachers were still mainly Russian speaking, cribs in that language were provided.

By 1960 it was established that a hundred students, five from each main northern nationality should be admitted to Leningrad each year. These are tenth grade students, and they follow a course broadly similar to that of the majority of students of the Herzen Institute, namely a three-year academic course followed by two years professional training. However, the students from the North remain for a sixth year to prepare for their specific assignments to "promote a bilingual education, and to perfect their knowledge of Russian, of the appropriate national language, and to acquaint themselves with the problems of using the minority language for teaching subjects up to the 8th grade". (Lewis, 1962c, 14). Special grants and accommodation are available to the students from the Far North both in the Herzen Institute and in the Faculty of Northern Peoples in the University of Leningrad. In 1962 the Minister of Education of the RSFSR spoke of the "special attention being paid to the development of the network of teacher-training schools in the national republics, in the districts of Siberia and the Far North, to meet similar demands to those then being met at the Herzen Institute and the University of Leningrad" (Afanasenko, 1962).

This kind of provision for teachers in bilingual schools embraces a comprehensive system of in-service training also. In the national language schools, for instance those in the North Ossetian Autonomous Republic, the main problem, as the administrators see it, is the teaching of Russian as a second language. Monthly courses are organized in the summer for students of the lower grades, with the intention partly of improving the competence of these pupils in Russian; but partly, if not mainly, to enable the teachers themselves to experiment with and to develop new techniques and materials. Russian language societies are also formed in each school and these are attended by the teachers, mainly of the lower grade pupils. "The training of teachers in the primary grades is arranged in such a way that in 3 or 4 years they will complete instruction at 2 year regular and correspondence advanced courses, thereby making it possible to employ Russian as the language of instruction in all primary grades" (Galazov, 1965, 49).

The whole problem of teaching children of the Northern Peoples and other nationalities as well, is the concern of the 'Scientific-Research Institute of the Nationality Schools' of the Academy of Pedagogical Sciences. This was set up in 1949 for the precise purpose of studying methods of teaching both Russian and other national languages. It has four branches in various ASSR's of the Russian Union Republic and experimental schools in others, for instance Mordvin, Buryat, Chuvash and Kabarda. Though the competence of the Academy of Pedagogical Sciences of the RSFSR does not extend automatically to other Union Republics it co-operates very intimately with associated institutes elsewhere, for instance the Tashkent Institute, the Institute in Tbilisi, and the Pedagogical Institute in Erevan which have separate Georgian and Russian, and Armenian and Russian sections respectively. Co-operatively these institutes study the situation of minority linguistic groups in the educational systems. They prepare textbooks for teaching the various tongues, as first and as second languages, and publish selected vocabularies. They also adapt text books in the Russian language on a variety of subjects of the curriculum for teaching in other national languages. Specially prepared general subject text books in Russian, for instance geography, do not seem to be available for those students who are speakers of other languages but who are being taught in Russian. (Lewis, 1962c, 14).

ii. *Non-Russian Minority Schools*

The liberal attitude to national languages during the first two decades of the Soviet regime was reflected in a concern for even small minority groups in most of the Republics, whether they were indigenous or immigrants. Thus up to 1925 the Ukraine provided schools for Jews (2.9% of the school population), Germans (1.4%), Poles (0.9%), Belorussians, Czechs, Hungarians and Tatars. There were separate Bureaux to conduct these schools and separate systems of inspection. The RSFSR had schools for Ukrainians who had a minority of 5.5% in the Republic. Of the total Armenian immigrant population in Russia 56% sent their children to Armenian language schools. This minority facility gradually declined, and in some cases even the principle of minority provision is no longer regarded. For instance, in the Ukraine the number of Jews and Poles attending their own schools was halved by 1935 and 5 years later, only Moldavians and Uzbeks were able to maintain their own schools. At present, apart from the provision for the indigenous minorities of the Republic, no schools for minorities are recorded in the RSFSR. Belorussian immigrant minority provision disappeared in 1959, and Ukrainian schools even earlier, 1937. A decline in minority provision has long been apparent in other Republics too. Armenian medium schools, which met the needs of 12% of the school population of Azerbaydzhan in 1940, now account for only 5.4% (1959 Census, Armenian vol., 102). It is not surprising that if the major national groups cannot succeed in safeguarding their own schools when they are minorities in exile, it is most unlikely that small nationalities can do so. Thus whereas in 1935 there were, for instance, Assyrian schools in Transcaucasia (Kolarz, 1952, 249), there is now no record of any such schools. It must not be assumed, however, that whenever a minority school is closed the children of the minority have adopted Russian as the language of instruction. Among the Poles in the Ukraine and Belorussia, who gave up their own schools, and among the Uzbeks of Tadzhikstan, who lost their minority schools, two-thirds chose to attend non-Russian national language schools and only one-third the Russian language schools. An even more interesting case is that of the Bashkir in their own area, who, on relinguishing their own national schools, chose to attend the Tatar schools in preference to Russian, largely because of their close cultural, ethnic and linguistic ties with the former.

It has been argued persuasively that because the number of children attending minority schools decreased only slightly from 35% in 1955 to 33% in 1964, there is no warrant for the conclusion that minority provision is greatly at risk (Lipset, 1967, 188). However, even if the official estimates are accepted without qualification, the argument does not sufficiently take into account the enormous increase in migration already described or the consequent need to distinguish precisely between minority provision for such immigrants and that for the long standing indigenous or native groups who are minorities only by administrative rule or *fiat*. The traditional minorities usually occupy compact and clearly delimited areas and to that extent are not minorities but traditional enclaves and in some instances they could have autonomous status.

The following languages are used as media of instruction in their own Union Republics only: Estonian, Latvian, Lithuanian and Belorussian. The following, though minority languages in their Union Republics are not minority languages in their own specific territorial areas within Union Republics, but they are confined as teaching languages to those areas, in spite of the fact that there are representatives of those groups spread unevenly in the RSFSR: Tatar, Chuvash, Mordvin, Bashkir, Udmurt, Mari, Komi, Avar, Buryat, Yakut, Kabardin, Dargin, Kumyk, Adygei, Lak, Khakass, Altai, Nenets, Evenki, Khanty, Chukchi, Koryak, Abazin, Nogai, Chechen, Even, Mansi, Tuvin, Karachai, Ingush, Tabasaran, Balkar, Kalmyk. Where there are minorities of these peoples outside their own administrative area their languages are not used as languages of instruction. On the face of it the number of minority languages used in the various Republics, but omitting the RSFSR, is impressive,

TABLE 35

Where and which languages are used in minority schools[a]

Language	Union Republics														
	RSFSR	Ukrainian SSR	Belorussian	Uzbek	Kazakh	Georgian	Azerbaydzhan	Lithuanian	Moldavian	Latvian	Kirgiz	Tadzhik	Armenian	Turkmen	Estonian
Russian	×	×	×	×	×	×	×	×	×	×	×	×	×	×	×
Ukrainian									×						
Finnish	×														
Kirgiz				×											
Abkhaz						×									
Ossetian						×									
Lezgin							×								
Moldavian		×													
Hungarian	×														
Polish		×						×							
Turkmen				×									×		
Armenian						×	×								
Azerbaydzhan	×					×									
Tadzhik				×	×							×			
Kazakh				×								×	×	×	
Uzbek					×							×	×	×	

[a]   Source: *Kulturnaya Strana SSSR* 1956 and Lipset, 1967, 185-186.

but it will be noted that of these languages Uzbek (4), Kazakh (4), Tadzhik (4), Tatar (2) and Armenian (2) represent language groups living along the borders of the Republics concerned or in very close proximity. In fact most of the minority schools that remain exist, almost without exception, for long standing indigenous minorities or neighbouring enclaves rather than for new populations. This can be exemplified by the case of the Tatars, 50% of whose Tatar medium schools are outside the ASSR (*Natsionalnyye shkoly RSFSR* 1958, 180). Nearly all of those outside the Autonomous Republic are in the neighbouring Bashkira with which it has extremely close linguistic and cultural affinities.

Finally we should record not only the minorities which were, until recently at any rate, provided with their own schools, but the sometimes very large minorities which have not been able at all to have their own schools in exile. For instance, according to the 1970 Census, there were 578 thousand Tatars in the Uzbek Republic, 284 thousands in Kazakhstan, 69 thousands in Kirgizia, 71 thousands in Tadzhikstan, but they have had no minority schools since well before 1959. There were 125 thousand Gagauz in Moldavia, 25 thousand Uygurs in Kirgizstan who were also without schools in their own languages. There were over 50 thousand Uzbeks, 21 thousand Kirgiz, 96 thousand Azerbaydzhanis and 23 thousand Turkmens in the RSFSR and in some other parts of the western areas (Moldavia, the Ukraine, Belorussia and the Baltic) without their own schools. In fact the undoubted decline of minority schools has been commented upon in the Soviet press. For instance, Khanazarov wrote in 1960: "During the period of developing Socialist construction, in the 1938-1939 school session Uzbekistan provided schools where instruction was conducted in 22 languages [...] The provision even made it possible for a Polish family to have its child taught in the mother tongue [...] The policy has recently led to parents choosing to send their children not to the minority school but to Russian medium schools. There are in Uzbekistan now schools for minorities in only 7 languages, and these are the neighbouring Central Asian languages, in addition to Russian. At the same time, 50% of the Russian medium schools consist of Ukrainian, Belorussian, Jewish, Armenian, Mordvin, Kazakh and other minorities.' (*Voprosy razvitiya*, 340).

Although the situation of minority schools in the RSFSR is the most extreme case it is not, perhaps, untypical of what is happening to these schools throughout the USSR. After the period of *korenizatsiya* the only minorities who have anything like a satisfactory provision are those who are either indigenous to the administrative area of the Union Republic, have close linguistic or cultural affinities, like the Central Asia Nationalities, or are historical enclaves bordering on large nationalities. For instance, apart from the Azerbaydzhanis all the minority languages which are used for teaching in the RSFSR are spoken by nationalities which are historically native to the areas in which they live and have, in many cases, Autonomous status. Moreover, if we take account of how widespread is the incidence of the Peoples of the North, sometimes large language communities, the relatively small number, 600, of their national language schools, anywhere in the North, is noteworthy. The spread of minority school provision is severely limited.

iii. *Bilingual or Parallel-Medium Schools*

The school language policy pursued in the USSR reinforces the tendencies towards greater penetration by Russian. This means the probable decline of traditional bilingualism as the smaller minority groups are assimilated. For instance, the Yagnobi and Pamiri groups no longer maintain their national identities in any real sense but regard themselves as Tadzhiks, though they retain their own languages to some extent. It also means, as we have seen, a considerable rise in the number of non-Russian students who are bilingual in the novel sense of having received their formal schooling in their second language, Russian. This is the undoubted long-term aim of educational policy; and such an aim, it is argued more and more cogently by Soviet educationists, is best achieved by creating schools where there is parallel instruction – in Russian and the 'national language,' rather than by increasing the exclusively Russian medium schools for non-Russian children or separate 'national' or minority schools. These bilingual or parallel-medium schools are not a new phenomenon in what have now become parts of the USSR. For instance, between 1860-1889, Ibrahim Altensarin (Altynsarai), who considered himself a Kirgiz, though he worked hard to establish the Kazakh language, founded several such schools in which both Russian and Kazakh were used as teaching languages. His intention was mainly to promote Russian without depressing the status, or loosening the hold of the national language on those who spoke it. Usually, however, in the 19th Century the two languages were taught to all children in what were, therefore, dual or mixed, rather than parallel medium schools.[2] This was the custom during the first decades of the Soviet regime also. From 1930 onwards, however, dual medium schools were forbidden, and where both languages are used the different language groups have to be separated according to the wishes of the parents (De Witt, 1961, 112). These become 'parallel medium' schools.

Soviet scholars are profoundly interested in bilingual education and the Alma Ata conference of 1962 after calling for studies of languages in contact in the different areas goes on to specify the need for a further conference to consider types of bilingualism, its nature in the USSR and how school organizations can best promote the advantages to be derived from it (*Voprosy Razvitiya*, 373-7). Without question the inclusion of information about the degree of bilingualism involving non-Russian indigenous languages in the 1970 Census was one of the results of the 1962 conference. That information, in Tables 2 and 25 combined, gives a picture of very high levels of bilingualism, and even when allowance is made for the undoubted fact that very large numbers are common to both tables the level of bilingualism must still be significantly high. This and the political recognition of the need to promote bilingualism accounts for the attention the question receives from such periodicals as *Russkiy yazyk v natsional'noi shkole*, where it is recognized that the "Soviet people, as a clearly defined historical community, is characterized in

---

[2] A dual medium school employs both languages at different times in teaching all the children, though not necessarily in all subjects. A parallel medium school separates the children into parallel language groups, and uses only the native language with each. A mixed medium school is one which may use both languages in the same lesson.

respect of language by the development of a stable, durable and purely voluntary bilingualism." At the same time while it is not surprising, considering that the professed aims of the journal are to promote the teaching and use of Russian, it is nevertheless disappointing to educationists interested in an enlightened bilingual policy to find that the Journal interprets the question largely if not exclusively in terms of acquiring Russian as a second language – "A constantly growing number of parents send their children to Russian schools or raise the question of the change-over in a greater or lesser degree, of national schools to the Russian language of instructions." (*Russkiy yazyk v shkole*, No. 6, 1963, 4-5).

Many educationists however are disturbed by the segregation of the ethnic and linguistic groups brought about by exclusive types of different language medium schools, often in the same neighbourhood. For several reasons, therefore there is a drive towards the establishment of schools where different language groups are brought together, while safeguarding the principle of choice of medium for the individual child. Usually, but not invariably, the languages concerned are Russian and the 'national languages'. Sometimes three languages are used in schools which have three language tracks like Collective Farm 10, near Stalingrad during 1962 – Russian, Uzbek and Tadzhik (Personal observation). There are instances of schools in which four languages are used – Kirgiz, Uzbek, Tadzhik and Russian (*Narodnoye obrazovaniye*, 1965, 3, 9).

The rationale for the establishment of such schools is complex. In the first place, it is sometimes stated quite openly that though the child attending such schools may not actually be taught in Russian, yet since Russian tends to be the language of play, he acquires a ready facility in it. It is in any case recognized that in such schools the "common language of the pupils in all extra class activities is Russian, which is the language of school administration." (*Norodnoye obrazovaniye*, 1965, 3, 9). On the other hand more liberal motives are sometimes acknowledged. Secondary School No. 55 in Riga was reported in 1966 as having provided parallel Latvian and Russian classes for over six years, with the result that 'more than 1,000 Latvian and Russian children learned to live as one family.' Both languages were used in all out of school activities. There are now over 240 such schools in Latvia, enrolling more than a third of the total school population; and the intention is that any new schools that are established should follow this pattern. The Director of School 55 claims that the experience of the joint instruction of Latvian and Russian children in such schools fosters mutual respect among the two linguistic groups (*Pravda* 5-4-1966). That this estimate of their achievement is not an empty boast is borne out by the experience of a foreign observer who, in 1965, visited the Central Asian Republics. He agreed that "multi-national co-education [...] apart from its primary aim of Russiffication and *sblizheniye*, in practice means that from their earliest years young Slavs, Kazakhs, Kirgiz, Tadzhiks and many other Asian nationalities [...] are working and playing together. This co-education may go far to destroy the racial and linguistic barriers among the Central Asian nationalities, which were formerly endemic here." (*Central Asian Revien*, XIII. 1, 1965, 13).

Bilingual schools were fairly popular in some areas during the early period. In 1927 nearly 7% Ukrainian children of elementary age were in such schools, which provided for 2.1% of the total school population. In Kharkov province the figure was as high as 49% (*Statistika Ukraini*, 1928, 20. 21). In the thirties in Turkestan 12.0% of the pupils attended bilingual schools, but this type of school became less popular there, the percentage dropping from 12.0% to 7% in 1956 (*Kulturnaya Strana*, 1940, 74, and 1956, 186). The number of Azerbaydzhan-plus-Russian bilingual schools increased from 158 in 1940, 183 in 1953, 231 in 1959, to 295 in 1963, accounting for over 16% of the total (*Azerbaydzhan v tsifrakh*, 1964, 192-193). In Uzbekistan the percentage of such schools rose from 10% in 1960 to 17% in 1963, accounting for a total of over a thousand schools (*Voprosy filologii*, 1963, No. 6, 11). In the Tashkent Oblast, 50% of the pupils attended bilingual schools. In Kirgizia there were 300 parallel medium schools in 1964 (*Kommunist*, 1964, 12, 19). In Kazakhstan there were 1,962 schools with classes in Russian and one or more of the 'national' languages in 1962. Boarding schools are very often 'bilingual' in one or other of the forms we have described (*Pravda*, 29-5-1962).

The bilingual schools, whatever theoretical justification may be offered for their establishment, are often convenient organizations when there are insufficient numbers to constitute different and separate language medium schools. Short of creating separate nationality schools, which for various reasons parents are becoming more reluctant to demand, the parallel medium school seems to them to offer the best of both worlds, ensuring a command of Russian that is likely to be more advanced than when it is promoted only by class teaching of the language, and maintaining the mother tongue, at least during the period of elementary education. Nevertheless, the official support for their establishment is a combination of concern to establish the Russian language as 'a second mother tongue' and to avoid the possibly adverse consequences of early segregation. The 'bilingual school' in the USSR as in most countries where any two languages do not meet on equal terms is generally an intermediate stage to final subordination of the 'national language'. In the long term it is bound to facilitate Russification, though in the short term it maintains some support for national languages more effectively than does a Russian medium school where the mother tongue has very little chance of maintaining its role in the bilingual partnership.

iv. *Russian Medium Schools for Non-native Speakers of Russian*

When we come to consider the position of the Russian medium school for non-native speakers of Russian the developments have been very different from those in which the previous types of schools have been involved. This fact is not difficult to understand in view of the complex linguistic situation in many areas, to say nothing of the ideological, and political pressures to which communities are exposed. The Russian schools in the non-Russian speaking areas are usually *multi-national* organizations. All schools in Daghestan cities receive children from 5 to 25 nationalities. School No. 7 in the city of Maikop in the Krasnodar region is attended by children of twelve linguistic groups. In the city of Kzyl-Orda, in Kazakhstan, there is one school, Saken Seifullin School, which recruits members of 30 nationalities, while in Frunze, School No. 23 has 19 different linguistic groups. In 1964 there were 317 such multi-national Russian language schools in Kirgizia, and the number is increasing rapidly (see Table 36).

In the 1966-1967 school year there were at least 400 such schools in Daghestan, nor is this surprising. For example in the little village of Tataiurt in the Babaiurt region the 508 children included representatives of 16 nationalities of whom the Russians, 113, were the majority, followed by 109 Chechens (the native population), Kumyks, 70 etc. Every class has at least one representative of each nationality. In the Daghestanskie Ogni settlement, of the 2,000 children in 1968 the native Dargins accounted for only 174, while the other linguistic groups included Kumyks (52), Mountain Jews (22), Ossetians (10), Avars (9), Laks (9), Tatars (8), Ukrainians (9), Rutuls (6), Armenians (5), Belorussians, Greeks, Aguls and several others. In such an area it is impossible to set up either separate schools or schools in which all the languages are used. The almost inevitable result is a school in which the lingua franca, Russian, is the sole language of instruction. The parents of School No. 4 in the city of Derbent, it is said, insisted on the school becoming a Russian language school since it was difficult for 9 nationalities among the 1,400 children, including Azerbaydzhanis (917), Tabasarans (211), and Lezgins (46) to receive comparable education, each in his own language. (Garunov, 1970, 10-13).

The situation as might be expected is even more severely aggravated among the small indigenous minority nations in the RSFSR, as Table 37 indicates.

In the early liberal period however, there was no great disparity between the proportion of the children attending Russian schools and the proportion of Russians in the locality: the Russian school was in the early days meant to cater to the native speakers of Russian. In the Ukraine, for in-

TABLE 36

Use of Russian and other languages as media of instruction in Union Republics[a]

	% of Russian medium schools	% of pupils in Russian sections	No. of languages used
USSR	59	65	59
RSFSR	90	94	45
Ukrainian SSR	14	26	5
Belorussian SSR	5	22	2
Uzbek SSR	6	20	7
Kazakh SSR	43	66	6
Georgian SSR	7	20	6
Azerbaydzhan SSR	5	23	4
Lithuanian SSR	3	11	3
Moldavian SSR	27	33	3
Latvian SSR	21	33	2
Kirgiz SSR	19	49	5
Tadzhik SSR	2	16	6
Armenian SSR	5	9	4
Turkmen SSR	7	21	4
Estonian SSR	6	22	2

[a] Source: *culturnaya Strana SSR* 1956, 186-187.

TABLE 37

Percentage of pupils in autonomous Republics, regions or districts attending Russian medium schools[a]

Area	% of pupils	Area	% of pupils	Area	% of pupils
Bashkir ASSR	65	Tatar ASSR	63	Komi Permyak	
Buryat-Mongol		Udmurt ASSR	85	Region	71
ASSR	88	Chuvash ASSR	56	Koryak Permyak	
Dargin ASSR	61	Yakut ASSR	55	Region	87
Kabardin ASSR	76	Adygei Region	89	Evenki Permyak	
Komi ASSR	76	Altai Region	85	Region	98
Mari ASSR	71	Khakass Region	94	Nenets Permyak	
Mordvin ASSR	77	Cherkess Region	91	Region	96
N. Ossetian ASSR	81	AGA Region	68		

[a] Source: *Kulturnaya Strana* 1958, 206-209.

stance the percentage of Russians in the population was 9.2, and the percentage of children in Russian schools was only slightly greater in the elementary classes, 10.6, though rising quite considerably in the secondary schools to 15%. By 1935, with only a small change in the proportion of Russians in the communities the proportion of children in Russian schools at the elementary level had reached 12.7% (Weinstein, 1942, 130-142).

The number of schools catering for the Ukrainians in their own language compared with the number of Russian schools dropped. In 1940 Russian schools accounted for 10% of the total but by 1959 this had risen to 15%. This increase in the number of schools meant, inevitably, that an even greater proportion of the pupils were being educated in Russian because the urban-rural disparity operated to favour the Russians who attended the very much larger city schools. Furthermore the city schools reflected the greatly Russianized proportion of the population (Goldhagen, 1968, 48, Note 35). Thus, while the percentage of Russians in the city of Kiev at the time of the 1959 Census was only 23, nearly 60% of the schools were Russian. In Belorussia, similarly, the demand for Russian medium schools has grown from 11.7% in 1927 to 22.5% in 1959, and from 14% (of the number of schools) in 1959 to nearly 16% in 1964 (*Bilinsky*, 1968, 419).

Among Turkmens also there has been a considerable rise in the number of children taught in Russian: from 13.2% in 1938 to 22% in 1955, and the trend has continued, until it reached 28% in 1964. In the cities the tendency is even more marked, naturally. In the city of Ashkabad, Turkmens accounted for 30% of the population and of these over 96% claimed Turkmen as their native language. However, of the 24 schools in the city, 21 (87%) were Russian medium schools. Since fewer than half the Turkmen-speaking children were taught in their mother tongue (13.7% of the 30% who comprised the Turkmen element in the population), it can be assumed that Russian schools claimed not only the Russified Turkmens but a considerable number of Turkmens who still regarded their national language as the mother tongue. (*Kult. Str. Turk. SSSR*, 1963, 76). The same is true of the Azerbaydzhanis among whom the number of Russian schools declined slightly between 1938 and 1963 – from 173 to 166, but where the proportion of children taught in those schools rose from 18.8% to 23.4%. Of those attending Russian schools or Russian streams of bilingual schools, a considerable number still claimed Azerbaydzhan as their mother-tongue – 12% in 1940, rising to over double that figure in 1960 (Allakhiarov, 1966, 36). In 1959 it was said that a quarter of Kazakh children were attending Russian schools (*Kommunist*, 13, 1959). In Uzbekistan at the same time, 10% of the children attending Russian language schools were non-native speakers of that language (Khanazarov, 1963, 201). In the Baltic Republics though there are differences between the three members of the group, the move towards the use of Russian as the teaching language, though noticeable has not progressed so far or so rapidly as in other Republics. In Lithuania the increase has been from 10.1% to 12% in the twelve years between 1953 and 1965.

Some of the changes in the proportions of children being taught in Russian have been due to increases in the proportion of Russians in the contributing populations. However, there is a considerable disparity, even allowing for such increases, between the proportion of Russian immigrants and the proportion of children taught in that language. One reason for this is that other immigrant groups choose Russian rather than the national language of the Republics in which they live, partly because separate schools for minorities are provided too rarely, and partly because since parents have to select a non-native language school in any case the advantage is in favour of Russian. But even allowing for this further consideration, it remains a fact that sometimes nearly as many as three times more children choose Russian than might be justified by the numerical composition of the population. Such is the case in Belorussia, Moldavia and Armenia. In Georgia the ratio is 2 to 1, as it is in Azerbaydzhan also. The disparity is not as great in the other Republics, and it will be noted that it is lowest among the Baltic Republics where the figure is 11 to 9. Tables 36 and 37 show that, whatever the disparity, Russian is used to teach a considerable and an increasing number of pupils for whom it is in effect a second language. It may even be the third language, if they are brought up in traditional bilingual areas. Consequently Russian is rapidly becoming the only common element in a large number of different bilingual or multi-lingual repertoires of individual children from an early age.

C. TEACHING RUSSIAN AS A SECOND LANGUAGE[3]

The fourth aspect of bilingual education in the USSR is the teaching of the Russian language in all schools, whatever the medium of instruction may be. It is the only language which is granted this privilege. In consequence, the undoubted usefulness of Russian as a lingua franca and its prestige as a language of wider communication are not only reflected in but strongly reinforced by its compulsory inclusion in all curricula, from the first grade onwards. The resolution of the 7th All Russian Conference of the Communist Party, April, 1917, called for the 'abolition of a compulsory state language', but after twenty years, in 1938, it was decreed that Russian should be introduced in all schools. So far as education is concerned it is to all intents and purposes a compulsory state language and is regarded as such. For some time after 1938 its teaching commenced in the third class, but it is now the common practice to commence formal teaching wherever possible in the middle of the first year. Furthermore, there has been every encouragement to establish preparatory classes, preschool instruction, especially in the rural areas, in order that children should at least become acquainted with the sounds and vocabulary of

[3]   See table 25, chapter 4, p. 148.

what is virtually a foreign language, before they are taught other subjects in that language when they enter the elementary school. In 1946 it was decreed that preparatory classes should be created for the Daghestan group of nationalities, North Ossetian, Buryat Mongols, Kabardin and Yakut, together with those of the Oirot, Adygei, Khakass and Tuva autonomous regions. This provision has been constantly extended and in 1965 classes for even younger children were introduced. Experience has shown, it was claimed, "that this training is most effective in the kindergarten [...] In the North Ossetian villages where there are no kindergarten it is necessary to create health centres for children entering the first grade and to direct students in teaching colleges to them for practice teaching." (Galazov, 1965, 51).

From the beginning, to support the pressure on the teaching of Russian, there was scholarly interest in the theoretical, academic and practical problems of second language pedagogy. Even during the turmoil of war, in 1940 onwards, a Commission of Education was created to discuss the main difficulties of second language teaching and this resulted in a circular on 'Teaching the Russian Language in non-Russian Schools' (1941). At this time too, Chistiakov (1941), published his standard textbook on second language methodology. Between 1938 and the issue of the 1941 circular, however, others had been active preparing materials for second language teaching. 165 textbooks were published, many of them designed for particular non-Russian language groups, over 43 of which were catered for. In 1956 Tashkent was chosen for the venue of the first Inter-Republican Conference on The Study of Russian in National Schools with special reference to Muslim nationalities. The discussions produced practical suggestions concerning the relevance of the oral approach and the more economical use of a readjustment of the time available for teaching Russian. Between 1960 and 1964 new syllabuses and textbooks were produced and though there have been some modifications of these, affecting different grades successively, and designed usually to reduce the amount of theoretical grammar and the weight of vocabulary, the 1964 models are still employed. This was observed recently among Karakalpak and Uzbek school children (Personal observation).

Considerable attention has been given to the preparation of teachers who in very many instances were not trained initially to teach Russian or any other second language, particularly in elementary schools. One of the resolutions discussed at the Tashkent Conference of 1956 concerned the training of teachers of Russian to speakers of other languages and the possible creation of special institutes. Soon after the war a beginning was made to improve this training. The Kazan, and especially the Zhdanov Institutes are early instances of places where this work was done. Nevertheless the early 60's witnessed considerable uneasiness about the quality of Russian teaching. Specialist teachers of the language were used in elementary schools, but they were too academic and their use was wasteful. It was proposed in *Uchitelskaya Gazeta* that all primary school teachers should be trained in Russian second language pedagogy. (*Uchitelskaya Gazeta*, 25-9 and 22-11-1962). In 1963 was created the Tashkent Institute to recruit and train students from the whole of Central Asia, not dissimilar in conception to the Institute for the Peoples of the North at the Herzen Institute of the University of Leningrad. At the end of 1963 it had 1,700 students, and 2,200 in 1969.

In addition, professional journals appeared with special articles or symposia on Russian as a second language. The main professional journal for all teachers of Russian, *Russkiy yazyk v shkole* 'The Russian Language in School' regularly deals with second language issues; but the journal which is specifically concerned with our particular problems is *Russkiy yazyk v natsional'noi shkole* 'The Russian Language in National Schools', with some support from *Russkiy yazyk za rubezhom* 'The Russian Language Abroad'. Separate journals appear in the different Republics devoted in part to the specific difficulties arising out of the interference of the national language. Instances are *Ruskiy yazyk v kazakhshkoi shkole*, *Russkiy yazyk v azerbaydzhanskoi shkole*, *Russkiy yazyk v armayanskoi shkole* 'The Russian Language in Kazakh', 'Azerbaydzhan and Armenian schools', respectively. There has been a markedly scholarly and forward looking approach to, and interest in, teaching Russian and other Soviet languages as second languages prior to the Revolution among notable linguists. Some studies were produced by Russians, but the most interesting came from scholars of other nationalities: A. Altansarin for the Kazakhs, I. S. Gogesbashvili for Georgians, I. T. Iakovlev for Chuvash, I. Davis for Baltic languages and K. Nacyri for Turkic languages. Textbooks on the teaching of Russian in non-Russian schools have proliferated following the early example of V. M. Chistiakov. The most noteworthy are those by S. D. Purtseladze for Georgian children (1966), A. V. Mirtov for Uzbeks (1962) and another for Azerbaydzhanis (1956); V. D. Kudriavtsev for Buryat children (1965) and I. C. Cherednichenko for the non-Russian schools of the Ukraine (1957).

At the same time as the problems of teaching Russian to non-Russian speaking children is being considered the specific difficulties of those who speak fairly extreme dialects of Russian, especially in areas of close contact with other languages, is being investigated – for instance among the children around Voronezh on the Don, the Ashkabad area, the Balkir ASSR, the Komi-Permyak National Region, work undertaken mainly under the direction of Tekuchev, Kolkov and others. Nevertheless there are always many complaints about the shortage of competent teachers of Russian, or teachers of Russian of any sort for that matter. Because of this shortage Russian was not taught for some time in rearly 200 schools in the Tashkent area, 70 in Samarkand oblast and 100 in the Andizhan oblast. (*Uchitelskaya Gazeta*, 22-11-1962). At about the same time the number of teachers of Russian in Kirgizia had to be increased as part of an emergency programme from 500 to 2,000 in less than five years, and the teacher training plan had to be changed to produce 33% more teachers of Russian (*Pravda*, 30-5-1962).

In view of the planned promotion of Russian as a medium of instruction to non-native speakers of the language, and the considerable effort that had been and is being made to improve the teachers of Russian as a second language, it is surprising that so little research has been conducted on the several difficult problems arising out of the use of the second language as a teaching medium. Using the same language to teach non-native speakers the subjects being taught to native speakers of the language is full of complicated pedagogical and linguistic issues. The "temptation to provide the content before the skill has been acquired to understand what is being said [...] whether it is in geography or cultural patterns of various sorts" has been criticized (Twaddel, 1964), and there is no questioning the "undesirable inefficiency of attempting to learn the medium and the content of the subject simultaneously." (Prator, 1952). Time and again experienced teachers and investigators have drawn attention to the fact that when pupils are being taught the general subjects of the curriculum in a language they cannot understand easily they fail to stand up to the running stream of the language, unless both the linguistic and the substantial content of the lessons are very well graded and controlled (Lewis, 1965). There is little evidence, either in the literature or from direct observation, whatever may have been done to improve the syllabuses and the text books used in teaching the Russian language, that similar attention has been given in the USSR to modifying the syllabuses in subjects other than languages, when the second language is used to teach them. On the contrary, it is generally claimed as a virtue that these syllabuses are modelled on and more often than not are identical with those used for speakers of Russian. The need to ensure or to advance educational homogeneity is satisfied at the cost of pedagogical prudence.

This weakness in pedagogical thinking has, without doubt, contributed to the admitted inefficiency in teaching Russian to speakers of other languages. There is another problem which is always prominent when a lingua franca is used as an instrument of federalizing or assimilating different cultural and linguistic communities. It has been apparent for instance in the approach to the English language abroad: at the Commonwealth Conference on Teaching of English as a Second Language in 1961, it was clear that some countries were interested in the use of English as a key to a particular culture and tradition while others, often on the same sub-continent, were concerned mainly with teaching the English language as a means of wider international communication. This is very much the case with Russian in the USSR also. The main difference of opinion is between those who consider the chief purpose of the Russian language course to be mainly linguistic and 'communicative', and those who wish to direct the teaching of Russian towards the inculcation of Russian culture, and in consequence to the furtherance of an ideology. The second group of teachers are in the ascendancy. The senior classes in Republics as remote culturally as they are geographically from the Russia of classics such as 'Dead Souls' and 'War and Peace' (the whole background of which is entirely alien to the experience of the children) are expected to study them and to profit from understanding not only the language in which they are written but the values which they express. This is because the teachers are convinced that "Russian (classical) literature is the most effective of all school subjects in inculcating the moral qualities of a builder of communism." Others believe that the teaching of the Russian language should be considered separately from the use of Russian literature as an instrument of ideological education, and for that reason they recommend that the Classics of Russian literature should be studied in the native languages of the various nationalities. From whichever angle the problem is regarded the result is to create difficulties for the children who are learning Russian as a second language.

It might be expected that because of the considerable pressure to advance the case of Russian, the strong motivation of large sectors of the population to acquire it, and the pervasiveness of the language in public media, the standard of Russian would be high: in fact it is complained that it is not even satisfactory. The role envisaged for Russian is to become the second mother tongue, and there are some observers like Tekuchev, who, the facts not withstanding, maintain that "populations of the Republics have assimilated into Russian culture and have mastered Russian as a second language" (1967, 16). But this seems an expression of official aspiration rather than an objective conclusion. Khanazarov, however, does not envisage, even in the fairly distant future that knowledge of Russian will be as high as that of the mother tongue, but only that eventually it will assume equal importance. He points out that even in the Russian environment of urban schools 6th and 7th grade children after several years teaching are hardly able to recognise Russian words (*Uchitelskaya Gazeta*, 20-11-1967). At the Inter-Republic Conference on the improvement of Russian in non-Russian areas to which we have referred, a member of the Presidium of the Central Committee of the Party alleged that in spite of their efforts non-native speakers of the language are still severely handicapped by their unsatisfactory acquaintance with Russian. As late as 1963 a Tatar literary critic maintained that while the teaching of the other languages was improving the status of those languages "it was still too early to speak about making Russian the native language of all Soviet people." (*Voprosy literatury*, 1963). This is the view of Baltic observers too, where the evidence indicates that "while some have acquired a fluent knowledge of Russian [...] there are many indications from official sources which point to [...] shallow acquisition." (Maciuika, 1963, 346-347). It is not unlikely that the situation of Russian in the USSR, outside Russia itself, is similar to that of the English language in India on the eve of independence – the perpetration of the same methodological and administrative mistakes, wide diffusion and considerable acquaintance with the language among the intelligentsia, but few and parched roots for the language among the vast majority of the population, even among school children who are instructed in it.

D. THE TEACHING OF FOREIGN LANGUAGES

i. *Criticism of Standards and General Provision*

There is one more element in the evolving pattern of bilingualism, however halting the developments may be, namely the considerable emphasis on, and the very early introduction of the foreign language, as well as the establishment of special foreign language schools. For Marx a foreign language was a weapon, and Lenin and his wife Krupskaya, among other leaders of the Revolution, always attached importance to the study of a foreign language. After the initial impetus to an extension of the pre-Revolutionary élitist attraction of foreign languages into a system of mass teaching of those languages, part of the concern of the regime has been expressed in pointed criticism of the teaching. One reason for the spate of criticism which has appeared was the need to counteract what had come to be recognized as the adverse consequences of the theories of Marr, one effect of which as it concerned teaching, was a growth of formalism first of all enthusiastically encouraged and later as severely criticized. Until the teaching of language came to be directed, in theory, towards the development of speech the formalism of the whole language course was even greater than it is at present. This formality was criticized intensely in official statements, in conferences convened officially, by the Ministries of Education of various Republics and by teachers. The criticisms can be said to begin in 1927 when there appeared the first of a series of decrees concerning the level of student achievement. In 1931 and the following year came official pronouncements concerning the contribution of the elementary and middle-school respectively to the teaching of a second language. Because of the war and its aftermath and as a result of the influence of Marrist linguistics, official interest in the teaching of second languages was muted until 1954 when it was accepted that "the graduates of the secondary schools are correct to call the schools to give an account of themselves. They do not know a foreign language even after six or eight years study [...] Even with the aid of a dictionary they do not understand a piece of writing, because they have studied only the formal grammar and not the living language." (Gomojunov 1954, 28).

At the end of the year, following a highly critical conference, a new programme was issued, which made more realistic demands on students. In 1956 reference was made to the "unsatisfactory state of foreign language teaching" (*Pravda*, June), and to the causes of the poor teaching, namely "the overburdening of the curriculum with grammatical and lexical materials, which [...] makes it impossible for students to master reading and conversation. Consequently the students study formal grammatical rules but cannot use them because they have no ability to speak the language". The programme of language teaching was still further modified following a meeting of nearly 400 prominent educationists called by the Ministry of Education and the Academy of Pedagogical Sciences. Arakin submitted detailed criticisms of language pedagogy, among which he included deficiencies in organisation, the establishment of language departments in schools which lacked competent teachers; the dispersal of the available teachers too widely and thinly, and the lack of interest among heads and directors of schools. Among defects of actual teaching, Arakin pointed to the unsatisfactory quality of the text books and materials, poor methods of teacher training, the failure to communicate new ideas to practising teachers, together with a lack of stimulating environment in the classrooms. It is significant that these criticisms were repeated as late as 1966. "Attention to languages has been intensified; the aims and methods of teaching them have been reviewed so that imitative mechanical approaches have been abandoned and the speech development of students emphasized." (Sidorov and Shekhter 1966). This improvement may be said to stem from the new programme introduced in 1960. The following year the USSR Council of Ministers noted a little improvement though it remained, the Ministers thought, for the teachers to improve the position still further. Others still found the curriculum in languages, whether mother tongue or second language, overloaded with grammar (Mirolyubov, 1961, 45).

The responsibility of the State for the promotion of foreign languages within the broad strategy of bilingual policy extends beyond simply criticizing achievement, or improving materials and creating experimental or new types of schools. It specified both the languages to be taught in the Union and the numbers who are required to study each of them. In 1961 the Council of Ministers stated: "in the practice of schools there are disproportions in the foreign languages studied. The special features of the Union Republics are not taken into account in selecting the languages to be studied at school and higher education institutes. The Council of Ministers of the Union Republics and the USSR Ministry of Higher Education and Special Education have been directed to determine within three months the most advisable relationship in the foreign languages to be studied at schools and to provide facilities for the study of the most widely spoken languages of Asia, Latin America and other peoples." Following the directive Tass reported three years later that within seven years, i.e. in 1970, 50% of the students would be studying English, 20% each French and German and 10% Spanish and other languages. It was also envisaged that 45% of the first year University and Institute students would be studying English, 20% French, 15% German and Spanish respectively and 5% other languages (Tass, April, 1963). The teaching of foreign languages is governed very strictly by the overall 'nationalities policy' and by the general plan for languages in the USSR.

ii. *Special Foreign Language Schools*

One of the most influential factors within the language policy of the Soviet system of education, has been the establishment of secondary schools to ensure very intensive foreign language teaching. At the beginning of the fifties such schools were established in the largest cities, especially Kharkov, Kiev, Leningrad and Moscow. They allocated nearly three times the amount of time devoted to languages in the ordinary secondary schools, and at certain stages some subjects, for instance Modern History in the 8th Grade and a science in the 10th, were taught in the foreign language (Lewis, 1962c). Within ten years many more such schools were established in the cities already named as well as in Stalingrad, Kazhan, Rostov and some other large cities. Article 5 of the 'Law on Strengthening Ties between School and Life' so far as it affected the RSFSR, stated: "further expansion should take place of secondary general education schools, labour polytechnical schools conducting instruction in a number of subjects in a foreign language." This article appears in the Law as it was adopted by other Republics and in some of them, for instance Belorussia, it is given great prominence. Other Union Republics, however, did not adopt it, prominent among them being Armenia, Azerbaydzhan, Latvia and Moldavia (De Witt, 1961, 556). It cannot be doubted that those who did not follow the Russian line on extending such special schools were concerned with the already very complex linguistic situation their schools had to cope with, which would be even more difficult if a special category of schools were expanded.

In 1961 came the Council of Ministers' meeting and as a result, directives were issued to implement Article 5. This resolution also envisaged the organization at Universities and Pedagogical Institutes as from 1961-1962, of courses for teachers of general subjects taught through the medium of a foreign language, following the pattern, to some extent, of the training that had been provided for teachers of national minorities in Russian medium schools (*Pravda*, 4 June, 1961, 156). In April, 1963, Tass reported that by 1965, 700 more specialist schools where teaching was to be given in a foreign language – English, French, German, Spanish, Arabic, Chinese, Urdu and Hindu were to be opened (*Tass*, April, 1963). In 1963 there were already 503 such schools in the RSFSR, Belorussia and the Ukraine. These developments were generally welcomed, but they were not immune from criticism either. One critic wrote that it was "alarming that the specialist language secondary schools here and there are beginning to remind us of 'lycées' for the children of well-to-do-parents" (*Pravda* October, 1965, 158).

iii.   *Early Introduction of Foreign Languages*

Another aspect of the drive towards the acquisition of a foreign language has been the very early introduction of the foreign language, at even three or four years of age. This has been done partly to prepare pupils for the Special Language Schools already referred to, and has affected kindergartens and the first grades of general education schools. Ordinarily foreign languages are taught from the fifth grade in general education schools. But the Council of Ministers decided on more radical provision, and a special meeting of the Ministry of the RSFSR, December 1958, subsequently discussed the teaching of languages to pre-school children.

A 1961 resolution stated that "the USSR Council of Ministers has proposed the organization, if parents so desire, of foreign language groups at kindergartens and in the elementary grades of general education schools. The RSFSR Ministry of Education and Academy of Pedagogical Sciences have been instructed to publish syllabuses and method manuals for foreign language instruction in such groups" (*Pravda*, 4th June, 1961). In consequence parents and teachers in several large cities took the initiative and "in spite of a whole series of difficulties" which teachers met in attempting this work, the advance was sufficiently encouraging to justify a continuance of the experiment on a larger scale (*Pravda* 15-6-1966). Furthermore, the new 'boarding schools' were also especially valuable in promoting this development in lower elementary grades. Here, several different approaches have been adopted. One school gives one whole day to the teaching of a foreign language and its use for teaching some subjects. In other schools (very well equipped by British and U.S. standards), sophisticated language laboratories have been installed. The

results, as they were observed personally, appeared to be highly satisfactory (Lewis, 1962c and later).

Interesting though the introduction of foreign languages into the
lower elementary grades undoubtedly is, the developments in kindergartens occupy the attention of many scholars, but teachers and policy
makers even more. There has been a long history of very early teaching
of a second language in Russia and a great divergence of opinion about
its advisability and the advantages to be derived from it. In the 19th
Century it was felt by some educationists that such a programme served
only to alienate the children from their Russian heritage. Among those
who took an interest was the influential teacher Ushinskii (Ushinskii,
1939, 1, 154, etc.). His approach was moderate: he argued the desirability of consolidating control of the mother tongue before the child
was taught a foreign language at somewhere around 7 years of age. This
need to consolidate the mother tongue was stressed by A. I. Thomson also
(1960); the mastery of the mother tongue is so integrally a part of the intellectual development of children and their acquisition of basic concepts,
that everything should be done to avoid interfering with the development
of the first language. When children learn a foreign language too early,
Thomson argued, this interference is apt to be accentuated. He advocated
delaying the introduction of a second language though he stressed the
desirability of introducing it as early as an acceptance of the qualifications he had introduced would permit (Thomson, 93). Traditionally,
therefore, the intellectual and educational leaders of Russia cannot be
said to have been unqualified supporters of introducing foreign languages
into kindergartens. However, the new knowledge derived from the
disciplines of neurology and psychology, but above all the accumulation
of experience in teaching as second languages either Russian or non-
Russian national languages in the various republics, has brought a
growing awareness of the advantages of similar early introduction of a
foreign language. In this way a policy of 'indigenous bilingualism' has
served to promote the interest of early foreign language instruction, and
this in turn has made even more complicated the pattern of a comprehensive bilingualism which Soviet planning promotes.

One of the most prominent advocates of this development in recent
years, and one who has been most actively concerned in careful research,
is V. S. Ginsberg of the Herzen Institute. He reported in 1960 the complaint of many of those who attended the 1958 conference, about the absence of objective information, and the need for sound observation of the
teaching of very young children. More research and experimental developmental work was required before any sound conclusions could be
stated concerning the theory and the practical possibilities. Particularly,
it was necessary to discover the possible effects upon general psycholog-

ical and social development and the acquisition of his mother tongue; presumably it would be at least equally necessary to investigate the implications for those children who were already learning two or more indigenous languages: their ethnic language and Russian (Ginsberg, 1960, 21).

Pioneer work was undertaken at the Herzen Institute and the Leningrad kindergartens, which were related to the Institute, three of which, representing the three languages, English, German and French, participated in the experiment. Lessons were given to groups of 13-15 and of 28-30 children, though the size of the group turned out not to correlate significantly with the success of the teaching. At the same time as the kindergartens were being taught, the same teachers taught groups in the second and fourth grades of two general education schools in the same city. At the end of the project, Ginsberg concluded, factors which might quite easily have a negative effect on the child's general development and on his acquisition of the mother tongue would have to be studied in much greater depth. Nevertheless, the general conclusion favoured the continuance and expansion of the work in the kindergartens. The number of kindergarten and lower grade elementary classes undertaking the work has increased, but it would be wrong to exaggerate the importance of the foreign language component in the ordinary elementary schools since the time devoted to it is small and the number of competent foreign language teachers of very young children is limited (Ginsberg, 1959, 81).

Whatever degree of importance attaches to the teaching of these young children and however modest the present provision may be (when it is seen against the background of the total languages provision), it cannot be denied that foreign language instruction at a very young age in kindergartens, and from the first grade of the elementary school to groups of no more than 25 children and sometimes fewer, as well as its use as a medium of instruction in some schools – all these features of the programme represent a significant part of language policy in the USSR. A foreign language which is regarded in this way and taught with such intensity ceases, for such children, to be a foreign language in the traditional sense. It enters into the pattern of their bilingual education. The learning of Russian and a foreign language in this fashion necessarily affects the attitude of the younger generation of children to the maintenance of the ethnic language when this is the language of the minority in any area, or where it does not carry the prestige which parents prize.

E. THE PLANNED PENETRATION OF THE RUSSIAN LANGUAGE[4]

In 1965 it was decided that Russian should replace the native language
as the medium of instruction for all children in the Kabardin-Balkar
ASSR, immediately on their entry to school and at all stages subsequently.
This process began in 1960 when half the first year classes were transferred to Russian. In 1964 the training of teachers for native language
primary school classes in the Autonomous Republic ceased altogether.
This is a representative example of the process by which Russian is
planned to penetrate farther and farther into the non-Russian sectors of
the education system. The reasons given for the decision in this instance
are also a fair reflection of the justification usually and more generally
advanced. The Minister of Education for the Republic maintained that
it was the desire of the parents, as much as the difficulty of catering for
several native languages in a small set of schools, that forced the decision
on the administrators (*Russkiy yazyk v natsionalnoi shkole* 4. 65). Nevertheless, it is clear from the Minister's statement that the problems of sub-
stituting Russian as a teaching language were no fewer or less bothersome
than the continuation of the existing policy of using the native languages.
Teachers qualified to teach Russian and to use it for other subjects, text
books and other materials, were not forthcoming. Most of the rural
schools had to resort to pre-school classes in order to instil some acquaintance with the rudiments of the language. The real reasons for the administrative change were more numerous, and more political or ideological than were stated.

In the light of such determination to pursue a policy which raises as
many difficulties as it resolves, it is not surprising that the Russian language, at least superficially, has penetrated so extensively into the school
systems. It has been a very privileged language, since it is the only one
which is 'official' in every sense of the term and in every part of the USSR.
Other languages are 'official' in their own Union Republics and for specific and limited purposes; but Russian is universally so. The political
and ideological support for Russian which arises from some of the considerations we have already adduced, has been reinforced by administrative steps, like the decision to make the teaching compulsory. Perhaps the
most decisive consequence of political pressure was the series of changes
resulting in the Laws of 1958-1959, tending towards placing Russian on
an equal footing with the national languages as the medium of instruction
of non-Russian children in all Republics. The opposition arguments
to the proposals were well articulated and even after enactment teachers
were criticized, as in Latvia, "for being restricted by nationalist feelings

[4] See table 25, p. 148.

and remaining stagnant" in the face of the new policy (*Sovetskaya Latviya* 10-6-1940). It became clear that the penetration of Russian through the operation of the optional clause was being resisted elsewhere since several local school administrators were being accused from the centre of frustrating the wishes of parents to have their children placed in Russian medium schools (*Partiinaya zhizn.* 23, 1962).

In spite of or perhaps because of this continuing resistance on the part of many parents powerful voices have always been raised to question the need to continue a national languages policy at all, and so to allow the strongest language to prevail. The termination of national language publications among small ethnic groups, the possible prohibition of students from studying or using the 'national languages', the administrative difficulties of conducting national schools, especially in the remote areas such as the Far North, and the uneconomic returns from publishing textbooks in the minority languages – all these arguments have been advanced in influential circles (*Voprosy razvitiya*, 320-321). It is also true that though attempts are sometimes made to interest Russian children in learning a 'national language' (Pennar, 1969, 10), neither Russian nor other monorities are required to study any local language. In the Ukraine the Polish, Hungarian and Moldavian minorities more often than not teach, not Ukrainian but Russian in their minority schools (Kolasky, 1968, 72). Even before 1958 it was becoming abundantly clear that the Russian medium schools did not propose to teach the national languages of the Republics in which they were established. In some instances the languages were actually dropped from the curriculum. Outside school, also, Russians evinced little interest in speaking the local languages. An observer noted in 1965 that Russians or Ukrainians were cynical about the need to learn the language of those among whom they lived, and in fact made no attempt to get acquainted with other major languages, such as Tadzhik, Kazakh, Kirgiz or Uzbek. Personal observation of similar attitudes among Russians in Georgia and Armenia reinforce this evidence (Lewis, 1962c).[5] The shifts of population have also depressed the status of national languages locally. Where there is considerable language contact and mélange there is always the inescapable practical need for a lingua franca. In Daghestan Arabic served this purpose for a long time, (until, in fact, the late 20's of this Century), while several languages were used in the schools (Kolarz, 1952, 203). Similarly, it is to be expected that Russian should be found a useful and sometimes necessary lingua franca. And for that reason, apart from any other, more and more parents have turned to it as the most suitable language of education for their children.

---

[5] An examination of the figures for second language learning among the Russians is conclusive on this point, considering how well they are represented among so many non-Russian nationalities. (Table 2, p. 44).

The importance of the appeal to "parents' wishes" which is put forward with almost ritual regularity in these discussions cannot be ignored or disputed. Even in the absence of the planned promotion of Russian, parents would have been attracted towards it as the teaching language in schools, partly because of the imbalance within the curriculum caused by a superfluity of languages. Thus Uygar children had to study four languages, even in their undeveloped system of education: Uygur up to grade 7, Kazakh, Russian and a foreign language. It simplified matters to opt out of at least one of these languages – and the only realistic candidate for omission was the native language. Russian offers substantial advantages in its own right; it had a literary prestige prior to the Revolution, and this has been reinforced since by other considerations, political and ideological as well as purely literary. Russian has a standing as a world language of science and technology. The knowledge which other nationalities require to advance the higher education of their children cannot be realistically provided in all of even the major languages of the USSR, so that Russian became the means of entry to international scholarship and into the province of scientific advance. Even if the present multi-national structure of the Soviet state were to disintegrate or had not come into existence, it would remain true that for many of the nationalities any prospect of advanced education and progress would entail a considerable knowledge of Russian.

Parents are also influenced by the consideration that since Russian is a compulsory language in every type of schools (an aspect of policy which is not generally criticized even by those who argue very strongly in favour of instruction in the other national languages as well), it is more economical of time and effort that the whole education of their children should also be in Russian. This line of argument is reinforced by the realization that sooner or later, whatever type of school the child may be attending, he will have to transfer to Russian medium courses. This has been the line of policy for a very long time in most of the nationalities, especially the scattered and more remote ones. Thus during the 1950's in five Alma-Ata Rayony Uygur children were taught in their own language only in the first grades of primary school. After completing grade 4, they transferred either to Kazakh or Russian, usually the latter. At the same time there were no facilities to train teachers to use Uygur beyond grade 4. In Daghestan during the same period, Russian became progressively the language to which national and minority school children transferred beyond grade 5. Some Daghestan schools, like the Uygur, were unable to recruit teachers competent enough to use the native language of instruction to which the children were accustomed in the primary grades (Koutaisoff, 1951, 122). This was equally the case with Turkmen schools, where the three top grades of secondary schools had to be taught in

Russian, thus catering for 79% of the school population of that age (*Kulturnaya Strana*, 1940, 74). These developments during the 1950's set the direction of parent's interest so that their expectation for the education of their children came to be identified with proficiency in Russian. Once parents' minds had been oriented in this way the use of Russian in secondary schools came to be regarded not only as inevitable, but natural, and it was virtually impossible to halt it.

This is even truer of post-secondary education. In the Specialised Secondary and Higher Institutes even foreign languages came to be taught in Russian – a contradiction not only of more enlightened teaching of such languages in other countries, but of the fundamental principles of Soviet theory itself (*Central Asian Review*, XIII. 2. 183). The teaching of other subjects in Russian is general even in teacher training colleges and Pedagogical Institutes though not in faculties of Medicine and Engineering (Bilinsky, 1968, 431). Even where Russian is not the medium of post-secondary education there is always the difficulty of obtaining native language textbooks which are standard for their subject. In 1964 was issued 'On Improving the Teaching of Russian in the Higher and Secondary Special Education Institutes of the Union and Autonomous Republics' which remarked on the vital need for Russian in acquiring new knowledge, and as the foundation for being able to work anywhere in the USSR. For these reasons Russian replaced a foreign language as a compulsory subject for VUZ students who had been taught in another language at School. Since such a large part of the curriculum of higher education is conducted in Russian, students from non-Russian schools have to sit an entrance examination in it. Even so, not only has the proportion of non-Russian taught students in higher education declined but a disproportionate number of those who manage to obtain entry fail to complete their courses (De Witt, 1961, 357). Because of these considerations students and their parents wish to ensure their acceptance and to safeguard their final success in higher education by beginning instruction in Russian early and by entering Russian medium schools.

The future educational prospects of their children are not the only factors which parents obviously take into account: they are guided in their choice of school to some extent by the superior provision which is available, immediately, at elementary and secondary Russian medium schools. Textbooks in any language are always somewhat scarce. During 1967-1968, the supply of books in the Central Asian Republics was markedly deficient, falling short by over 20% of the demand in Uzbekistan and Tadzhikstan. Russian books are far more easily obtainable because the supply within any Union Republic can be supplemented from elsewhere in the USSR (Sheey, 1966, 154). The difficulties as we have noted apply particularly to post-secondary education. Even in terms of the proportion of Russians in the whole of the USSR the volume of textbook publication in that language far exceeds those in other languages: 92.5% of the books for special secondary education in 1966-1967 (*Pechat. SSR 1966. Stat. mat.* 1967, 50). The books in Russian are also of better quality. The teacher of local languages has to improvize or to use translations. And though this practice is often commendable in the circumstances, it eventually becomes self defeating (Galazov, 1965). In one Republic 60% and in another 50% of the textbooks were produced locally and it is these which, in the eyes of experienced teachers, are most open to criticism because of their poor quality (Sheey, 1968, 155).

To the general disadvantages under which the non-Russian schools labour must be added the disadvantage of their being located mainly in the rural areas. It is recognized in the USSR "certain problems are noteworthy here: school standards are not high enough to enable students to compete equally with town students for admission to VUZ" (*Pravda Vostoka*, quoted in *World Survey of Education*, UNESCO, 644). This is due partly to poor equipment, which has frequently to be produced by students themselves. While the shortage of books affects town and rural schools alike the urban areas are able to operate a useful second-hand book trade which is not available to rural schools. The rural schools, again, are usually very small: in some districts 75% of them are one-teacher schools (*Uchitelskaya Gazeta*, 16-1-1968). In Kirgizia in 1966 there were 250 schools with numbers sometimes as low as 10 for all age groups. The rural secondary school with no more than a single form entry annually cannot justify the appointment of well qualified and specialist teachers in all subjects in the way a large urban secondary school can (*Uchitelskaya Gazeta*, 15-3-1966). Rural schools also need to attract teachers from outside the area. In some instances the position has not changed very much since 1949 when 60% of the teachers of children in the schools of the North were drawn from other nationalities. The Minister of Education for the RSFSR has pointed out that the conditions in which the teachers taught and lived were not such as to attract many or to retain those who had come. "There are still a number of places where the locality remains indifferent about them. Many teachers in the area of Novosibirsk have to rent accommodation and this is unsatisfactory when they need to prepare lessons. As a result many teachers leave the area. The same is true of places like Pskov and Ulianovsk" (Afanasenko, 1962, 13). It was reported in 1967 that 200 schools in Tashkent Oblast were unable to teach Russian for reasons of staff shortage, and in the Altai region of Kirgiztan 19 new teachers left at the end of one year (*Uchitelskaya Gazeta*, 20-11-1967). Such shortage of staff has meant that the standard of education is often unsatisfactory, and when the teaching of Russian is affected special measures are taken. As a general rule, it was decided in 1966-1967, that wherever possible classes in which Russian is taught should not be larger than 15 to 18, whereas in urban schools the normal size of such classes is 35-40.

But these considerations are not the only ones which affect the parents' choice of schools for their children. The Russian schools are favoured by the organization of the curriculum and by the differences in the amount of time allotted to some subjects. Reference has been made to the problem of the overloaded curriculum of the national schools and an administrator in Yakutia claimed that 50% of the student's classroom time was taken up with the study of language. Such a disproportionate allotment means neglect of other subjects (*Russkiy Yazyk v natsionalnoi shkole*, 1959, 22). Whatever the cross currents of argument might have revealed in the 1958-1959 Education Laws debate, no one doubted the need to rationalize the curriculum. A comparison of Russian and Uzbek schools in the latter Republic shows that children attending national schools were required to spend 480 hours longer at their school lessons each year. While the amount of time for most major subjects was the same in each type of school, the national school had 51 hours fewer for foreign languages, 36 for drawing and singing, etc. In 1966 a decree of the USSR Council of Ministers stipulated that students in national schools should spend two or three hours more at school per week. There is considerable disparity in treatment of Russian as the first language in Russian medium schools on the one hand and Uzbek as the mother tongue in the national schools of that Republic on the other, Russian being favoured by a ratio of approximately 4 to 3 (2,521 hours to 1,796). As second languages in the respective schools the ratio in favour of Russian is 4 to 1. Put in another way, the amount of time given to Russian as a *second* language is almost equivalent to the time given to Uzbek as the *mother tongue*. In Russian medium schools the disparity between Uzbek as a second language and Russian is of the order of 1 to 6 in favour of Russian. It is hardly surprising that forward looking parents are apt to choose Russian medium schools in preference to those where the children are taught in their national language.

The disparity is reinforced by the manipulation of the mass media. For instance, a Television Schedule was reported in Sovetskaia Kirgiziia for September 19th, 1970, where the programme from the local station provided $1\frac{1}{4}$ hours of broadcasting in Kirgiz and $4\frac{1}{2}$ in Russian. The Second Programme, which was broadcast from Moscow was entirely in Russian and provided 5 hours entertainment and instruction. On the following day there were programmes in Russian for over 11 hours, distributed between two stations and only 4 hours from the same stations in the local language.

F. CONCLUSION

The implementation of a language policy in the system of education of the USSR both reflects the shifts of emphasis within the nationalities policy which were analyzed earlier, and at the same time it helps to bring about those changes of stress between centralizing and decentralizing tendencies. Political conditions and ideological pressures help the schools to ensure the increasing penetration of Russian into the whole of Soviet society, and this penetration is planned directly or indirectly – indirectly through the manipulation of manpower movement across the whole of the Union and by the changes in the languages themselves, alphabets and vocabulary especially. Directly, by the supply of teachers who are competent in the various languages, of textbooks and other materials and by the promotion of certain decisions such as the compulsory teaching of Russian and the transfer from teaching through a 'national language' to Russian as the child moves from elementary to secondary and to post-secondary classes. The teaching of Russian as a second language is not notably successful, on the evidence of Russian educationists themselves, and the problems arising from the use of Russian to teach the curriculum to non-native speakers of the language raises problems, in the solution of which there does not appear to have been any significant advance over the outmoded approaches adopted by British educationists in African or Asian schools at the end of the first quarter of this century. Maximum language saturation of the child is substituted for scientific, economic and therefore more effective methodology of language teaching.

This penetration of Russian, facilitated by the educational system, has produced more extensive Russian related types of bilingualism among school children, and this process has several noteworthy characteristics. In the first place, though historically determined and fortuitous bilingualism is still an impressive feature of the Soviet Union (Table 2) the forms of bilingualism that really matter are being planned and programmed by the creation of types of 'bilingual schools'. Outside the RSFSR nearly all schools are bilingual since they have to take into account the existence of at least two languages – the 'national language' and Russian (the second mother tongue). Some schools in the autonomous areas of the RSFSR do so as well; and many schools in the other Republics may have three or more languages to cope with. However, different kinds of school organization differ in the emphasis which they give to these languages in the school programme. Some are single medium schools in which another language, whether Russian or the national language is taught as a second language. Other schools use more than one language to teach other subjects: among such schools some may use both languages to teach all children, sometimes in the same lesson (mixed medium), or in different lessons (dual medium); and some may use both languages but with separated language groups – parallel medium schools. In all these schools a foreign language is becoming an increasingly important component of the child's linguistic programme. The foreign language is being taught so intensively and introduced so early, as well as being used so much more frequently to teach other subjects that in very important ways it is no different from Russian in the curriculum of children in some of the more distant non-Russian republics.

Consequently the bilingualism being promoted so carefully by the educational system is no longer an élitist characteristic as it was in the 19th century. Nor, is it mainly an oral bilingualism as it was before the advent of mass literacy and the use of the vernacular in the schools. Where bilingualism arising simply out of historical contact situations is concerned the system of education has transformed 'oral bilingualism' into 'literate bilingualism', and this embraces bilingualism involving the languages of even small minorities. So far as this new kind of bilingualism includes Russian as an important element, it is indeed a *predominantly* literate bilingualism – since it depends for its entire existence, almost, on the availability of the press and the schools.

Chapter 8

SECOND LANGUAGE PEDAGOGY — AN ASPECT OF LAN-
GUAGE PLANNING

A. INTRODUCTION

Soviet planning is directed to produce a homogeneous and some would
say a uniform society. In the social services, and especially in education,
such planning is required in proportion to the speed and the extremity of
the changes being introduced. A revolutionary society such as that of the
Soviets, requires planning more than most. Population growth has been
and is still being planned, over vast areas and this is important from the
point of view of pedagogy since population studies have shown that in
developing countries, among which we can include several parts of the
Soviet Union, there is a close link between population growth and technical change. Growth produces new needs, including new educational
needs affecting the organization of different kinds of schools, innovations
in the curriculum and modifications of method. These new needs cannot
be satisfied economically without the intervention of technology. The
prestige attaching to technique in other areas of social operations transfers to educational planning. But independently of success in other areas a
planned technique is required to solve pedagogic problems; a general
technique is welcomed because it helps to produce changes in methodology which are predictable and controllable. What was previously a
matter for individual teacher choice is now determined by large and remote organizations. The teacher, of languages as much as of other subjects, in such a situation becomes the medium rather than the source of
educational advance. In short the character of the Soviet system is such as
to place a great emphasis on uniformity of approach to classroom practice, uniform application of centralized research programmes as well as

centralized development of teaching materials and guide lines to teachers. As a result there is a tendency towards formality which affects the teaching of languages particularly. However, there are compensations: the rapid and phenomenal increase in literacy among all nationalities could not have been achieved without considerable planning as well as a stern insistence on adherence to a set programme. The tremendous advance, beyond the development simply of a literate population, in the general and especially higher education of the masses, some of whom were primitive by modern standards, required strict standardization of courses, textbooks, equipment and the training of teachers of all subjects including languages. Standardization inevitably leads to uniformity of approach and consequent formality in teaching.

The influence of technique increases as society goes beyond relatively primitive means of living and has to rely on institutionalized education. The more technologically advanced a society becomes the more it relies on institutionalized instruction, which becomes progressively standardized and uniform. We tend to think of technique and technology as relating to the physical sciences and in particular the science of mechanics. It is not so limited, for not only has every science its appropriate technology, but every human activity of the disciplined sort has its technology and technique of achieving success – its formulated and standardized methods. Technique is an attitude of mind characterized by the acceptance of prescribed rules and formalized approaches to problems, together with standardized, and objectively determined norms. Such an attitude of mind imposes definite restraints on human freedom of action: "no technique is possible when men are free", and the converse is equally true that no man is free in a system dominated by 'technique'. Technique, in teaching as in other activities, has for its objective the elimination of human variability; and the greater the scope of the activity the greater the need for a predictable performance. The aim is "to leave little to the acuteness and strength of wit, and indeed rather to level wit and intellect. For as in drawing a straight line or accurate circle by the hand much depends on its steadiness and practice, but if a ruler is used or a compass there is little occasion for either" (F. Bacon, 1608, LXI). A mass system of teaching languages cannot rely upon high level ability in all teachers and for that reason, if for no other, technique takes over from individual inspiration and flair. Where planning and technique take over uniformity and formality enter. In so far as technical approaches to teaching depend on standardized procedures, methods, equipment and materials, less is required of individual excellence. This is what the Soviet system of language pedagogy and education in general requires. Specifically, it needs to achieve its results in a limited time and with the least expenditure of resources.

The actual classroom practice of teaching languages is characterized by the same concept of planning and 'social engineering' as is found elsewhere in the Soviet system: the formulation of a languages policy is justified in the light of political and ideological principles as well as demographic tendencies, and classroom practice is justified by the principles derived from linguistic and psychological research. Therefore policy, and methods of implementing it, are derived from a matrix of abstract principles. Most educational activities in the Soviet Union are largely determined within a well articulated ideology, and that ideology encourages uniformity. It is for this reason that in attempting to analyse the approach to language teaching in the Soviet Union we need to take into account an important characteristic, which in this respect approximates more nearly to the prevailing attitude of the U.S.A. than of Britain: namely the pronounced care taken to build practice on theory. In Britain, until recently, an unlikely combination of tradition, empiricism and pragmatism prevailed in the development and evaluation of teaching approaches, more than did scientific theory. This has safeguarded a welcome degree of stability and continuity which is not evident to the same extent in the U.S.A. In the USSR that stability and continuity are ensured by dogmatism. Whatever may be said about the quality of Soviet research or the validity of Soviet theories concerning language learning and teaching (and they compare with the best ideas advanced research workers can offer elsewhere in the world), it is impossible to ignore either the extent to which new developments in teaching language are planned specifically to take account of the most recent research, and the use of scientific theory to justify such new developments, albeit within the ideological consensus. In this way class teaching of languages, whether the mother tongue or indigenous and foreign second languages cannot be understood without reference to research into fundamental concepts of language acquisition and the ideology which guides the research, on which such teaching is based. It will emerge from such an analysis that the planning, 'interventionism' or engineering which prevails in other sectors of Soviet education is emphasized as one of the critical features of actual pedagogic practice also.

The theory of language teaching reflecting the ideological tenets to which reference has been made emphasizes the primary importance of social experience, and the possibility of manipulating the social environment, especially the school and classroom environment, not only to give some substance to the act of communication, but to modify linguistic behaviour and to accelerate its development. This is the motivating force of Soviet language teaching theory and practice, and it can be seen to be another factor conducive to planned and specifically promoted bilingualism. A second current characteristic of this theory, and derived from more fundamental psychological principles of learning, is the avoidance of the 'peripheral', more mechanistic behavioural approach. This has important consequences for attitudes towards the relationship of the mother tongue and a second language. The basic concepts of language learning all tie together to give theoretical justification to the concept of education as psychological and social engineering, to an extent that is alien to the prevailing climate of educational thinking in Britain. This does not mean that it is any the less valid for that reason.

B. LINGUISTIC RESEARCH

Russia and some of the other countries which come together to form the USSR have had a long tradition of philological and linguistic studies, which has been enriched in recent years. So far as affects second language pedagogy reference need only be made to non-Russian though indigenous languages which in conditions of considerable population mobility and consequent mixed language communities need to be taught as second languages. Furthermore in many instances the general acceptance or adoption of a standard form, where it exists, has a long way to go, so that even within the same language community a standard language has to be taught to speakers of extreme dialects, very much as a second language. Consequently the work on the dialects of Tadzhik by Rastorgueva, of Uzbek by Polivanov, Azerbaydzhan: by Sheraliev, and Nogai and Karakalpak by Baskakov are significant to our enquiry. Similar importance attaches to the work on the languages and dialects of the smaller language communities of the Caucusus such as those on Tat and Talysh by Miller and Dzhavakhishvili respectively.

   Some of the most fruitful ideas in contemporary linguistics were contributed by scholars working in Russia before the revolution. Fortunatov, Shazmatov, and others contributed to European general linguistics as much as they did to Slavic, Turkic or Caucasian studies. In spite of their alleged 'idealist and psychological trends' the contemporary Soviet assessment of this work is very favorable. The most prominent among these, Baudoin de Courtenoy, first suggested and emphasized what became the essential and characteristic features of contemporary linguistics, and to him both Saussure and Trubetzkoy, who taught in Russia before the Revolution, were indebted. First at Kazan and later at St. Petersburg, his pupils, particularly Shcherba and Vinogradov, played an important part in rectifying the eccentricities of the Marrist interlude. Though the pre-revolutionary lines of linguistic enquiry may have changed, with the adoption of the materialist standpoint and adherence to a belief in the irreducible character of socio-historical considerations, the present emphasis on the importance of language in education was always there. In consequence eminent linguists like Shcherba participated actively in improving language pedagogy. They took steps to relate school grammars more closely to scientific grammars of the indigenous languages; and, to take one instance, Shcherba's discussions of Russian syntax, the parts of speech, and lexicology had a profound effect on teaching. He entered vigorously into discussions with teachers and published studies on detailed aspects of language pedagogy (Shcherba, 1947).

In spite of the continuity of Russian and Soviet scholarship the Revolution placed linguists and teachers in an acute dilemma. On the one hand there was a gradual realization of the need to take advantage of the results of foreign research and of new ideas in many branches of science and technology, as well as to train able students and university teachers, the precondition of social and industrial mobilization. This need to keep open the channels of foreign influence meant that the study of languages had to be maintained. The vigorous and sometimes biting controversy about the theoretical bases of this teaching served only to stress the regard with which it was held in the schools and its relevance to society.

The USSR Council of Ministers has on more than one occasion expressed its views 'Concerning the Improvement of the Instruction of Foreign Languages' and this interest has derived from the "realization that the growth of the Soviet Union's international contacts is lending greater importance to foreign language study in the higher education institutes. It is most important to make the student realize that today it is impossible to be a fully fledged specialist making full use of the latest foreign and domestic achievements in science and technology without foreign languages." (*Pravda*, 4-6-1961).

On the other hand the political system has tended to be suspicious of external contacts and to restrict any access to 'bourgeois and counter revolutionary influences', especially among the young. One consequence of this dilemma was a tendency for Soviet linguistics, and the theory of language pedagogy to isolate themselves from the main stream of Western European and American ideas. For instance, though Saussure was influenced by de Courtenoy's ideas, he was strongly criticized for arguing that language as a system must be studied independently of its history, and the character of the society speaking it. Saussure's conviction that "linguistics has as its sole aim the study of language in and for itself" was unacceptable to Soviet linguists. Serdyuchenko (1949), one of Marr's pupils and a later exegisist of the latter's views, attacked the alleged unhistorical bases of Saussure's theory, and especially his claim that "the influence of history only distracted the linguist from his path".

The same writer criticized Sapir, similarly, for refusing to consider seriously the question of the origin of language. Soviet linguists thought it important not only to know language as it is but to investigate how it became what it is (Marr, 1949, Vol. V, 422). Vinogradov draws attention to this comparative-historical character of Soviet linguistics, stressing the fact that contrary to the prevailing European theories the Soviet approach has centred on the "essential nature of language as a social phenomenon [...] and the historical development of national languages". Western linguistics, it was alleged, rested on an unprofitable philosophical dualism, itself a product of a disintegrating atomistic society. (Vinogradov, 1950, 145). The American variety of structuralism therefore played a relatively unimportant part in Soviet linguistics and only gradually came to influence the preparation of teachers, teaching materials, and methodology. The fundamental postulates of synchronic linguistics, likewise, were not always accepted by even major figures like Vinogradov. Consequently, it is not unusual to find text books for language courses drawing their exempla from different periods of the historical development of a language.

C. N.Y. MARR

This temporary isolation from the most powerful forces in general linguistics, the divorce from the mainstream of Indo-European scholarship, as well as the break with the tradition of classic Russian studies come out most clearly in the theories of N. Y. Marr, who though he proclaimed himself the true advocate of Marxist linguistics was ironically enough officially refuted by Stalin (1950b). The public discussion which followed the latter's intervention illuminated the most characteristic features of Soviet linguistic isolation where education is concerned, and outlined the main components of the orthodox Soviet approach. The most serious error for which Marr's linguistics was indicted is the separation of language and thought, the so called "freeing of language from the natural matter of language", active reflection, which led Marr's linguistics into the "swamp of idealism". (Stalin, 1950b). This in turn, according to Vinogradov resulted in an "erroneous conception of what should be the natural relationship between the pupil's native language and the language he is taught subsequently". Such misconceptions led to an "underestimating of the role played by the native language in learning a second language and to belittling the importance of the theory and practice of translation." (Vinogradov, 1950, 143). In fact, it was language pedagogy which experienced the most harmful consequences of Marrist influences, because it created considerable confusion among teachers in institutions of higher education, who found it impossible to work out a consistent methodology on Marrist foundations. The teaching grammars which were set out under his influence were contradictory and inconsistent. The organization of teaching and research became less and less well co-ordinated. (Ellis and Davies, 1951, 232). It is not surprising that the most critical views of Marr's linguistic theories were expressed by the advisers to the Ministry of Higher Education of the USSR, the Ministry of Education of the RSFSR, and the authors of text books and school syllabuses.

Marr was also criticized for his unhistorical approach to the study of the grammar of language, and, because of his 'stadal' theories, his underestimation of linguistic continuity. The period of greatest opposition to his views coincided with the political realization of the need to reinforce and support the nationalities of the federation, after the strains of German propaganda and invasion. Minorities had to be assured that their languages would be maintained, and for this reason the theoretical opposition to Marrist linguistics emphasized that "languages possess great stability and a tremendous power of resistance to forcible assimilation". Contrary to Marr's view that "grammar was an empty formality" the stability of languages was seen by his critics to derive from the continuity of the grammatical system determined not by class but by underlying and evolving national characteristics. Whatever scientific justification there may or may not have been for criticism of Marr's theories, Stalin's intervention which served as the stimulus to the expression of those criticisms, was politically inspired by the strategic need to remove a source of concern among the leaders of national and linguistic minorities.

Marr participated in the linguistic analysis of several of the national languages and was instrumental in setting up a 'Committee for the Study of the Caucasian Peoples' which became later the 'Committee for the Study of the Ethnic and National Cultures of the Soviet East', and finally took the form of the 'USSR Nationalities Institute'. But in spite of this engrossing interest in the nationalities and their languages he looked forward to a time when in "the new classless society not only will the system of spoken languages be done away with but a unitary language will be created, as far and even farther removed from articulate language as the latter is from gesture." (Marr, 1949, Vol. III, 118). In another place he writes "in the same way as mankind is moving from multiplicity towards a common world economy and a single common order ... so language is moving in gigantic strides from multiplicity to a single language'.[1] (Vol. II, 135). His followers took their cue from these pronouncements for which they were severely criticized. They were said to have "completely ignored the specific features of national languages, and

---

[1]   It must be confessed that an objective interpretation of Marr's standpoint does not indicate any great difference between this view and those of one of his principal critics, Vinogradov, who argued for the priority of Russian in the educational system because "it is creating suitable conditions which in the future will shorten the path to one single language for all mankind" (Vinogradov, 1945, 113).

approached the development of national languages in an oversimplified and vulgarized manner [...] The result was a break in the way in which the national languages were regarded, which in turn led to many difficulties in the mastery of the grammar of the languages, chaos in orthography etc..." Marrists, it was alleged, interpreted the relationship of languages mechanistically and conceived of the role of Russian for instance, "in the development of the national languages as the mechanical merging of the latter with Russian". Not only did Marr's views as interpreted by his successors create difficulties for the study of language but they interfered with the procseses of language planning as they were then being developed. "The drawing together of languages as they saw the process, created difficulties for their real relationship" (Mordvinov, 1950, 82, 83).

Again, Marr's concern with semantics, partly because of his tendency towards the acceptance of what was alleged to be idealist and universalist as opposed to materialist considerations, laid him equally open to Stalin's prevailing ideological preoccupation. Semantics, according to Serdyuchenko (1950, 35) was Marr's first and foremost concern. But, his critics claimed that his semantics ignored one of the most fundamental of Soviet educational postulates, not so much the parallelism but the identity of thought and language. Marr considered that language and thought were brother and sister, but though they rose into being autogenetically and phylogenetically simultaneously, they were not at any point identical. He argued that ideas could arise in the mind of man prior to their being expressed. He disregarded the concept of language as the direct reality of thought, and so his semantic theories were associated by Vinogradov and others with idealist theories and the philosophy of logical syntax, for which America was held responsible, and which led to "an extratemporal or omnitemporal system of arbitrary symbols divorced from historical reality, from social development and struggle [...] The kind of criticism, the formalization and mathematization of language engaged in by the modern positivists of the Vienna school, by their British adherents and by the American semanticists is one of the most extreme manifestations of idealism" (Vinogradov, 1950, 22) to which Marr is alleged to have succumbed.

Compared with Marxist materialism, Marr's 'idealist' philosophical propensities meant a total divorce of language and thought, and a consequent underestimation of the importance of the mother tongue in general development and in learning a second language. His erroneous concept of the determination of language by social class as opposed to national characteristics directed language teaching into unprofitable paths. Furthermore "he refused to treat as linguistic data the manifest resemblances and relationships between languages", and could therefore do very little to establish right relationships in the study of the various national languages, and in teaching indigenous second languages (Vinogradov, 1950, 21-22).

D. PRINCIPLES OF LANGUAGE ACQUISITION AND LANGUAGE PEDAGOGY

For Soviet psycho-linguists the most disturbing feature of Marr's theories was the support they gave to those who stressed the separation of the development of language in the individual child from its material foundations, physiological and social. Following the pronouncements of Lenin, and Pavlov's enquiries it has been an essential postulate of Soviet educationists' thinking that the mind of man must be studied in its "dependence on the objective conditions of existence". Human psychological processes develop in society and are the product of mainfold reflex physical activity. This is the only foundation, it is argued, on which we can understand scientifically the acquisition of language and its functioning. Language is a socially determined second signal-system, standing in for the immediate signals received from the environment through the child's sensory receptors. To that extent language is one step removed from reality and reflects the aspects of the physical and social environment impinging on the organism in only a generalised form. If the child is to grow up normally this generalized character of the language has to be fed by, remain rooted in the immediacy of concrete activity and be confirmed by it. Though this second signal system is unique in that it possesses very great powers of self-regulation it is still subject to the same material forces and laws which govern the first signal system.

Investigations show how very gradually and according to precisely defined stages speech comes to take over from immediate physical stimuli the task of regulating behaviour. Some psychologists have described the relationship of speech and behaviour, without attempting to explain the nature of such a relationship. Other investigators like Piaget have been epistemologists and have analysed the constitution of each successive pattern or stage of intelligent behaviour, and the different functions of language at each stage. Neurolinguistic investigations, such as those undertaken in the USSR, it is claimed, go beyond these limits of enquiry: they explain the nature of intellectual and linguistic functions, analyse the constitution of psycho-linguistic development as well as the physiological and neurological conditions which permit increasingly complex forms of behaviour.

Soviet neuro-linguistics is tied to the principles of dialectical materialism, and the 'Leninist Theory of Reflection', which argues that learning takes place through the action of the human organism on society, and through the active manipulation of the environment. The child's earliest speech utterances are directly related to his actions upon the real world. As the child's activities grow more complex so does language become increasingly involved in the co-ordination of the various aspects of those activities. It is his action upon the variety of objects by which he is surrounded that sets in motion and shapes his linguistic and intellectual development (Vygotsky 1934), 22). It is in social activity, above all social play going beyond the narrow limits of the random or fortuitous manipulation of objects, that the child develops language (Rahmani, 1966, 157). Memorization and the ability to recall, on which so much intelligent behaviour relies requires first the use of external devices which are gradually set aside, and reactivated whenever difficulties are faced (Leontev, 1961). Behind the linguistic expression of abstract ideas lie discarded forms of material activity. As a rule, utterances of the twins Yura and Liosha for instance acquired meaning only in a concrete, active situation. They understood speech that was directly related to an object or action in which they were engaged but were unable to understand speech that was not so directly related or which was 'distanced' from it (Luria and Yudovich, 1959, 40, 50).

This stress on the concrete and active character of the fundamental processes of language acquisition is reflected also in the Soviet aim to relate education in general to the productive forces of society. In spite of fairly recent educational changes tending towards the relaxation of the emphasis on productive work for all school children the conviction still holds that only by active participation in society can an individual child be offered the opportunity for full psychological and intellectual development as a precondition for language acquisition. The arguments advanced by Khruschev and others "concerning drawing the school child into productive work" were aimed not simply to ensure the cohesiveness of society by safeguarding the school's relationship with the larger world, but also to make certain that the mental development of an individual child was promoted satisfactorily through the maintenance intact of its concrete and material foundations (*Pravda*, July 1958). There is no doubt, either, that the insistence of the teachers of language on the 'productive' aim of language teaching was meant in part to ensure that language development remained firmly rooted in considerable classroom activity, rather than in the arid and academic practices of the former grammatical language courses.

Acting upon the environment, the necessary base for the acquisition of language, is not a temporary phase in the development of the child. Action is not discarded when the more abstract symbolic system of language takes over. Such concrete, 'enactive' ways of thinking and acquiring language, themselves develop and change in the course of schooling and acquire new functions. The initial active and material forms of intelligent behaviour out of which language grows and which the process of second language acquisition also requires continue to develop with the more abstract forms of language. It is only to be expected therefore that incipient articulatory activity accompanies all language learning. For instance covert articulatory activity accompanies the identification of new sounds in a second language: "it is impossible to distinguish new sounds clearly or to associate them with specific phonemic categories without an accompanying articulatory activity however covert: kinesthetic analysis of speech sounds [...] plays an essential part in the hearing of phonemes and neurolinguistic analysis has confirmed this" (Luria, 1967, 40). Nearly every intellectual operation is accompanied by minutely determined activation of the organs of speech. Similarly any one aspect of language behaviour involves the active participation of several areas of brain activity: for instance writing involves the activation not only of the brain area which controls the general programme of the writing process, but areas of the brain concerned with processing auditory, kinetic and visual-kinesthetic inputs (Luria 1967, 68). The exclusion of speech activity before the establishment of abstract intelligence, or a restriction of incipient speech activity in the performance of those intellectual operations including aspects of language behaviour other than speech, may severely handicap the child's language development (Lane, 1964, 256).

There are interesting parallels between the views of Soviet psycho-linguists and those of the 'transformationists' concerning some aspects of language learning. Soviet workers frequently refer to the work of Piaget also with respect. But though they find it possible to agree with some aspects of both 'transformationist theory' and the genetic-epistemological theories of Piaget they differ from them on two related issues, namely the possible innateness of language and the role of experience in learning. These two differences are crucial to the Soviet justification of psychological and linguistic engineering. Soviet psycho-linguistic theories, though they tend more and more to postulate mediating cognitive factors in the learning of language, differ from transformational theory because Soviet linguists subordinate the innate, internal factors to the social and historical processes. The structures, the existence of which Soviet psycho-linguits are prepared to accept, are not given but the product of the psycho-genetic process. They do not determine *ab initio* the whole of the processes which produce language. Rather they provide, simply, a point of departure on which the environmental and developmental cognitive processes work. The possibility of internalizing linguistic structures so as to ensure the more developed and abstract kinds of thinking lies in the existence of antecedent structures, possibly in the genetic code itself, DNA and RNA. But the structures, as they concern the linguist are neither innate nor immobile, though they are certainly more consistent and stable than early naive behaviourism would wish to admit. The relation between the organism and the environment so far as language development goes may be seen as a cybernetic loop ensuring that individual language development both selects and is conditioned by the environment (Saumjan, 1965, 142 ff.).

Vygotsky, as early as 1926, criticized the hypothesis of innate linguistic factors or a special capacity for language learning, which has come to characterize Chomsky's system. "It is not upon inborn capabilities but on anatomical and physiological characteristics [...] that capacities are built." (Menchenskaya, 1967, 12). True there are very deeply embedded innate factors, but these undergo qualitative changes in the course of development. The innate internal conditions are "themselves the result of a socio-historical process and have been formed as a result of external action". Consequently the creative role is assigned not to the inherited characteristics exclusively, as Chomsky tends to suggest, any more than to the external forms exclusively as is implied by Skinner, and other empiricists, but to the central processes activated and operated by the interaction of these two factors. Chomsky's idea of innate linguistic universals producing a pattern of linguistic features to which the child's acquisition of language conforms is contrary to the Soviet standpoint, which insists that the central structure which is the base for the development of language ability is "produced not postulated". Internal schemas or structures are formed during development in society, though the effect of external social agents can never be actually to create the central schemas. "There is always a mobilization of the cognitive processes, a fresh analysis leading to change and development" (Leontev, 1957a, 234).

Maturation therefore does not determine the child's development or his increasing mastery of language – it is simply the precondition of such a mastery. The important characteristic of the learner's mental activity is its extraordinary plasticity, "because of which nothing is intractable, everything may be achieved, changed for the better, *provided* only that the proper conditions are created" (Pavlov 1941, 144). Spontaneous, maturationally determined development belongs in the main to the area of biological growth and the view that "nature brings nothing to light other than that, which maturing within itself, strives to emerge" (Comenius) is diametrically contrary to Soviet thinking. Consequently among Soviet workers there is approval for work which goes, first to demonstrate the value of *directed* experience and second to show that improvement of instruction makes it possible to increase the language learning capacity of children (Menchenskaya and Saburova, 1967, 5, 8). Even Leontev who goes as far as any Soviet psychologist in emphasizing that development and learning are independent in some circumstances, regards the processes of 'spontaneous' development as themselves in the long term the results of social evolution (Leontev, 1957b, 243). Soviet thinking stresses the specific and irreducible character of the social-historial level and consequently it has no place for innate entelechies, immanencies or innate mental functions. The whole process of learning a language changes with time and is an essentially public, social and active process (Vygotsky, 1934, 22).

As it affects the acquisition of language this attitude to learning has marked affinities with Piaget's. In spite of Soviet suspicion of the latter's alleged idealist philosophical tendencies they have much in common. Piaget speaks of an inner schema which, having become increasingly verbal during successive stages of development is synonymous with what he calls a 'capacity to respond' or set. Furthermore although, at least for the purposes of enquiry and investigation if not in actual theoretical explanation, he places far greater emphasis on autonomous development and the possibility of isolating the innate factors in such development, he like the Soviet psychologists concludes that "recourse to innate factors never resolves problems; it merely passes them on to biology" (Piaget, 1964, 15). Like Leontev he argues that it may "always be supposed that modification resulting from environmental influences will be found at the origin of innate mechanisms".

For neither the Genevan nor Soviet school is there any polarization of the external or social, and the innate psychological forces, and the notion that 'the external operates through the internal' is common to both schools of thinking. For Piaget and Leontev the assimilation of social experience affects the structure of the cognitive processes which are identical with or necessary to the learning of language. In both cases the theory of learning, including language, regards the basic structures as not simply factors in promoting development, including language, but as products of learning as well. Chomsky on the contrary bases his theory of the acquisition of language on the assumption that certain mental structures are innate, and though capable of transformation are by their nature immutable. There is considerable ambiguity within Chomsky's own writings and apparent differences between Chomsky and some of those influenced by him, about the nature of these structures. Chomsky argues that the general features of grammar are common to all languages and that these universals of language are not learned but are an innate property of mind (Chomsky, 1957, 59). They are not only a necessary but almost a sufficient condition of knowledge of language. Language is not acquired through experience but "is a matter of growth and maturation of relatively fixed capacities [...] The form of the language that is acquired is largely determined by internal factors." McNeill who is of the same school of thought speaks of the innate universals of language providing a child with a set of templates, and it is only in so far as the language the child hears from his parents and others conforms to this in-built set of templates (grammatical structures) that the language of his society is useful to him (McNeill, 1966, 36). The child is assumed to have the capacity to fit the blueprints he is born with upon the language he is surrounded by, and to accept only what is already contained in the blue print. Language acquisition which is independent of the processes of learning and experience is regarded by the transformationist school as being autogenic. "It is not clear to them how the hearing of a language affects the child's acquisition." (Jenkins, 1966). Such an extreme pre-formationist standpoint neutralizes the possibility of both linguistic ontogeny and phylogeny – we are operating within a closed, if internally mobile or transformationist system; an eternally predestined plan whose gaps are inexplicable and imperfections ineluctable.

The transformationist assumption that the child possesses an inborn faculty for language which experience does not modify is as unacceptable to the Soviet psycho-linguist as it is to the Genevan school. Language acquisition is neither separate from nor identical with innate or with external factors exclusively, but is the fruit of their interaction. Soviet and Genevan theorists differ in their estimate of the relevance of school teaching, and formal instruction as a way of facilitating this interaction, but this we refer to later. From our point of view the important fact is that the views of psychologists and linguists in the USSR concerning the material and social foundations of languages, and their conviction that modification of these environmental influences are reflected in changes in the process and rate of language acquisition provides one of the necessary justifications for the conscious planning of language programmes, and the precise control of classroom teaching to promote the same purpose. Political and social considerations tie in with the educational and psychological factors in promoting the language policy and pedagogy.

E. THE IDENTIFICATION OF SPEECH AND THOUGHT

The adult's behaviour is so completely under voluntary control that it is difficult to analyse the processes by which that control comes to be exercised. In the young child however it is possible to trace behaviour from the point where it is dominated by external stimuli, through the stages of its dependence first on adult verbal commands, subsequently on the child's understanding of his own spoken commands, to the point where behaviour is almost entirely regulated by internalized or inner speech. The speed with which a child acquires the ability to understand and use words is rightly emphasized by teachers and psychologists, but it is deceptive. In the present climate created only partly it is true by transformation theory, with its nervous insistence on the speed with which language is acquired, it is not as clearly recognized that it takes a relatively long time for the language which the child has learned to function, or that acquisition and functioning are different parts of the same process.

The relation of mastery of the system and the functioning of that system in regulating behaviour is central to the consideration of the relationship of the first and second languages. The relationship is influenced not only by how much of the first language has been acquired before the second language is introduced but also by the extent and the direction of the influence of the first language on important cognitive operations which inevitably affect the ease with which the second language is acquired and its effective functioning in social contexts. When it is appropriate to introduce a second language and how a first and second language, acquired simultaneously, should be handled in school or in the home, are questions which can be answered only in the light of investigations into how the primary language, the mother tongue, operates in general development, especially up to the age of puberty. This is an area to which Vygotsky and his disciples, such as Luria, have contributed greatly. In the area of concept formation they distinguish those which are acquired very early and owe nothing to words; those, the formation of which language facilitates and which in any case language is required to explain; and those that are fundamentally and essentially verbal – their core is a word without which the concept could no longer be an element in thought. In so far as the mother tongue enters into concept formation, therefore, it does so at various levels which extend over several years of the child's development, from the ages of 6 or 7 (Luria 1961b, 12) ripening to make its main contribution somewhere around 12 years (Vygotsky, 1934, 58). These processes therefore are continuing at the same time as very many thousands of Soviet children are probably being exposed to the second, though not necessarily a foreign, language. That second language is not an independent functioning system as a game of chess for instance might be, but draws upon the same range of experiences and the same social context as the first language.

Discriminating and ordering experience, the bases of concept formation, are outward-oriented linguistic functions, in the sense that the child is attempting to control his environment. At the same time language is being used progressively as a means of controlling personal behaviour, an inward-oriented functioning of language, the child learning to act on or control his reactions to the environment. The inward-oriented, or regulating function of speech means the capacity to initiate, control and direct action in response to verbal stimuli originating first from adults and subsequently from the child himself. In this latter case the verbal stimulus accompanies and then prepares for the child's action. This pragmatic as distinct from the designative function develops in several stages, the first of which is the impellant or initiatory phase which may appear from as early as the 2nd year. The second phase is characterized by the use of language to inhibit rather than to initiate action. Before he is able to use language to stop action which is stimulated by a statement or command a child will continue an action already begun in spite of a new and contrary instruction; and this process by which words actually influence a child in delaying a proposed action is complex and long in maturing. The third phase of the development of the regulating functioning of language is its role in preparing beforehand for future action, not simply to trigger action or to stop ongoing action, but organizing action in advance of its actual occurrence. In this phase language acquires a conditional function – action takes place if certain conditions are fulfilled, these being articulated lingistically.

The directing, preparatory role of language is important not only for itself but because without it other cognitive functions could not be performed. The control of conditional operations enables the child to reflect upon the activities he is performing now or likely to perform in the future, a capacity which is developed only towards puberty and serving to distinguish childhood from adolescence. Thus language becomes part of three of the most vital aspects of advanced learning at a time when the child who is learning or being exposed to a second language at all is deeply involved in that process. These are hypothesizing, that is the formulation of possible answers to questions or an anticipation of the results of an enquiry; the formulation of aims, and the organization of objects and the manipulation of people according to a plan – all three vital and advanced cognitive processes.

"Any complex behaviour is determined by a programme which ensures not only that the subject reacts to actual stimuli, but within certain limits foresees the future, foretells the probability that a particular event may happen, will be prepared if it does happen, and as a result formulates a programme of behaviour [...] The creation of these action programmes is taken with the closest participation of the abstracting, generalizing and regulating function of speech." (Luria, 1967, 531). There is no doubt whatever that all the highest functional formations with which psychology is concerned are in greater or lesser degree linked with this regulating function of speech, locks in an existing system of connections, which in normal behaviour becomes dominant and which defines the course of all subsequent actions of the child. These processes which are central not only to development in general but to second language learning, (if we conceive of the latter as a developing rule-governed behaviour), are gathering momentum at the time when most Soviet schildren are learning or being exposed to a second, though not in the majority of cases a foreign language to which they are introduced later.

Language moves, then, from having interpersonal functions mainly, being simply a form of communication, to having intra-personal directive functions – participating in the interpretation of the social and physical environment, regulating actions, then securing the transition to complex forms of meaningful play and ending by becoming the most important factor in the development of conscious behaviour" (Luria and Yydovich, 1959, 47). The language of the child acquires a psychological in addition to its original social significance, and the child's mother tongue establishes itself not only as an objective means of making contact with other people, but as a principle which governs the nature of those contacts. Contrary to transformational theory, with which he shares some important concepts, for the Soviet psychologist language comes to be identified with thought. In Chomsky's view the acquisition of language is independent not only of the experience available in society, as we have shown, but of the child's intelligence. Not only are language and thinking not identical at any stage, as is the Soviet argument, but for the transformationist there appears to be "little useful analogy between the linguistic structures and other systems of mental organization", nor is there "much promise in extending the concepts of linguistic structures to other cognitive structures." (Chomsky, 1968, 53, 56). This of course is completely at variance with the Soviet view. In Soviet thinking it is true that ontogenetically thought and speech have two genetically different origins, with a pre-speech phase of intelligence reflected first in sensory motor activity, and at a later stage in imagery. It is also their belief that speech and intelligence continue along parallel and separate lines until about the age of two when the curves of speech and cognitive development begin to converge. Thereafter comes a close integration between speech and motor intelligence (the enactive phase) and between speech and imagery (the ikonic phase) (Bruner, 1966). Progressively the vital aspects of behaviour are represented by verbal thought (Vygotsky, 1934, passim). In other words, so far as the most important areas of every day life are concerned thought and intelligent behaviour become identified with the use of words.

Soviet psychology explains this gradual identification of thought and speech by the process of internalization. This is not a peculiarly Soviet contribution nor is it a recent theory in Soviet studies of intellectual and speech development. It was put forward by Pavlov nearly 40 years ago, and it is well over a century since Sechenov maintained that when a child thinks he invariably talks at the same time. Thought in five-year-olds is mediated through words or whispers, silently through movements of tongue and lips, and this is frequently true though perhaps in different degrees, of the thinking of adults. The work of Leontev, Galperin and

Luria following upon that of Vygotsky has tested, refined and elaborated the early suggestions, and they have shown that as it helps more and more to determine the child's actions his social speech becomes less frequent, it is more abbreviated, the grammatical constructions revealing contractions, breaks and telescoping of propositions into single words, and is transformed to whispers. "On the basis of psychological and electromyographic investigations of internal speech it may be concluded that the real process of thought in individuals who are able to speak is always connected with the language though at certain moments or phases of thinking the speech action may be inhibited [...] The internal speech which manifests itself in the thinking process is not an epiphenomenon, but a really acting mechanism of human thought. Internal speech organizes and directs this thought, maintains its purposive character and leads to a logical completion of the whole process. It is a form of speech which possesses a highly dynamic and changeable structure and is adapted to the performance of the functions of thinking. At the moment when thoughts arise it may be reduced only to a few hints of some of the most generalizing or 'key words' (Sokolov, 1971, 90). As the child begins to move away from using speech in order to direct attention to an object, from simply orienting himself to the environment, and more and more to understanding the environment and to making statements about it, the language he uses concentrates almost exclusively on the predicative element. The subject and all words qualifying it are omitted, the predicate alone being retained, and "a single word is saturated with the meaning which many words in social, adult speech would be required to convey" (Vygotsky, 1934, 148).

Thus every intellectual operation begins with external action and is then gradually transformed by a process in which external, extended speech participates. It is finally linked with internal speech, and this internal speech, based on condensed verbal kinesthesia, is the mechanism responsible for the performance of complex mental actions. A study of the function of inner speech in the acquisition of a second language recorded electrical disturbances from the tongue and lips while students were learning English, and greater muscular movements when subjects were reading English than when they read their mother tongue, Russian. "For example, during reading texts in foreign languages micro-movement of the speech organs may be recorded" (Sokolov, 89). This muscular activity increased as the text became more difficult, being most pronounced among students with poor command of the second language. As the students' competence in English approached their ability in Russian differences in the amount of subvocal activity declined. The conclusion is that motor-activity feedback is necessary in learning any language and especially the second language.

Because of the identification of thinking and speech, and the fact that language from being only a form of communication develops into a principle of mental growth, or a part of the process of psychological development, there are deeper layers to language acquisition and learning than can be accounted for by the traditional associationist theories. In fact Soviet schools have in the past been criticized within the USSR for failure to abandon the behaviourist-associationist theories of language as pure habit-formation. The primary school courses, it has been alleged, have been used mainly to instil habits mechanically (Zankov, 1963, 4). It is not denied that the accumulation of linguistic habits is important but these habits should be regarded as only the secondary manifestations of a 'more profound understanding of the laws of language'. Since language and thought are so inextricably intertwined and identified with each other, mechanical or unreflecting habit formation is not a satisfactory explanation of acquisition. In fact surveys of language courses in the USSR have shown that successful habit formation in the early stages is not necessarily accompanied by any substantial linguistic progress. It is incorrect to reduce the mastery of speech to habits, and habits to systems of conditioned reflexes or associations as was traditionally the case (Artemov, 1967, 15). Instead, language teaching should be directed, in Ushensky's words, to awakening the active thought of the pupils or "the consciousness of the purpose of the action" to be performed, and should lay greater emphasis on the cognitive aspects of linguistic education, and on the theoretical knowledge of language (Zankov, 1963, 8).

The cognitive structure created by, or identified with speech, is given a variety of names. Pavlov refers to a certain impetus towards the creation of a 'dynamic stereotype' (Pavlov, 1926, Vol. II), which provides the possibility for the creation of whatever habits have to be acquired in learning a language, the habits being only the realization of a more general competence or 'skill'. All the possible variations of the child's linguistic performance stem from this competence, *gotovnost* 'disposition'. This fundamental precondition or presupposition of actual performance is called a 'set' by the Georgian school of psychologists, a term which Luria had employed very much earlier to refer to the abbreviated internal *schema* which become identified with speech and which determine the acquisition of language through an understanding of the laws which govern it. (Luria, 1932, 68 et seq.). For the Georgian psychologists the 'set' is a 'facility for correct speech' (Natadze, 1957, 308) and constitutes the basic form of a language, and determines its acquisition. Beliaev refers to what is virtually the same concept as a 'feeling for language' (1963, 91), or dynamic stereotype (194), that which permits a student to have practical knowledge of the language. The central schema, stereotype, skill, set or feeling for language, whatever it may be called is a dynamic constant, on the basis of which alone it is possible to learn a language. As such it bears very close resemblance to the concept 'linguistic competence' later developed by Chomsky.

F. INTERACTION OF FIRST AND SECOND LANGUAGES

As we have seen the whole of Soviet linguistic theory tends to the postulation of deep seated cognitive, as opposed to peripheral, associationist processes. It is because the learning of language involves these that the learning of a second language and its interaction with the first language have such profound implications not only for the linguistic but for the more general development of the child as well. Interesting work on the psychology of bilingualism was initiated in Georgia by Uznadze, followed by Imedadze. In their view the two languages of a bilingual child, to begin with, constitute a single verbal repertoire, and components of both languages are used indiscriminately in the young child's communication with adults. After a short period, at about 1.8 years, the two systems begin to separate until at about 2 years independent vocabularies are recognised by the child, and two independent grammatical systems are gradually formed. Nevertheless though in appropriate settings or speech situations the two languages operate independently, the interaction between them is significantly complex (Luria, 1932, 213). Such observations are not new, and several psychologists especially in North America have refined the concept of two related but independent systems. Nevertheless little has been done by these researchers to analyse the deep psychological as distinct from linguistic consequences of the interaction. It is as if they had been content simply to investigate the separate but related levels of *performance* without considering the reaction upon the deeper levels of *competence* common to performance in each language.

Well before 1934, when the first edition of his 'Thought and Language' was published in Moscow, Vygotsky had pointed to the dependence of the second language on the processes which had led to the acquisition of the mother tongue. He had also made suggestions about the nature of that dependence, using what is to all intents and purposes the twin ideas of *competence* and *performance*. Vygotsky makes the point that the second language belongs to the 'exterior, social, physical aspects of verbal thought', akin to *acquired* scientific concepts; while the native tongue is identified with the development of *spontaneous* concepts, those mental structures which are dependent on the unfolding or maturing of the inherent possibilities of the organism's endowment. In learning the mother tongue the child unconsciously develops his competence without explicit awareness of phonetic, grammatical forms because the mother tongue develops naturally and necessarily with the gradual evolution of the neurological system, which makes any kind of learning possible. There is an essential difference when it comes to learning the second language. "The later stage does not repeat the course of the earlier one [...] analagous systems develop in reverse direction at the higher and lower levels, each system complementing the other and benefitting from the strong points of the other." The gradually acquired complex system essential to the working of the mother tongue can be assumed to exist when the second language is introduced and in consequence explicit, more formal "intellectualist theories of language, such as Stern's which place a full grasp of the relationship between sign and meaning at the very beginning of linguistic development, contain a measure of truth in the case of the second language", though they do not explain the acquisition of the first language. *Competence* can be assumed in learning the second language and the area of language acquisition which is peculiar to the latter is that of performance: "the exterior, social and physical aspects of verbal thought are acquired in the reverse order to the mother tongue, that is by *conscious* employment of linguistic rules and strategies" (Vygotsky, 1934, 110). In the eyes of Soviet psychologists the understanding of the relationship of these two levels of language acquisition has considerable relevance to the teaching of a second language as well as to the observation of first language development. This understanding of the importance of the mother tongue in learning the second language is part of the concept of rule governed language learning which leads to an emphasis on 'consciousness' in learning.

In their insistence that the bases of language learning need to be acquired only once, subsequent languages being built on a common foundation of *competence*, Soviet psycho-linguists, like the generative theorists, turn away from traditional associationism. For the latter all language learning is on one level, the learning of the second language repeating all the processes of acquiring the first. The two languages not only function independently but in learning them there is no common foundation, plan or schema. The learning of each language depends on the acquisition of the two assemblages of verbal associations each of which constitutes the whole of a language and of that language alone. This traditional associationism is rebutted by Imedadze's account of the bilingual child's acquisition of the two languages. The first stage of the child's language development, characterized by the undifferentiated use of elements from both languages indicates that what the child is concerned to do is by using materials from both languages without restraint to create one system, which only later becomes differentiated into separate languages. The undifferentiated stage corresponds to the development of *competence*, the differentiated stage corresponds to the level of performance, in either language.

At this later stage of performance the two languages interact with advantages to both as Vygotsky argues, sharpening the consciousness of the rule governed process in both languages. The interaction affects the level of performance by sharpening the student's consciousness of the regularities of both languages and so refining his control of all aspects of the two languages. The interaction can also have considerable retroactive influence on the deeper level of competence. Interaction on the performance level can influence the deep seated mechanisms which are the precondition of *performance* in either language. Both languages reflect the existence of basic common *competence* or *set*, the non-conscious factor in cognitive behaviour. If there is a conflict in the situations in which the two languages are used, or where performance is relevant, there is a very profound emotional disturbance which produces a deterioration in the child's verbal responses. This is of considerable importance in the Soviet Union since it affects the learning of Russian as a second language by all those for whom this language is virtually compulsory from an early age, and other indigenous second and even third languages, learned by many thousands of immigrant children moving from one national and linguistic community to a very different one, as it might be those moving from the West into Central Asia. Such children are inevitably brought up against very considerable differences not only in language but in the social contexts in which the languages are spoken.

Awareness of differences is one of the ways in which an individual comes to create a concept of self, of personal identity. Such an awareness is apt to be more intense among bilinguals, especially bilingual immigrants in profoundly different cultural and linguistic settings. It produces among them one of four possible results – first the immigrant may be highly conscious of his ethnic origins and conceive himself as distinctively differentiated from others, so that he may develop hostility towards them. Nevertheless he maintains a consistent if negative attitude and is unlikely to be emotionally insecure. A second alternative is uncertainty in his ethnic identification patterns, life on the margins of his own and the dominant culture setting. Thirdly, he may go out of his way not to be identified with his own group and in fact seek to avoid commitment to any community – he tries, in this respect to be completely non-allied. Finally the immigrant child may succeed in preserving a stable relation with both language groups having made clear to himself, or having accepted, the demarcations and appropriate roles for his relevant languages.

In different ways and with different intensities the marginal and the unattached child or adolescent is alienated from both possible linguistic milieux, and a state of alienation may produce a total crisis of personal identity and emotional life. In so far as the two languages he has acquired are concerned uncertainty in the choice of one or other will depend on several factors, some of them affecting the adolescent more than the younger immigrant. For instance one of the factors is whether the occasion on which he is called to make a choice is a private or public one; whether the occasion involves problems of group or ethnic identification; what the prestige of the two languages, public attitude towards them or degree of tolerance may be; whether the occasion is a threatening one, an occasion when the young person is concerned with being adequate and making a good impression, especially as he progresses up the school and his level of aspiration is high, so that he becomes concerned with problems of correct linguistic usage. And finally whether the setting in which the language-alternative is offered touches central rather than peripheral layers of personality. Soviet workers emphasize that there is no necessary or inevitable conflict between the use of the two languages, but conflict may arise from the incompatibility of the settings of the two languages, and the way a child is able to handle the transfer from one to another. "These disturbances are referred not to the difficulty of associating ideas in a foreign language but exclusively to the necessity of transferring from one established setting to another." (Luria, 1932, 216). Speaking a certain language, an individual becomes habituated to a particular setting and "transfer to a new setting with the removal of the former setting is evidently sufficient to create neuro-dynamic disturbances." (Luria, 1932, 213). It should be sufficient to bring into collision such language settings in order to create a conflict of two very complicated structural systems. Luria has shown that when such a transfer occurs suddenly or where there is no predictability about the way in which such transfers are organised "a series of very interesting and serious disturbances occur [...] Sudden transfer to another language is combined with a very great destructive process." (Luria, 1932, 215).

The danger is characterized by Soviet psycho-linguists as a reversion to more primitive mechanisms of thinking such as those which Piaget has named syncretism. In such cases an individual will adopt capricious linguistic responses in both his first and second languages. This is consequent on the lowering or destruction of the 'functional barrier' which normally enables the child to exercise an inhibitory, restraining influence – to interpose a barrier between stimulus and response. One form of the distortion which the lowering of the 'functional barrier' produces is spasmodic speech behaviour and hesitancy. Luria has pointed out that the time expended in speech responses in situations of language conflict fluctuated, and together with rapidly flowing associations he had very slow ones. The individuals were unable to produce reactions with a degree of stability. The phenomenon relates to sudden transfer of language "the subject when exposed suddenly to an unfamiliar word or one with which he is only slightly familiar attempts to think it out, assimilating it to words whose meaning is known to him in the other language." (Luria 1932, 52). Thus when confronted with the need to interpret the English word *letter* a speaker of Russian responds with the English association *summer* because of the association of the Russian *leto* which means summer.

The Soviet position with respect to language acquisition is not dissimilar to that adopted by the generative theorist, and in fact Luria refers favorably to the potential value of Chomsky's linguistic analyses. However, whereas a generative grammar according to Chomsky does not provide a 'model for the speaker', and is irrelevant to the problems peculiar to second language learning (Chomsky, 1957, 14; 1965, 202), Soviet psychologists using basically the same concepts offer a very cogent explanation of second language learning and of the psychological interaction of the two languages and possible consequences of such interaction.

G. IMPLICATIONS OF SOVIET THEORY FOR LANGUAGE PEDAGOGY

From what we have seen Soviet theory proposes language as a crucial factor in intellectual development, and for that reason, pedagogy ensures that the mother tongue is recognized as the basis for the acquisition of any subsequent languages. Any general educational programme therefore has to be built around language teaching; and the teaching of the second language, so far as Soviet theory is concerned, is conceived mainly in psychological rather than strictly linguistic terms. Whatever may be the importance of the natural sciences the whole programme of Soviet national development so far as it is reflected in education must in the last resort depend on a satisfactory programme for languages. Not only is the mother tongue central to general education, it is also the basis on which the second language is acquired. Therefore general national development relies for a great deal of its success on the establishment in the classroom as well as in society at large of a right relationship between the several languages individual children are required to learn. The educational theories we have so far discussed reflect the general emphasis in the USSR on the child's consciousness of language processes and consequently on a language pedagogy which justifies intense adult intervention to promote those processes. Language teaching is based on a concept of language as rule governed behaviour in preference to the establishment of habits; the student is to be made consciously aware of the theory which ties together these rules and of the structure of the language he is acquiring. Explicitness and consciousness are guiding considerations, and this means that the teacher is central to the language acquisition process. Very much the reverse of the situation in Britain, though perhaps not so far removed from trends in the USA, the *teaching* rather than the *learning* of language is the principal point for consideration, adult direction of acquisition rather than an emphasis on personal discovery of the characteristics of the language.

i.   *The Use of the Mother Tongue in Learning the Second Language*

The information which forms the theoretical foundation for second language learning may be given in the student's mother tongue. Transiation also gives to the mother tongue a prominent place in second language learning. The Marrist inability to conceive of a necessary relation between linguistic and cognitive development resulted, Vinogradov maintained, in errors concerning the relation that should exist between the pupil's native language and the second language. It "led Marrists to underestimate the role played by the mother tongue in learning the foreign language and to belittle the importance of the theory and practice of translation" (Vinogradov, 1950, 22). Shcherba had offered a theoretic justification of the use of the native language but it was not until the development of psycho-linguistics in the hands of Leontev, Galperin and Luria following the lines laid down by Vygotsky that it was realized fully how important was the mother tongue in producing linguistic *competence*, and so providing the necessary basis for second language learning.

Psychology provided as we have seen one justification for the importance attached to the first language but linguistics too provided an important theoretical justification. Translation is only one form of the conscious-comparative method and to some extent the more mechanistic interpretations of this principle of comparison and formal translation as it was outlined by Raxmanov have recently been severely criticized and greatly modified. It is now agreed that "translation should be used only for revealing the peculiarities of thinking in the foreign language, and not as the basic means for giving the meaning of the foreign words or for understanding the foreign language speech." A combination of the principles of conscious theoretical learning and a sympathetic attitude towards the possibilities of using translation-comparison methods meant that Soviet linguists developed their own theory of 'contrastive analysis'. The theoretical information communicated to the student need not duplicate what is already known to him from his acquaintance with his mother tongue, but should refer only to what is uniquely characteristic of the second language. "It assumes that the explanations and exercises should take into consideration the difficulties encountered by pupils because of differences between the language they are studying and their native language. Comparisons should be made only when they help the pupils master the phenomenon being studied." (Galazov, 1965, 51).

Though developed from a different angle, the use of contrastive analysis is as theoretically well founded in the Soviet Union as it is in the U.S. However there is only a limited acceptance of the pedagogic value of that theory and the approach is adopted much more selectively than in the U.S.A. Nor does it depend to the same extent as in the U.S. on exhaustive comparative analyses of the relevant languages.

Another difference between the development of contrastive analysis in the USSR and the US is that whereas in the case of the latter, until very recently, it has been related mainly to foreign languages, in the USSR it has developed from the beginning out of the study of the problems of interference between the great variety of indigenous languages all of which to some extent are taught as second languages. Such problems of interference have received considerable attention in the USSR. Serdyuchenko (1955), Rastorgueva (1952), Grunberg (1960) and Ubryatova (1956) in particular have drawn attention to this linguistic problem. Stress is laid on the advisability of studying Russian in texts prepared locally "because they take into account the specific features of the national language and are a great help in mastering those aspects which are difficult for the Ossetian children" (Galazov, 1965, 52). Linguistic investigations relating to Uzbek were used to identify phonetic difficulties encountered by students, and these "showed for instance that Russian listeners heard the length and volume of the stressed vowels as the basic component of stress while the Uzbeks hear the volume and pitch of the fundamental tone" (Artemov, 1960, 44). Mirtov (1962) has worked on the linguistic problems arising from differences between Uzbek and Russian, as well as Azerbaydzhani and Russian (1956); Purtseladze on Russian and Georgian (1960-1966); Kudriatsev on Russian and Buryat (1965); and Cherednichenko on Russian and Ukrainian (1957). Similar work has been done for Armenian. The work on indigenous languages has been extended to cover some of the more important foreign languages. Lithuanian linguists have made a study of the contrasts between Lithuanian and English (Schmalstieg, 1963) and there are several approaches to the comparison of Russian with French, German and English.

However Soviet teachers are reluctant to rely on theoretical contrastive analysis exclusively and they are encouraged to supplement linguistic analysis with observation of actual difficulties and error analysis. Furthermore the use of comparison, translation and the mother tongue during the language lesson is not allowed to dominate classroom practice nor to create a too intellectualist approach to teaching. 'Consciousness', on which all these approaches are based, is not only intellectual awareness, it is also an attitude. Knowledge, as Leontev is fond of stressing is meaning, and an understanding of meaning or the significance of the linguistic features being presented depends as much on attitude and the student's motivation as upon the objective nature of the knowledge to be acquired.

ii. *Structure and Consciousness*

It has often been said that 'structuralism' has no part in Soviet language pedagogy, but if we interpret structuralism non-restrictively, it must be recognized to be part and parcel of Soviet linguistic and language teaching theory. It would be extremely odd if it were not so. The concept of language as structure, implicit in the work of Boas and Sapir, has a very wide connotation. These implications were somewhat restricted in the studies of Bloomfield and his followers, among whom structuralism came to acquire special connotations and to be employed very largely as a term of art. It is unfortunate that the theory of 'structuralism' has been confused with and has overshadowed the more general 'concept of structure,' for the confusion has led to suspicion both of the concept and the theory. Structure in the broad sense is a characteristic of all mental activity: intelligence, like language, becomes more effective according to its "greater complexity of structure" (Piaget, 1951, 6). It is the structuring of behaviour which constitutes its cognitive aspect (Bruner, 1968, 72), and when it comes to using language to improve behaviour or to facilitate intelligence structure again is an inevitable factor in that process. If the child is to learn fully from experience he must be given "an understanding of the fundamental structure of whatever subjects we choose to teach" (Bruner, 1960, 11).

If structure in its more concrete, elementary but nevertheless comprehensive meaning were not important to Soviet teachers they would hardly emphasize as they do the value of teaching grammar, nor would linguists have complained that Marr underestimated the importance of grammar and system. Nevertheless it cannot be denied that Soviet teachers have never been drawn towards structuralism as a theory, basically because it attempts to do what Marr was accused of doing, setting up a dualism between form and content, between structure and meaning. In 1960 an observer from the U.S. reported that 'in the Soviet Union it is not generally realized that linguistics has any particular application to foreign language teaching. Whenever I asked about this at the schools, institutes or universities I either received a definite no as an answer or they were puzzled to understand what I was talking about." (Quoted in Ornstein, 1963, 179). My own conclusions two years later (Lewis, 1962c) and during more recent visits and in talks with teachers of English visiting Britain confirm this impression of indifference or puzzlement. During the last six years interesting work has been conducted at the newly formed Department of Structural Linguistics in the Russian Language Institute of the Academy of Sciences of the USSR, under S. K. Saumijan. But the main interest lies in structure which is not abstracted from what they conceive to be the full reality of the language, and which, therefore, includes meaning. The stress on meaning abstracted from the grammatical system in which it is embedded led Marr towards the semanticism of the logical-positivists, while the stress on structure investigated and taught without regard to meaning led to the unreal formalism of some American linguistics.

The Soviet teachers are interested in a linguistics which has a regard for language in a living social situation, not a semantic or structural abstraction. For instance in spite of the attack on the alleged idealist semantics of Marr, Stalin in order to stress the concrete reality of language made it a point to note that "semantics is one of the important aspects of linguistics. It is only through building up a large stock of meanings that the relevance of language can be ensured." (Stalin, 1950b, 40). The fundamental tenet of Soviet psychology, namely the identification of language and thought as much as their social-materialist philosophy leads them to this view. Though there are some Soviet researches which suggest that concern for meaning may hinder the acquisition of the grammar of the language in the very early stages (Benediktov and Iarnatovskaia, 1960, 63), the emphasis in teaching structure is almost invariably on understanding. It is for this reason and not because they are not interested in structure that Soviet teachers of language are either indifferent to or puzzled by what is meant by 'structuralism', which has played an unimportant part both in Soviet linguistics and in the theory of language teaching.

In stressing their own ideas about the place of 'structure' in language pedagogy Soviet teachers have been supported by the views of theorists and research workers concerning the place of theoretical explanations, and of the transmission to the students, from a comparatively early age, of information about language – the mother tongue as well as subsequent languages. In warning his colleagues as early as the twenties that if they ignored the problem of consciousness they block themselves from access to the investigation of complicated problems of human behaviour Vygotsky began an interpretation of Pavlovian theory which consistently led Soviet psychology away from both naive associationism, and the American operant-conditioning theory which is part of the justification of the audiolingual approach. Current language pedagogical theory in the USSR has long stressed the principles of conscious acquisition. This requires that pupils be taught so as to instil in them a thorough understanding of the linguistic materials with which they are presented, and not simply to enable them to repeat the drills. Shcherba puts 'conscious automation' at the centre of linguistic pedagogy – a progression to ultimate unconscious control and a feeling for or intuitive understanding of the language, through explicit and conscious appreciation of the characteristics of the language, and their relation to each other. The teacher is told that conditions must be created to maximize the child's conscious awareness of the rules governing the operation of the language. This stress on consciousness implies a 'rule governed learning' and a 'rule using teaching' system. The firmness with which the material is assimilated, though benefiting from repetition of the patterns, depends not so much on repetition, as on the student's awareness of the structural significance of what is drilled. The student has to understand why these particular structures are being repeated and how they relate to the general pattern of the language he is studying.

Language learning therefore is conceived in accordance with Ushensky's proposition concerning the 'intellectual origin of habits'. He was foremost in criticizing the abstractness and unreality of the learning theories and psychology of his time, and based his own psychological system on practical experience and educational needs. His penetrating research into the nature of understanding, which he conceived as the process of concept formation, ensured that language learning was not regarded as the accumulation of unrelated experiences or habits simply, but of habits as the manifestation or exemplification of a logically prior intellectual system. In the performance of any linguistic operation or skill the pupil needs to have a general theoretical awareness recognised as the foundation for habitual performance (Zavatskaia, 1963, 14). The teacher of languages aims to impart practical mastery of the language but such a mastery depends on the communication to the student of theoretical information about the language (Beliaev, 1963, 95). Though it is subordinated to practical mastery, from the standpoint of the teacher, theory precedes the inculcation of habits and skills. For these reasons though the basic orientation of the language course should be practical and though the changes in the language courses in recent years have reduced theoretical information, the principle of basing practical teaching on the conscious understanding of linguistic theory is still adhered to firmly. Theory facilitates the practical mastery of the material. Consequently even in the innovations recently made in the language programmes pupils are introduced to the abstract ideas of the parts of speech, not so much to teach them to recognize and produce the correct forms in each case "but to acquaint them with certain laws of language. It is very important that they not only know how to distinguish the parts of speech in terms of subject matter, but also in formal grammatical terms" (Zavatskaia, 1963, 12). The provision of such theoretical information facilitates the student's own systematization of the linguistic experience to which he is being exposed, but in addition to this instrumental or practical value, it is important in itself as being largely identical with intellectual development (Rozhdestvenskiy, 1967, 32).

iii. *Formalism*

Because of the use of the mother tongue and the tendency to make explicit the rules governing language, as well as consciousness of the structure both in the mother tongue and a second language there has been and continues to be considerably greater formality than in Britain, for instance. With increased emphasis on speech this formalism has come under the critical scrutiny of teachers and in official statements. Formalism has been reflected, first, in the place accorded to language as a subject in the curriculum, and in its relationship to other subjects. During the early years of the existence of the Soviet school system attempts to inculcate grammatical rules explicitly were regarded as pedantic. The formal understanding of the operation of language, later emphasized, was thought in the early days to depend more on implicit discovery techniques. In those years of more progressive language teaching "the idea was born of teaching even grammarless grammar" (Vvedenskiy, 1918), i.e. organizing language studies without the memorization of definitions, terminology and classifications. In conformity with this attitude too the Dalton plan was favoured. The teaching of languages, especially though not exclusively the mother tongue was regarded as part of the 'complex project method'. Russian, either as the first language, or the second for those who were not native speakers of the language, was eliminated as an independent subject from Soviet curricula. The same applied to other languages. In 1922 the State Scientific Council of the People's Commissariat for Education directed that all instruction should be imparted under three headings – nature and man, labour, and society. An explanatory note to the 'New Curriculum' of 1923 outlined the theory. This meant rejecting systematic courses and text books of language, and their replacement by work books. Any suggestion that there was a need for specific language methodology was largely ignored. A result was the adoption of lax concepts in first and second language pedagogy which in turn affected the teaching of the foreign languages. It was only after resolutions of the Central Committee of the Communist Party in September 1931 that practical expression was given to the disillusionment of teachers, and language teaching began to swing towards greater formalism.

Formalism is also reflected in the fact that from beginning to end the language course is conceived, in theory to consist of separate linguistic levels, each taught independently of the other, the independence becoming progressively more marked. In 1940 faculty members of the Gorky Teachers Foreign Language Institute criticized the organization of a language curriculum by mechanical amalgamation of separate aspects of language – vocabulary, grammar, phonetics – and pressed for a course that was more organic and well integrated from start to finish. Instead of separate teachers for each aspect they pressed for one language teacher for each class and for the presentation of the grammatical and phonetic material in less abstract and more situationally determined form. (Benediktov and Iarnatovskaya, 1960). Yet the Curriculum of the Pedagogic Institutes of Foreign Languages still showed this separation several years after the criticism had been made, and separate allocations of time as well as separate departments are providing for the teaching of phonetics, grammar, practical training, analysis of texts and written practice, translation, lexicology and the introduction to linguistics (Rosen, 1963, 52-53). While school teaching does not reflect this extreme fissiparousness there is no doubt that the handling of the lessons in primary and secondary classes is influenced by the formal separation of language levels in the teacher training course.

For instance, a great deal of attention is devoted to phonetics separately, especially in teaching Russian as a second language: the use of data on phonetics, and the reliance on it (for instance in the study of declensions of nouns, and of some orthographical rules) have become customary and almost mandatory in the normal Russian language instruction in Soviet schools. In line with the separation of the various aspects of language in the teacher training course separate spelling and dictation instruction have a significant place in school teaching of Russian as a first and second language and this has influenced the teaching of foreign languages. Thus although the aims of language teaching are stated by the Assistant Director of the Research Section of the Academy of Pedagogical Sciences to be 'the thorough mastery of speech' (Monoszon, 1962) the evaluation of success is based very largely on the detailed examination of spelling tested by dictation. Shcherba very early directed attention to spelling in his 'Bad Spelling and its Causes' (Shcherba, 1927), and the concern for this aspect of language has not declined. In much the same way the mastery of correct punctuation is inculcated by formal methods in separate lessons and based on theoretical discussions. Grammar is introduced early and taught formally while parsing is regarded as a convenient and effective device for language learning.

iv. *Adult Intervention in Learning – Stress on Planning and Instruction*

Vygotsky criticized Piaget, in the main for his lack of interest in adult intervention and the explicit direction of learning. Vygotsky, for whom teaching is the real basis of psychology, claimed that Piaget took as the starting point of his theory the hypothesis that development of such intellectual operations as the acquisition of language is "independent of the child's actual school learning". This, he alleges, is a question of principle for Piaget. The tasks which Piaget investigates and on the basis of which he bases his conclusions about child development are "entirely foreign to any school work." (Vygotsky, 1934, 21). There is much in Piaget's writing which tends to substantiate Vygotsky's observations. Piaget argues that "the success of teaching is subordinated to the stage of development [...] to the mechanism of development, and does not project the organism beyond what the level of development of the mechanism permits" (Piaget, 1968, 291). In his 'Comments' upon Vygotsky's *Language and Thought* Piaget while prepared to accept the possibility of acceleration of learning maintains that what is transmitted by instruction is assimilated only if it represents the achieved level of development or "corresponds to the structure the child had already formed himself." (Piaget, 1962, 11). Vygotsky stands Piaget's formulation on its head – instead of good teaching, in order to be successful, accommodating itself to the level of development "the only good teaching is that which outpaces development". (Vygotsky 1934, 31). And this is the more recently expressed view of practising Soviet teachers also: "education and teaching do not await the maturation of mental functions but stimulate, condition their development." Vygotsky in fact postulates two zones of development, the level of task performance which necessitates or relies on guidance and adult assistance; and the level of performance where the child is successful independently of intervention. The gap between the two zones or levels is the area available to the teacher, where instruction can improve maturationally dependent performance. Teaching which is based on too optimistic an assessment of the extent of the gap, or of the efficiency of intervention, and which therefore proceeds at too challenging a pace, it is acknowledged, "far from furthering the development of mental abilities in fact smothers them" (Kostyuk, 1956, 39). Following this line of thinking Luria formulates the Soviet justification of intervention and very challenging instruction, by rejecting "the static principle of the child's independent performance of a given task in favour of that of comparing the success of his independent performance with that achieved with adult help". The theory is that "if the higher mental functions are in fact formed in the course of social relationships, and if today the child can do on its own what yesterday he could only do with adult help, then is it not of equal importance, and essential to prognosis to ascertain how far the child can make use of such help and how he applies its results to his independent activity thereafter?" (Luria, 1961a, 20). This is the view expressed by Leontev also, who while agreeing that "the extent and the forms taken by the teacher's participation in the act of the learner can vary greatly [...] yet learning in the strict sense of the word always requires participation of the teacher." (Leontev, 1957b, 243-5).

The extent of the importance which Soviet psycho-linguists attach to actual instruction in languages can be gauged if we compare their approach to that of the transformation theorist. As both McNeil and Lenneberg have pointed out: "we do not know that a child needs tuition, nor is it even certain that he profits from the tuition when it is given to him" (Jenkins, 1966, 351). In fact the farthest they will go is to say that a "child learns from his parents' speech habits how to choose among a narrow set of possibilities defined by the innate properties we call linguistic universals." (McNeill, 1966, 65). Patterns of development and of language learning emerge according to a "maturational schedule in every child raised in an adequate environment. The emergence of such patterns is independent of training procedures and extrinsic response shaping." (Lenneberg, 1967, 127). The speed with which a child learns a language is taken by the transformationists as an indication if not a proof of the innateness of language; but the Soviet theorists, while acknowledging the speed of acquisition, first of all emphasize the time it takes for language actually to function in psychological development. And second, they explain the apparent speed of acquisition by the fact that the child in acquiring language is exposed to an experience which is already generalized and processed: the experience we call language is not amorphous, without shape, but already possesses form, and is therefore easier to assimilate. Moreover, even on empiricist interpretations the child does not acquire uncategorized units but classes of sounds and of words.

The doubt expressed by Chomsky's school about the need for or the efficacy of instruction involves consideration of the problems of practice and the value of reinforcement techniques, which in functional terms can be described as ways of bringing to bear on the learning process the consequences of those processes, by reinforcing performance positively or negatively, or confirming or negativing the results. It has been part of Chomsky's classic criticism of Skinner's work on verbal behaviour that such reinforcement is of little value. (Chomsky, 1959). Lenneberg too maintains that we have neither a good theoretical model nor any practical insights into how we can teach an organism to respond to plurality, third person-ness, let alone how we can train him to use these responses in the correct order and verbal contexts of original sentences. (Lenneberg, 1964, 66-67). While the Soviet theorists would not dissent from some of Chomsky's criticisms of Skinner they attach, as we have seen, great importance to instruction, and to reinforcement (interpreted liberally) as a component of instruction. This in turn suggests that Chomsky's valid critique of aspects of Skinner's explanation of verbal behaviour does not as a necessary consequence invalidate the positive contribution of the neo-behaviourist contribution to linguistic pedagogic theory, represented by Soviet psycholinguistics to which Chomsky makes little reference.

Adult intervention or instruction is not only theoretically justifiable, it is in fact effective. Vygotsky studied the abilities of children in various learning situations, some working independently and some working with adults, and found that the achievement of the latter was significantly higher, and their intellectual development more advanced than the former (Leontev, 1957b, 231). Specific and formal instruction in aspects of language can result in the language courses being brought forward into earlier and earlier grades. Kostiuk and Zankov found that the school programme in language could be covered in three rather than four years if more complex materials were introduced in earlier classes (Menchenskaya, 1967, 11). The introduction of special speech training accelerated the language development of one of the twins Luria studied and helped him to advance well beyond the other who had not been given specific instruction. It was also only the twin who had been taught systematically who was able to develop an appropriate theoretical attitude towards speech, on the basis of which alone language functions satisfactorily in the control and regulation of behaviour. (Luria and Yudovich, 1959, 119).

The intervention of the teacher and the form of instruction, especially in foreign languages, cannot be left to the teacher's intuitive judgement, but must be handled according to precise methods based on careful analysis (Artemov, 1960, 44). Such conclusions were put to the test in the so-called Lipetsk project, in which lessons were arranged so as to present the maximum amount of material for assimilation. The time available was planned precisely and economically so that a number of lesson items, such as vocabulary, dictation, discussion of writing exercises, short compositions etc. could be included almost obligatorily. Finally a system of evaluation, the lesson mark, based on formally established procedures and norms, became a universal feature of the class work in the project. The results of the experiment were set out in guidelines to teachers and though the extension of the experiment was not always successful, the teaching of language became more effective partly because it was so rationalized. Material which had previously been introduced in the 3rd grade was taught successfully to first graders and the high level of difficulty, rapid coverage of the curriculum and the inculcation of theoretical knowledge of the language promoted not only a higher standard of language competence but more confident children as well (Tekuchev, 1967 and Zavatskaya, 1963).

H. CONCLUSION

The character of Soviet language pedagogy naturally reflects language policy, and in turn the success of the regime in pursuing that policy depends as much on what happens in the class room as on other important factors, historic, political, demographic and administrative. The natural historical development of bilingual and multilingual contacts which prevailed in the USSR before the Revolution has given place to language contact planned carefully to achieve precise aims. The teaching of a foreign language has to be envisaged as part of this plan. Just as the growth of literacy has changed patterns of largely preliterate or oral-bilingualism of the previous centuries, involving scores of indigenous languages, to patterns of literate bilingualism, so bilingualism which was fortuitous in its provenance and diffusion is now explicitly planned and encouraged as part of the state system of education. And foreign languages which at one time were the privilege of even a minority of that minority which was educated, are now a vital part of the education of nearly all. An understanding of second language pedagogy in the USSR necessitates, therefore, some understanding of the relation of those classes of languages, the mother tongue or first language, indigenous second languages, of which there are nearly fifty in Russia alone, and foreign languages. Pedagogic research in the USSR is directed towards the understanding of the psychological, sociological and linguistic relations between these three groups, in order to facilitate an immense linguistic and educational planning operation.

An examination of the direction in which Soviet research into language acquisition, language development and language pedagogy is proceeding, as well as a consideration of the fundamental bases of such research and its main characteristics serve to remind us of the intimate relationship between the ideas which inform the general character of Soviet ideology and those which govern the place of language in the practice of education. Whether we regard language development and teaching from the standpoint of psychology or of sociology the emphasis in Soviet theory is upon the manipulation of the process of learning, and the possibility of directly influencing the nature of that learning, (whether linguistic or general), as well as the speed with which it proceeds. This element of planning and manipulation of the learning process itself, whatever may be said of the administration of aducation is alien to British ideas, though, I fancy, not quite unnacceptable in the United States. By the insistence on 'conscious learning' as distinct from the reliance on spontaneous maturation Soviet theory justifies adult intervention in formally controlling linguistic and other forms of learning. Similarly, the stress on language learning as only one aspect of social interaction justifies the conscious and formal manipulation of the school and general environment for such learning, and the considerable attention which is paid to the planning of the operation of the factors operating in that environment. Psychological and social theory justifies a regard for language pedagogy as itself an aspect of planning, as much as it does the contribution which language pedagogy makes to more general social planning. This contribution to general social engineering is seen also in the character of the research which supports the demand to relate very intimately first and second language learning. The social environment as well as the psychological 'setting' in which both languages are learned and used need to be characterized by high level consistency, if considerable social and psychological disadvantages are to be avoided. This demand for a consistent relation between the learning and use of the two languages is calculated to support the general aim of linguistic 'raprochment' and social uniformation. In effect linguistic pedagogy is an essential element in the 'nationalities policy' and the planning which is essential to it.

Chapter 9

HETEROGENEITY AND LANGUAGE PLANNING – SOME CONCLUSIONS AND GENERALIZATIONS

A. THE USSR AND COMPARATIVE STUDIES

So far, the present study has been devoted almost exclusively to the analysis of the data concerning the historical development, the social position of some of the languages in the Soviet Union and the factors which have operated in creating that position. The present paucity of objective information, and the practical difficulties which students may have in validating theories and generalizations by an appeal to first hand experience are such that theorizing becomes a highly hazardous, though an attractive exercise. We need a large number of detailed studies before the pattern of Soviet socio-linguistic relations can come into focus, and the best that can happen at present is a modest exploration in order to define the area of study and set the outlines of part of the map of such relations. For the same reasons it would have been equally unprofitable in this study to attempt prematurely to interpret and present Soviet data within formulae which have been devised to explain other linguistic complexes, policies and socio-cultural groupings, and which (for very cogent reasons) do not take the Soviet situation into account in the comparisons and correlations. Before we can attempt to apply to the USSR formulae respecting 'plural and pluralistic', 'developing and developed', polities, or different 'categories of language situations' we have first of all to understand the USSR as 'a thing in itself', as if it were *sui generis*, which in the last resort of course it is.

For instance Banks and Textor (1965) advance a positive correlation between the number of students enrolled in higher education and in primary and secondary schools with linguistic homogeneity: but in fact this is reversed in the USSR where intensification of existing linguistic heterogeneity is accompanied if not facilitated by greatly increased school and college attendance and literacy. The hypothesized positive correlation between a totalitarian political system and linguistic homogeneity is likewise reversed. In fact the political system of the USSR is instrumental in promoting increased, if from the official point of view temporary or transitional, heterogeneity. The discrepancy between the two possible interpretations arises from the fact that it is possible to take either the Soviet state (the Federation) or a Union Republic as the unit of reference in comparative studies. If we take the former it is difficult if not impossible to find any one comparable unit elsewhere, to say nothing of a sufficient number, to make a reliable correlation possible. If we take the Union Republic as the unit we are met by the difficulty that these are not, like the usual units of comparison, nation states – they do not for instance, in practice, however much it might be possible in theory seek to acquire a measure of effective and independant control over the behaviour, linguistic or otherwise of their members, which in the USSR is the prerogative of central state organizations and the Party. A society like the USSR looks very different according to the level of observation, whether it is the State as a whole, a separate Union Republic, Autonomous Republic, Oblast etc. According to the level of observation on which we chose to operate the relationship between the variables will turn out to be very different.

Furthermore the revolutionary origins and the continuing revolutionary dynamic in several areas of Soviet society, as well as its long periods of deliberately fostered isolation makes the USSR less amenable than other countries to cross-national or comparative study, so far as concerns the languages of the Union. It is true that there has always been a close relationship everywhere between linguistic heterogeneity and political, religious, and even military conflict, whether in Africa, parts of Western Europe like Belgium, Ireland and to a lesser extent Wales; in India or Canada. It has always been the case in such countries that an individual has been forced to choose between conflicting attitudes in several spheres of social and cultural activity. In the Soviet Union, however, whatever historical conflicts of a similar nature may have existed have been transformed during the last fifty years by more deep seated and intense politico-linguistic conflict. At the same time, potentially at least, the conflict in the USSR has embraced vaster numbers of the population.

Apart from its political character the revolution of the last fifty years has had a four fold character – there has been first of all a revolution in the amount and nature of the knowledge which has an impact on the every day life of some of the meanest and the most remote people, and this affects their attitude to the languages in which communication of the information is conveyed. Second, there have been profound changes in the interpretation of the knowledge which the people were accustomed to handle, with similar consequences to their attitude to the languages. Third, there has been an upheaval in the people's consciousness of their ethnic/ national, and their international/supra-national obligations including attitude to languages, with an exacerbation of conflict between the two sets of obligations.[1] And finally there has been what is often referred to as a 'communications explosion' which has directly affected relationships between languages, their relative social value, and which disseminates and intensifies the consequences of other revolutionary processes.

It is true, of course that these processes are not peculiar to the Soviet Union, but naturally their operation there is highly characteristic. The extent of the linguistic heterogeneity, the conjunction of geographic spread and the number of languages which are viable in political and educational contexts is unusual. Second, the degree of political sophistication in control of the planning of this vast complex is also unusual, possible comparative areas being China and India. Though African states, too, we are reminded, are without exception linguistically heterogeneous, their indigenous languages and the related communities do not display to anything like the same extent the range of differences in levels of development. Heterogeneity in most other states compared with that of the USSR affects one dimension only or mainly. In the USSR there is exceptional vertical as well as horizontal diversity – both of equal significance – languages and families of languages of great dissimilarity (the horizontal dimension) and great multiplicity in levels of development (vertical dimension).

These reservations are offered as a precaution against accepting the generalizations and rather lightly adumbrated theories that are offered in this chapter, as anything but modest and tentative suggestions of ways in which the Soviet Union can be compared with other linguistically heterogeneous countries, or in which we can produce helpful formulae for the further study of the USSR itself.

B. THE ETHNIC/NATIONAL BACKGROUND TO LINGUISTIC DIVERSITY

We have already outlined the great diversity of ethnic groups and nations which constitute the horizontal dimension of Soviet heterogeneity, and it will have been apparent in the discussion of the mobility of these groups, their levels of literacy, the kinds of educational provision which exists for them, the difference among them in the take up of places in

---

[1] These may be said to correspond to 'group culture' and 'civic culture' obligations, respectively.

higher education and the different lengths of time they have had in which to develop their educational systems satisfactorily, that they vary greatly in levels of national development – their heterogeneity along a vertical dimension. For our purposes, at the present stage of studies of Soviet so-ciolinguistic situations, the most satisfactory criteria to measure or describe this diversity are the simplest. For this reason it is useful to refer to Deutsch's distinction, within the total population of a country, be-tween those who are and those who are not socially mobilized – suscep-tible or not to intensive communication (the mobilized/underlying popu-lation): and among those who are socially mobilized, the further distinc-tion between those who are already speakers of the predominant language or not (the assimilated/differentiated population) (Deutsch, 1966, 123-150). The nationalities, we know, vary enormously in size, and they differ also in respect of the proportion of the population which is on one or other of the development levels referred to. The Russians for instance are highly mobilized and assimilated and so are the Ukrainians, Georgians, the Armenians, the Baltic nations, as well as the major nationalities of the Central Asian Republics, though these to a much less uniform extent, and at a very much later point in time. Less mobilized are those of the Daghes-tan groups, and the Peoples of the North, among which are examples of very low mobilization.

We also find, however, among some nationalities that, contrary to the predicted working of Deutsch's model, while the degree of assimilation may be high, their level of social mobilization is relatively low, partly be-cause of the nature of their economy-nomadic central Asian groups and the hunters and fishers of the North for instance. They are in large num-bers literate in their national language, but how far their literacy is a usable commodity, socially significant, and therefore a factor in mobiliza-tion, is to be doubted. This suggests perhaps the need to reconsider the way in which the distinctions are formulated.

Another useful and simple model has been proposed (Sjoberg, 1966, 260-73) which correlates levels of social development (preliterate, pre-in-dustrial civilized and industrial) with levels of literacy. There are several Soviet languages which have not been given written form (Serdyuchenko, 1962 and 1965) and some whose new alphabets have been allowed to lapse. Some degrees of illiteracy still remain among literate communities. There are also communities where functional literacy is effective only in the urban areas – for instance among the Bashkirs and to some extent the Kazakhs; while other nationalities have widespread or universal literacy. Then again there are many nations who boast a long tradition of literacy and which are organized at different points along Fishman's scale of 'Great Traditions' (1968c, 497). The Russians and the Georgians are or-ganized around a single tradition; and some, such as the Ukrainians (if we include for example the Yiddish tradition) or some Central Asians (if we include both Christianity and Islam) treasure more than one Great Tradition; while a large number of nations have no Great Tradition.

However we examine the ethnic background of the Soviet Union we are met by a number of different types of groups and, more importantly, a multiplicity of developmental levels. At the same time one is aware that current development is towards greater uniformation, and that this tendency in the long term leads to identification with Russian. Nevertheless, whatever the ultimate position, the present situation is highly complex revealing conflicting and reciprocal tendencies of the most varied sort. Thus the movement between Kurdish and Turkmen cultures is reciprocal. The Kurdish have taught Turkmen women to knit the *jorap*, the bright woollen sock, and Kurdish designs appear very frequently in Turkmen rugs. Simultaneously Turkmen influence on Kurdish is very pronounced. Not only are the 'nationalities' drawn towards Russian but there is evidence of Russians and other Slavs being drawn towards other cultures, though not necessarily towards other languages. For instance in Central Asia though Russians neglect the native languages, patterns of behaviour which are associated with the upper classes in the traditional khanates have become prestige symbols for the new-type party and government officials, many if not the majority of whom are Russians. Where the process is limited to already fairly homogeneous groups it often happens that the process of change is not modelled on imported Russian cultural traits but generalizes those which previously characterized only a segment of the total native group. Thus, changes in the steppe way of life take the form of emulating the oases patterns of behaviour, rather than those of the migrant Slavs. The initial differences between oases and Steppe disappeared quickly under the impact of collectivization and industrialization. But these two forces tended to operate as catalysts for internal uniformation rather than to impart entirely new or alien ways of behaving. Most rural and a large number of town Tadzhiks still adhere, in dress and culinary habits to the national tradition. Even those who on a 'civic culture' level accept the Marxist ideology are slow to change the central traits of their national culture. Behaviour to women and girls has changed only very gradually and the family still maintains its importance in very much the traditional form (Kisliakov, 1954, 162). Their religion means a great deal to a very large number of Tadzhiks, and this is a powerful factor in ensuring that the Tadzhiks do not become submerged by a Russian culture or by the more general 'civic' Soviet culture, entirely dehumanized and mechanical. In this effort too they are supported by their consciousness of a long literary tradition embracing the Persian classics. Whether they are justified in their intense attachment to this as their national heritage is not strictly relevant since they believe it is so.

The same is true of the Azerbaydzhanis. For instance, a contemporary poet of that language speaks passionately of his love for his mother tongue and attacks those who would subordinate it to Russian (*Azerbaydzhan*, 1962, 3). At the same time those who promote the official centralist attitude complain of the lack of any creative inspiration in the 'official' literature. Furthermore "some poets consign the militant traditions of Soviet poetry to oblivion". The whole corpus of literature intended to express the 'civic' affiliation is found to be "cold and dreary [...] full of dejection and sentimentality" (*Edebiyat ve indzhesenet*, March 23, 1963). Then again when Central Asians do change they are more often attracted to the cultural patterns of their Central Asian neighbours than to Western forms. The opera was popularized in Central Asia by Azerbaydzhan touring groups, and the Central Asian intelligentsia took to wearing the Tatar skull cap in Summer. What we find, at present, is not a predominant and uniform levelling out of culture differences but culture changes on several levels. Some changes are perceived as foreign, and constitute 'enclaves' in the normal way of life. Some innovations no longer appear alien, but they are not regarded with sympathy. Others have become part of the normal way of life. But most changes at the present time, among most nationalities, are at a prior stage to this last stage. They are optional or alternative patterns of behaviour within the same, often quite intimate local community (Shils, 1971, 157).

So the picture of the Soviet Union at present is one of considerable diversity between cultures or languages, and within any one culture or language group. Consequently Soviet ethnic/national heterogeneity has to be measured by more than the simple criterion of enumeration. Nevertheless, we would be wise not to exaggerate the depth of the change, the rate at which it is occurring or the uniformity of its diffusion. On these matters there is disagreement among serious Soviet scholars and observers. N. S. Dzhunusov (1966, 51) of the USSR academy of Sciences claims that during the last fifty years the Soviet peoples have moved far more towards uniformation than during the whole three centuries of the Tsarist state's existence. What changes have occurred are perhaps more apparent in aspects of material culture: facilities for the sale of mass produced consumer goods have led to changes in the popularity of some fabrics, and in the use of ready made clothing and footwear. Native costumes incorporate some elements of what may be regarded as the 'universal-type urban' dress. In so far as the changes affect deeper psychological and sociological features it is perhaps in the realm of religion and even more in the official status of women that changes are most apparent. Women enjoy full civic rights and entry into the professions. There are women agronomists, doctors, operators of complex farm machinery, to say nothing of teachers at all levels of education. Nevertheless any comparison with the Tsarist state is meaningless because of the stagnation of those three centuries to which Dzhunusov referred. Furthermore the reality of the changes is doubted by some Soviet observers, though the doubt is implicit in their arguments rather than explicitly articulated. L. M. Drobizheva refers to the retention of basic characteristics, for example, religion. Not only are these characteristics of national cultures retained but the people cling to them tenaciously (1967, 77).

One consequence of this difference in degree of attachment to a tradition and of the selectivity which most people exercise in the process of culture change in the USSR is a cleavage between two areas of cultural existence. There is the area which includes all the deep seated national distinctivenesses, which over the centuries a 'national psychology' and other factors have helped to establish, and which in turn have helped to reinforce that psychology. Most moderate Soviet social anthropoligists recognize the importance of a careful approach to the preservation and further development of valuable elements in the cultural heritage of the nationalities. Unless this happens whole branches of excellent manifestations of the human mind in art and in work will disappear. Local climatic conditions, for instance, make it necessary to adapt whatever is valuable in the new ways of thought and in economic development to national traditions of behaviour, of dress and habits of work. At the same time it is recognized by the moderates that it is possible to make a fetish of many aspects of the heritage. This is the attitude in general which supports the continuation of what might be called 'group culture' affiliation. In the main this affiliation is to the immediate ethnic or national entity. However, one of the tendencies which have been noted is the extension of this affiliation to embrace less immediate groups without however losing the sense of 'group identification'. In fact this is what is happening most frequently as changes are introduced. The local group is embraced by a larger local group, the Pamiri by the Tadzhiks, the Kurds and the Beludzhi by Turkmen. We can identify therefore a 'primary group identification' and a 'secondary group identification', and this is generally without loss of the fundamentally important traits of the national or ethnic heritage.

There is however a very different kind of affiliation which is being promoted by immense efforts in the USSR: this is a 'civic culture' affiliation. Although this is not an entirely new development, it is in the kind of mass society of which the Soviet Union is an example that it has found its most complete realization. Its basis is the incorporation of all the members of a state in a culture which is determined by the ideology of that state rather than by the inherited endowments of communities of various kinds which have gone into the establishment of the state-ethnic, and the religious communities in particular. In the USSR this civic culture, which, in theory, is coterminous with the adult population of all nationalities, is characterized by elements of meritocracy, technocracy and managerial proficiency, and economic egalitarianism. So far as the element of ethnicity is concerned this culture is international and superimposes "a Marx-Leninist world view, a communist moral outlook and attitude to work, socialist realism in all forms of art" (Gardanov et al., 1961) upon the traditional social attitudes of the local groups. Much of the controversy among Soviet theorists is only a reflection of this cleavage between a 'group culture' and a 'civic culture' affiliation.

Even if to some members of the society itself changes appear to be far reaching, they do not affect more than a small part of the total culture which characterizes the group for quite a long time; and such changes as do occur spread themselves unevenly over the total membership of the nation. For instance in rural settlements and among kolkhoz chairmen in several Republics there is a great fear of novel ideas and innovations. They cling to the tried customary way of doing and looking at things. Attitudes to women change only with almost imperceptible degrees of gradualness – polygamy and child marriage still survive. *Pravda* remarked on the tenacity with which people cling to obsolete and archaic national characteristics, vestiges of traditionalism (May 23, 1963). Complaints are made because of the fact that so many people, many of them young are still attached to their traditional faiths (*Komm. Tadzh.* Dec. 26th, 1963). Those nationalities which have had long historical contact with Russia (the Ukraine especially, and Georgia) have naturally enough not rejected even crucial and fundamental Russian cultural elements, and under compulsion they have taken over a great deal more than they would normally consider expedient or beneficial. But they have compartmentalized the alien traits into a co-existent system which, though it is never so separate as to constitute an alternative culture, is nevertheless recognized as an instrusive element. The social system of the family, religious practices (and even as important, the memory of such religious forms), art and music, material traits like domestic architecture, interior decoration, food habits and dress, and especially language all react to outside influences differently, and the culture is never felt to possess the integrity of the traditional culture – the new elements are important but they have not been absorbed, they are adopted but not 'lived'. These divergencies are the consequence of several types of discontinuities some of which may result from area variations, as is the case between Russia and Ukraine or Russia and the Baltic Republics. Other changes occur in spite of accentuated territorial or geographical obstacles, as is the case with Georgia and Armenia in relation to Russia. Others again are introduced over great distances as is the case with the Central Asian peoples, so that there may

be few overlaps between the cultures or the people. All these considerations ensure that innovations are never distributed evenly over the USSR,
they do not proceed at the same pace everywhere, and they are not assimilated by the members of the various groups uniformly.

It would of course be strange if the processes of innovation within the
relatively short period of the Soviet's existence had been anything but
limited. Although change is to be expected even in quiet periods, major
revolutionary change has to be seen against a background of deep seated
stability. Alsace still constitutes a recognizably distinct community after
centuries of contact, and in spite of successive conquests by French and
Germans, which have been no less harsh than those experienced in areas
of the USSR. The dialect is still the mother tongue of a large proportion
of the inhabitants. Similarly the consciousness of nationality is still strong
in Wales and the language a vigorous medium of literary expression and
of education, after over 7 centuries of conquest and over 150 years of
massive industrialization and English immigration. Neither has conquest
eliminated the languages or identities of the peoples historically subservient to Russia. Whatever political, demographic and educational
strategies may be employed in the Soviet Union it is difficult to believe
that the characteristic historical processes will be fundamentally reversed. The enormously slow rate of cultural and linguistic assimilation is
recognized in the USSR, where it is argued by many scholars that even if
extensive assimilation is achieved differences will remain for a long time
even "after the victory of the proletariat on a world wide basis." (Terakopayan 1967, 246).

Naturally, Soviet scholars themselves consider it normal to find dis-
crepancies between the various possible indices of ethnic affiliation –
formal identification of nationality, religion, retention of material aspects
of culture and language (Gantskaya and Terentova, 1965, 8). Of these
manifestations of difference in the rhythms of change it is the relative
independence of language which is most crucial. Of course language,
more particularly but not exclusively vocabulary, is affected by changes in
the environment of a people or in their way of life, but linguistic change
and development on the one hand and social/cultural change, even of a
revolutionary character, on the other do not exhibit the same contours.
Stalin upbraided those who had supported Marr, because they insisted
that language necessarily changed with the culture it was related to, "but
culture and language are two different things": and while cultures change
inevitably as part of a historical process "languages possess a great
stability and tremendous power of resistance to change" (Stalin 1950b,
14, 17, 18). Nor is the stability of a language necessarily radically affected
by differences in the cultural milieu in which it is spoken. The stability of
the four languages of Switzerland, for instance, is independent of the

Cantonal cultural milieu in which any of them is spoken, or in which it developed.

The relative independence of lingusitic from more general cultural, and social change can be affirmed for all advanced countries, and for most developed nationalities in the USSR, like Georgia and Armenia. Where the contours of linguistic and of broader cultural change conform at all closely, as they may be said to do in the Baltic Republics, for instance, it is because the extent of any change is relatively small (Gantaskaya and Terenteva, 1965, 7).

C. LINGUISTIC HETEROGENEITY

i. *Multiplicity of Developmental Stages*

There are several standpoints from which, theoretically, it might be possible to observe the linguistic heterogeneity of the USSR, but unfortunately at least one of them is not feasible in practice – it would be impossible to do justice to the complexity of the pattern or to analyse it satisfactorily if we were to "use the nation as the basis for general sociolinguistic description" (Ferguson, 1962, 25), or at least those aspects which concern us. Not only would it be repetitous and uneconomical to do so, but the Soviet picture would inevitably be distorted, since the demographic and linguistic overlap among the nationalities is of the essence of the total Soviet situation. Furthermore, both the politico-social and the linguistic considerations, and especially the planning, are governed firmly by a common central policy which a description based on the several and separate national units would find it difficult to take into account. Even the crudest of the criteria of diversity, simple enumeration of the languages and language families, however much it is the foundation for all other descriptive approaches, postulates the whole Soviet Union as the unit.

a. *Dialect Levels*

However, simple enumeration does not take us very far. Just as the ethnic/national cultural diversity of the USSR possesses a 'developmental' as well as an 'extensive' dimension, so does linguistic heterogeneity. There is among the scores of languages of the Union what Karl Mannheim called a "contemporaneity of the non-contemporaneous" and Gilbert Murray referred to as a "chronological conglomerate". There are within the total pattern instances of dialects which, because of the influence of a contact language, have formed separate languages. This is the case of Dolgan, now recognized as a language, rather than a dialect of

Yakut or Evenk, which was the language of contact. There are also dialects which have so far not reached the status of languages, and are at different points of the progression. Khakass is a case in point, for the language, which has been provided with an alphabet, is still to a considerable extent a congeries of dialects – Sagay, Kachin Koybal, Beltire and Kuzyl. Eskimo has three dialects none of which has advanced towards standardization to any significant degree nor are they likely to in view of their numbers. Sometimes, of two dialects, like for instance Khanty (Ostayak) and Mansi (Vogul) one may have been reduced to writing and be considered a literary language though the dialect is not, in fact, serving any extended literary or broad social purposes. On the other hand a language like Mordvin, an East Finnic language, has two mutually unintelligible dialects, Erzya and Moksha, both of which have achieved literary status.

Among the best examples of groups of dialects in which the members are at considerably different levels of development towards standardization and literary use are, first, the Pamiri group of languages consisting of four categories of dialects, the most advanced group being the Shugnan-Rushan which itself includes five separate and almost mutually unintelligible dialects, only one of which, the Shugnan dialect (spoken along the main reaches of the river Piandzh) is considered for possible standardization. Whether it ever actually achieves this status is doubtful since Tadzhik serves most of the purposes of these bilingual groups very well. The second group of dialects, the Tatar consists of two branches, North Western and South Western, the former having nine separate dialects. All these are at different developmental stages but Volga Tatar is the one which is used as a literary language. In most dialects the levelling off process is very apparent, and no language better exemplifies this than Tadzhik. Most people of that language group continue to speak one of several regional dialects, the use of the standard language being cultivated, to all intents and purposes almost exclusively by the intelligentsia. At the same time the regional dialects are converging, partly because of the natural influence of better communications and partly because of the existence of the standard forms.

Any consideration of the levelling out of dialects has to take the presence of Russian into account. It is natural that the impact of Russian on the local languages varies according to whether the local dialects are urban or rural. Since most Russians live in the cities it is the urban dialect which is most influenced. It is also the case that where the local language is in process of standardization it is the urban dialects which are used to form the base for such a process. In addition those who are in contact with Russians in the towns and cities are heavily influenced by the literary Russian rather than by oral and especially dialect forms. For all these reasons Russian tends to have considerably more influence on the literary forms of local languages rather than on the dialects and to that extent it is a factor in standardization. This has been the case with Ukrainian and is tending in the same direction with Tadzhik.

At the same time, while some groups of dialects are moving together there are instances of languages becoming dialectized. For instance among the South Caucasian languages are those of the Mingrelian, an ethnic group of 300,000, Svan (13,000) and Laz (living along the border with Turkey and amounting to less than two thousands) which, because of the diffusion of Georgian and its status as the literary language of the whole area, are now regarded as little more than dialects of Georgian. They are not recorded in the 1970 Census. It is a process which greatly affects more well established languages as well. Because of the coercive measures which have placed Russian in an even more dominant position among the Slav languages than its numbers and the greatness of its literature would, in any case, justify, less favoured Slav languages, even Ukrainian, are, very gradually it is true, being near dialectized. This is not a novel phenomenon for in the late 19th century the Imperial Academy concluded that Ukrainian was not a separate Slav language, and the government banned Ukrainian publications on the strength of the opinion that it was a dialect of Russian.

Conversely Moldavian, a parallel variety of Romanian, is gradually establishing itself as a separate indigenous Soviet language because of Soviet policy to accentuate differences between languages which are spoken both inside and outside the USSR. Though political, geographic and other forms of separation do not necessarily result in variants of the same language becoming independent languages separation of one kind to another does help and it has happened more than once in the USSR. During the 19th century Ukrainian was so subordinate to Polish and Russian that it had little chance to develop as an independent literary language. During the first phase of the Soviet nationalities programme it was able to establish some modicum of separation. It was allowed a degree of independence, was regarded as an official language for many purposes – education especially, and in consequence it moved towards becoming an entirely independent language. The same is true to some extent of Tadzhik in relation to Persian, and of Kazakh and Kirgiz.

b. *Standardization Levels*

Apart from the differences between languages at various stages of standardization there is a considerable variety within the standardized languages themselves. Of the levels of standardization which Kloss (1968, 78) categorizes examples can be adduced among Soviet languages. Russian, Georgian and Ukrainian, for instance, are *fully modernized mature standard* languages, suitable for all levels of employment. Kara-Kalpak (236,000) a member of the N.W. group of Turkic languages is a *small group standard* language, as is Komi-Permyak (153,000) which is closely related to Komi (287,000) and Udmurt (704,000). Together they constitute a large linguistic group but for various reasons, mainly their subordination to major standardized languages, the Central Asian in the case of Karakalpak, and Russian in the case of Komi-Permyak, they are unlikely to advance to the position of modernized standard. The central Asian languages like Tadzhik can claim in some respect to have close affinities to, without actually being *archaic standard* languages. Central Asians before the Revolution read the classical literature of other Turkic peoples without difficulty and however much these now Sovietized languages have diverged from each other, and from Arabic and Iranian associations they possess the same historical, literary and linguistic traditions. There are traces of literary Uzbek as far back as the XVIth century and the foundations for this were laid in the XIth century. Turkmen has a literary tradition going back to the XIVth century, and Tadzhik as the Central Asian form of Persian has had a continuous literary record over very many centuries. But in spite of affinities with the category of 'archaic standard' languages the major Central Asian languages should now be regarded as being at an intermediate stage between 'fully modernized standard' and 'young standard'. A better instance of 'archaic standard' is Church Armenian.

Many Soviet languages are *young standard* languages having gone through part of the process of standardization since the Revolution. To some extent this is true of the Baltic languages. Although Lithuanian literature of a documentary nature survives from the 16th century, not until the last century did it become the medium of literary expression; and not until its independence in 1918 did it emerge as an official national language. Even then it was lacking in words which might enable it to serve the purposes of a modern society. Latvian, until the beginning of the last century was spoken only by peasants, the urban population preferring German or Russian. The standard language began to emerge only after Latvia became independent in 1918. In the case of Estonian the speakers still maintain a considerable pride in the regional dialects, which are used in the literature. A standard language did not come into being until the period 1918-1940.

Then again some languages have *written forms but are unstandardized*, and to this category belong some of the Paleo-asiatic languages. Of the *preliterate* group there are still several cases of languages which have either not been given alphabets, or having been given them at the beginning of the regime have been compelled to see them lapse because of reduced populations and the difficulty of finding any significant use for them (Serdyuchenko, 1961).

Ferguson's three point scale of standardization is not incompatible with Kloss's categories though it is marginally less useful in the circumstances of the USSR (Ferguson, 1962). The zero standardization category (St0) does not enable us to take into account the levels of development towards standardization we have described and illustrated. As Ferguson himself suggests the second category (St1) requires refining and he instances Armenian as a *bi-modal standard.* Like Albanian with Northern and Southern standards, Armenia has two standard written languages, based on Eastern and Western dialects. It would be possible from some points of view to include Tadzhik as a bi-modal standard language also. Most Soviet languages, like Ukrainian, and Georgian are *uni-modal standard* languages. The third category (St2), languages without significant dialect varieties, applies in the USSR to standard languages spoken by relatively small groups and even they have variants which may or may not be accounted dialects. Komi is a case in point. Where very large numbers are involved, as in the case of Russian, Armenian, Tadzhik, Estonian or Tatar, there are several regional dialects to say nothing of the gradual establishment of important social differences between rural and urban varieties.

ii. *Status of Languages and Their Formal Currency*

a. *Official Languages*

Since the authoritarian character of the Soviet Union implies a considerable degree of control of communication beyond the area of interpersonal relationships, the currency of Soviet languages is very much a matter of official promotion and recognition. Consequently the most satisfactory approach to the categorization of the socio-linguistic status of the languages of the USSR is in terms of the number and significance of their roles. The highest in the hierarchy of roles is that of 'official language' but since there are no 'state languages' it is difficult to give the designation "Official Language" any real and consistent meaning.[2] This statement should be qualified by the recognition that the constitution of the Georgian SSSR, Armenian SSR and Azerbaydzhan SSR recognizes the Republican language in each case as 'state languages' which means no more than that it is the eponymous language. An official language is one which is declared to be so, usually by enactment. It has to be current in the formal spheres of social life especially, in government, law and administration,

---

[2] Under Article 140 of the Soviet Constitution laws passed by the Supreme Soviet must be published in the languages of all Union Republics (eponymous languages). Laws adopted by the Supreme Soviet of each SSR are published in the languages of the nationalities and peoples which constitute the Republic.

education and commerce, but it has also to be set apart categorically and specifically. This is not the case in the USSR. In theory all languages are recognized for some official purpose. The very fact that a language is used for publications and for radio communication implies a degree of official recognition. Any language that is spoken by a sufficient number of people is 'recognized'. This means it can be used in courts of law. The fact that there are languages like Yukagïı spoken by about 500 people, which are recognized means that recognition and official status are liberally interpreted.

Consequently so far as the USSR is concerned one has to make the distinction between an 'official language' and a 'language used for official purposes'. In this sense an official language in any Union Republic is that which is given precedence in practice, employed for *most* of the highest official purposes, but it is allowed no statutory superiority. They are the eponymous languages of the Union Republics. By and large a language has the same status within and outside its administrative area – Union or Autonomous Republic etc. Russian is privileged – for instance it is taught compulsorily.

This state of affairs is exemplified by the constitution of the Tadzhik SSR (1961), which can be taken to represent other constitutions also. It stipulates that all laws are to be published in Russian, Tadzhik and Uzbek throughout the Republic. In certain areas where minorities are strong they will also be published in the relevant minority languages – Kirgiz in the Murgab and Ozhirgatal raiony. In legal proceedings Tadzhik is to be used, but in the rayony where the majority speak Russian, Uzbek or Kirgiz, the appropriate language is to be used. Even this does not limit the number of languages officially recognised even in the realm of law – any person who does not speak any of the languages already mentioned has the right to have translations and an interpreter.[3] Government, law and administration are the strictest of the domains of formal recognition and even here there is considerable latitude, arising out of the basic fact that, from well before the establishment of the Soviet regime it was an important part of policy that there should be no 'state' languages. Nevertheless one language, Russian, stands at the head of the league of languages used for official purposes, because it is the only language which in fact is recognized for use in all formal domains in all Union or Autonomous Republics.

Since there is so much latitude in the most formal of the domains it is not surprising that nearly all languages are used and recognized in other administrative or formal situations. In addition a few languages, more particularly the languages of the Far North and Far East, are tolerated

[3] Stipulated in Article 10 of the Soviet Constitution; and in respect of the Tatar ASSR, to take one case, in Article 78.

officially without being promoted for formal employment. But locally even they are always recognized for even the strictest formal usages. Only one language, Yiddish, can be said to be in most senses proscribed or discouraged actively, since though it is the language of 2,151,000 Jews (and claimed by over a third of a million) it receives no recognition in education or administration.

b. *Formal Domains and Use for Writing*

It goes without saying that in the formal domains the extent to which the language is used for writing is a factor to be considered in an assessment of its status. Some (though they have not been given an alphabet) are used even in the courts of law, since they are the only languages a litigant may be able to speak. Others, like several of the newly standardized languages are normally used for writing but mainly for non-specialized interpersonal affairs, and for education. Others again, like Armenian and Georgian are used for writing over a wider range of highly specialized work, in science for instance, economics and law. But they do not rank with Russian as the language of international written communication, or as languages into which scientific works are translated, for the convenience of other Soviet nationalities.

So far as organized cultural activities are concerned, for instance the mass media, newspapers are printed in all the languages which are used in administration. Thus in Tadzhikstan the majority of newspapers are in Tadzhik, but there are regular Russian, Uzbek and Kirgiz publications as well. Radio broadcasts occur, but in only the four languages referred to; and the theatre gives performances in Dushanbe, but only in Tadzhik and Russian. The language used in commerce depends upon the level of commercial transaction, and this is the case also with technology and industry. At the highest level in each case, that which involves central state organizations, scientific and industrial research and industrial management, Russian is well ahead of other languages in Tadzhikstan. At lower levels, especially on the floor of the factory or of the store the language employed will depend very largely upon the locality. Thus in the Gorno-Badakhstan Oblast both Tadzhik and Kirgiz are normally used, in the Murgab raion Kirgiz is normal, while in Dushanbe the tendency, from personal observation, is for a speaker to assume that Tadzhik is the appropriate medium, until it becomes necessary to switch, usually to Uzbek or Russian or Kirgiz, in that order of probability. The same flexibility is noticeable in quite formal kolkhoz meetings or sessions of the local party organizations. Some members use Tadzhik and some Uzbek, with Russian as the language of convenience.

Official recognition then is no different at any level of formal transaction, whether it be law and government or during discussions of administration at local level. Official recognition has to be measured, not stipulated as a category, and the measurement has to be according to the extent of use in each of the main domains. In the present study an attempt has been made to do this for education. The juridicial and administrative domains can be handled in the same way, and from such an analysis a profile of the status of the language may be assembled. However, such a profile would have to take into account one important consideration, namely the standing of a language not only inside but outside its eponymous area. One will find that a profile for Armenian inside Armenia will be very different from that produced for it in Georgia, and different again in the RSFSR, in both of which there are considerable numbers of Armenians, 452 and 299 thousands respectively.

These are some of the considerations which have led to the view that the admittedly powerful model which Ferguson has produced for obtaining a normal national socio-linguistic profile, would be inappropriate for the USSR, in spite of Ferguson's conviction that even such a "socio-linguistic giant as the USSR" could be handled by it (Ferguson 1962, 25). Ferguson distinguishes three categories of criteria. First he makes a distinction between a major and a minor language in terms of the overall size and the percentage of the total population they represent, together with the official status and use in secondary education. At this level too, he distinguishes languages of special status[4] which so far as the USSR is concerned would affect the languages of religion, for instance Yiddish, Hebrew and the main Muslim languages. The second set of distinctions he makes include differences between vernaculars, standard languages and hybrids, the last of which do not concern us. The third set of distinctions is according to the use of languages – whether they are 'ethnic group languages', official, used or taught in schools, lingua franca or international languages.

Apart from the fact that so far as the USSR is concerned the three sets of distinctions overlap quite considerably, there are other difficulties which will have been noted. For instance, it is now probably clear that official status is not a satisfactory discriminator. Nor is size or proportion of the total population if Ferguson's criteria are adopted. For instance, Udmurt (704,000), Komi (222,000) and Mari (599,000) could not rank as major languages since they could not claim over a million speakers nor represent over 25% of total of their Union Republic. Consequently, they would not be differentiated on this scale from other languages like Khakass (67,000) or Abkhaz (83,000). Consequently if we stipulate a proportion of the total population as a necessary criterion, we group together

---

[4] Since no language in the USSR has a special status, and least of all in religion, a more appropriate phrase in our case, would be 'language of particular significance or importance'. This would cover Hebrew.

small and large language groups, which may be major languages in terms of numbers, but not in terms of proportion of the population of the recognized administrative area. We would have to omit cases like Udmurt, Bashkir, Komi and Mari, in spite of the size of the group. Furthermore, 'national' in the context of the Soviet Union as an administrative concept may equally well refer to Union or Autonomous Republics, or even smaller units like Oblasts, since the frontiers are predominantly ethnic/national and linguistic. At the Union level Udmurt is not, but at the Autonomous Republic level it is a major language by Ferguson's standards. Using 'national unit' as the criterion, in fact, creates too many anomalies in the study of the USSR. If we are to perservere with a territorial unit of reference we are left with the necessity of dealing with the whole of the Soviet Union as one unit for socio-linguistic description, and this unit is too unwieldy.

Again, Ferguson's model is difficult to use in this study because of the existence of a multiplicity of developmental levels in conjunction with the diversity of languages and groups of dialects which we have already described. This conjunction of variables would require very considerable refinement of the categories if the analysis is to yield reliable conclusions. It is, for instance, impossible to stipulate absolutely a category of standard language since the standard languages range themselves along a graduated scale. Then again the category of "languages used primarily for communication within a particular speech community marking it as an identifiable group or nation" is in fact as true of the languages of highest social importance or demographic currency – for instance Armenian (3,559,000), Ukrainian (40,753,000) or one of the Central Asian languages, Tadzhik (2,134,000) as it is for the smaller languages like Nanai (10,000) or Even (12,000). This criterion can only be used if it relates to a scale for measuring the relative or graduated importance of usefulness for ethnic identification, and this involves the use of scales which measure the extent of other domains of use of the language.

D. PROVISIONAL MODEL FOR SOCIO-LINGUISTIC DESCRIPTION IN THE USSR

Since the whole Soviet Union is admittedly too large and too diverse to be taken as the unit of reference, and since the use of other sociopolitical units give rise to so many anomalies, it follows that the unit of reference should not be territorial at all but linguistic. The model which is now proposed very tentatively does not accommodate sufficient detail nor does it refine the various subcategories or levels so delicately as Fishman proposes (Fishman 1964), but it could serve an exploratory purpose by distinguishing in the USSR levels and domains of linguistic operations in broad terms, and so providing the base for a more refined system of description. This first-stage model would consist of five levels, each level consisting of several scaled components. Three of the scales are quantitative and two qualitative. It is fundamental to this profile that account is taken of the internal and external status of the languages. The formula for the profile might be set out as follows, using *Tadzhik* as the example.

Level 1 Major or minor status – according to size of language group inside and outside the area.
Majority Status = 1 Million + speakers

Numbers	Up to 2,000	2-10th	10-50th	50-100th	100-250th	250-500th	500-1m	1-5m	5m+
Inside								√	
Outside						√			
Total								√	

Level 2 Degree of currency in governmental domains

	Very Often		Often		Sometimes		Seldom		Never	
	In	Out	In	Out	In	Out	In	Out	In	Out
Law	√					√				
Administration	√					√				
Party Literature			√							√

Level 3 Degree of currency in formal non-governmental domains

	Very Often		Often		Sometimes		Seldom		Never	
	In	Out	In	Out	In	Out	In	Out	In	Out
Press and radio	√					√				
Science and Research					√					√
Industry – Higher							√			√
Lower				√						√
Literature	√							√		
Translations – Science					√					√
Literature				√				√		
Education – Primary	√					√				
Second				√				√		
Higher							√			√
W.C.								√	√	

Level 4 Degree of standardization and modernization

a	Standardization	Mature Standard	Small group Standard	Archaic Standard	Unstandard alphabet	Preliterate
		√				
b	Wr. Index W1					
	W2	√				
	W3					

There is another category of language to which we have not referred directly in the present discussion, namely the *lingua franca*. It is an important category historically and because of the current diffusion of Russian it is a matter of considerable interest in the socio-linguistic description of the Soviet Union. In the past Chagatay, Arabic in the Caucusus, Persian in the towns of Central Asia, Nogai as a trade language, Avar, Kabardin and even Lezgin each served as a lingua franca. Lermontov's and Tolstoy's stories of the Caucusus show how Tatar was used as a lingua franca among non-Turkic nationalities. The presence of several dialects in an area – Yagnobi and Pamiri, for instance, make the national languages, in this case Tadzhik, a convenient lingua franca. The exigencies of contemporary migration also have sometimes promoted the use of a local language, as a lingua franca. Thus in the Tashauz Oblast in Turkmenia because Uzbeks form about 47% of a mixed population their language acts as a lingua franca. But in such a case the common language is limited in its usefulness and restricted to a small locality. The general policy of the Soviet Union has been to discourage the promotion of any language but Russian to act in this capacity, though this is impossible to ensure. Russian is deliberately promoted, at the lowest level because it is an administrative convenience, and at its presumed highest level, as an ideological force facilitating the creation of a new society. Apart from Russian, therefore, it is doubtful whether the category of lingua franca is a significant one for Soviet socio-linguistic description, save in severely limited areas.

But the use of Russian as a lingua franca raises important issues. In spite of its promotion in education and in the dissemination of Russian literature of all kinds, which means not only the use of the language, but safeguarding its stabilization in so extended a currency, Russian is threatened with the dangers (or offered the possibilities) that every other lingua franca has experienced. Where the speakers of a language are widely dispersed and especially when those who speak it are originally or currently native speakers not of different dialects but of widely different languages, there are three possible consequences, in addition to the improbability of its remaining unaffected by the new circumstances of its employment. It may split into several languages, an unlikely outcome in the USSR, because the political prestige of Russian, its administrative and educational support, its continued reinforcement by immigrant native speakers, and the sheer size of the reservoir of those native speakers all conduce to its stabilization no matter how far its writ may run. On the other hand Russian may remain an apparently uniform language, but at the risk of an increasing rift, particularly in the more remote areas, between literary and colloquial levels. This too is an unlikely occurrence for a very long time to come, if at all, since the acquisition of Russian is governed by the formal processes of education. The variant of Russian which most people acquire, certainly the younger generations, is a highly literary variant, and the dangers which have been noted are not slackness in its use but hypercorrectness.

What is most likely to happen over time is the development of a Russian *koine*,[5] which is not the same thing at all as the development of a colloquial as opposed to a literary dialect. A spoken koine can possess all the characteristics of an artificially formalized and over-correct use of the language. Russian as a lingua franca cuts across numerous linguistic boundaries, many of which are not only geographically but linguistically far removed from Slavic. The great mass of the Central Asian populations, and even a great proportion of those of the Far East and Far North complete, at most, the equivalent of only lower secondary school education. Thereafter their exposure to Russian is limited to the appearance of party bulletins, official pronouncements and civil service variants of different kinds, the vocabulary of kolkhoz bulletins and activist propaganda. Those who live in the villages or follow the herds have little cause to acquire a colloquial Russian. Even for those who live in towns Russian is experienced through the veils and mists of numerous other native languages. The Russian language is inevitably distorted and coloured by experience of and familiarity with numerous other languages. For those who speak it, excepting perhaps the intelligentsia, it is a highly simplified means of communication, pruned of its native nuances, its colours toned down to a dull unidiomatic monochrome. However, the language has even here one valuable support, namely the fact that it is also the one Soviet language which is a viable language of world communication. This

---

[5] Meillet recognized this in the case of French: "The fact that French is spoken at the present time in Paris by a majority of provincials and of foreigners and descendants of foreigners is believed of great importance. At first sight the effects are not appreciable, but the fundamental result is that Parisian is disappearing, drowned in a sort of Koine". (*American Speech*, 4, 1929).

fact will reinforce the internal agencies of education, etc. to which we have referred. In the forseeable future the Russian language will probably survive most of the dangers of a lingua franca because for most people its functions in Soviet society will be limited to the more formal domains, to political, scientific, administrative affairs. The traditional colours of the Russian language will be largely irrelevant.

There is, then, a fifth level in the socio-linguistic profile of any Soviet language, relating to its use as a lingua franca. This level would need to be described according to the following criteria-method of acquisition of the lingua franca (whether formal or informal); extent to which its use is literate or simply oral; the domains of its use (whether formal or informal in the main); where it is used (locally, or widespread); and whether its use is progressing or declining. Each of these can be described along a six point scale, but it is important to note that the alternatives within any criterion are not mutually exclusive. Thus a lingua franca may be acquired in the main at school (formally) but sometimes informally. The following are suggestions of how such profiles would appear for Tadzhik, and for Russian in Tadzhikstan. In the case of Russian it would be necessary to provide a different profile for its use as a lingua franca in different Union Republics. The situation is such that this would not be necessary for the other languages.

Level 5 Use as a lingua franca (Tadzhik)

Scale	How acquired		Degree of literate use		Where used		Domains of Use		Prognosis	
	Formal	In-formal	literate	Oral	Local	Wide-spread	Formal	In-formal	Prog.	Declin
Always										
Mainly		√		√	√			√		
Generally										√
Sometimes							√			
Seldom	√		√			√				
Never										

These profiles indicate that Tadzhik as a local lingua franca is acquired in the ordinary course of social contact rather than formally, and seldom used for reading and writing. Its domains of use are informal and its future as a lingua franca is not encouraging. So far as Russian in Tadzhikstan is concerned it is acquired as a lingua franca formally in the main, that is in school, though informal contacts in towns and cities help. Its

Russian (In Tadzhikstan)

Scale	How acquired		Degree of literate		Where used		Domains of use		Prognosis	
	Formal	In-formal	Literate	Oral	Local	Wide-spread	Formal	In-formal	Prog.	Decline
Always						√			√	
Mainly	√		√				√			
Generally										
Sometimes		√		√				√		
Seldom										
Never										

use is widespread throughout the Union Republic and is not even confined to the urban areas since Collective Farms in the Rural areas make use of it. At the same time although it is a spoken lingua franca it is much more a literary medium. Consequently its domains of use are mainly formal. Its use as a lingua franca is spreading.

E. TYPES OF SOCIO-LINGUISTIC CONTACT

i. *Levels of Contact*

From the point of view of the present study the interest and attraction of Soviet linguistic heterogeneity, however it is measured, is only partly the phenomenon of heterogeneity itself. To some extent a more absorbing feature is the diversity of types of *contact* which characterize the heterogeneity. These types of contact can be considered at four developmental levels. The lowest level of socio-linguistic contact is simple, geographically contiguous co-existence of linguistic groups. This has persisted over many centuries among many peoples, perhaps the best examples being among those of the N. Caucusus, the Pamiri highlands, and the Ferghana valley. The bilingualism which has resulted has, with a few exceptions, been stable many centuries, but the stability does not arise from a distribution or separation of complementary social functions. Because the social relations between the communities are stable, awareness of linguistic differences is not obtrusive and explicit. The bilinguals resort indifferently to either language in most situations, because the situations themselves are not well differentiated. The life of the communities has changed very little over the centuries, and in consequence the impetus towards assimilation, linguistic or otherwise was negligible. As with Daghestan languages, this has been the case of Uzbek-Tadzhik relations in the Chust-Kassansai areas. With innovations which affect the way of life of the peoples, an intensification of political consciousness, and urbanization, there is, almost automatically, a growth of linguistic self-consciousness, an awareness of differences between the linguistic groups, and between the roles different individuals and their languages play. Awareness of differences between the groups leads to incipient conflict, and differentiation of social roles leads in a bilingual community to appropriation of different languages for those roles.

The second level of contact provides for a greater tendency towards assimilation, and can be characterized as dynamic bilingualism – the bilingualism of peoples on the move socially and geographically. Social mobility, role differentiation and appropriation of different languages for those roles prepares the ground for assimilation. One instance of this has been the Tat-Azerbaydzhan situation in the North Caucusus. The Azerbaydzhan language is aggressive, partly because it has become the language of political power in the locality. There is general social instability, and the languages fit at different levels into the pattern of social prestige. The Tats are gradually being assimilated and Tat-Azerbaydzhan bilingualism is moving towards the elimination of Tat. This is true of the relations between the Shagdag language group and Azerbaydzhan, and for the same reasons. Some dialects of Shagdag, like Hinalug and Kriz have become dialects of Azerbaydzhan.

The third level is where two or more languages assume overlapping functions. We have noted that the juridical roles which are set down for the various languages overlap, and in most cases there is little juridical complementarity of function. This is the result of the theoretical liberalism of the USSR concerning languages. For instance Russian and Tadzhik are both used for the publication of laws, and the local languages too are permitted in legal processes – Kirgiz in the case of that minority. There are some areas of function where such overlap is not apparent. So far as religion is concerned and the more traditional aspects of national life, marriage and death rituals, the delimitation of linguistic function is strict. We can distinguish in such cases between the 'civic' and 'group culture' roles, and the languages appropriate to the former are obvious: Russian, and well behind it in prestige, the 'national language' of the Republic. It is certainly the case that the co-existence of Russian and the local languages at present depends entirely on a delimitation of function – one performing a civic, international service, the other assuming a group culture or local role. One interest of the study of bilingualism in the USSR is the mapping not simply of the demographic penetration of Russian or the increasing control of the language by more and more non-Russian speaking people, but the appropriation by Russian first, of a part in some functions where it overlaps with other languages, and then exclusiveness in operating those functions.

The fourth level of contact is one of almost complete assimilation, where bilingualism is vestigial and often only symbolic, characterizing a small and diminishing minority. The transfer from one language to another, usually as we have noted, Russian, is facilitated by the acquisition of an intermediate language. The Pamiri usually adopt Tadzhik before they learn Russian, and the smaller N. Caucasian peoples learn Georgian before Russian, except in the urban areas and where the education system provides for exclusive Russian medium education. This shift of language affiliation is one of the consequences of population movement in the USSR, but it is not a simple issue. Long distance migration where the language group is severed from its base best exemplifies this operation. Where migration involves the urbanization of the immediate surrounding rural population the tendency is for the newcomers to the towns to delay the process of switching to the new language, and to rejuvenate an otherwise receding local language in the urban area. This happened for a long time in Baku. With each seasonal invasion of the shepherds who migrated into the town during winter for occasional employment the speakers of Azerbaydzhani received a new lease of life. Then again, so far as small immigrant groups are concerned, it is usually the case that their retention of the native language is limited to oral command and more often than not of a dialect rather than the standard language. This has been noted among immigrant groups everywhere – the Welsh and the Irish in England for instance, and among immigrant groups in the USA. "Where trained linguists distinguished only several regional dialects, peasant immigrants readily recognized many differentiating features between their own local speech and that current a few miles away from their native village. And it was precisely this parochial tongue, the speech of their kin and dear ones, rather than the national language that peasant immigrants appeared to have been attached to." (Nahriny and Fishman, 1965, 313). For this reason the demographic resources of the language in the enclaves become attentuated. When several dialects are represented among the small minority using that language, in any locality it becomes more difficult to ensure its maintenance. Even when dialect problems do not exist among the immigrants they are unable to maintain a standard of literacy in that language. Even Armenians who remain bilingual in exile seldom continue to be functionally literate in their own language. The opportunities to read and write their native language in exile are frustrated because of the lack of a literature which they can read in the mother tongue. Literacy therefore is a factor which though it conduces to the survival of the main national languages has the reverse effect on the

stability of the immigrants' language. The prestige of literacy and the
necessity in Soviet society to be literate if only for minimal, civic, purposes, places an inordinate value on the languages in which the need for
literacy is satisfied.

ii. *Types of Contact and of Bilingualism*

a. *Oral/literate Bilingualism*

Among language contact situations one of the most important distinctions to be observed in certain societies is that between bilingualism where
the speaker is literate in neither language and where a speaker is literate
in either or both languages. It is clear that one consequence of Soviet
planning is that bilingualism acquires the new dimension of literacy,
where previously there may have been largely fortuitous and oral bilingualism only. This transformation has led to two contradictory consequences. In so far as the great majority of the bilinguals are literate in only
one of their languages there is a tendency for the language in which they
are literate to take over, in the first instance, the most prestigous and
then all the significant roles in communication. Soon bilingual speakers
cease to include any real command of the language in which there is only
oral competence. In so far as the bilinguals are literate in both languages
it has been observed that a complementary type bilingualism occurs, but
in terms not of linguistic function as of social grouping. Both languages
are used for almost all roles indifferently, but varying in emphasis on one
language or the other according to the primary language of the speaker.
Where complementarity involves differentiation of *linguistic* roles we
find that it is, to begin with at least, a function of that kind of bilingualism
where only one language is available for literacy. The differentiation in
such a case is between formal and colloquial transactions. This has been
the case among the Kirgiz in contact with Tadzhiks in Tadzhikstan. It is
certainly the case in the relationship of Russian and the local languages.

b. *Bi-dialectalism*

Bi-dialectalism is a frequent phenomenon and involves two dialects of
the same, or of different languages. For instance there are two groups of
Tadzhik dialects, northern and southern, and though there is a standard
written language based largely on the classical language, it frequently
happens that in the Darvazsky khrebet for instance, speakers of the
Tadzhik dialects have to make a mutual accommodation in their attempts
to communicate in the same language. The same is true of speakers of the
Shugnan-Rushan group of mutually unintelligible Pamiri dialects –
Shugnan, Rushan, Bartan, Oroshor, and Chuf, spoken along the upper

reaches of the river Piandzh and its several tributaries. In Tadzhikstan too we find numerous examples of bilingualism resulting from a dialect of Tadzhik and of Uzbek which overlap in several areas, and of an Uzbek dialect and the standard Tadzhik.

c. *Diglossia*

There is no agreement at present about the meaning to be attached to the term *diglossia*. For some it is applied to a phenomenon which is indistinguishable from bilingualism where different languages are adopted for different and complementary rather than overlapping roles in the community. This is the view adopted by Fishman (1967) and by Even-Zohar (1970). Since in normal circumstances there are bound to be cases where though the two languages are used normally for different roles but may nevertheless quite frequently be used for the same roles by certain groups of people, it is difficult to distinguish between bilingualism and diglossia in any useful way, using such a definition. Others confine the use of the term to intra-lingual situations, to "the use of variants of the *same language* that are distinguishable by their use for different and stable complementary roles and by structural linguistic differences". This is the view taken by Ferguson (1959).[6] Martinet tends to the same view – for him diglossia distinguishes multiple norms for the same language in a single community, whereas bilingualism distinguishes multiple norms of a single speaker of two or more languages (1959, 139). In the situation of the USSR, whatever may be the case elsewhere there is little point in applying the terms "diglossia" to the use of different languages. The language contact situation there is too complex and necessitates the recognition of too fine gradations from one type to another to permit us to speak of the relationship of two languages as diglossic. There are very many instances where in the same community some groups restrict the use of a particular language to particular domains of function, while other groups do not. Such cases occur in other societies too. We do need a term for the specific phenomenon described and illustrated by Ferguson and it is doubtful whether a useful purpose is served by extending its use.

Instances of diglossia in this sense though not infrequent in the Soviet Union do not constitute a significant class of contact situations. It does occur in the case of Tadzhik, where the standard written language is largely based on the classical language and there exist clearly identifiable groups of regional dialects among which are 'high' and 'low' variants. Though it is claimed that there exists a standard spoken language, said to be the same as the standard written form, it is almost certainly the case

---

[6] Ferguson defines diglossia as "a particular kind of standardization where two varieties exist side by side throughout the community, each having a definite role to play" (325).

that most of the intelligentsia, even those who would be proficient in both the written standard and the spoken standard if it exists, revert to one or other of the dialects in intimate conversation and in ordinary every day informal communication. Even in personal writing it is the dialect which determines the style in such communications. This is coming to be more and more the case in Uzbek also where the written standard based on urban dialects around Tashkent is used in teaching, in all publications and in the oral transaction of official or formal business. But the non-urban dialects though coming to be considered inferior are often the media of conversation and casual private transactions, even in Tashkent itself, on account of infiltration from the rural areas. The same local dialects are the ones which are heard in the playground and in the shops. One interesting instance of diglossia occurs in Armenia, where in addition to the two standard dialect varieties there is also Church Armenian. It is an 'archaic standard' in current highly limited use. Without conforming entirely to Ferguson's definition it suggests itself as a possible candidate for inclusion in the category of diglossia. Some linguists would refer to the relationship between Russian and Ukrainian in the 19th Century as one of diglossia, though since the 19th Century the development of the latter permits it to be regarded as an independent language rather than a variant. During the 18th and 19th Centuries however it was the case that Russian and Ukrainian tended to be regarded as the High and Low variants of the same language, with important structural differences and both equally widespread in the Ukraine.

d. *Élitist/Mass Bilingualism*

This is a distinction in type of bilingual contact which, in the main, moulds the relationship of foreign and indigenous languages. The traditional oral bilingualism of the USSR affected the uneducated mass of the population, though not necessarily very large proportions of them. Élitist bilingualism, historically, involved the learning of a foreign language, which in very many instances was preferred to the mother tongue. This was the case not only in Russia, where for the élite French was a second mother tongue, but, as we have noted, in Latvia and other Baltic countries where German was preferred. The command of Russian in addition to one's mother tongue also constituted élitist bilingualism until the incidence of mass migration and mass education, with compulsory Russian.

Élitist bilingualism involving a foreign language, too, is becoming a mass phenomenon on account of universal secondary education, the compulsory learning of a foreign language, intensive teaching of it and its use as a medium of instruction in many schools. In fact, though Russian is regarded in the Soviet Union as 'a second mother tongue', the competence of many students and the pressure behind the teaching of a foreign language places the latter not very far removed from Russian as an element in mass bilingualism. Soviet, non-Russian teachers who have visited Britain during the last ten years to my knowledge have often revealed not only almost native competence in English but a control of the language which is as great as, greater sometimes than their control of Russian, a fact which if pressed they will themselves acknowledge.

e.   *Transitional/Long Term Bilingualism*

The analysis of the figures for language maintenance shows that some languages are more likely to be involved in widespread and persistent bilingualism than others. But the social contact is not the only factor which determines which of the alternative types of bilingualism, transitional or long term characterizes a particular combination of languages: there are many entirely personal factors to be taken into account. The reasons why one particular speaker of the two languages may move rapidly to the substitution of one language for the other, while another retains both may be entirely personal and idiosyncratic. Sometimes both languages are retained in spite of conditions which overwhelmingly favour one language. This has happened with speakers of Ukrainian in some Komosmol territories of the Far East where conditions favour the local languages or Russian. However, whatever personal factors may be involved the social conditions of the two languages in contact usually determine the rate of assimilation or the permanent retention of both. This applies particularly to such languages as Yukagir and Tat.

f.   *Venicular/Cultural Bilingualism*

There is a distinction to be made between vehicular, and cultural or comprehensive bilingualism,[7] in situations of contact where one of the languages is used for very limited purposes only, or for transactions which are impersonal and make no demands upon the speaker in respect of his cultural affiliations. Like the distinction between transitional and permanent bilingualism this category too has personal as well as societal dimensions. The same language, in the same social situation may be acquired by one person as a vehicular language and by another as the means of entry into the total culture related to the language. But in general the conditions in which the two languages operate, and the social pressure promoting either language create the conditions of choice. An Uzbek or Kirgiz who acquires Tadzhik within Tadzhikstan is more likely to be involved in a more comprehensive type bilingualism than a Kirgiz, Uzbek or Tadzhik who acquires Russian in Tadzhikstan in spite

[7]   As was noted in Chapter 2 this is an important aspect of the relative importance of the specifically linguistic and the broad ideological value of Russian.

of the intense support for Russian. Partly because of the cultural distance between Russian and Central Asian or for that matter Caucasian languages, the identification of Russian with a revolutionary and to that extent an unhistorical ideology, as well as the narrow bases on which the acquisition of Russian is founded, Russian related bilingualism in a large number of cases, even among the non-Russian intelligentsia, leads to vehicular rather than comprehensive bilingualism. To a lesser extent, it is true, but not unlike English in Africa or S.E. Asia for instance, Russian is developing the capacity to operate independently of its related group or traditional culture in most areas of the Soviet Union. In other areas where the tradition of contact with Russian is very much longer and the community of cultures fairly intimate, as it is in the Western Republics, Russian operates according to a pattern which conforms more closely to that of French in Africa, where the French language is thought of as part of a total complex – the French way of life.

In any socio-linguistic profile of the languages of the USSR it will be necessary to add to the 5 levels of the provisional model already suggested a sixth level which describes the extent to which the language is involved in any of the above types of contact, the names of the other languages in contact being stated.

iii. *Profile of Contacts*

Level 6 Tadzhik in contact with the named languages[8]

Contact Languages	Type of Contact [8]										
	Oral	Literate	Bi-dialect	Elite	Mass	Trans	Long Term	Vehic.	Compr.	Scattered	Concentrated
Foreign language		√		√			√	√	√		
Uzbek	√	√	√		√	√		√	√		
Kirgiz	√	√	√		√	√		√	√		√
Tatar	√	√			√	√		√		√	
Turkmen	√	√			√	√		√		√	
Pamiri	√	√			√	√		√			√
Russian		√		√			√	√	√	√	
Ukrainian	√				√	√		√		√	
Arabic	√	√			√	√		√		√	
Iagnobi	√	√			√	√		√		√	
Dungan	√	√			√	√		√		√	
Gypsy	√				√	√		√		√	

[8] It will be noted that no slot is provided for Diglossia, since this is a category which

F. LANGUAGE PLANNING – AN INTEGRAL PART OF SOVIET POLICY

i. *The Political Influences on Language Planning*

The great diversity of languages, the multiplicity of stages of development, and of types of contact situation are to a great extent the result of the working of historical factors, but they have been influenced during the last half century by massive and multiform exercises in social engineering. At one end of the scale of such planning procedures are major forms of economic and industrial planning involving the movement of whole industries, the opening up of virgin lands, the creation of immense cities where there were formerly, by most standards, only small townships or even villages, together with movements of peoples, sometimes whole nations, across enormous distances. At the other end of the scale, less spectacular almost minute operations take place in the linguist's study, involving the production of alphabets, or in the educationist's office involving the creation of various types of schools to accord to the general plan, and even in small classrooms involving teaching methods designed to reinforce that general plan.

These we have attempted to analyse, and though there ought to be no reason to apologize for including pedagogy and especially language pedagogy as part of social planning, the political relevance is so seldom examined that a case for its inclusion may be expected. A theory of instruction and a theory of language planning, certainly so far as the USSR is concerned, and I suspect this is generally the case, are aspects of a political theory or a political philosophy, since in both cases a great deal of the concern which both motivates and directs language pedagogy and planning is with the mobilization of the society, and consequently with the distribution and consolidation of political power. Studies of social planning have hitherto given too little attention to the functions of language planning, and with the exception of Haugen (1966a and b), students of language planning have given too little consideration to social-political aspects of its motivation. Language pedagogy, whatever else it is, is an aspect of language planning. The latter cannot succeed unless the teacher is able to translate the decision of the planning agency into actual use of a language, or into acceptance of changes in a language. Pedagogy is certainly more than an instrument of social policy, and language pedagogy is more than an instrument of language planning, but they are no less.

In the last resort language planning has to do with how people are

---

according to the definition accepted for this study is internal to the language itself and involves no outside contact. Furthermore it requires only a yes/no answer. It need not be built into the model but it should be noted in the profile.

educated, with the choice of instrument for education and with how the chosen medium can be made more efficient, which includes enabling it to deal with information more adequately along a 'rising scale of intellectualization'. Finally planning has to do with the acceptability of the language, which means considering the attitudes of those who use them. Bearing these aspects of language planning in mind the educator or planner who proceeds without specific regard to the economic, social and practical considerations surrounding the choice and implementation of pedagogic method, for instance, or of the social aims and possible political consequences of the purely linguistic aspects of language planning, is likely to put the relevance of his work at risk. Innovation whether in linguistic theory or practice is never without its impact upon the organization of society, which is an aspect of political theory. In most countries, perhaps, the political consequences are subordinated to more theoretical or academic considerations, or more usually are left to take care of themselves. This is not the case, as we have seen, in the Soviet Union, where it is the judgment of the balance of political advantage and disadvantage which directs language planning and pedagogical endeavours.

For instance the three criteria we have referred to, efficiency, adequacy and acceptability have invariably been interpreted in the USSR in the light of political considerations, though the manner of satisfying those criteria, that is 'the level of formal elaboration' (Haugen, 1966a, 17) has been left to the specialists to determine. The decision to use a Latin alphabet in Central Asia rather than to continue with Arabic was politically motivated in the main – to help ensure the separation of some Soviet languages and nations from their Arabic or other non-indigenous associations. Then again, as far as concerns the adequacy of the Soviet languages in meeting the needs of new sciences and technology the insistence on using new resources of vocabulary is governed by political intentions, though the linguistic aspects of the adaptation of the loan words phonically and morphologically has been the concern of the linguists. All the machinery at the command of the regime has been used to promote and make acceptable the linguistic innovations and the consequences of pedagogical and linguistic planning – this machinery includes the central control of printing and publishing, for instance, as well as radio and the educational system. This political motivation and direction of aspects of language planning have been aimed to attain three objectives – the reinforcement and acceleration of the tendency towards uniformation within communities, and thus to extend the area of social mobilization. Simultaneously with this has been the attempt to insulate as far as possible those languages which might have associations outside the USSR, as well as to accentuate the differences between languages and communities within the USSR, which if allowed to form a block might threaten the predominance of Russian.

For instance the Mountain ASSR of the North Caucusus appeared to the new regime to be too well consolidated a political area on the flank of the RSFSR. In September 1921 Kabarda was detached, followed in January 1922 by the separation of the Karachai who were joined to the Cherkess. At the end of the year the Chechens were made independent of the Mountain Republic and became a separate and autonomous province. Finally the Ossetians and the Ingushi completed the disintegration of the Autonomous Republic. Similarly care was taken to frustrate the formation of a possible pan-Turkic block. At one time educated Uzbeks and Tadzhiks questioned the need for a Tadzhik literary language since both groups were trained in Uzbek and Persian. Representative Turkic groups outside the USSR do not recognize the separation of the two languages or the independent existence of the Tadzhiks. They tend to regard Uzbeks and Tadzhiks to be far more united than divergent groups. Nor did the Tadzhiks regard themselves or their language as specifically national units. They saw themselves first and foremost as tied to the Iranic heritage and to a Central Asian community. Even within Tadzhikstan there were considerable differences. The Tadzhiks of the plain who spoke Farsi, the Persian dialect which became the standard Tadzhik language, had little contact with other groups, and the adoption of Farsi was engineered to ensure that there was as little contact as possible with other, non Tadzhik groups in Central Asia. Language planning was directed so as to ensure that the Tadzhiks were first of all separated as far as possible from Iranic groups outside the USSR, and second to consolidate a 'nation' different from others who might have identified themselves with the Tadzhiks inside the USSR.[9]

A third intention of language planning generally in the Soviet Union has been to extend directly the influence of Russian. This explains the decision to change the newly created alphabets in Latin form to Cyrillic, as well as the intensive promotion of Russian loan words. The heart of Language Planning is "the exercise of judgment in the form of choices among available linguistic forms", (Haugen, 1966b, 52) and though the implementation of the initial choice and the success or failure of the attempt depend largely on the specialist work in linguistics and education, that initial judgment, in the USSR certainly, is political.

It may seem odd that this political orientation and direction of language planning cannot be assumed without the need for what must appear at the moment to be special pleading. Nevertheless, however one looks at

[9] This process of separating small communities and proliferating independent administrative units, having achieved its purpose of ensuring that there would be no 'anti-Russian blocks', the theorists are now promoting the idea of the cultural legitimacy of 'regional units' such as the N. Caucasus, again, in the main, as a means of ensuring political uniformation within the USSR (See Chapter 2).

it language, either symbolically or instrumentally, is integral to everything that is attempted in social planning. Language symbolizes ethnic/national consciousness in ways which are immensely significant. It is not only a part of what we regard as our ethnic/national identity, it also crystallizes that consciousness, makes it explicit, and formulates its meaning for us. Language has a dual character – being part of what we mean by our nationality, and at the same time ensuring that such a consciosuness is more than an insubstantial, incohate feeling. It is because of this dual character that language can, in Fishman's terms be "ideologized", and so exist as an independent force or field of attraction. When almost everything else that defines our ethnic or national identity has evaporated language can symbolize it without necessarily perpetuating its possibly obsolete associations. As a symbol of ethnic consciousness, linguistic nationalism may have disadvantages. These the participants of the 1969 conference of Sociologists at Cannes (Tajfel, 1970) realized, when they stressed the "many undesirable consequences to the intensification of ethnic and national awareness in many countries in the course of primary and secondary education".

In some respects, therefore, it can be argued very persuasively that the Soviet Union has only reacted to anticipate these adverse possibilities. Intensified national language consciousness can undoubtedly raise barriers to all kinds of innovations which promote social mobilization and uniformation in the USSR. Some of these barriers are cultural – the basic values of the group mainly encapsulated in the national language, or symbolized by it. Some barriers arise from differences in social structure – types of family grouping and the network of authority, and these are strengthened and preserved by the common language. There are psychological barriers – stemming from differences in learning styles and processes among different peoples, and these again at the important learning levels, are intertwined with language, or influenced by linguistic differences. It is also the case that with the obsolesence of other indices of national identity, for instance religion, economic organization, and the exclusive or predominant occupation of a common territory, the concept of nationality itself becomes increasingly irrelevant. The tendency in these circumstances is to exaggerate the claims of language. As the foundations of national consciousness are eroded and opportunities for its expression circumscribed feeling for language becomes more intense and strident. The national language becomes a progressively divisive agency as the reasons for the consciousness of difference lose weight.

However this need not occur. Whatever may have been the case in periods of much greater national isolation, or in areas of the USSR where communication between peoples was and is discouraged or restricted, it is plausible to argue that since isolation is yielding to the forces of change the value of a national language is no longer commensurate with the intimacy of its relationship to a national culture. Of the various ties that bind human beings together those of a common language appear at present to be losing whatever strength they had. Other bonds protect language rather than language them. Where in any land different languages are spoken in different parts, those parts are not isolated because the people speak a different language, but they speak different languages to the extent that they are isolated. This is certainly true of the Soviet Union.

However, as an independent institution capable of operating independently or of being disassociated from the uniqueness of its cultural concomitants or its ethnic/national correlatives language need not automatically lend itself to an exacerbation of national differences and divisiveness. "There are grounds for thinking that linguistic nationalism is one of the more attractive aspects of nationalism" (Haugen 1966b, 63). In the USSR it symbolizes national consciousness in ways which are compatible with international development, and for this reason "conscious and even ideologised language differences need not be divisive" (Fishman, 1968a, 45). It has been part of the argument of this study that Soviet policy looked at objectively and intensively, has only the appearance of inconsistency or contradiction though it is ambiguous, and explained very often by tortuously devious arguments. The ambiguity arises largely, though not exclusively from the fact that the USSR is committed to the strategy of 'the two fronts', and recognizes a dual obligation – international and national. The national languages have been promoted (out of necessity, it is true, but promoted nevertheless) as instruments of social mobilization through literacy; and whatever other national institutions, religious, economic or juridical have been undermined or eliminated, and whatever restrictions may be placed on some uses of the national languages the balance of advantage is ultimately immensely in their favour. Furthermore whatever has been done to increase their instrumental value in the above sense their symbolic value increases also, though the substance they symbolize has changed. As political loyalties relate to ever larger *civic* groups (as opposed to ethnic/national communities), or become focussed not upon a people as upon an ideology or even a Party, institutions which are capable of providing more concrete foundations for affiliation without necessarily being associated with potentially political entities (the former nations and nationalities) acquire a rich symbolic value. Consequently Soviet languages and Soviet linguistic nationalism, because they can operate independently of a national political consciousness, can become the means of giving reality to community life which is less extensive than civic and international political loyalty, and at the same time compatible with it. It is the ability of national languages satisfactorily to meet these two equally exigent demands which is the justification of their promotion – they instantiate better than any other aspect of national life the concept 'national in form and socialist in content', which may be two-faced but not contradictory.

ii. *Implementation Techniques*

Haugen in his analysis of language planning in Norway (1966a) distinguishes in any movement towards change two stages – initiation and implementation, and we have accepted this as operating in the USSR. This study has argued that so far as the Soviet Union is concerned the level of initiation, which Haugen identifies with the selection of a norm, is largely motivated by political considerations. And from Haugen's general analysis of the Norwegian situation this would appear to be the case there also. The level of implementation, in strict linguistic terms, is identified by him with "the elaboration of function". There is another aspect of implementation, however, which is again largely political in character – that aspect of language planning which Punya Sloka Ray (1963) and Haugen have stressed, namely acceptability. There are, without question, entirely linguistic aspects of acceptability, for instance, a judgment of how far the proposed norms diverge from or how near they are, or should be, to existing popular norms. But even so there is a further level of implementation which has to do with techniques of ensuring that these linguistic choices, whatever they are, become realized in practice. At this level of implementation the administrator, educationist and the political agent intervene to influence attitude.

The success of Soviet endeavours in the general area of language planning depends as much on the attitude of the speakers as upon the validity, the reliability and the authenticity of the work of the linguists. Consequently though attitude to language is one of the most fugitive concepts of socio-linguistics it has to be taken into account, especially where language planning-occurs in the context of very widespread and radical social change. As the individual in the Soviet Union ceases to be immersed in a single, and possibly isolated group, attitude to language changes. Where there is considerable cross cultural contact the attitude to the relevant languages cannot be the same as it is in periods and areas of isolation. This change, when it occurs, is independent of the inherent character of the cultures in contact – change of attitude has very little to do with how different or how close the ways of life may have been. It is the element of change itself which is significant. For instance, perhaps one of the most important forms of change affecting language has been urbanization, and urbanization produces characteristic effects, independently of the culture groups which become urbanized. The change is not a modification of previous attitudes, but a new creation. It has been shown that the differences between urban and rural children as classes, irrespective of country, are very much more significant than the differences between urban children in different countries, or between rural children in different countries, or between sub-sets of the same class in the same country. Once the horizons are extended a whole new way of life appears to be created which bears little relation to the original patterns of behaviour. Nor does the extent of a citizen's urban sojourn matter very much. When everything else is the object of comparison, as it is in the process of urbanization, language cannot be expected to remain immune.

Changes in attitude however, are not uniform and members of the same group may adopt different attitudes according to whether they regard the language from within a *group* culture or within a *civic* culture. The wider the interest of the group the more likely it is to change its attitude. Similarly, attitude to language as we have noted varies with generational differences and with sex. But the vital fact about attitude to language is that it can easily become institutionalized – formalized in the case of USSR in terms of an ideology. Because it is formalized attitude becomes more sensitive and responsive to other institutional pressures, or is more easily available for manipulation by such agencies. The Soviet Union has operated upon three levels of such manipulation.

One of these is simple and crude imposition, or its converse, namely deprivation of a particular language from opportunities to participate in important domains of employment, like education. Imposition and deprivation have affected such minorities as the Jews especially, but not uniquely. It is difficult to draw the line between imposition/deprivation, and the second level of implementation, that is regulation. One is tempted to argue that the difference lies in the fact that it is the tendency for imposition to be arbitrary. This is not a satisfactory distinction. A probably more satisfactory way of differentiating the two levels of implementation is to include within regulation some element of consultation with the language group affected. For instance, the Irish and the Welsh languages were forbidden in the schools of the respective nationalities and this was done by due process of law. It was not arbitrary. It was nevertheless implementation by imposition because those who were most affected were hardly consulted if they were consulted at all. Regulation on the other hand assumes consultation and is concerned with articulating the necessary constitutional framework for implementation. Yiddish has been the subject of imposition/deprivation, while the role of Tadzhik is the subject of consultation with those who are most intimately involved. The consultation leads to the preparation of a constitutional instrument which provides for the implementation of the processes of language planning – use in law, in schools, etc. and what form of Tadzhik to use, for instance Tadzhik written in Cyrrilic. The same system of regulation affects the relation of Tadzhik with other languages.

However, the most characteristic Soviet technique for attempting to resolve problems arising out of linguistic heterogeneity is the administrative or managerial.[10] This technique involves the use of linguists and others concerned with language planning in only a severely limited capacity; they are not independent practitioners of their art, or a theoretically and academically autonomous body of scholars. Though the administration or management of language planning requires them as a scientific and technical cadre, or a source of essential information, the manager or administrator is not bound to their proposals for language planning. The control is in the hands of an entrenched and powerful lay élite. It is possible, even probable, that because of the complexity of Soviet linguistic heterogeneity 'management' of language planning is bound to be paramount; but whether this should be so or not is hardly the point – it is so.

The complaints which are made in Tadzhikstan, for instance, are not against imposition or deprivation, or against the constitutional position of the Tadzhik language, but against the administrative arrangements which are made for the maintenance of the constitutional position. Supply of paper can favour publication in one language, usually Russian rather than another. The dilemma expressed in the Journal *Nedelya* indicates the possibilities of management of publication priorities to ensure the success of a particular policy: "there arises the question of publishing bigger editions of certain major works of importance for ideological work and economic and cultural construction, as well as the most popular works of classical literature. In this case however extremely rational editions have to be fixed for many hundreds of thousands of other books, mainly of a specialist nature." (*Nedelya*, No. 13 1971). If, to this difficulty of deciding on priorities, is added the disinclination to give the appropriate attention to native writers, so that "it is difficult to find on sale the works of Mirzo Tursunzade, Mirsaid Mirshakar, Boka Takhimzade and other outstanding Tadzhik writers" it is possible to understand the frustration produced by managerial manipulation. In fact "in the Tadzhik Republic in recent years the publication of books has fallen 50%. Readers have been waiting a long time for books, but their publication is carried over from one plan to the next." (Mullodzhanov, 1970). But the managing of publication priorities is only one aspect of this process. The arrangements for the admission of students to state universities and institutes of higher education can be manipulated also (without changing the statutory

[10]   The Soviet Union best exemplifies the operation in contemporary Society of the three conjoined characteristics – bureaucracy, meritocracy and technocracy. The Managerial approach arises from an amalgam of all three, and governs the present development of languages.

obligations on admission) so as to favour non-national students, or the national students who are most proficient in a particular language – Russian. The medium of instruction in secondary schools is obviously an area for management and manipulation.

However, one of the most effective ways of managing the language planning process is through the constitution of the local bureaucracy and the qualifications demanded of its members. As in the Greek and Roman Empires, and in a way which was never true of the British Empire, the Soviet bureaucracy is multinational as well as supra-national. It not only constitutes a unified élite but a unified élite composed of different nationals with different national languages. Nevertheless their ability to operate supra-nationally is seen to depend on their acquisition of a common language, Russian. The opportunities for promotion which exist for the hundreds of officials depend on their acquiring Russian, and to an equally important degree on their attitude to Russian and other languages. Furthermore, trans-national exchange of speakers of Russian depresses the value of the local language. The level of implementation which is most important for language planning is therefore undoubtedly the level of management, partly because it can manage not only the realization of a policy or of a constitution for the language, but even the interpretation of that constitution. It is also the most effective because it is the level of implementation which is nearest the point of impact, and facilitates or frustrates at will, and immediately.

G. CONCLUSION

In attempting to draw some general conclusions from our study of multilingualism in the USSR perhaps the first judgment we have to make is on the difficulty of discovering among the formulae which have been proposed as models for socio-linguistic studies of such linguistically complex areas any one, or for that matter any combination of existing formulae which can do justice to the Soviet situation. The difficulty appears to be less surprising when the study has been completed than when it was begun, and this in itself is a measure of our (or my) ignorance of the Soviet position. The difference between the USSR and other multi-lingual areas lies partly in the number of variables of which account has to be taken, and partly in the existence of variables which do not appear to operate elsewhere or to operate on such a low level of significance elsewhere as to negative any possibility of comparison. These variables have been distinguished along two dimensions, the first of which, a vertical co-ordinate, is related to the multiplicity of development stages of ethnic groups and their languages. So far as languages go the developmental dimension extends from almost extinct dialects to major and world languages such as Russian. Between the dialects and languages there exists also a great variety of developing or changing relations from assimilation, convergence, mutual influence, to separate and stable co-existence. These relations concern both the ethnic groups and their languages, and there is no certainty that what characterizes the relations of the ethnic groups characterizes the relationship between the languages the groups speak. This is particularly important so far as Russian is concerned since it is moving into a position which English has already attained, where the adoption of the language is independent of the adoption of any particular attitude to the related national or 'group' culture, or political status of any English speaking community, such as Britain or the U.S.A.

The second dimension has to do with classes of situations – contact situations, in the main between the ethnic groups and between their languages. We have tried to distinguish types of contact in the USSR, ranging from the historical and traditional contact where the languages or dialects are not distinguished according to their characteristic roles, to contact situations where the languages do have distinguishable roles, but which, however, overlap in the process of extending the coverage of one language at the expense of the other. A third type of contact is the situation of a complementary stability which is the result not of historical contact but of new forces of social and geographical mobility. This type is of importance since the complementarity seems to exist between two clusters of linguistic and cultural roles, which we have hesitatingly called a *civic culture* cluster and a *group culture* cluster. The importance of this type of contact for us is that it concerns the relation between Russian and the major 'national languages' (the eponymous languages of the Union Republics) on the one hand, and the local or minority languages on the other. And finally we have tried to observe the operation of what may be called vestigial bilingualism, especially as this affects the attitude of some ethnic groups to their historical identity, expressed in the Census claim for the possession of a particular native language.

This typology of bilingual situations in the USSR has tried to take into account also the changes which have taken place in the USSR during the last fifty years, involving a movement from a mainly oral to a literate bilingualism, and within literate bilingualism a difference between a largely élitist literate form, based on the aristocracy, and a mass literate bilingualism arising from expanded and improved education. But in all the attempts at categorization the interesting feature has been the change from a largely fortuitous to a planned pattern of language contact, brought into existence by political policy, economic and demographic arrangements, educational administration, as well as pedagogic systematization and planning of courses and methods, together with linguistic standardization, directed towards social and political ends. The planning is handled in several ways but the most characteristic form in the USSR is management, which often bears only a very tenuous relationship to the statutory obligations of the managers, and is governed largely from the centre.

However, in spite of the extraordinary care and drive of the USSR in pursuing its language planning processes by whatever strategies and techniques, what most strikes the observer in the end is the resilience of the large number of 'national languages', several of them quite small, and the tenacity with which they are maintained. The well documented, but almost mystical unwillingness of languages to submit to their own demise accounts in a large part for this. But part of the explanation so far as concerns the USSR, and all countries which have been involved with mass literacy campaigns and mass education, is the undoubted fact that however the language complex is managed the vernaculars have to be used and for that reason they have to be safeguarded and improved for a variety of social roles, especially education. The 'policy of the two fronts' (*dva potoka*) has to be implemented and the problem of the Soviet regime in nationalities policy and in language has been and will remain one of maintaining a judicious, which is not always the same as a just balance between the needs of the centre in promoting homogeneity and uniformation, and the claims, both 'sentimental' and practical, of the local languages. It looks as if the regime finds its solution in promoting the distinction between the two clusters of affiliations we have referred to (civic and group), and by ensuring that the instrument of group culture affiliation, the 'national language' becomes the means of expressing only 'the attractive forms of nationalism'.

References and Bibliography

Aamovich, A.,
   1962   "Towards a Single Socialist State", *Studies in the Soviet Union*, IV.iii: 203-210.
Abilov, A.,
   1964   Artcile in *Pravda* (July 1964).
Ablin, F. (ed.),
   1970   "Decision Making in Soviet Higher Education: a Documentary History", *Soviet Education* XIII.9-11.
Abramson, S. M.,
   1946   *Ocherk kultury Kirgizskogo naroda* [A Study of the Culture of the Kirgiz Nation] (Frunze).
   1962   "Otrazheniye protsessa sblizeheniya natsii na semynobytovom uklade narodov srednei Azii i Kazakh" [The influence of the Process of Increased Contact Between Nations on the Family Life in Central Asia and Kazakhstan], *Sovetskaya etnografiya* 3:18-24.
Afanasenko, E. I.,
   1962   "Concerning the Progress in Implementing the Law on Strengthening the Ties of School with Life etc.", *Uchitelskaya Gazeta*, July 26 (Trans. in *Soviet Education*, Nov. 1962).
Agayev, A.,
   1961   "V seme volnoi novoi" [In the Free and New Family], *Izvestiya*, Dec. 5th 1961.
Aghayan, E.,
   1958   "Twenty Five years of Armenian Linguistics", *Armenian Review* IV.iii.
Agheyisi, R. and Fishman J. A.,
   1970   "Language Attitude Studies", *Anthropological Linguistics* XII.v: 37-57.
Agurova, N. V.,
   1959   "An Experiment in Teaching English to first and second grades", *Inostraniye yazyki shkole* IV (Translated into English in *Soviet Education* II: 2).
Akhmanov, D. S.,

1960   *O Psikholinguistike* (Moscow).

Albert, V. M.,
1970   "Uncontrollable Population Shifts in the Soviet Union", *Analysis of Current Developments*, in the *Soviet Union* 62, 2 June.

Alito, S. B.,
1969   "The Language Issue in Communist Chinese Education", *Comparative Educational Review* xiii.i: 43-59.

Allakhiarov, G.,
1966   *Sblizheniye kultur sotsialisticheskikh natsii v period stroitelstva kommunizma* [The Merging of Cultures in Socialist Nations in the Period of Communist Construction], (Baku).

Allworth, E. (ed.),
1967   *Central Asia: A Century of Russian Rule* (New York).

Ananev, B. G.,
1957   "O Razvitii detei v protsesse obucheniya" [Child Development under Instruction], *Sovietskaya Pedagogika*, 7.

Apte, M. L.,
1970   "Some Socio-linguistic Aspects of Interlingual Communication in India", *Anthropological Linguistics* XII, March.

Aristova, F. F. and Vasilyena, E.,
1965   "Kurds of the Turkmen SSR", *Central Asian Review* XIII, 4:302-309.

Armstrong, J. A.,
1968   "The Ethnic Scene in the Soviet Union", in: *Ethnic Minorities in the Soviet Union*, E. Goldhagen, ed.

Aron, R.,
1968   *Democracy and Totalitarianism* (London).

Artemov, V. A.,
1960   "Some Problems of Speech Psychology in Teaching Students to Speak a Foreign Language", *Innostranniye iazyki v shkole* V (translated into English in *Soviet Education*, 1961).
1966   *Psikhologii a obucheniya innostrannym yazykam* [Psychological Foundations for Teaching Foreign Languages] (Moscow).
1967   "Basic Problems in Contemporary Psychology of Foreign Languages", *Innostranniye yzayki v shkole* I (translated into English in *Soviet Education*, 1967).

Arutiunian, Iu. V.,
1968   "Opyt sotsialno-etnicheskogo issledovaniya po materialam Tatarskoi ASSR" [Preliminary Social-ethnographic Investigation of Tatar Materials], *Sovetskaya etnografia* 4: 3-13.

Avtorkhanov, A.,
1964   "Denationalization of Soviet Ethnic Minorities", *Studies in the Soviet Union* II.

Aymanov, K. A.,
1967   "Razvitiye narodnogo obrazovaniya v Kazakhstane", [The Development of Public Education in Kazakhstan] *Sovetskaya Pedagogika* 5.

Azizyan, A.,
1961   "Stroitelstvo Kommunizma i razvitiye natsionalnykh otnosheniy", [Relations between Soviet Nationalities in Communist Construction], *Kommunist* 10: 47-57.

Bacon, E. E.,
   1966   *Central Asia under Russian Rule* (Ithaca, Cornell University Press).
Bacon, Francis,
   1608   *Novum Organum-Aphorismi et consilia* (London).

Badalbayan, S.,
   1968   in: *Razvitiye natsionalnykh otnosheniy na sovremennom etape kommunisticheskogo stroitelstva* [Development of National Relations at the Present Stage of Communist Growth], (Pyatigorsk).

Banks, A. S. and Textor, R.,
   1965   *A Cross Polity Survey* (Cambridge [Mass.], M.I.T.).

Banner, R. A.,
   1959   *The New Man in Soviet Psychology* (Cambridge [Mass.], Harvard).

Barbu, Z.,
   1953   "Language in Democratic and Totalitarian Societies", *Orbis*: 73-81.

Barghoorn, F. G.,
   1954   "Nationality Doctrine in Soviet Political Strategy", *Review of Politics* XVI.iii: 283-304.
   1956   *Soviet Russian Nationalism* (New York).

Baskakov, N. A.,
   1951   *Karakalpakskiy yazyk* (tom I.i; 2) [The Karakalpak Language] (Moscow).
   1960   *The Turkic Languages of Central Asia: Problems of Planned Culture Contact*[2] (translated) (Oxford, Central Asia Centre).
   1960   *Tyurkskiye yazyki* (Moscow).

Belyaev, B. V.,
   1963   *The Psychology of Teaching Foreign Languages* (translated) (Oxford).
   1965   "The Basic Method and Methods of Foreign Language Instruction", *Innostranniye yazyki v shkole* III (translated into English in *Soviet Education* XIII, 7).

Bendriakov, K. E.,
   1960   *Ocherki po istorii narodnogo obrazovaniya v Turkestane* [Outline History of Public Education in Turkestan] (Moscow).

Benediktov, B. A. and Iarnotovskaya, E.,
   1960   "Metodika prepodovanii inostrannogo yazyka" [Methods of Teaching Forreign Language], *Vestnik vyssheii shkole* 9.

Bennigsen, A.,
   1967   "The Problems of Bilingualism and Assimilation in the North Caucasus", *Central Asian Review* XV: 205-211.

Bennigsen, A. and Quelequejay, Ch. M.,
   1961   *The Evolution of the Muslim Nationalities of the USSR and Their Linguistic Problems* (Oxford).
   1967   *Islam in the Soviet Union* (Oxford and London).

Bereday, G. and Pennar, J.,
   1960   *The Politics of the Soviet Union* (New York).

Bereday, G. and Stretch, B.,
   1963   "Political Education in the USA and the USSR", *Comparative Educational Review*, June, 9-16.

Bidwell, C. E.,
   1962   "Language, Dialect and Nationality in Yugoslavia", *Human Relations* 15.

Bilinsky, Y.,
    1962   "The Soviet Education Laws of 1958-1959 and Soviet National Policy",
            Soviet Studies XIV, 2: 138-157.
    1964   *The Second Soviet Republic: The Ukraine after World War II* (New Jersey).
    1968   "Education of the Non-Russian Peoples in the USSR 1917-1967", *Slavic
            Review* XXVII.3: 411-439.

Binder, M. A.,
    1967   *Gosvorstvenno-pravovye problemy v zaimopomoshchi Sovetskikh narodov* (Alma
            Ata).

Bogoyavlenski, O. N. and Menchenskaya, N. A.,
    1963   "The Psychology of Learning", translated in: *Educational Psychology in the
            USSR*, B. Simon and J. Simon, eds.

Boiko, V. I.,
    1970   "Naprevleniye i motivy potentsialnoi migratsii narodov Nizhnego Amvra"
            [Direction and Motivation of Potential Migration of the Peoples of the Lower
            Amur], *Izvestiya Sibirskogo Otdeleniya Akademii Nauk SSSR* XI.3: 57-63.

Borhek, J. T.,
    1969   "Ethnic Group Cohesion", *American Journal of Sociology*, 33-45.

Borodolina, M.,
    1966   "Thirst to Know Languages" *Pravda*, Oct. 26th.

Borovkov, A.,
    1952   *Tadzhysko-Uzbekskoe dvuyazychiya* [Tadzhik-Uzbek Bilingualism] (Moscow).
            (Akademiya Nauk CCCP).

Bozeman, A. B.,
    1960   *Politics and Culture in International History* (Princeton, University Press).

Brezhnev, L.,
    1966   *23rd CPSU Congress Report* (Moscow).

Bright, W.,
    1966   *Sociolinguistics: Proceedings of the UCLA Sociolinguistics Conference, 1964*
            (Mouton), The Hague.

Brazeau, E. J.,
    1958   "Language Differences and Occupational Experience", *Canadian Journal of
            Economic and Political Sciences* XXIV.4: 532-540.

Brumberg, A (ed.),
    1967   "Nationalities and Nationalism in the USSR", *Problems of Communism* XVI:
            5.

Bruner, J.,
    1960   *The Process of Education* (Cambridge [Mass.], Harvard).
    1966   *Toward a Theory of Instruction* (Cambridge [Mass.], Harvard).
    1968   "Culture, Politics and Pedagogy", *Saturday Review*, May 18th.

Bruner, J., et al.,
    1966   *Studies in Cognitive Growth* (London).

Burg, D.,
    1960   "Notes on Foreign Language Teaching in the USSR", in: *The Politics of the
            Soviet Union*, G. Bereday and J. Pennar, eds.

Carr, E. H.,
    1950   *The Bolshevik Revolution 1917-1932* (London).

Central Asian Review
    1965   "The Second Mother Tongue", 4: 310-322.

Chadwick, H. M.,
1945 *The Nationalities of Europe and the Growth of National Ideologies* (Cambridge University Press).

Cherednichenko, I. G.,
1957 *Metodika prepodovaniya russkogo yazyka v shkolakh s ukrainskim yazykom obucheniya* [Russian in Ukrainian Medium Schools] (Moscow).

Chistiakov, V. M.,
1941 *Osnovy metodiki russkogo yazyka v nerusskikh shkolakh* [Russian in non-Russian Medium Schools] (Moscow).
Chislennost, Sostav i Razmeshcheniye Naseleniya SSSR [Population, Composition and Distribution of Soviet Peoples] (Moscow, 1961).

Chomsky, N.,
1957 *Syntactic Structures* (The Hague, Mouton).
1959 Review of B. F. Skinner, *Verbal Behaviour, Language* XXXV.
1966 *Cartesian Linguistics* (London).
1968 *Language and Mind* (New York).

Coleman, A. P.,
1935 "Language as a Factor in Polish Nationalism", *Slavonic and East European Review* 13: 155-172.

Conquest, R.
1960 *The Soviet Deportation of Nationalities* (London). (Expanded edition, *The Nation Killers* [London, 1970]).
1965 *Russia after Khruschev* (London).
1967 *Soviet Nationalities Policy in Practice* (London).

Dahlstedt, K. H.,
1953 "Du bilinguisme et de l'influence laponne sur les patois suedois en Asele Lappmark", *Orbis*: 82-93.

Dallin, D. and Nicolsvesky, B.,
1947 *Forced Labour in Soviet Russia* (Yale, University Press).

Danilov, V.,
1959 "Problema izucheniya trekh yazykov v yakutskoi shkole" [Studying Three Languages in a Yakut School], *Russkiy Yazyk v Natsionalnoi Shkole* II.

Davidson, T. T. L.,
1969 "Indian Bilingualism", *Lingua* 22.

Davletshin, T.
1965 "Soviet Colonization in Turkestan", *Studies on the Soviet Union* V.iii.
1967 "Moscow still Bent on Russification", *Analysis of Current Development in the Soviet Union* 478.
1968 "Soviet Tatars, an Underprivileged Minority", *Analysis of Current Developments in the Soviet Union*, February 13th.

Denison, N.,
1968 "Sauris: A Trilingual Community in Diatypic Perspective", *Man* 3: 578-591.

Deroy, L.,
1956 *L'Emprunt Linguistique* (University of Liège, Paris).

Desheriev, Yu. D.,
1952 *Batsbiiskiy yazyk* [The Batsbi Language] (Moscow).
1958 *Razvitye mladopismennikh yazykov narodov SSSR* [Development of the National Languages of the New Nationalities] (Moscow).
1966 "Razvitye yazykov narodov SSSR v sovetskaya epoxu" [The Development

of National Languages in the Soviet Period], in: *Vazyki narodov SSSR* Part I. (Moscow).

Desheriev, E., et al.,
  1966 "Razvitiye i vzaimnoe obucheniye yazykov narodov SSSR" ,The Development and Mutual Enrichment of the Languages of the USSR], *Kommunist* XIII: 55-56.

Despres, L. A.,
  1967 *Cultural Pluralism and National Politics in British Guiana* (Chicago).
  1967 "Anthropological Theory and Complex Societies", *Current Anthropology*.

Deutsch, K. W.,
  1942 "The Trend of European Nationalism", *American Political Science Review* 36.
  1966 *Nationalism and Social Communication*² (Cambridge [Mass.], M.I.T.).

De Witt, N.,
  1961 *Education and Professional Employment in the USSR* (Washington, D.C.).
  1963 "Strategic Problems of Educational Policy in the USSR and USA", *Comparative Educational Review*, June 4-8.

Diebold, A. R.,
  1961 "Incipient Bilingualism", *Language* XXXVII.i: 97-112.

Dmitriev, N. K,.
  1940 *Grammatika bashkirskogo yazyka* [The Grammar of the Bashkir Language] (Moscow-Leningrad).
  1948 *Grammatika kumykskogo yazyka* [The Grammar of The Kumyk Language] (Moscow-Leningrad).

Dmitirev, N. K. et al.,
  1952 *Ocherki po metodike prepodovaniya russkogo i rodnogo yazykov v Tatarskoi shkole* [Outline of Method for Teaching Russian and Native Languages in Tatar Schools] (Moscow).

Doob, L. W.,
  1961 *Communication in Africa* (London).

Dozier,
  1956 "Two Examples of Linguistic Acculturation: the Yaqui of Sonora and Arizona, and the Tewa of New Mexico", *Language* 32: 146-157.

Drobizheva, L. M.,
  1967 in: *Istoriya SSSR* I: 77-90.

Dulling, G. K.,
  1968 "The Turkic Languages of the USSR: a New Development", *Central Asian Review* XVI, 2.

Dzhunosov, N. S.,
  1966 *Voprosy Istoriya* 4: 16-30.

Dzhandildin, N.,
  1959 "Nektorye voprosy internatsionalnoi vospitaniya" [Some Problems of Relations of Nationalities in Education], *Kommunist* 13: 30-43.
  1966 "Edinaya mnogonatsionalnaya kultura" [A Single Multinational Culture], *Kommunist* 5.

Ellis, J. and Davies, R. W.,
  1951 "The Crisis in Soviet Linguistics", *Soviet Studies* II.3: 209-264.

Emeneau, M. B.,
  1956 "India as a Language Area", *Language* 32.

Entwistle, E. and Morrison, W.,
  1949   *Russian and the Slavonic Languages* (London).
Epstein, E. H.,
  1967   "National Identity and the Language Issue in Puerto Rico", *Comparative Educational Review*, June, 133-143.
Ermoyan, H.,
  1950   "Inside Soviet Armenia", *Armenian Review* 3.iv.
Eudin, J.,
  1941   "Soviet National Minority Policies 1918-1921", *American Slavonic and East European Review* XX: 31-55.
Even-Zohar, I.,
  1970   "Lebirur Mahuta vetitkuda šel lešon hasifrut hajatta badiglosija", *Hasifrut* 2 (English Summary).
Fedenko, P.,
  1963   "The Nationality Question", *Studies on the Soviet Union* II,3: 98-111.
Ferguson, C. A.,
  1959   "Diglossia", *Word* 15.ii: 325-340.
  1960   "Linguistic Diversity in South Asia", *International Journal of American Linguistics* 26.iii.
  1962   "The Language Factor in National Development", *Anthropological Linguistics* IV.i., January.
  1966   "National Socio-linguistic Profile Formulas", in: *Sociolinguistics*, ed. W. Bright.
  1868a "Language Development", in *Language Problems of Developing Nations*, J. A. Fishman et al.
  1968b "St. Stefan of Perm and Applied Linguistics", in: *Language Problems of Developing Nations*, J. A. Fishman et al.
Feshbach, M.,
  1966   *Manpower in the USSR: A Survey of Recent Trends and Prospects in New Directions in the Soviet Economy* (Washington D.C.).
  1970   "Observations on the Soviet Census", *Problems of Communism*, August, 58-64.
Fishman, J. A.,
  1964   "Sociolinguistic Perspective on the Study of Bilingualism", see Fishman et al 1968 b.
  1965   "Domains of Language Behaviour in Multilingual Settings", see Fishman et al 1968 b.
  1966a "The Historical and Social Contexts of an Enquiry into Language Maintenance", in: *Language Loyalty in the United States*, J. A. Fishman et al.
  1966b "Language Maintenance in a Supra-ethnic Age", in: *Language Loyalty in the United States*, J. A. Fishman et al.
  1966c "Language Maintenace and Language Shifts as a Field of Enquiry", in: *Language Loyalty in the United States*, J. A. Fishman et al.
  1966d "Some Contrasts between Linguistically Homogenous and Linguistically Heterogenous Polities", *Sociological Enquiry* 36.ii.
  1966e "Bilingual Sequences at the Societal Level", in: *On Teaching English to Speakers of Other Languages* 2.
  1966f (ed.) Readings in the Sociology of language (The Hague, Mouton).
  1967   "Bilingualism With and Without Diglossia; Diglossia With and Without Bilingualism", *Journal of Social Issues* XXIII,3.
  1968a "Sociolinguistics and the Language Problems of Developing Countries", in: *Language Problems of Developing Nations*, J. A. Fishman et al.
  1968b "Nationality-Nationism and Nation-Nationalism", in: *Language Problems of Developing Nations*, J. A. Fishman et al.

1968c "Language Problems and Types of Political and Socio-cultural Integration; a Conceptual Summary", in: *Language Problems of Developing Nations*, J. A. Fishman et al.

Fishman, J. A. et al.,
1966 *Language Loyalty in the United States* (The Hague, Mouton).
1968a *Language Problems of Developing Nations* (New York).
1968b *Bilingualism in the Barria* (Washington D.C., Office of Education). Also, 1971, Bloomington (Indiana), Research Center for the Language Sciences Monograph, 7.

Fonlon, B.,
1969 "The Language Problems of Cameroon", *Comparative Educational Review* 5.i: 25-49.

Fox, R.,
1968 "Multi-lingualism in Two Communities", *Man* 3: 456-465.

French, R. A.,
1966 "Recent Population Trends in the USSR", in: *St. Antony's Papers on Soviet Affairs* 4. 68-95 (Oxford).

Friedrich, P.,
1962 "Language and Politics in India", *Daedalus*, Summer.

Fromen-Maurice, G.,
1968 "La Femme Sovietique entre le travail et la famille', *Ann. d'URSS Droit, Econ., Soc. Politique* (Paris).

Gadzhiyev, N.,
1962 "Kultury sotsialisticheskikh natsii, ikh nastayashchee i buduschhee", [The Culture of the Communist Nations, Their Present and Future], *Kommunist* 1.

Gafurov, B. G.,
1959 *Nektorye voprosy natsionalnoi politiki KPSR* [Some Problems of Soviet Nationalities Policies] (Moscow).

Galazov, A.,
1965 "The Native and Russian Languages in our Schools", *Narodnoye Obrazovaniye* II (trans. into English in *Soviet Education* VII.12).

Gantaskaya, O. A. and Terenteva, L. N.,
1965 "Etnografichskiye issledovanniya natsionalnykh protsesov v pribaltike", [Ethnographic Study of National Process in the Baltic], *Sovetskaya Etnografiya* 5: 5-8.

Gardanov, B. K. et al.,
1961 "Osnovnye napravleniya etnicheskikh protsessov v narodov SSSR", [Study of Processes of National Development in Soviet Nations], *Sovetskaya Etnografiya* 4: 9-29.

Garin, M. and A. Druzenko,
1970 "Man and his Work: At the Same Village Crossroads", *Izvestiya*, 12th July (Summary in *Current Digest of the Soviet Press* XXII.33: 1970).

Garunov, E.,
1970 "Schools with a Multinational Composition", *Narod. Obraz.* iii. (Trans. in *Soviet Education* XIII: 4-16).

Geiger, B. et al.,
1959 *Peoples and Languages of the Caucasus* (The Hague, Mouton).

Genko, A. N.,
1955 *Abazinskiy yazyk* [The Abazin Language], Moscow, Academy of Sciences.

Gessain, R. D. M.,
1946 "Facteurs compares d'assimilation chez des Russes et des Armeniens", *Population* I: 99-116.

Ginsberg, V. S.,
1959   "Opyt obucheniya inostrannym yazykam detei doshkolnogo i mladshego shkolnogo vozrasta" [Experiment in Teaching Foreign Languages to Preschool and Lower School Children], *Inostranniye yazyki v Shkole* 2.
1960   "An Experiment in Teaching a Foreign Language to Pre-school Children", *Sovetskaia Pedagogika* 5 (trans. in Soviet Education II.2).

Gitelman, Z.,
1967   "The Jews", *Problems of Communism* XVI: 92-101.

Glaser, N.,
1966   "The Process and Problems of Language Maintenance: an Integrative Review", in: *Language Loyalty in the United States*, J. A. Fishman et al.

Goldhagen, E. (ed.),
1968   *Ethnic Minorities in the Soviet Union* (London, Praeger).

Gomojunov, I.,
1954   "Vo vlasti formalizma" [On formalism in Teaching], *Inostranniye yazyki v Shkole* III: 24-40.

Goncharov, N. K.,
1964   "Rodnoe slovo v pedagocheskoi sisteme K. D. Ushenskogo", [The Native Language in the Pedagogical System of Ushensky], *Sovetskaya Pedagogika* XXVIII:10.
1966   "On Certain Lines of Development of Pedagogical Science", *Sovetskaya Pedagogika* VI (trans. in *Soviet Education* III).

Gordienko, A. A.,
1959   *Sozdaniye sovetskoi natsionalnoi gosudartsvennosti v srednei Azii* [The Creation of Soviet Nation Statehood in Central Asia] (Moscow).

Gorokhoff, B. I.,
1963   *Language Development in the Soviet Union* (Washington D.C., U.S. Office of Education).

Graffeberg, E. G.,
1963   *Narody Srednei Azii i Kazakhstana*, Chapter 2 (Moscow).
1969   *Beludzhi Turkmenskoy SSR* (Leningrad).

Greenberg, J. H.,
1956   "The Measurement of Linguistic Diversity", *Language* 32.i.
1958   *Essays in Linguistics*[2] (University of Chicago Press).

Grunberg, A. L.,
1960   "On the Question of Linguistic Influence", *Bulletin of the Oriental Institute of Moscow*. Summary provided by Serdyuchenko (personal communication).

Guffenheim, F. and A. Hoem,
1967   "Cross Cultural Attitudes of Lapp and Norwegian Children", *Journal of Social Psychology* 73.

Guseinov, V. and V. Korchagin,
1970   "Questions of Labour Resources", *Voprosy Ekonomiia* 2: 45-59. (trans. in *Current Digest of the Soviet Press* XXIII: 18).

Guxman, M. M. (ed.),
1960   *Voprosy forminovaniya i razvitiya natsionalnykh yazykov* [Problems of Formation and Development of National Languages] (Moscow).

Gryzynskaya, I.,
1929   "Kritika knigi Epsteina *Mysleniye mnogoyazychie*", [Criticism of Epstein's *La Pensee et la polyglossie*], *Inostranniye yazyki v Shkole*.

Hammerich, I. L.,
  1954   "The Russian Stratum in Alaskan Eskimo", *Word* X.4: 408-414.
Hans, N.,
  1959   "Learning Languages in the USSR", *Education*, November, 746-748 (London).
Harris, D. L.,
  1963   "Education of Linguistic Minorities in the USA and the USSR", *Comparative Educational Review* 6.ii: 191-198.
Haugen, E.,
  1950   "The Analysis of Linguistic Borrowing", *Language* XX.vi: 210-231.
  1953   *The Norwegian Language in America* (Philadelphia, University of Pennsylvania Press).
  1956   *Bilingualism in the Americas* (New York, American Dialect Society).
  1966a *Language Conflict and Language Planning: the case of Modern Norwegian* (Harvard University Press).
  1966b "Linguistics and Language Planning", in: *Sociolinguistics*, ed. W. Bright.
  1966c "Dialect, Language and Nation", *American Anthropologist* 68: 922-935.
  1968   "The Scandinavian languages as cultural artifacts", in: *Language Problems of Developing Nations*, J. A. Fishman et al.
Herman, S. N.,
  1961   "Explorations in the Social Psychology of Language Choice", *Human Relations* 14: 149-164.
Herman, S. N. and G. Schild,
  1960   "Ethnic Role Conflict", *Human Relations* 13.
Hill, T. and S. Jackson,
  1950   "The Language Discussion", *Anglo-Soviet Journal* XI.iii.
Honeger, H.,
  1957   "Some Observations on Bilingualism and Language Shift in Italy from 6th-3rd Centuries B.C.", *Word* 13: 415-440.
Horecky, L.,
  1967   *Basic Russian Publications: a Selected and Annoted Bibliography on Russia, Soviet Union* (Chicago).
Hymes, D. (ed.),
  1965   *Language in Culture and Society* (London).
Ignatov, O.,
  1966   "In a United Family. Consolidated Schools Using Latvian and Russian", *Pravda*, 5th April.
Imedadze, N. V.,
  1960   *K psikhologichskoi prirode rannego dvuyazychiya* [The Psychological Characteristics of Early Bilingualism], *Voprosy psikhologii*.
  1967   "On the Psychological Nature of Child Speech Formation under Conditions of Exposure to Two Languages", *International Journal of Psychology* 2: 129-132.
Inkeles, A.,
  1964   "Soviet Nationality Policy in Perspective", *Problems of Communism* XIII: 25-34.
Isort, P.,
  1964   *Essai sur les solutions sovietique au probleme colonial Russe* (Aix-en-Provence).
Isupov, A. A.,
  1964   *Natsionalnyy sostov naseleniya SSSR* [Ethnic Composition of the Peoples of the USSR] (Moscow).
         Itogi vsesoyuznaya perepisi naseleniya 1959 goda

(1959 Census. There are 16 volumes embracing the Union Republics separately) (Moscow, 1962-1963).
Izmenie sotsialnoi struktury sotsialistcheskogo obshchestva, materialy vsesoyuznoi teoritcheskoi konferentsii v Minske [Changes in the Cocial Structure of the Soviet Society]
(Sverdlovsk, 1965).

Jakobson, R.,
1945   "The Beginnings of National Self-Determination in Europe", *The Review of Politics* 7, 29-42, and in: *Readings in the Sociology of Language*, ed. J. A. Fishman.

Jenkins, J. J.,
1966   "Reflections on the Conference", in: *The Genesis of Language*, F. Smith and G. A. Miller.

Jernudd, B.,
1965   "The Language Situation in Tadzhik SSR", *Anthropological Linguistics* 7.iii: 76-83.

Kalashnikov, A. G. (ed.),
1927-29 *Pedagogicheskaya Entsiklopediya* (Moscow).

Karapetian, S. K.,
1940   *Sovetakan Hayastan* [Soviet Armenia] (Erevan).

Kari-Nyazov, T. N.,
1968   *Ocherki Istorii Kultury Sovetskogo Uzbekistana* (Tashkent and Moscow).

Katz, J.,
1966   "Bilingualism and Biculturalism in Canada", *Comparative Educational Review* II.2: 113-118.

Khanazarov, K.,
1963   *Sblizheniye natsii i natsionalnykh yazykov v SSSR* [Rapprochement of Nations and Nationality Languages in USSR] (Tashkent).

Kharpov, I. and A. Myrolubov,
1957   "40 Let sovetskoi metodiki prepodovaniya inostranykh yazykov", *Inostranniye yazyki v shkole* [Soviet Methods of Teaching Foreign Languages During 40 Years].

Kholmogorov, A.,
1969   "Sblizheniye i rastsvet sosialisticheskikh natsiy" [Assimilation and Flourishing of the Socialist Nations], *Kommunist Sov. Latvii* (Riga).

Kirk, D.,
1946   Europe's Population in the Inter-war Years (Geneva, League of Nations).

Kisliakov, N. et al.,
1954   "Kultura i byt Tadzhikskogo krestyanstva: po materialam kolkhoza G. M. Malenkova Leninabadskogo raiona Leninabadskoi", *Akademiya Nauk SSSR Institut Etnografiya* XXIV (Study of Tadzhik Life and Culture in a Kolkhoz).

Kloss, H.,
1966   "Types of Multilingual Communities", in: *Explorations in Sociolinguistics*, ed. S. Lieberson.
1967   "Bilingualism and Nationalism", *Journal of Social Issues* XXIII.2.
1968   "Notes Concerning a Language and Nation Typology", in: *Language Problems of Developing Nations*, J. A. Fishman et al.

Kochan, L. (ed.),
1970   *The Jews in Soviet Russia since 1917* (London).

Kohn, H.,
    1953   *Nationalism in the Soviet Union* (London).

Kolarz, W.,
    1954   *The Peoples of the Soviet Far Eeast* (London).
    1952   *Russia and Her Colonies*[2] (London).

Kolasky, J.,
    1968   *Education in the Soviet Ukraine: a Study in Discrimination and Russification*
            (Toronto).

Kononov, A. N.,
    1948   *Grammatika Uzbekskogo yazyka* [The Grammar of the Uzbek Language]
            (Tashkent).

Kosinski. L,,
    1969   "Migrations of Populations in East Central Europe 1939-55", *Canadian Sla-
            vonic Papers* XI.iii: 359-373.

Kostiuk, L.,
    1956   "Some Aspects of the Inter-relationship Between Education and Personality",
            in: *Psychology in the Soviet Union*, ed. B. Simon.

Kosygin, A. N.,
    1965   in: *Plannovoye Khozaistvo* 4.

Koutaisoff, E.,
    1951   "Literacy and the Place of Russian in the non-Slavonic Republics of the
            USSR", *Soviet Studies* III.2: 113-130.

Kreusler, A.,
    1961   "Bilingualism in the Non-Soviet Russian School", *Elementary School Journal*
            62.ii.
    1962   *The Teaching of Modern Foreign Languages in the Soviet Union* (Leiden).

Krupyanskaya, V. et al.,
    1961   "Osnovyye problemy etnograficheskogo izucheniya narodov SSSR", [Ethno-
            graphic research on Soviet nationalities], *Sovetskaya Etnografiya* 3: 3-11.

Kucera, J.,
    1954   "Soviet Nationality Policy: the Linguistic Controversy", *Problems of Com-
            munism* II.2: 22-29.

Kudriatsev, V. D.,
    1965   *Prepodovaniye russkogo yazyka v v-viii klassakh buryatskoi shkoly* [Teaching
            Russian in v-viii Grades of Buryat Schools] (Moscow).

Kulischer, E. M.,
    1949   "The Russian Population Enigma" *Foreign Affairs*, April, 497-501.

Kulturnoye stroitelstvo SSSR, statisticheskiy sbornik
            [The Cultural structure of the USSR, a Statistical Compilation] (Annual
            publication, and separate for each Union Republic).

Kuper, L. and M. G. Smith,
    1969   *Pluralism in Africa* (University of California Press).

Kuznetsova, Z. V.,
    1958   *Pavlodarskaya Oblast* [The Pavlodar Oblast] (Alma-Ata).

Labov, W.,
    1963   "The Social Motivation of Sound Change", *Word* 19.iii: 273-309.

Lane, H.,
    1964   "Programmed Learning of a Second Language", *International Review of
            Applied Linguistics in Language Teaching* II.4: 249-301.

Leach, E. R.,
  1954   *The Political System of Highland Burma* (London).

Leasure, J. W. and R. A. Lewis,
  1967   "Internal Migration in the USSR 1897-1926", *Demography* IV.2: 479-496.
  1968   *Population Changes in Russia and the USSR – a Set of Comparable territorial Units* (San Diego).
  1968   "Internal Migration in Russia in the Late 19th Century", *Slavic Review* XXVII.3: 375-394.

Lenin, V. I.,
  1929-35 *Sochineniya* [Works] (Moscow).
  1956   *O Natsionalnom i natsionalno-kolonialnom voprose* [The National and National Colonial Questions] (Moscow).

Lenneberg, E. H.,
  1964   "The Capacity for Language Acquisition", in: *The Structure of Language – Readings in the Philosophy of Language*, J. A. Fodor and J. J. Katz, eds. (Englewood Cliffs, N.J., Prentice Hall).
  1967   *Biological Foundations of Language* (London).

Leontev, A. N.,
  1957a "Teoreticheskie problemy psikhicheskogo razvitiya rebenka" [Questions Regarding the Theory of Mental Development], *Sovetskaya Pedagogika* 6.
  1957b "Learning as a Problem in Psychology", *Voprosy psikhologii* I: 311 (trans. in: *Recent Soviet Psychology*, O'Connor, ed.).
  1959a *Ob istoricheskom podkhode v izuchenii psikhiki cheloveka* [The Genetic approach to the Study of the human mind] (Moscow).
  1959b *Problemy razvitiya psikhiki* [Problems of Mental Development] (Moscow).
  1961   in: *Voprosy filosofii* 1.

Lepeshkin, A. I.,
  1962   "Konstitutsionnoye razvitiye sovetskovo soyuznovo gosudarstva" [Constitutional Development of the Soviet Union State], *Sovetskoye gosudarstvo i Pravo*, 32.

Lewis, E. G.,
  1952   *The Place of English and Welsh in the Schools of Wales* (London, ed. for Ministry of Education).
  1956   *Bilingualism in Education* (London, UNESCO, U.K. Commission).
  1962a "Introduction" to *Colloque Sur le Multilinguisme*, E. G. Lewis and W. H. Whiteley eds., (Conseil Sc. pour l'Afrique Pub. 87) (Brazzaville).
  1962b "Conditions Affecting the Reception of an Official Language", in: *CCTA*, Pub. 87.
  1962c *Foreign and Second Language Teaching in the USSR, ETIC paper I* (London).
  1970   "Immigrants and their Languages", *Trends in Education*, 19 (London).
  1971   "Migration and Languages in the USSR", *International Migrations Review*, July.

Lewis, R. A.,
  1969   "The Post-War Study of Internal Migration in the USSR", *Soviet Geography* X.4: 157-166.

Lieberson, S.,
  1964   "An extension of Greenberg's Measures of Linguistic Diversity", *Language* XL: 526-531.

Lieberson, S. (ed.),
  1964   *Explorations in Sociolinguistics*, The Hague (Bloomington and Mouton).

1965   "Bilingualism in Montreal: A Demographic Analysis", *American Journal of Sociology* 21: 10-25.
1970   "Measuring Population Diversity", *American Sociological Review*, April, 850-862.

Lipset, H.,
1967   "The Status of National Minority Languages in Soviet Education", *Soviet Studies* XIX.ii: 191-199.

Liublinskaya, A. A.,
1961   "The Development of Children's Speech and Thought", (Moscow), (trans. in: *Psychology in the Soviet Union*, B. Simon, ed.).

Lorimer, F.,
1946   *The Population of the Soviet Union* (Geneva, League of Nations).

Lozovan, E.,
1954   "Expatriation et bilinguisme", *Orbis*: 56-60.

Lubarskaya, A.,
1929   Opyt Analiza dvyuazychiya v svyazi s rabotoi Epsteina Mysli v mnogoya-zychiya", [Analysis of Bilingualism as Treated in Epstein's Work], *Inostran-nye yazyk v Sovetskoi shkole* 1.

Luria, A. R.,
1932   *The Nature of Human Conflicts* (trans. 1967 ed.) (New York).
1955   "The Role of Language in the Formation of Temporary Connections", *Vo-prosy Psikhologii* I (trans. in: *Psychology in the Soviet Union*, B. Simon, ed.).
1956   "The Disturbance of Reading and Writing in Polyglots", *Fiziologicheskiy Zhurnal SSSR Sechenova* 2.
1957   "The Genesis of Voluntary Movements", *Voprosy Psikhologii* 6 (trans. in: *Recent Soviet Psychology*, O'Connor, ed., 165-185).
1958   "Brain Disorders and Language Analysis", *Language and Speech* I.i.
1959a   "Experimental Analysis of the Development of Voluntary Action in Children: the Role of Speech in Child Development", in: *The Central Nervous System and Behaviour*, U.S. Department of Health, Education and Welfare (Washington, D.C.).
1959b   "The Directive Function of Speech", Parts I and II, *Word* 15.
1960   "Verbal Regulation of Behaviour", in: *The Central Nervous System and Be-haviour*, M.A.B. Brazier, ed. (New York, Macy Foundation).
1961a   "Speech and Development of Mental Processes", in: *Psychological Sciences in the USSR* I (Washington).
1961b   *The Role of Speech in the Regulation of Normal and Abnormal Behaviour* (Oxford).
1963   *Human Brain and Psychological Processes* (Moscow) (trans. London).
1967   "Problems and Facts in Neurolinguistics", *International Social Science Jour-nal* XIX.i.
1968   *Human Cortical Functions and their Disturbance in Local Brain Damage* (London).

Luria, A. R. and O. S. Vinogradova,
1959   "An Objective Investigation of the Dynamics of Semantic Systems" *British Journal of Psychology* 50.

Luria, A. R. and F. Ya. Yudovich,
1959   *Speech and Development of the Mental Processes in the Child* (London).

Maciuika, B. V.,
1963   "The Baltic States under Soviet Russia", mimeographed, (University of Chi-cago, Ph. D. Thesis).

Madyeva, G.,
  1929   *Nekotorye voprosy sopos tav itelnoi grammatiki russkogo i avarskogo yazykov*
         [Certain Problems in Comparing Russian and Avar Grammars], (Makhach-
         Kala).
Magner, T. E.,
  1967   "Language and Nationalism in Yugoslavia", *Canadian Slavic Studies* I.iii.
Manevick, Ye.,
  1969   "Problems of Manpower, Reproduction and Ways to Improve the Utilization
         of Labour Resources in the USSR", *Voprosy ekonomiki* 10 (trans. in: *The
         Current Digest of Soviet Press* XXII.i: 1970).
Mansurov, E.,
  1969   *Summary of paper given at the Cannes Conference of Sociologsits in 1969*, in:
         Aspects of National and Ethnic Loyalty, H. Tajfel.
Marr, N. Y.,
  1949   *Izbrannye raboty* [Selected wroks] (Moscow).
Martinet, A.,
  1959   *Elements of General Linguistics* (London).
  1962   *A Functional View of Language* (Oxford).
*Materialy sesii instituta natsionalnikh shkol Akademii Pedagogicheskikh Nauk RSFSR i
         Ministerstva prosveshcheniya Bashkirskoi ASSP po voprosam prepodovaniya –
         russkogo i rodnykh yazykov v natsionalnoi shkole* [Minutes of Meetings of
         Russian and Bashkir Institutes on Teaching Russian and National Langua-
         ges in National Schools] (Pedagogical Institute, UFA).
Matossian, M. A. K.,
  1962   *The Impact of Soviet Politics in Armenia* (Leiden).
Matthews, W. K.,
  1947   "The Language Pattern of the USSR", *Slavonic and East European Review* 25:
         427-453.
  1950   "The Soviet Contribution to Linguistic Thought", *Archivum Linguisticum* II:
         114-121.
  1951   *Languages of the USSR* (Cambridge).
  1956   "Developments in Soviet Linguistics Since the Crisis of 1950", *Slavonic and
         East European Review* 34: 123-130.
Maxwell, R. (ed.),
  1962   *Information USSR* (London).
Mayer, K.,
  1956   "Cultural Pluralism and Linguistic Equilibrium in Switzerland", in: *Demo-
         graphic Analysis*, Spengler and Duncan eds., (New York).
McNeill, D.,
  1966   "Developmental Linguistics", in: *The Genesis of Language*, F. Smith and G.
         A. Miller, eds.
Medlin, W. K. and W. M. Cave,
  1964   "Social Change and Education in Developmental Areas: Uzbekistan", *Com-
         parative Educational Review*, October, 166-176.
  1965   *Education and Social Change: a Study of the School in a Technically Developing
         Society in Central Asia* (University of Michigan Press).
Mcillet, A.,
  1952   *Linguistique Historique et Linguistique Generale* II (Paris).
Menchenskaya, N. A.,
  1967   "Fifty Years of the Soviet Psychology of Learning", *Sovetskaya Pedagogika*
         10 (trans. in *Soviet Education*, April 1968).

Menchenskaya N. A. and G. G. Saburova,
   1967   "The Problem of Instruction and Development", *Sovetskaya Pedagogika* 1 (trans. in *Soviet Education*, July 1967).

Miller, B. V.,
   1953   *Talyshskiy iazyk* [The Talysh Language] (Moscow).
           Minsk Conference, 1965 – See under "Izmenenie sotsialnoi struktury".

Miroliubov, A.,
   1961   "Developing Habits of Foreign Speech in School Children", *Naradnoye Obrazovaniye* 3 (trans. in *Soviet Education* III, 9).

Mirenenko, Y.,
   1958   "Ethnic and National Changes in the USSR", *Bulletin of the Institute for Study of the Soviet Union*, October.
   1965-66 "The Population", *Studies on the Soviet Union* V.i.
   1967-68 "A Demographic Survey", *Studies on the Soviet Union* 7.

Mirtov, A. V.,
   1956   *Ocherki po metodike prepodovaniye russkogo yazyka v azerbaydzhanskoi shkole* [Studies on Methods of Teaching Russian in Azerbaydzhan National Schools] (Moscow).
   1962   *Ocherki po metodike prepodovaniya russkogo yazyka v uzbekskoi shkole* [Russian Methods in Uzbek National Schools] (Moscow).

Mlikotin, A. M.,
   1967   "Soviet Methods of Teaching Foreign Languages", *Modern Languages Journal*, October: 337-343.

Mnataskanyan, M.,
   1966   "Natsiya i natsionalnaya gosudarstvennost", [Nations and National Statehood], *Voprosy Istoriya* 9: 27-36.

Monoszon, E. I.,
   1962   "Methods and Results of a Study of Pupils' Knowledge", *Sovetskaia Pedagogika* 9 (trans. in *Soviet Education*, November, 1962).

Mordvinov, A. E.,
   1950   "Razvitiye yazykov narodov SSSR", [Language Development in Soviet Nationalities], *Voprosy filosofii* 3: 75-95.

Mordvinov, A. E. and G. Sanzheev,
   1951   "Nektorye voprosy razvitiya mladopismennykh yazykov narodov SSSR" [Some Problems of the National Languages of the Peoples of the USSR], *Kommunist* 8: 38-49.

Mullodzhanov, M.,
   1970   "From Plan to Plan", *Izvestiya*, 19th June (Summary in *The Current Digest of the Soviet Press* XXII, July).

Nadezhdin, M. and M. Solomonov,
   1956   "The Korenizatsiya of the National Schools", in: *The Nationalities Problem and Soviet Administration*, R. Schlesinger, ed.

Nadzhafov, A.,
   1955   "Formirovaniye i razvitiye Azerbaydzhanskoi sotsioalisticheskoi natsii" [Principles of Formation and Development of Azerbaydzhan], *Baku* 1.

Nahriny, V. C. and J. Fishman,
   1965   "American Immigrant Groups: Ethnic Identification and the Problem of Generations", *Sociological Review* XIII: 311-326.

Narodnoye khozyaistvo SSSR – Tsent. Stat. Ubr. [The National Economy of the USSR] (Moscow, 1956-1966), (Ref. as Nar. Khoz).

Narodnoye obrazovaniye SSSR tsifrakh [Periodical publication. Statistics of Public Education in the Soviet Union] (Moscow).

Natadze, R. G.,
  1957   "Voprosy myshleniya i rechi v trudakh psikhologov gruzinskykh SSR" [Questions of the Relation of Thought and Speech in Georgian Research], *Voprosy Psikhologii* 5: 91-107.

Natsionalniye shkoly RSFSR [The national schools of the RSFSR] (Moscow, 1958).

Natsionalniye sostav proletariata v SSR [National Composition of the Peoples of the USSR] (Moscow, 1934).

Newth, J. A.,
  1959   "Some Trends in the Soviet Population, *Soviet Studies* X.iii: 252-278.
  1964   "Nationality and Language in Turkmenia", *Soviet Studies* XV.iv: 459-463.

Nikolsky, V. K. and N. F. Yakovlev,
  1949   "Osnovnye polozheniya materialisticheskogo ucheniya N.Y. Marra o yazyke" [Fundamental Principles of Marr's Materialist Theory of Linguistics], *Voprosy Filosofii* I: 265-285.

Nove, A.,
  1969   "History, Hierarchy and Nationalities. Some Observations on the Soviet Union", *Soviet Studies* XXI.i: 77-92.

Nove, A. and J. Newth,
  1967   *The Soviet Middle East* (London).

Novichenko, L.,
  1967   in: *Druzhba Narodov*, January.

O'Connor, N. (ed.),
  1961   *Recent Soviet Psychology* (Oxford).
  1966   *Present Day Russian Psychology* (Oxford).

Oinas, F.,
  1956   *Russian Calques in the Baltic Finnish Languages*, in: *Indiana Slavic Studies*, (eds. Ginsburg and Shaw).

Okladnikov, A. P.,
  1968   *Yakutia – Before its incorporation. Arctic Institute of N. America Publications* 8 (Montreal).

Organizatsiya uroka v peredovykh shkolakh Lipetskoi oblasti [Lesson Organization in a Pilot Study] (Lipetsk, 1937).

Ornstein, J.,
  1959   "Soviet Language Policy. Theory and Practice", *Slavic and East European Journal*, Spring: 1-24.
  1963   "Foreign Language Teaching (in the USSR)", in: *Current Trends in Linguistics*, T. A. Sebeok, ed.
  1964   "Patterns of Language Planning in the New States", *World Politics* 17.
  1968   "Soviet Language Policy. Continuity and Change", in: *Ethnic Minorities in the Soviet Union*, E. Goldhagen, ed.

Oskotsky, V.,
  1965   *Druzhba Narodov*, January.

Osnovniye problemy metodiki prepodovaniya rysskogo yazyka v natsionalnykh shkolakh [Problems of Method of Teaching Russian in National Schools] (Moscow, 1956).

Ostapenko, V.,
  1970   "Derevnea Gadyshi segodnia" [The village of Gadyshi Today], *Sovet. Etnografiya* 5, 102-111.

Osterberg, T.,
　1961　*Bilingualism – in a Swedish dialect Area* (Umea and Uppsala).

Park, R. E.,
　1922　*The Immgirant Press and its Control* (New York).

Pavlov, I. P.,
　1926　*Conditioned Reflexes* (trans. Anrep) (London).

Pennar, J.,
　1967　"Soviet Nationality Policy Redefined", *Analysis of Current Developments in the Soviet Union* 460, (Institute for Study of the Soviet Union, June).
　1969　"The Changing Nature of Soviet Education", *Bulletin of the Institute for Study of USSR* XVI, 12.

Perevedenstev, V. I.,
　1965　"Relationship between Population Migration and Ethnic Convergence", in: *World Population Conference Transactions*, 513-518. And in: *Voprosy narodnoi i demograficheskoi statistiki* 106-151 (Moscow).
　1965b　O Vliyanii etnicheskikh faktorov na territorialnoye pereraspredelneiye naseleniya", *Izvestiya Akademii Nauk Sr. Geogr.* IV (Summary in *Central Asian Review*, Ethnic Factors in Population Movement").
　1966a　Population Movement in Economy and Science", *Literaturnaya Gazeta* March 10 (Account in *Current Digest of the Soviet Press*, XVII, 11).
　1966b　*Migratsiya naseleniya i trudovye problemy Sibiri* [National Migrations and Economic Problems in Siberia], (Novosibirsk), (trans. in *Soviet Sociology* VII, VIII and IX).
　1967　in: *Narodonaseleniye i Ekonomika* [Population and Economics] 99-119 (Moscow).
　1970a　"Soviet Population Census 1970", *Literaturnaya Gazeta* 29th April.
　1970b　"Population Migration and the Utilization of Labour Resources", *Voprosy Ekonomiya* 9 Sept. (trans. in *Current Digest of the Soviet Press*, XXIII.2).

Petrovic, R.,
　1971　"The Numerical Strength and Territorial Distribution of the Nations and Nationalities of Yugoslavia", *Yugoslav Survey* XII, Feb. 1-14.

Piaget, J.,
　1951　*The Language and thought of the child* (London).
　1962　*Comments on Vygotsky's remarks* (Cambridge [Mass.], M.I.T. Press).
　1964　*Entretiens sur les notions de genese etc.* Congrès et Colloques, Paris.
　1968　*Six Psychological Studies* (London).

Pieris, R.,
　1952　Bilingualism and Culture Marginality", *American Journal of Sociology*.

Pipes, R.,
　1954　*The Formation of the Soviet Union: Communism and Nationalism 1917-1923* (Cambridge [Mass.] Harvard University Press).
　1964　"The Forces of Nationalism", *Problems of Communism* XXIII.i.

Pisarev, I.,
　1962　*Narodnoye naseleniya SSSR* [The Population of the USSR] (Moscow).

Podiachickh, P. G.,
　1961　*Naseleniye SSSR* [Population of the USSR] (Moscow).
　1969　*In Vsesoyuznoye soveshchaniye statistkov, 22-6 aprela 1968 goda* [All Union Conference of Statisticians April 22-6, 1968] (Moscow).

Pokshishevskii, V. V.,
　1951　*Zaseleniye Sibiri* [The Settling of Siberia] (Moscow).

1962 "Perspektivy migratsii naseleniya USSR", *Geografiy Naseleniya Vostochnoi Si-biri A. K. nauk SSR.* (Moscow).
1966 *Geografiya naseleniya v USSR* [Soviet Population Geography].
1969 "Population Migration and its Evaluation in Lenin's Work", *Geografiya v shkole* 8 (trans. in *Soviet Education* XII.iii: 86-100).

Pokshishevskii, V. V. et al.,
1964 On Basic Migration Patterns trans. in Soviet Geography (V.10: 3-18).

Prator, C. H.,
1952 *Language Teaching in The Philippines* (Manilla).

Purtseladze, S. D.,
1966 *Osnovy metodiki prepodovaniya russkogo yazyka gruzinskoi vosmiletnei shkole* [Methodoligcal Bases for the Teaching of Russian in Georgian Eight Year School], Parts I and II (Tbilisi).

Radzhabov, S. A., and A. Nikolaev,
1965 *Istoriya Tadzhikskogo naroda* III.2. (Moscow).

Rahamani, C.,
1966 "Studies on the Mental Development of the Child", in: *Recent Soviet Psychology*, N. O'Connor, ed.

Rakowska-Harmstone, T.,
1970 *Russia and Nationalism in Central Asia: the Case of Tadzhikstan* (London).

Rashin, A. G.,
1956 *Naseleniye Rossii za 100 let 1811-1913* [The Population Shifts of Russia over 100 years] (Moscow).

Rashulov, R.,
1957a *O psikhologicheskom analize razvitiya rechi v yazyk azerbaydzanchev c tochki zreniya vzaimodestiviya c rodnoi rechi* [Analysis of Psychological Proceess of Acquiring Russian in Azerbaydzhan] (Moscow).
1957b '*O psikhilogicheskom analize protsessa formirovaniya dvuyazychiya*'' [Analysis of the Psychological Procees of Development Bilingualism] *Dokladi Akademii Pedagogiki nauk RSFSR* 3 (Moscow).

Rastorgueva, V. S.,
1952 *Ob ustoichivosti morfoligicheskoi yazyka po materialam severnykh tadzhiyskikh govorov* [On the Stability of the Morphology of Tadzhik] (Moscow).
1952-61 *Ocherki po tadzhikskoi dialectologii* [Outlines of Tadzhik Dialectology], 4 Vols. (Moscow).
1954 *Kratkiy ocherk grammatiki tadzhikskogo yazyka* [Short Outline Grammar of Tadzhik] (Moscow).

Raxmanov, I. V.
1956 *Metodika obucheniya yazyka v starshix klassax* [Methods of Language Teaching] (Moscow).

Ray, P. S.,
1960 "Language Planning", *Quest* 31.
1961 "The Value of a Language", *Lingua* 10.
1962a "Formal Procedures of Standardization", *Anthropological Linguistics* 4.iii.
1962b "Language Standardization", in: *Study of the Role of Second Languages in Asia, Africa and Latin America*, F. A. Rice, ed.
1963 *Language Standardization: Studies in Prescriptive Linguistics* (The Hague, Mouton).

Rayburn, W. D.,
1956 "Problems and Procedures in Ethnolinguistic Surveys – An Outline Based on

a Study of Multilingual Areas (Honduras and Nicaragua)", mimeographed.

Rayfield, J. R.,
  1970   *The Languages of a Bilingual Community* (The Hague, Mouton).

Reimekis, T.,
  1967   "The Evolving Status of Nationalities in the Soviet Union", *Canadian Slavic Studies* I.iii: 406-423.

Reshetov, V.,
  1956   "*O vzaimodeistvii uzbekskikh i uzhonkirgizskikh govorov*" [References to the teaching of Uzbek and Kirgiz languages], *Trudy instituta yazyka i literaturii kirgizskoi Akademii Nauk* 6 (Frunze).
  1955-60 *Rodnoi i russkiy yazyk v shkolakh Severnogo Kavkaza* [Russian and local languages in the Northern Caucasus] Vol I, in: *Two Volumes of Collected Studies*, Serdyuchenko ed., (Moscow Pedagogical Academy,).

Rice, F. A. (ed.),
  1962   *Study of the role of second languages in Asia, Africa and Latin America*, (Washington D.C., Center for Applied Linguistics).

Riza, B.,
  1971   "The Cultural Heritage", *Studies on the Soviet Union* XI.i: 66-76.

Roff, M.,
  1967   "The Politics of Language in Malaya", *Asian Survey* VII.v.

Rogachev, P. and M. Sverdlin,
  1963   "Sovetskiy narod – novaya istoricheskaya obshchnost lyudei", *Kommunist* 9: 11-20.

Roof, M. K.,
  1960   "Recent Trends in Soviet Migration Policies", *R.E.M.P.Bulletin* 8.i: 1-18.
  1961   "Soviet Population Trends", *Soviet Survey* July-Sept.

Roof, M. K. and F. A. Leedy,
  1959   "Population Redistribution in the Soviet Union 1939-56", *Geographical Review*, April, XLIX.ii.

Rosen, S. M.,
  1960   *Report on Soviet Education Reform: Source Book*, *U.S.* Office of Health, Education and Welfare, (Washington D.C.),
  1963   *Higher Education in the U.S.S.R.* (Washington D.C. U.S. Office of Education,).

Rosetti, A.,
  1944   "Langue mixte et mélange de langues", *Acta Linguistica* IV.iii: 73-78.

Roszhdestvenskiy, N. S.,
  1967   "Composition and Structure of the Russian Language Syllabus", *Nachalnaia shkola* 5 (trans. in *Soviet Education* X.2: 1967).

Rubin, J.,
  1968   *National Bilingualism in Paraguay* (The Hague, Mouton).

Rundle, S.,
  1946   *Language as a Social and Political Factor in Europe* (London).

Russett, B. M.,
  1967   *International Regions and the International System: a Study in Political Ecology* (Chicago).

Russett, B. M. et al.,
  1964   *Handbook of Basic Political and Social Indicators* (Yale University Press).

Sadvakasov, G.,
  1961 "K nekotoiym voprosam slovoobrazovaniya v sovremennom vygurskom yazyke" [On some problems of word formation in Uygur], *Izvestiya Akademii Nauk Kazakhskoi SSR* 1: 62-71.

Salys, A.,
  1967 "The Russification of the Lithuanian Vocabulary under the Soviets", *Lituanus* 13.2

Sapir, E.,
  1949 *Language* (First Edition), (New York).

Sarafian, V.,
  1955 "The Soviets and Armenian Church", *Armenian Review* VIII.ii.

Saumjan, S. K.,
  1965 "Cybernetics and Language", (trans.) *Diogenes* 15. Autumn.

Schmalstieg, W. R.,
  1963 "Lithuania", in: *Current Trends in Linguistics*, T. A. Sebeok, ed., Vol .I.

Schapiro, I.,
  1970 "Introduction" to *The Jews in Soviet Russia Since 1917*, L. Kochan, ed.

Schlauch, M.,
  1946 "Early Behaviourist Psychology and Contemporary Linguistics", *Word* II: 25-36.
  1947 "Mechanism and Historical Materialism in Semantic Studies", *Science and Society* XI.2.

Schlesinger, R.,
  1956 *The Nationalities Problem and Soviet Administration: Selected Readings*, (London).
  1959 "The Educational Reform", *Soviet Studies* X: 432-444.

Sebeok, T. A. (ed.),
  1963 *Current Trends in Linguistics* Vol. I (The Hague, Mouton).

Semenov, P. G.,
  1966 "Natsiya i natsionalnaya gosudarstvennost" [Nations and National Statehood], *Voprosy Istoriya* VII: 72-81.

Serdyuchenko, G. P.,
  1949 "N. Y. Marr", *Vestnik Akademii Nauk SSSR* II.
  1950 "N. Y. Marr and Materialism in Linguistics", *Anglo-Soviet Journal* XI: 31-39.
  1955 "The Language of the Abazins", *Information Bulletin of the Academy of Science* V (Personal summary from author).
  1962 "The Eradication of Illiteracy and the Creation of New Written Languages in the USSR", *International Journal of Adult and Youth Education* 14.i: 23-29.
  1965 *Elimination of Illiteracy Among the Peoples Who Had No Alphabets* (Moscow, USSR, Commission for UNESCO) (trans. Paris).

Serdyuchenko, G. P. (ed.),
  1961 *Voprosy prepodovaniya russkogo iazyka v stranakh narodnoi demokratii* [Problems of Teaching Russian in the Schools of the Nations] (Moscow).

Seton-Watson, H.,
  1964 *Nationalism and Communism* (London).

Shaheen, S.,
  1956 *The Communist Theory of Self Determination* (The Hague).

Shcherba, L. V.,
  1927 "Bezgramotnost i ee prichiny", [Bad Spelling and its Cause], *Voprosy Pedagogiki* II.

1947 *Prepodovanniye innostrannykh iazykov v sredney shkole* [Teaching Foreign Languages in Early School] (Moscow).

Sheey, A.,
1966 "Population Trends in Central Asia and Kazakhstan 1959-65", *Central Asian Review* IV: 317-329.
1968 "Primary and Secondary Education in Central Asia and Kazakhstan", *Central Asian Review* XVI: 2 and 3, 147-158 and 189-204.
1970 "The Baluchis of the Turkmen SSR", *Mizan* XII: 43-54.

Shils, E.,
1971 "Tradition", *Comparative Studies in Sociology and History* XIII.2: 122-159.

Sidorov, N. and I. Shekhter,
1966 "Once Again on the Study of Foreign Languages", *Pravda*, Jan. 15.

Simon, B. (ed.),
1957 *Psychology in the Soviet Union* (London).

Simon, B. and J. Simon, (eds.),
1963 *Educational Psychology in the USSR* (London).

Sjoberg, A. F.,
1966 "Socio-Cultural and Linguistic Forces in the Development of Writing Systems", in: *Sociolinguistics*, W. Bright, ed.

Slobin, D. I.,
1966 "Soviet Psycholinguistics", in: *Recent Soviet Psychology*, N. O'Connor, ed.

Smirnova, Y. S.,
1967 "Natsionalno smeshannye braki v narodov karachayevocherkessi" [Ethnograhpic Study of Karachai and Cherkess Peoples], *Sovetskaia Etnografiya* 4.

Smith, F. and G. A. Miller, (eds.),
1966 *The Genesis of Language* (Cambridge [Mass.], M.I.T. Press).

Sokolov, A. N.,
1971 "Internal Speech and Thought", (trans.), *International Journal of Psychology* VI.i.

Solovkhin, V.,
1962 in: *Lateratura i zhizn*, 6th Febr.

Sommerfelt, A.,
1954 *Language, Society and Culture* (Oslo).
1962 *Diachronic and Synchronic Aspects of Language* (Oslo).

Sorensen, A. P.,
1967 "Multilingualism in the North West Amazon", *American Anthropologist* 69: 670-684.

Sovetskaya stroeltsvo (Periodical publication: *The Structure of the USSR*(-Moscow).

Sovetkin, F. F.,
1959 *Natsionalnye shkoly RSFSR za 40 let* [Forty Years of National Schools in Russia] (Moscow).

SSSR v tsifrakh [The USSR in Figures] (Moscow, 1958).

Stalin, J. V.,
1936 *Marx and National and Colonial Questions* (London).
1949-52 *Sochineniya* (Moscow), (Supplementary volumes 1-3: Stanford, U.S., Hoover Institute, 1967).
1950a *Natsionalnyy v vopros i Leninizm* [Nationality questions and Leninism] (Moscow).

1950b *Marxizm i voprosy yazykozaniya* (Moscow), (trans. *Concerning Marxism in Linguistics*, London, Soviet News Booklet).
1953 *Collected Edition*VI, English trans. (London).

Stavruly, M.,
1935 "K voprosy o dvuyazychii", [Problems of Bilingualism], *Protsveshchenie natsii nasnei* 4.

Strana sovetov za 50 let [Soviet Union During 50 Years] (Moscow, 1969).

Sultan, G.,
1968 "Demographic and Cultural Trends among Turkic Peoples of the Soviet Union", in: *Ethnic Minorities in the Soviet Union*, E. Goldhagen, ed.

Szalai, A. et al.,
1966 "Multilingual Comparative Research", *American Behavioural Scientist* 10.IV.

Taagepera, R.,
1969 "National Differences within Soviet Demographic Trends", *Soviet Studies* XX.iv.

Tajfel, H.,
1970 "Aspects of National and Ethnic Loyalty", *Social Sciences Information* IX.iii.

Tanner, N.,
1967 "Speech and Society among the Indonesian Elite", *Anthropological Linguistics* 9.iii.

Tanter, R.,
1966 "Dimensions of Conflict Behaviour Within and Between Nations, 1958-60", *Journal of Conflict Resolution* 10.i.

Taskin, G. A.,
1964 "Kazakhstan. Changes in Administrative Status, etc.", *Bulletin Institute for Study of USSR*, February, 34-41.

Tekiner, S.,
1963 "Developments in Azerbaydzhan", *Studies on the Soviet Union* II.iii.

Tekuchev, A. V.,
1965 "Akademik L. V. Shcherba v metodike i o metodike kak nauk" [Study of Shcherba's Pedagogic Theories], *Russkiy yazyk v Shkole* 4.
1965 *Osnovy metodiki orfografii v sloyakh mestnogo dialecta* [Teaching Orthography Within a Local Dialect] (Moscow).
1967 "Major Landmarks in the Development of Soviet Methodology for Teaching Russian 1917-67", *Russkii iazyk v shkole* 4-5 (trans. in *Soviet Education* X.iii).

Terakopayan, L.,
1967 *Druzhba narodov* 1.

Terhune, K. W.,
1970 "From National Character to National Behaviour", *Journal of Conflict Resolution* XIV.2: 202-263.

Terletsky, P.,
1936 "Kultbazy Komiteta Scvcrov" [Culture Bases of the Committee of the North], *Sovetskiy Sever* 1: 36-47.

Thomson, A. I.,
1960 "On Learning Foreign Languages in Secondary Schools", *Pedagogicheskii Sbornik*, October, 1891 (See *Soviet Education* 2.XI: 1960).

Tillet, L.,
1967 "Nationalism and History", *Problems of Communism* XVI.v: 36-45.
1969 *The Great Friendship: Soviet Historians on the Non-Russian Nationalities* (Chapel Hill).

Timasheff, N. S.,
   1948   "The Post War Population of the Soviet Union", *American Journal of Sociology*, Sept., 148-155.

Tolstov, S. P. et al.,
   1962   Narody Srednei Azii i Kazakhstana [Central Asian and Kazakh peoples], *Akademiya Nauk SSSR* (Moscow).

Trudovyye resursy SSSR [Manpower Resources in the USSR] (Moscow, 1961).

Tsamerian, I. P. and S. L. Ronin,
   1962   *Equality of Rights between Races and Nationalities in the USSR* (Paris, Unesco).

Twaddel, W. F.,
   1964   Report of Conference on Teaching English Abroad (Washington, C.A.L., mimeographed).

Ubryatova, E. I.,
   1956   in: Reports and Notes of the Language Institute IX (Moscow), (Summary communicated by Serdyuchenko personally).

Umurzakova, O. P.,
   1961   K voprosy o periodizatsii formirovaniya i razvitiya Uzbekskoi sotsialisticheskoi natsii" [Problems of the Stages in the Development of the Uzbek Nation], *Obs. nauk Uzb* 8: 11-19.

Ushinskii, K. D.,
   1939   *Izbrannye sochineniya* [Works], 2 Vols. (Moscow).

Uznadze, D.,
   1966   *The Psychology of Set* (New York).

Vardys, V. S.,
   1965   "Soviet Colonization in the Baltic States. 1940-65", *Baltic Review* 29.

Vdovin, I. S.,
   1954   *Istoriya izucheniya paleoziatiskikh yazykov* [Development of Paleoasiatic Languages], (Moscow-Lengingrad).

Vsesoyuznaya perepisi naseleniya 17 dekabrya 1926 g. Kratkiye svodki vypsuk IV: Narodno i rodnoy yazyk naseleniya SSSR [1926 Census – Fourth Print of Short Summary Relating to Nationalities and Native Languages] (Moscow, 1928).

Vestnik Statistiki [Periodical publication: Statistical Handbook].

Vildomec, V.,
   1963   *Multilingualism* (Leyden).

Vinogradov, V. V.,
   1945   *Velikiy Rysskiy yazyk* [Great Russian Language] (Moscow).
   1950   "O linguisticheskoi diskussii i rabotakh I.V. Stalin po voprosam yazykoznaniya" [On Stalin's Discussions of Language Problems)], *Bolshevik* 15: 7-23.
   1952a *Trudy I.V. Stalina po voprosam yazykoznaniya* [The works of Stalin on Linguistic Problems], *Izvestiya Nauk SSSR* IX.1.
   1952b "Soviet Linguistics on a New Path", *Anglo-Soviet Journal* XII.

Vogt, H.,
   1945   "Substrat et convergence dans l'evolution linguistique; remarques sur l'evolution et la structure de l'armenien, georgien, de l'ossete, et du turk", *Studia septentrionalia* 2.
   1954   ' Language Contact", *Word* X.ii-iii: 368-379.

Volkova, N. C.,
1967 "Voprosy dvuyazychaya na Severnom Kavkaze" [Problems of Bilingualism in the N. Caucasus], *Sovetskaya Etnografiya* 1: 27-40.

Voprosy razvitiya literaturnykh vazykov narodov SSSR v Sovetskuyu epokhu [Problem of the Development of National Literary Languages in the Soviet Period], (Alma-Ata, 1964), (Ref. as Vop. raz.).

Voprosy dialekticheskogo i istoricheskogo materializma v trude Stalina – Marxisma i yazykonaniya [Dialect Problems and Historical Materialism in the Work of Stalin-Marxism and Linguistic Problems] 2 volumes (Moscow, 1951-52), (Ref. as Vop. dial.).

Voprosy trudovykh resursov v rayonakh Sibiri [Questons of Labour Resources in Regions of Siberia] (Novosibirsk, 1961).

Vygotsky, L. S.,
1934 *Myslenie i rech* (Moscow), (trans. *Thought and Language*, 1962).
1956 *Izbranniye psikhologicheskiye issledovaniya* [Selected psychological studies], Leontiev and Luria, ed. (Moscow).

Vvedenskiy, D. N.,
1918 *Grammatika bez grammatiki* [Grammarless Grammar] (Rostov).

Vysshaya Shkola SSSR za 50 let 1917-67 [50 years of Soviet High School Education] (Moscow, 1967).

Wadekind, K. E.,
1964 "Internal Migration and Flight from the Land in the USSR", *Soviet Studies* XVIII.ii.

Waterson, N.,
1960 Appendix to *The Turkic Peoples of the USSR*, N. A. Baskakov.

Weinreich, U.,
1953a *Languages in Contact. Findings and Problems* (New York).
1953b "The Russification of Soviet Minority Languages", *Problems of Communism* 46-57.

Weinstein, H. R.,
1942 "Language and Education in the Soviet Ukraine", *American Slavonic and East European Review*.

Wexler, P.,
1971 "Diglossia, Language Standardization and Purism", *Lingua* 27: 330-354.

Wheeler, G.,
1964 *The Modern History of Soviet Central Asia* (London).

Winner, T. G.,
1952 "Problems of Alphabetic Reform among the Turkic Peoples of Soviet Central Asia 1920-41", *Slavonic and East European Review*.

Wittermans, T.,
1967 "The Frisians: an Ethnic Group in the Netherlands", *Sociology and Social Research* 36.i.

Wolff, H.,
1967 "Language, Ethnic Identity and Social Change in S. Nigeria", *Anthropological Linguistics* IX.i: 18-24.

Woolner, A. C.,
1938 *Language in Politics and History* (London).

World Survey of Education 3 volumes (Paris, 1957-1961, UNESCO).

Worth, D. S.,
   1960   "Russian Borrowings in Kamchadal", *Orbis* IX.

Wurm, S.,
   1954   *Turkic Peoples of the USSR* (Central Asian Reasearch Centre, Oxford).
   1960   Appendix (Comments) to *The Turkic Languages of Central Asia*, N. A. Baskakov.

Yarmolenko, A.,
   1949   *K voprosy o psikhologii mnogoyazychiya. Materialii universitetskoi psikhologicheskoi konferentsii* [Problems of the Psychology of Polyglotism], (Leningrad, State University).
   1955   *K voprosy o mnogoyazychii, ucheniye zapiski* [Problems of Polyglotism], *Seriya Filologicheskikh Nauk* 8 (Leningrad).

Zaionchouskaia, Z. H. and N. I. Perevedentsev,
   1964   *Sovremnaya migratsiya naseleniya krasnogarskogo kraya* [Study of National Migrations in the Krasnogar krai] (Novosibirsk).
   1967   in: *Nauchniye Problemy geografiy naseleniya (Scientific Problems of Population Geography)*, 128-191 (Moscow).

Zankov, L. V.,
   1963   "Problems of Primary Education", *Sovetskaya Pedagogika* 11 (trans. in *Soviet Education* VI.6).

Zaslavsky, D.,
   1949   "Velikiy yazyk nashei epokhi" [The great Languages in World History], *Literaturnaya Gazeta* Jan. 1.

Zavatskaia, M.,
   1963   "The New System of Primary Education in Action", *Narodnoye obrazovaniye* 12 (trans. in *Soviet Education* VI.vi).

Zhdanko, T. A. (ed.),
   1961   *Materialy k Istoriko-Etnograficheskomu Atlasu Srednei Azii i Kazakhstana* [Material for a Historical-ethnographic Atlas of Central Asia and Kazakhstan].

Zhirkov, L. I.,
   1924   *Grammatika avarskogo* [The grammar of Avar] (Moscow).
   1926   *Grammatika darginskogo* [The Grammar of Dargin] (Moscow).
   1955   *Lakskiy yazyk-fonetika i morfologiya* [The Phonetics and Morphology of Lak] (Moscow).

Zlatopolsky, D. L.,
   1968   *Natsionalnaya gosudaristvennost soyuznykh republik* [The National State System of the Union Republics] (Moscow).

Subject Index

Index of Nationalities and Languages-
Soviet and Non-Soviet

Index of Names